THE WAR PLANS
OF THE GREAT POWERS
1880~1914

THE
WAR PLANS
OF THE
GREAT POWERS
1880~1914

Edited by
PAUL M. KENNEDY
BA, D.Phil., FR Hist. Soc.
Professor of History, Yale University

Boston
ALLEN & UNWIN
London   Sydney

Allen & Unwin, Inc.,
Fifty Cross Street, Winchester, Mass. 01890, USA

George Allen & Unwin (Publishers) Ltd,
40 Museum Street, London WC1A 1LU, UK

George Allen & Unwin (Publishers) Ltd,
Park Lane, Hemel Hempstead, Herts HP2 4TE, UK

George Allen & Unwin Australia Pty Ltd,
8 Napier Street, North Sydney, NSW 2060, Australia

First published in 1979
Paperback edition 1985

Library of Congress Cataloging in Publication Data

   The War plans of the great powers, 1880–1914.
Bibliography: p.
Includes index.
1. World War, 1914–1918—Causes—Addresses, essays, lectures.
2. Europe—History—1871–1918—Addresses, essays, lectures.
3. Europe—Military policy—Addresses, essays, lectures.
I. Kennedy, Paul M., 1945–
[D511.W33 1984]   940.3'11   84–20377
ISBN 0-04-940082-7 (pbk.: alk. paper)

British Library Cataloguing in Publication Data

   The war plans of the great powers, 1880–1914.
1. European War, 1914–1918 – Causes – Addresses, essays, lectures
2. Europe – History – 1871–1918 – Addresses, essays, lectures
3. Europe – Military policy – History – Addresses, essays, lectures
I. Kennedy, Paul Michael
940.3'11   D511   78–41059

ISBN 0-04-940056-8 Cased
ISBN 0-04-940082-7 Paper

Typeset in 10 on 11 point Plantin by Trade Linotype Ltd, Birmingham
and printed in Great Britain by Mackays of Chatham Ltd

Declaration of Copyright

Foreword

by Fritz Fischer

Despite the experiences of the Second World War and all its global consequences, the First World War has never lost its place in the historical
consciousness of the combatant nations, who still regard it as forming the
deepest caesura in their recent history. When, therefore, the defeat of
Germany in 1945 caused most of that government's past records to fall into
the hands of the Allies, who soon made them free for scholarship, it was
natural that historians should turn again to the question of Germany's aims
and role in the origins of the First World War. In the 1960s and 1970s the
opening of the archives of the Entente powers and the United States has
made possible research into the war plans and political intentions of those
countries as well. A comparative study of these developments is now at last
possible.

The First World War represents the high point of the age of imperialism,
during which technical and economic developments led to increased rivalries
between the European great powers, and also the United States and Japan.
In particular, those nations conscious of having come 'too late' on to the
world scene inevitably found themselves challenging the established countries
and their overseas empires, and this in turn led to repeated fissures and re-
formations in the existing alliance systems and to a 'destabilisation' of the
precarious European and global equilibrium, eventually culminating in a
general war. The populations of all those countries, influenced to a greater
or lesser extent by social-Darwinistic assumptions, came to expect that in
such a turbulent world a conflict was unavoidable and should, moreover, be
prepared for. Such preparations, especially in the military and strategic
domain, are the chief concern of this present collection of essays. They
show the impact of the Industrial Revolution upon the technical aspects of
warfare, but even more they reveal how the majority of states were obliged
to refashion the organisation of their military leadership by creating a
permanent General Staff. The model which was cited on so many occasions,
for example, in the British Army reforms and creation of an Imperial
General Staff following the Boer War, was that of the immensely successful
Prussian General Staff in the 1866–70 period – although, ironically enough,
that 'model' had lost a considerable amount of its effectiveness by 1911–12,
that is, even before the First World War broke out.*

*As was noticed by acute foreign observers, like Colonel Repington of *The Times*:
see the new study by B.-F. Schulte, *Die deutsche Armee 1900–1914: Zwischen
Beharren und Verändern* (Düsseldorf, 1977).

The operations plans, which the respective general staffs had to prepare, could be more or less binding, more or less flexible (as certainly was true of the much-debated Schlieffen Plan), and could therefore restrict the freedom of action of the political decision makers or leave them relatively untouched. In most of the states concerned – Russia and Austria–Hungary were the exceptions – the political and military leaders also had to grapple with the question of how far the navy or the army was to be considered as the more decisive and thus more important arm: in the German case, for example, the fleet appeared to be the more prominent for some years, but after 1912–13 the army recovered its traditional primacy since it could be seen that the chief theatre in any future conflict was likely to be on land; whereas in England the army (British Expeditionary Force) and the new General Staff began to gain ground after 1905, and by August 1911 had achieved a position in the national strategy which displaced the navy, the more especially since the Admiralty's ideas about the deployment of the fleet were neither coherent nor convincing. This was, in the history of British strategy, a quite epoch-making change of course, even if not fully realised at the time.

Closely connected with these controversies was the problem of waging war in coalition with one's allies, for it was hardly likely that a nation would find itself fighting alone against two or more enemies in view of the formal (or sometimes only moral) bonds and obligations of the various alliance partners in pre-1914 Europe. The difficulties which arose here, it is clear, could not be satisfactorily solved by either of the alliance *blocs* before the war or at the outbreak of the conflict itself.

The articles in this collection also offer an extensive contribution to the debate upon the problem of 'Militarism', whether in the more general question of the militarisation of a society, or in the specific area of the relationship between the political and military leadership in a state. If this ambiguity about the relations between statesmen and the military existed in all the countries dealt with here, it nevertheless becomes clear that the different cultural, social and constitutional circumstances of the various states led to quite diverse consequences. Whereas in France and Britain the political leadership retained its preponderance, despite the rising importance of the armed forces and their staffs, in Germany (and similarly in the fellow-empires of Russia and Austria–Hungary) the authority of the civilians was circumscribed both by the sheer weight of the military in social life and by the constitutional structure: for example, because the monarch was the *de facto*, and not merely the *de jure*, commander-in-chief; because the government was dependent upon him, and not upon Parliament; and because he possessed the power to decide over peace and war. What still remains questionable, however, is the notion – put forward in some of the contributions to this book, and in many other places – that there was so great a distinction between the political and military leaders of the Wilhelmine Reich: for there appears to me to have existed a co-operation between both elements in preparing for a conflict, and also in the decision for war, which was justified by their commonly expressed reference to the necessity of strengthening Germany's position in Europe and in the world. This was the unified aim of both, and is not simply to be attributed to the military argument that 'victory is still possible at present, in a few years' time it will have gone'.

However that may be – and those issues will no doubt be further researched and discussed in the future – this present collection offers a great deal to the reader: first, by presenting an extensive coverage of the war planning of all the powers concerned; and secondly, by the controlled comparative approach of the editor's introduction. *The War Plans of the Great Powers* gives us deeper insights into the connections between the military-technical-organisational aspects of war and the political-economic aspects, and also the legal and diplomatic, thus enlightening our understanding of present-day problems with these examples from a past epoch.

Hamburg, December 1978

Acknowledgements

My thanks are due, first of all, to the various authors and original publishers of the articles contained in this collection, for permitting me to reproduce them. I should also like to thank my agent, Bruce Hunter, and my publisher's editor, Keith Ashfield, for continued support of my ventures.

A number of old friends and colleagues, Professor Volker Berghahn, Dr Wilhelm Deist, Professor James Jones, Dr John Moses and Professor Len Turner, were once again kind enough to read draft manuscripts and to make comments upon my ideas. The introduction also benefited from being read to, and vigorously commented upon by, members of the War Studies Seminar (University of London) and Research in Progress Seminar (University of Sussex).

Finally, I should like to express my thanks to Professor Fritz Fischer, not only for kindly agreeing to write a foreword to this collection, but also for his friendship and encouragement to me over the past ten years. In dedicating this book to him in this, his seventieth year, I venture to make my own small acknowledgement of his path-breaking scholarship.

PAUL M. KENNEDY
Norwich, March 1978

Contents

To
Fritz Fischer

Editor's Introduction

The strategic planning of the Great Powers prior to 1914 has been a topic of continual fascination to historians for both military and non-military reasons. On the one hand, there has been the natural interest of the military writer in the operational, tactical and logistical contents of these plans and in the extent to which they anticipated the testing strategical conditions of the First World War itself. On the other hand, an equally intense concern has been shown by the student of politics in the broader, non-technical aspects of military planning: how far, for example, did the plans of the various General Staffs pre-empt their government's freedom of action and, to that extent, encroach upon the decision-making domain of the civilians? how far did they reflect the prevailing 'unspoken assumptions'[1] upon a country's foreign policy, the protection of national interests, and the nature of international relations and political morality? how far, indeed, were they actually responsible for the outbreak of that catastrophic conflict in the summer of 1914? It is precisely because this topic has always possessed both a military *and* a political aspect (frequently hard to disentangle, as much of what follows will show) that it has attracted so large an amount of historical attention.

However, a great deal of the earlier writing upon this topic was based either upon conjecture or upon incomplete knowledge, usually as a consequence of the selective revelations about prewar plans by the official naval and military historians of the major participants.[2] Even today there is still a great amount that is unknown, but sufficient investigation has been carried out in recent years, thanks to the opening of numerous archives and private papers, to clear up many mysteries and to permit us to come to reasonably firm conclusions about a large number of the more significant aspects of the war planning of the Great Powers. It is the intention of this book to bring together some of the most important of these contributions, hitherto only accessible in specialist journals, and at the same time, by comparing the contents of these new studies, to suggest what those conclusions might be.

From the military and the institutional points of view, a study of the operational planning of the major nation states in the few decades before 1914 is of particular importance, because this was the first time in a period of peace that the powers developed war plans in any systematic way. Compared with the elaborate staff organisations which evolved during and after the Second World War,[3] their predecessors around the turn of the century no doubt appear primitive but the fact remains that they had grown up remarkably swiftly. That this creation and expansion of military and naval staffs took place in the latter half of the nineteenth century can be attributed to a number of general causes, the most important being:

(1) the overall growth in the size of bureaucracies and governmental structures, this itself being a reflection of the increasing complexity of Western society as it underwent the processes of industrialisation and modernisation, and also a reflection of the desire of politicians and public to see more efficient organisations of state replacing ramshackle bodies often established centuries earlier.[4]

(2) the increasing pace of technological invention and change in both armies and navies throughout the nineteenth century, which was a further consequence of the 'Unbound Prometheus'[5] – the unstoppable and often unforseen interaction of technological breakthroughs which occurred once the Industrial Revolution had got under way. New weapons, new forms of propulsion, new methods of communicating information, all had military repercussions; and armies and navies had either to keep in touch with such developments or to suffer the consequences of their conservatism when they encountered opponents using more advanced weapons and techniques of war.[6] All this meant that the armed services required specialists who could encourage, test and report upon innovations and their implications, gather and assess information upon developments in foreign countries, and advise their leaders of the effect all this would have upon the conduct of war.

(3) the increasing complexity of warfare as those further consequences of the Industrial Revolution – mass production, vastly improved transport systems, and the more efficient organisation and employment of mass armies – made their impact. In an age when armies were beginning to total millions (including reservists and conscripts without much knowledge of military life), when railways were transforming all previous concepts of mobility, and when logistical preparations for a campaign could no longer rely upon the age-old system of living off the area in which the troops were billeted, organisation and planning became more exalted than ever before in the armed services. It was obviously crucial to control these huge war machines and to give them a direction.

(4) as a final consequence of all these developments, armies and navies were forced *nolens volens* to become more professional, that is, to contain and recruit officers who knew foreign countries and languages, who possessed the organisational ability to create and control a railway or ammunition supply system, who were well acquainted with technological innovations and who could study and assimilate the latest tactical and strategical writings. Improved educational qualifications upon entry and increased training of staff officers became the hallmark of late-nineteenth-century armed services;[7] and, in all this, the dominant role now being played by the 'expert' was but a mirror of trends which

were also in evidence in the foreign and colonial ministries, educational departments, commercial and financial offices and virtually all other sectors of government and administration.[8]

But the most important short-term impetus to the formation of General Staffs and the development of operational planning in the later nineteenth century was the undoubted success of the Prussian military system in the wars of 1864, 1866 and 1870–1, for these conflicts provided what seemed to be near-perfect examples of the way in which war should be conducted. Universal military service, and the planned deployment of a vast number of reservists in the front lines, became the norm in almost all European armies. Moltke's clever use of the German railway network to transport and supply his large armies produced great admiration – and emulation – in foreign states. And, in a similar fashion, the Prussian General Staff, the 'brains' behind this new military colossus, became the model for other powers to copy, some countries, such as Japan, Turkey and certain Latin American states, going so far as to invite the Germans to reorganise their entire military system. Even Great Britain and the United States, who, being insular, liberal states where the army's place was comparatively low in political terms, had resisted this trend for a while, were eventually forced by later circumstances – Britain by the pressures upon her worldwide empire at the close of the nineteenth century, the United States by the Spanish-American war – to conform. The frequency of imperial collisions and the growth of alliances and *ententes* between the Great Powers simply accentuated the desire to be prepared for war and to have an effective strategy against likely opponents. What we are examining here, in other words, are the early stages of something which has become one of the most important functions of the defence forces of every country: prewar planning.

This traditional interest for military reasons in the pre-1914 plans has received considerable support from another quarter as a consequence of the great controversy which has been raging since 1961 over Professor Fritz Fischer's interpretation of the origins of the First World War – for, in the allocation to Germany of the major responsibility for the outbreak of that conflict, Fischer and his school have paid particular attention to the role of the 'military party' in Berlin. According to this interpretation, the sheer influence of military as opposed to civilian values and powers was a noted characteristic of Bismarckian and Wilhelmine Germany. The Kaiser was commander-in-chief *de facto* and not only, as in Britain, *de jure*. A primitive form of 'military-industrial complex' had stoked up and exploited arms races to satisfy the needs of the vast armaments industry and to divert public attention from domestic political questions. Leading figures in both the central government and the military were seeking an excuse to go to war from the controversial *Kriegsrat* (War Council) of December 1912 onwards. A vigorous fulfilment of Germany's military alliance obligations to Austria-Hungary was regarded as axiomatic. Most important of all for our purposes, the Germans had only one war plan, that created by Count

von Schlieffen in 1905 and later modified by his successor as Chief of
General Staff, the younger Moltke: it was a plan which was so inflexible
that it meant going to war as soon as Russia even mobilised; which
threatened the overthrow of France as its first major aim, although that
power might not be directly involved in the *casus belli;* and which involved
a clear transgression of the territorial rights of those neutral neighbours,
Belgium and Luxembourg. With such aggressive forces at work in Berlin,
and with such an irresponsible operational plan to hand, it was scarcely
surprising that what had begun as a quarrel in the Balkans should have
escalated into a conflict involving almost all of the Great Powers.[9]

Critics of the Fischer school have not only sought to dispute the validity
of the interpretation which it has placed upon German policy itself but –
and this is the obvious riposte to the claim that one power or person was
responsible for a historical act – they have also argued that the outbreak
of the war cannot be fully understood by looking merely at one of the
players in the game. The policies, aims and decisions of the other participants deserve equal scrutiny, if a fair overall picture is to be drawn. When
this is done, they claim, it will be seen that Germany was not alone in
1914 in containing elements who looked forward to war or in possessing
inflexible and aggressive war plans. The French General Staff, thirsting to
regain Alsace-Lorraine, was only with difficulty restrained from invading
Belgium itself as a flank move against Germany if war broke out. The
Russians possibly possessed the most inflexible plan of all, and their
inability to mobilise separately against Austria-Hungary proved to be one
of the most fateful errors of the July crisis. In Vienna, too, there existed
both the ambition to engage in a war and the military plans, however
confused, to implement that ambition. Even Great Britain had, as a
consequence of her staff discussions with France between 1905 and 1914,
become drawn into a system of military checks and obligations which no
one power alone could control. Should any of these states decide upon war
in order to achieve its aims, it was unlikely that the others could keep out.
Militarism, and military planning, had set up the European states like a
row of dominoes; and it only needed one to fall in order to bring all the
rest to the ground.[10]

The gist of this criticism is, therefore, that the approach of the Fischer
school, by omitting any significant *comparative* element, has taken the case
of Germany's actions in 1914 out of its full international context. It will
be the main purpose of the present collection to emphasise, both through
the selection of the articles assembled here and through the editor's introduction, the comparative approach in order to satisfy such a demand and
to permit the reader to see the problem in its wider scope. To ensure this
aim, the articles which have been included deal not only with the war
plans of the European Great Powers, Germany, Russia, Austria-Hungary,
France and Britain, but also with those of the United States, which,
although aloof from those rivalries which led to the outbreak of war in
1914, had nevertheless felt the need to prepare for the possibility of
conflict with other states at a time when she was expanding commercially

and territorially outside her traditional boundaries. Thus even if, at the end of the day, the reader still feels (as many claim to do) that the issue of responsibility for the First World War is too complex to be encompassed within one historical interpretation or another, it is hoped that he or she will have gained a broader appreciation of the problems involved through looking at them in this comparative manner.

The first of the articles that follows is Professor Grenville's broad survey of American war planning between 1890, when the United States was just about to enter the ranks of the imperialist nations, and 1917, when she abandoned her neutral stance and partook in the First World War. It is, incidentally, one of the earliest published works to have been able to take advantage of the opening of defence records which had hitherto been 'security-classified'.[11] Grenville reveals the very primitive nature of Washington's planning in the 1890s, illustrated above all by the fact that at the outbreak of the Spanish-American war the only war plan was that drawn up by a young lieutenant two years earlier, and then traces the gradual, if halting, evolution of more effective planning organisations and more detailed operational preparations for war. Most important of all, this piece offers an outline of the strategical calculations which were made against Japan and Germany, the two most likely enemies of the United States, and thus, even if many further details have now been revealed to enhance or amend Professor Grenville's article,[12] its inclusion in this collection is a matter of course.

The work of Professors Herwig and Trask (Chapter 2) not only goes some way to supplementing Grenville's study but also introduces in a comparative form the country which more than any other developed and refined its war plans in those years – imperial Germany. By the end of the nineteenth century both the United States and Germany had expanded into the outside world and were uneasily measuring each other up as they came into conflict in such regions as China, the Philippines, Samoa and Brazil; and the contingency plans drawn up in Washington and Berlin were the real, if secret, manifestation of this mutual suspicion.[13] Yet, although Herwig and Trask show that there was much in common between the armed services of the two countries – for example, in their enthusiastic acceptance of Mahan's view that economic rivalry would eventually lead to a war – the basic fact remains that the Americans were planning for a *defensive* campaign whereas both the German military plan and political aim were *aggressive*, involving as they did a large-scale breach of the Monroe Doctrine, which the Kaiser and many of his entourage always detested. The German scheme was thus another reflection of that pent-up demand by Europe's most powerful military and industrial state for what her propagandists euphemistically termed 'world-political freedom'.

Whilst the Americans set up the General Board of the Navy, the General Staff of the Army, and the Joint Army and Navy Board to prepare a coherent defence strategy, the British, too, under pressure from foreign rivals throughout the globe, were compelled to give much more thought to the problems of preparing for war than they had needed to in those cosy, mid-Victorian decades when Britannia ruled the waves. Only with the establishment in 1902 of the Committee of Imperial Defence was a systematic study of naval and military requirements instituted, although it is true that earlier, less weighty bodies had sought to define the basic principles of imperial defence and to draft defence schemes for the colonies.[14] The article upon the strategy of imperial cable communications (Chapter 3) illustrates the way in which 'defence by committee' worked in this particular respect and also reflects more general developments which took place in British strategy in this period.

However, it would be erroneous to conclude from this that the Committee of Imperial Defence ever became an effective 'centre of strategic planning'[15] in the years before 1914. The first of its two major aims, the integration of Britain and the entire empire into an organic, unified defence system achieved only limited success, conflicting as it did with the wish of the self-governing Dominions for greater political and legal autonomy from Westminster and for a greater say in local defence matters.[16] The second aim, the bringing together of the strategies of the army and the navy so as to prevent a dichotomy in planning which would be disastrous in wartime, led to even greater dissensions. Much has now been written upon this furious strategical debate,[17] but the next two chapters (4 and 5) provide us with good analyses of its origin – and its outcome. Professor McDermott's contribution clearly shows the remarkable transformation which took place in British military planning between the end of the Boer war, when the problems of imperial defence (and, above all, the defence of India from a Russian attack) fully preoccupied the army, and the turn of the year 1905–1906, when the strategy of dispatching an expeditionary force to Belgium and northern France in the event of a German attack westwards during the Moroccan crisis was accorded the highest priority. This marks the beginning of the debate over the 'continental commitment' which was to last for more than three decades of this century.[18] It was, moreover, a strategical 'revolution' which not only reflected important changes in international affairs but also boosted the importance of the army vis-à-vis that of the navy, and as a consequence provoked the suspicion and antagonism of the senior service. Yet the latter, as Mr Haggie points out, was in no position to offer a viable alternative strategy, partly because it was impossible for battleships to prevent a German assault upon France, and partly because the fiery First Sea Lord, Admiral Fisher, had thwarted all efforts to establish a naval war staff which could evolve a suitable 'maritime' strategy. Thus it was that, when a war plan was hammered out in the aftermath of the second Moroccan crisis in 1911, the navy was forced to accept the inferior role after centuries of strategical predominance.[19]

French operational planning before 1914 has only recently received close historical analysis,[20] but even now there is much less secondary literature upon this topic than upon, say, civil-military relations in France in the political field. In the formulation of overall strategy, there was less ambivalence in France's objectives than in those of Britain – which is scarcely surprising, for ever since 1871 she had regarded Germany as her main foe, however much Bismarck had sought to reduce this revanchism and however much colonial quarrels with the British had distracted French attention; but with Germany allied to two Mediterranean powers, the French navy had been constantly afflicted by doubts as to whether to station its main force at Brest or Toulon. The 1912 'naval understanding' with London – an agreement which Fisher's successor at the Admiralty found unavoidable and, in certain respects advantageous in following the latest expansion of the German fleet in the North Sea – not only solved the French Navy's agonising strategical dilemma but brought with it a political advantage of immense importance, namely, it increased the British government's moral obligation to come to France's aid in the event of a German attack. With the Royal Navy protecting French interests in the Channel, and the French navy underpinning the British Empire in the Mediterranean, the inter-connectedness of strategical and political factors in the formulation of war plans is all too obvious.

If the French admirals had to pay considerable attention to defence problems in the Mediterranean, the generals concentrated single-mindedly upon preparations for a great campaign along their north-eastern frontier. The only real question for the French General Staff was: should their operational strategy be defensive or offensive? In the later decades of the nineteenth century, the former had been preferred in view of France's inferiority to Germany in terms of numbers and mobility; but the rise of the idea of an *offensive à outrance,* based upon the belief that the morale factor was all-important, soon had its effect upon the higher ranks of the French army. Under Joffre, as Professor Williamson convincingly shows (Chapter 6), the entire strategy was recast, with the famous Plan XVII – involving a vigorous forward move into the 'lost provinces' of Alsace and Lorraine – replacing all previous strategies. But this contribution is also of value in illustrating the relationship between the French General Staff and the Foreign Ministry, the French calculations about, and military conversations with, their Russian and British counterparts, and, above all else, the attitude towards the neutrality of Belgium. Respect for the latter was not only connected with the hope for British assistance, but it also ruled out of consideration the only other region in which Joffre could deploy large armies in an offensive operation.

Whereas the French politicians compelled their military leaders to abandon the notion of violating Belgian neutrality, the Germans had fewer scruples – or, to put it another way, German diplomacy was much more affected by military considerations, and its General Staff and Admiralty Staff had much more influence in decision making than their French equivalents. This blunt difference is amply brought out in Dr Steinberg's clever analysis of the German naval plan of 1897 to invade Holland and Belgium (Chapter 7). The astonishing part of this scheme, as he rightly remarks, is not the detailed logistical and technical discussion over its feasibility, but 'the nonchalance with which the neutrality of both Belgium and Holland was tossed aside'. The disregard for the rights of neutral neighbours, the bland assumption that a state's politicians and diplomats served the military rather than the converse, and the ideology of *Realpolitik* which is present in every paragraph of this German plan, should remind us once again of the interpenetration and indivisibility of military *and* political factors in this matter of war planning.

The scheme to seize *points d'appui* in Holland and Belgium as preliminary stages of an invasion campaign against England formed only one of a variety of plans drafted by the Germans between 1896 and 1914 to deal with their great naval and colonial rival, as the next contribution (Chapter 8) reveals. Here, too, neutral rights were little respected: for, while the German navy later preferred to see the Low Countries remain neutral so as to preserve trade with the outside world through their harbours, it always pressed for an occupation of Denmark which would close the Baltic to the Royal Navy; yet the army, on the other hand, was pinning all its hopes upon a grand sweep westwards and therefore strongly disliked the idea of diverting its forces to over-run the Danes. If the Schlieffen Plan dragged an unwilling Belgium into the First World War, it was also the chief reason why Denmark's neutrality was respected. The other feature of the naval operations plans against England before 1914, apart from the relative impotence and organisational weakness of the German navy's planners in general, was the oscillation between an offensive and a defensive strategy – a reflection of the contradiction between the ambitious aims behind Germany's naval expansion and the (as yet) still inadequate means to implement such aims.[21]

Because the German navy, despite Tirpitz's ambitions, was only the junior service, the plans of the General Staff have attracted far more attention – and rightly so, in view of both their military and their political implications. Professor Turner's lucid survey of the Schlieffen Plan (Chapter 9) is therefore a vital component in this collection. He not only explains why the more moderate scheme of the elder Moltke was rejected by Schlieffen in the 1890s but also shows how the latter's own plan was substantially modified later by Ludendorff and the younger Moltke, with the effect that this bold, aggressive concept was rendered less likely to achieve the necessary swift success when war did break out, even though it still carried the enormous political disadvantage of placing Germany in the position of being the aggressor, and that against a neutral neighbour. Moreover, Professor Turner also examines in detail the calculations which took place in Berlin during the first Moroccan crisis which was probably the best opportunity ever afforded to the Germans to deal with France, at least from the strictly military point of view. But German policy, too, could be affected at times by diplomatic and political considerations,[22] and the German sword remained in its scabbard. Eight years or so later, under far less promising circumstances, it was finally unleashed.

The adoption of Schlieffen's scheme to solve the military problems of a two-front war by placing all hopes upon an immediate assault westwards meant that Germany's eastern frontiers would be only weakly defended in the early stages of the campaign; it also implied, by extension, that the

Germans became ever more interested in the military support they could obtain from their long-standing ally, Austria-Hungary. The only trouble was, as Dr Stone relates in his contribution (Chapter 10), that the Austro-Hungarian General Staff also wished to crush another power – in their case, Serbia – before turning against Russia. Thus both Berlin and Vienna were interested in their ally's taking the offensive against their common enemy in the east whilst each secured a quick victory over a third power. Despite the agreement of 1909, therefore, it was a position ridden with mutual uncertainty; and at the outbreak of war itself the ironical situation occurred in which both the German and Austro-Hungarian armies were unable to undertake the offensive against Russia which they had promised each other because their respective General Staffs were concentrating almost all their attention upon their more immediate objectives, France and Serbia. In addition to exposing this lack of co-operation, Stone's chapter is also interesting in its analysis of the role – actual or alleged – of railway timetabling in restricting the flexibility of national strategy, which was yet another characteristic that Germany and Austria-Hungary had in common.

Precisely the same charge of indecision of policy and inflexibility of plan can be made, as Professor Turner points out in the final chapter (11), against Russian war preparations in 1914; and, on deeper probing, there is similar evidence to suggest that here, too, military leaders who wished for a more general (and, to them, more attractive and decisive) war used their 'expertise' to convince the civilians that the movement of vast numbers of troops by rail, once begun, was irreversible, and that partial mobilisation was impossible. Moreover, we see now that the role of the French in pressing the Russian General Staff into a full mobilisation, understandable no doubt in view of Paris's apprehensions about an immediate German assault, had the actual effect of triggering off the Schlieffen Plan which they so feared. Finally, here as elsewhere,[23] Turner reminds us of the lack of comprehension which existed in the minds of so many statesmen about the implications of ordering the mobilisation, whether complete or partial, of their country's armed forces.

What conclusions, then may be drawn from this collection of essays regarding the most important questions, military and political, which historians have posed about the prewar plans of the Great Powers?

From the purely military point of view, interest has concentrated upon how coherent and logical a national strategy has been; that is to say, what degree of ambivalence and/or flexibility was contained in the planning, and how effectively did the two armed services co-operate in pursuit of the defined major objective? Furthermore, how effectively was co-operation instituted with one's allies, and what additional problems of formulating and implementing a coherent strategy did this give rise to? How successful and realistic were the plans on the whole, when we consider them retrospectively? To what extent were the actual fighting conditions of 1914-18 anticipated and prepared for?

It is a rare event to discover complete coherence and single-mindedness in any Great Power's contingency planning, if only because it is likely to have more than one potential area of danger in a world where numerous nation states are protecting and enhancing their 'natural interests': strategical ambivalence is therefore the normal situation for all but a few countries, yet if one's armed forces are divided to meet these various threats, concentration of power is lost and one runs the grave risk of being beaten *en détail*. The United States, for example, although well clear of the European alliance system, was constantly torn between her Pacific interests (out of a fear of Japan) and her Atlantic interests (out of a fear of Germany), particularly at a time when no isthmian canal existed to shorten the journey between one theatre and the other. The logical solution, as the American gorvenment finally admitted in 1916, was to be strong in both oceans[24] – but no other state was wealthy enough to be able to implement such a neat solution to its problems. Great Britain, all too aware of a declining rather than a growing national strength, provides us with a classic example of strategical ambivalence, where eventually one aspect had to be sacrificed at the expense of the other. Since the time of the Tudors, the British 'Janus' looked both to the outside world, where it was building up an enormous and profitable empire, and to Europe, where it possessed a permanent interest in seeing that no one country dominated the continent.[25] For most of the nineteenth century the prospect of a dislocation in the European balance of power had not seriously existed; after 1905, it appeared to certain Britons to be very likely indeed and had to take priority. But this shift from an essentially maritime to an essential continental strategy was not effected without a great degree of bitterness.

The continental states, too, suffered from an ambivalence which affected their war planning. Austria-Hungary might recognise in Russia her most formidable foe; but this did not curb that passionate desire to deal with Serbia as soon as a war broke out. The dispatch by Conrad of the famous *B-Staffel* (the reinforcing army), firstly to the Serbian front, and then a week later to the Russian front in the early stages of the war illustrates the dangers inherent in not firmly resolving such an ambivalence beforehand.[26] In the German case, the dilemma seemed to be resolved by the adoption of Schlieffen's daring scheme; but this placing of all the German eggs in the basket of a hoped-for success in the west not only harmed Germany's image in the eyes of the world and brought her two additional foes in the shape of Belgium and Britain, but also gave the German strategy a rigidity which no other power possessed. Moreover, by watering down Schleffen's plan by 1914 his successors not only reduced the chances of its success but also revealed that they were still acutely conscious of their country's strategical dilemma. Russia's ambivalence was somewhat similar to that of the Central Powers: a wavering between a concentration upon the minor enemy, whom she would like to defeat first, and a need to defend herself against the major enemy, whose movements at the outbreak of war were uncertain. As the events of 1914 showed, St Petersburg had about as much success in reconciling these two military aims as Berlin and Vienna. Finally, the French, who had for centuries suffered as a consequence of divided military objects (against the Low Countries, against Spain, against the German states, against England), for once possessed a relatively unambiguous strategy as a consequence of the *entente cordiale;* for the arrangement with Britain not only removed the possibility of war with that country which had been strong until 1903 or so, but also reinforced the Italian desire to abandon the Triple Alliance and thus permitted France to concentrate upon the defence of her north-eastern frontier.

One subsidiary aspect of this vital problem of strategical coherence relates to the harmonisation of the aims of the military and naval branches of a country's defence forces. A state which was essentially continental, such as Russia and Austria-Hungary, had little trouble in this respect, for the navy served simply as an adjunct to the army; France, too, was similarly placed by 1914, with her navy being required chiefly to secure the lines af communication through the Mediterranean. For the United States in a period of isolationism, in contrast, the navy was all-important and the army was more or less a home-defence force.[27] Prolonged inter-service dissensions broke out only in Germany, where Tirpitz and the Admiralty Staff sought in vain to break free from the strategical dominance of the General Staff; and in Great Britain, where the Royal Navy struggled to maintain its traditional supremacy within the armed services at a time when circumstances suggested that only by adopting the army's scheme for a 'continental commitment' could the independence of France and the Low Countries be maintained. It is, perhaps, not surprising that it was in Great Britain that the furthest steps were taken to create an organisaion (the Committee of Imperial Defence) whose task was to ensure that the strategies of the army and the navy were integrated, since both sought primacy for their own operational schemes. Even here, no full harmony was achieved,[28] but elsewhere the creation of genuinely 'joint' planning bodies was far less advanced. Either, as was the case with the US Joint Army and Navy Board, there was no pressing need to give teeth to a (nominally) central organisation; or, as was the case in Russia, Austria-Hungary and France (despite the latter's formal *Conseil Supérieur de la Défense Nationale*), one service was clearly unchallenged in its primacy; or, as was the case in Germany, the Kaiser's concern about his own privileges prevented not only the creation of some equivalent to the CID but also any real emergence of a Cabinet style of collective ministerial government which would settle national policy. 'Who rules in Berlin?', Berchtold's famous question of 31 July 1914 about the contradictory messages emanating from the military and civilian wings of the German government, was one which had been asked many times before.

Co-ordination between allies was an even more difficult task to implement. The lack of true strategical harmony between Moltke and Conrad has already been pointed to – and the same disharmony occurred, incidentally, in the Austro-German naval arrangements in the Mediterranean at the outbreak of war - but other examples emerge from the *entente* side. Britain and Russia had never really made preparations to co-operate at all, and only in the summer of 1914 were tentative steps taken in the naval sphere.

As for Britain and France, the political scruples of the Liberal government ruled out any fixed promises of support, with the result that, although Joffre could regard British support as likely if Germany made an aggressive move westwards, he could never count with certainty upon the arrival of the British Expeditionary Force. Even the Franco-Russian military alliance, as Professor Williamson explains, was hardly of an intimate nature, joint planning being chiefly discussed at very formal staff meetings each year, with the two General Staffs keeping many aspects of their own plans to themselves. What held them together was a mutual fear of Germany; and the blunt fact that the Schlieffen Plan (whose general outlines were known in Paris and St Petersburg) dictated that the German riposte to a conflict with Russia was an assault upon France. Moreover, military arrangements between allies often added 'frictions', to use Clausewitz's term, to the already large problems facing the General Staffs. The French were always pressing for a Russian promise to advance before the latter's army was likely to be fully mobilised; Conrad demanded that Moltke agree to a swift German advance eastwards when Berlin's preferred strategy was to stay on the defensive in that theatre; Moltke, likewise, demanded an Austro-Hungarian pledge to assault Russia when Vienna wished to concentrate upon Serbia. Allies, in other words, might bring aid but they also brought further problems and uncertainties.

With regard to retrospective consideration of how successful and realistic, militarily speaking, the prewar planning of the Great Powers turned out to be, the evidence suggests that the 'experts' almost completely failed to anticipate the actual fighting conditions, and also forgot that in any case no country was likely to surrender quickly even if badly mauled in the field because of the existence of allies.[29] This seems all the more discreditable when one realises that there were in the late nineteenth and early twentieth centuries not one, but two, quite different projections of the course of future wars. On the one hand, there was the image of the elder Moltke's three swift campaigns against Denmark, Austria and France, and the belief that, since railways had vastly increased mobility and since modern indus-trialised states could efficiently mobilise millions of men, a war would be decided within weeks, if not days, of its opening. On the other hand, there was the image of the American civil war and the Russo-Japanese war, and the publication of such works as Ivan S. Bloch's *Modern Weapons and Modern War*, which suggested that future conflicts between the Great Powers would be long-drawn-out tests of endurance, where the defensive would have the advantage over the offensive and where the fighting would go on until one or both sides collapsed in economic ruin or recognised the stalemate for what it was.

Why, then, did the General Staffs plump so wholeheartedly for the first of these alternative scenarios, and disregard the second? Military considera-tions alone, as we shall argue below, cannot fully explain this choice; but the fact remains that in so many countries the General Staffs abandoned a strategy which appears in retrospect to have been more realistic. The elder Moltke's scheme for a defensive stand against France and a limited offensive against Russia appears, in view of the French disasters in Alsace-Lorraine and the disorganised state of the Russian army in 1914, to have had a better chance of success than Schlieffen's gamble; and in addition it would have taken from Germany's shoulders the onus of attacking Belgium, and possibly have kept Britain neutral. The French defensive strategy of the post-1871 period was also superior to Joffre's rush towards the Rhine, which simply played into the German hands. And would not the Russians have done better to have desisted from advancing into East Prussia, and the Austro-Hungarians from invading Galicia? One wonders, in addition, whether the British Cabinet would have been so willing to support their General Staff's strategy had they possessed any premonition that the war would not be over by Christmas. However, the adoption by the Great Powers of a defensive strategy would not only have contradicted what the generals believed to be those key military characteristics of speed and concentration, but they would also have indicated greater moderation in national objectives, a willingness to wait upon rather than to instigate events, and less conviction in the idea of an 'all or nothing' war which was so common in the summer of 1914.

Since this leads from the military to the political aspects of our topic, it will be as well to consider now the chief questions which have been asked about the role of war planning in the latter sphere. The first, and most important, aspect has always been concerned with the extent to which operational planning factors encroached upon the freedom of action of the central government itself, either by affecting its foreign policy or in actually provoking a decision for war. Were the military alliances a cause of the First World War? Did mobilisation mean war rather than a piece of diplomatic 'bluff'? Did railway timetabling replace decision making by human beings at the high point of the 1914 crisis? And how far were the fears of that old Liberal, Campbell-Bannerman, justified, when he argued that if General Staffs were created they would plan wars against other states and then probably ensure that their plans were realised?[30] The crucial topic of the proper balance in civil-military relations is involved in all of these questions, but it would be as well at the outset to remember that the constitutional position differed from country to country. The ability of the soldier to influence or even dictate policy was far less in the Anglo-Saxon countries, and also in France, than it was in the three conservative monarchies of eastern Europe.

That said, however, it is clear that the military factor encroached upon the civilian in all these countries, with only the United States government in 1914 still able to regard its military planners as working out academic contingency schemes. Even the 'non-commital' Anglo-French staff talks turned out to have implications which gave them a political dimension, as the critics of Grey's *entente* policy had forecast all along. In the first place, they made for an increasingly heavy *moral* commitment on Britain's part to support France in the event of war, not only because their respective General Staffs had worked so closely together but also because the November 1912 agreement had promised joint consultations between the governments when 'something threatened the general peace'; and while this did not legally bind London to the French, it compromised a truly neutral position – and, of course, completely ruled out the idea of Britain fighting on Germany's side, which by 1914 nobody thought possible. Furthermore, the Anglo-French naval understanding of 1912 bound the British in a much more concrete manner, for they accepted that it was as a result of this that the French left their Channel coast undefended by sea; thus on 2 August 1914, before any decision for war against Germany, the British Cabinet agreed with Grey's wish to assume responsibility for the defence of France's northern coastline. Even at this point neither France nor Germany – nor, for that matter, Grey and Asquith – was absolutely certain of Britain's actions, and it was more out of a sense of political and moral obligation to defend Belgium and the balance of power in Europe than as a consequence of some legally binding military treaty with France that Cabinet and Parliament voted to enter the war. The Anglo-French staff talks and the imposition of strategical unity by the CID in 1911 were more decisive in esablishing what sort of war Britain would fight *if* she came in than the question of *whether* she was obliged to come in; but they certainly caused many politicians and officials to regard intervention as being very likely.[31]

If the voice of the military planners was not all-powerful in Britain, the same was true in France, where the government was determined not to be the first to begin hostilities, nor to invade Belgium. On the other hand, it was also determined to fulfil its obligations to its Russian ally if the *casus foederis* occurred; yet even if the French had tried to wash their hands of that commitment, the Germans would not have let them, and on 1 August Berlin demanded not only French neutrality but also the occupation of some key border fortresses – which the German government calculated it would be impossible for Paris to agree to. In that sense, it was the exigencies of the German operations plan which brought France into the war even before her own alliance obligations did so.

The case of Austria-Hungary is perhaps the most interesting of all from one point of view, for in Vienna it was the civilian element represented by Berchtold which was pushing forward the military represented by Conrad into a swifter beginning to hostilities than the Chief of the Austro-Hungarian General Staff believed feasible. This in no way is to say that Conrad opposed the war – he had been anticipating it for years – but the diplomatic circumstances of late July appeared to Berchtold to favour action as soon as possible and he was probably the only statesman in Europe in this crisis who felt that mobilisation schedules were too slow! He also provides a good example of a 'militarised' civilian, one who was only too keen to see diplomacy replaced by hostilities. As for the role of alliances in causing war, it was admittedly true that only with Berlin's support could Vienna hope to undertake an action which might lead to a conflict with Russia; but it was also highly probable that the Austro-German alliance had deterred the Russians from attacking their weaker rival in the Balkans many times in the past and was therefore, particularly under Bismarck, a potential instrument for holding both Vienna and St Petersburg in check. In 1914, however, Germany was unwilling to restrain, and Russia was unwilling to be deterred; and it is to the capitals of those two powers that we must turn if we are to understand the key elements in the catastrophe.

The relationship between the civilian and military wings of government at St Petersburg in July 1914 was most complex. Undoubtedly, the existence of a military alliance with France made all the Russian leaders more willing to take risks than otherwise would have been the case – and the urgings of Poincaré of the French General Staff and the French ambassador, Paléologue, reinforced this consideration. Undoubtedly, too, no distinction can be detected within the Russian establishment about the anger felt at Austria-Hungary's aggressive reaction to Sarajevo and about the recognition that Russia would be obliged to defend Serbia. The real gulf emerged over the question of partial or general mobilisation. The Tsar favoured the former because he hoped to keep Germany out of the war; Sazonov also favoured it at first because he thought it could be used as a warning to Vienna without alarming Berlin. When the Russian military leaders declared that a partial mobilisation would dislocate their plans, it appeared that this strategy of 'bluff' had failed and that military incompetence and inflexibility had once again cramped the style of the civilians. Yet Professor Turner's chapter (11) puts all this in a new light by demonstrating that it could have been possible for Russia to institute partial mobilisation *had the generals so wished*, and also that Sazonov (who later changed his mind and urged full mobilisation upon the Tsar) was mistaken in his earlier calculation because even partial mobilisation would have been sufficient to send the German war machine into action, owing to the military terms of the Austro-German alliance and the inner logic of the Schlieffen Plan. To this extent Turner, and many others before him, have been correct in regarding the Russian decision to mobilise at all as one of the most fateful acts in this drama.

But it is in Berlin that the climax of any analysis of the influence of war plans must be found, if only because it was there that the crucial relationship between 'the sceptre and the sword' was most deranged, and because this imbalance had more far-reaching consequences than any other. Here again, we observe that common element of a government believing that it is obliged to support an ally, both in fulfilment of an international treaty and in defence of its national interests and honour. We also observe that tension between the diplomat, seeking to gain extra time, and the soldier, eager to ensure that his schedules run smoothly and countering any threat to them by the use of 'technical' arguments – witness Moltke's insistence on 1 August that the army could not possibly go on the defensive in the west. But it is here that comparisons begin to falter and we see that German war planning was, in certain respects, unique. For it was only the German plan which involved an attack upon another power (France), whether or not the latter wished to become involved in the war; it was only the German plan which involved the violation of neutral territory simply to satisfy military exigencies; and – most important of all – it was only in the German plan that mobilisation meant war. It is this fact, quite apart from the debate instigated by the Fischer school about the political and economic aims of German policy, which makes Berlin the centre of the 1914 crisis in military terms as well.

The British mobilisation of the fleet, and preparations to dispatch the expeditionary force, did not mean war; both measures could have been cancelled, and it was not until 5 and 6 August that the War Council and Cabinet respectively decided to give formal approval to the dispatch of the BEF. The French efforts to be ready in time also did not mean war; and Joffre was firmly restrained from any premature rush across the frontier which would put France in the wrong. Austro-Hungarian mobilisation also did not mean a jump over the brink; the declaration of war on Serbia itself was all-decisive, and the generals were straining to meet a deadline set by the diplomats. Even in the Russian case, a distinction had been drawn from 1912 onwards between 'the proclamation of mobilisation' and 'the order for the opening of hostilities';[32] and, although the Russian General Staff hoped and expected that the first would equal the second, there still existed the possibility of controlling events after mobilisation – and even for changing the general mobilisation back to partial mobilisation, as the Tsar did late on 29 July.

But the German plan was of a different nature; for Schlieffen, in attempting to solve the dilemma of a two-front war, had pinned all hopes upon defeating France whilst the more backward Russia was still mobilising. A Russian mobilisation *without the Powers going to war* until, say, a month or so later would totally upset this scheme, for the Russian 'steamroller' would then be in a position to invade East Prussia just as the bulk of the German army was moving against France – instead of six weeks later, as the German General Staff calculated! In other words, Russian mobilisation had to mean a declaration of war by Berlin. Thus Germany was the only country which drew no distinction between an act of 'brinkmanship' and the opening of hostilities. Criticism of Grey, Sazonov and other *entente* statesmen for not understanding this seems hardly fair, for it was surely difficult for them to conceive that that which still existed in their countries had no place in the German calculations; and it is therefore only by special pleading that one can regard the Russian decision to mobilise as the most fateful step taken during the crisis – since it was fateful simply because of a German operations plan which demanded the immediate opening of hostilities as its consequence. It may be that the Great Powers would have gone to war over the Austro-Serb conflict even if Grey had managed to get diplomatic discussions under way whilst all sides stood mobilised; but the exigencies of the Schlieffen Plan, together with the policy formulated in Berlin, precluded that possibility from ever being realised. Finally, there is the further evidence, provided in Fischer's latest book, that not only did Bethmann Hollweg himself privately admit that Russian mobilisation 'cannot be compared with those of the West European states', but also that the leadership in Berlin was only waiting for the news of a full mobilisation by Russia to give it the excuse to open up the war in the west. Thus the quarrel between the sceptre and the sword in Berlin on 29 July was solely concerned with conflicting views upon the reasons adequate enough to justify Germany's own offensive steps; and the degree of mobilisation of the Russian army appears to have been less significant in *military* terms – for Moltke, wanting to use its partial mobilisation as a reason, was declaring war in any case – than in *political* terms – since the Chancellor feared that the Chief of General Staff's proposal might too clearly expose the government's policy to the suspicious Social Democrats at home and the British abroad.[33] A comparative study of the war planning does not shift the focus of attention away from Berlin, in other words.

Was it, then, a 'war by timetable'?[34] Certainly not, as far as the British and French were concerned; even the latter's urgent pleas for a swift Russian mobilisation did not mean that war had to begin, for it was of course in the French interest to delay tthe outbreak of hostilities as long as possible, which was precisely why the German General Staff could not tolerate such a contingency. Even when we examine those critical occasions in which railway timetables appeared to affect the course of events in Vienna and St Petersburg, the evidence suggests that the soldiers were using false arguments to win over the civilians to their line of action: Dr Stone has shown that Conrad's statement that the dispatch of the B-Staffel troops to the Serbian front was irreversible was not true, and Professor Turner has shown the falseness of the Russian General Staff's claim that partial mobilisation was impossible. Only in the German case did the planning take all alternative strategies out of the government's hand, and as soon as Russia had mobilised Bethmann-Hollweg found himself reduced to being the diplomatic instrument of the Schlieffen Plan, his own concern being to present Germany's actions in the best possible light. Yet even in regard to the German operational scheme, alternative plans *could* have been devised, had the generals so wished it: the elder Moltke's strategy, for example, would have served the German government's purposes excellently in 1914. Was there not an advantage in keeping one's options open? Why place all hopes upon Schlieffen's *Va Banque* operation?

Part of the answer to this has to be found in the failure of politicians and diplomats to control their General Staffs. After all, even Clausewitz had admitted that 'the subordination of the political point of view to the military would be contrary to common sense' beause 'policy is the intelligent faculty, war only the instrument'.[35] Yet in 1914, in certain crucial cases, the relationship was reversed and military considerations were elevated to the primary position. Why did not the Russian government ensure that its army could carry out a partial satisfaction if that was required? And why, above all, did the German government not scrutinise more carefully all the implications which flowed from the adoption of Schlieffen's new scheme? It is scarcely adequate to answer that the technicalities of modern warfare made such scrutiny impossible, for we have only to turn to that famous CID meeting of 23 August 1911 to see that this was not always so in other countries. The host of questions put then to Admiral Wilson by such strong-minded, articulate and informed listeners as Churchill, Lloyd George,

Haldane and Asquith quite undermined the impractical Admiralty plan to launch an amphibious assault on the German North Sea or Baltic coasts in the event of war with that country. Moreover, although the army's alternative plan, of sending the BEF to France, was agreed to be the more realistic, Churchill and others had also challenged some of the General Staff's assumptions about the likely course of the land war in Belgium in its early stages.[36] It is true that the CID still had a long way to go if it was to become a true centre of strategic planning, but that meeting and several others (the 1903–5 and 1907–8 invasion inquiries, the 1912 Mediterranean decision) provide examples of the way in which civilians could scrutinise plans *if they so wished*.

This conditional clause leads us to the other reason why the war plans played such a decisive role in 1914, namely, the blunt fact that they encapsulated not merely the strategical calculations of military 'experts' but also many of the prevailing political assumptions of the establishments of the Western world at that time. To begin with, there was that belief in the need to take firm action in the defence of national interests, regardless of what were considered to be the eccentric notions of liberals and pacifists about international arbitration: 'my country, right or wrong' may have been coined by an American politician but it captures a much more widespread attitude. The Austro-Hungarian government regarded the Serbs as a grave threat to the empire's autonomy and was determined not to tolerate any slight to its prestige; the Russian government, humiliated in the Bosnian crisis of 1908–9, was now resolved to protect its Balkan interests, if need be by force; the German government felt itself bound to Vienna, its only remaining ally, and entitled to prepare for action against its Franco-Russian foes; the French government could not let Russia be eliminated by the Central Powers; the British government, conscious of its historic interest in the European balance of power, could not let France and Belgium be over-run by a hostile Germany. In this connection, we should also recall the American determination to brook no transgression of the Monroe Doctrine. Each of the war plans, it is worth noting, reflected the respective power's assumptions about what its political, diplomatic, economic and moral interests were. To ask for fundamentally different plans – say, British non-involvement on the continent, or Russian non-response while Serbia was being attacked by Austria-Hungary – is to ask for fundamentally different political attitudes.

But the military plans were also conditioned by background attitudes in another way, in that they reflected, through their inflexibility and demand for instant action, the mood of fatalism and determinism that was so strongly in evidence in the prevailing ideology. The social-Darwinistic notions of a struggle for survival; the hyper-patriotic feelings of the military men and the 'militarised' civilians; the cultural pessimism of elites alarmed at developing threats both within and without; the disregard for the concepts of international law and morality; the dislike of compromise, and the desire for 'total' solutions – is not all this to be witnessed in the war plans, giving them those characteristics which have appalled later critics?

The French stress upon *élan* and *cran* as integral parts of the strategy of revanche, which alone explains the folly of the rush towards the Rhineland; the Russian animosity towards its German foes and sense of its 'mission' in the Balkans; the fatalism of Conrad and Berchtold that only by a great war would the question of the future of the Austro-Hungarian monarchy be settled; and Captain Schröder's objections (in the German naval plan of 1897) to the 'artificially constructed clauses of international law', an attitude which of course the whole Schlieffen Plan fully reflected, are all part of a mentality which goes far to explain features of the prewar planning which otherwise appear bewildering. There were no defensive strategies, because they were not wanted; there were no alternatives, because inflexibility was as much in the mind as it was in the railway timetable; there were no schemes for stalemate and compromise, because a swift and absolute victory was what was demanded;[37] and there was little civilian control over the military because very often they both had the same objectives and shared a common ideology.

To put it in another way, the tensions which occurred between civilians and military in Berlin, Paris, St Petersburg and elsewhere following the Sarajevo assassination arose mainly out of a dispute over means, not ends. There is no doubt that the respective governments had generally failed to examine properly the means their General Staffs proposed to use in a crisis and were disturbed at the extent to which strategic exigencies curbed their freedom for diplomatic manoeuvre; but this, as we have argued, is an insufficient answer to the problem. Any proper inquiry into the war planning of the Great Powers in that period must in the end concentrate not so much upon the military technicalities as upon the political and ideological assumptions of which they were an expression. Only there can one discover the real meaning behind those carefully prepared, minutely timetabled and inflexibly conceived plans which took Europe over the brink of war in the summer of 1914.

NOTES

1 I take the term from Professor James Joll's seminal lecture, *1914: The Unspoken Assumptions* (London, 1968). It might be objected here that what is so clearly written down in an operations plan can scarcely be regarded as 'unspoken'; but, as Dr Steinberg has shown in regard to the German plan to invade Holland and Belgium (see Chapter 7 below), the most significant fact is precisely the way in which certain political and moral judgements within these operational writings were simply taken for granted by their authors and their intended audience, both having a similar cast of mind.

2 Compare, for example, the lack of detail about German plans to invade such small neighbours as Denmark and the Netherlands in the official naval history *Der Krieg in der Nordsee*, Vol. I (Berlin 1920), by O. Groos, with the revelations in Chapter 7 below.

3 See the complex of military (and civil) staffs and committees which has evolved in Great Britain by 1944 in J. Ehrman, *Grand Strategy*, Vol. VI

(London, 1956), appendix IV; and also Chapter X on 'The central organisation'.

4 G. Sutherland (ed.), *Studies in the Growth of Nineteenth-Century Government* (London, 1972); G. R. Searle, *The Quest for National Efficiency 1899–1914* (Oxford, 1971), pp. 14ff.

5 D. S. Landes, *The Unbound Prometheus: Technological Change and Industrial Development in Western Europe from 1750 to the Present* (Cambridge, 1969).

6 On this phenomenon generally, see W. McElwee, *The Art of War: Waterloo to Mons* (London, 1974), especially Chapter 4; and J. F. C. Fuller, *The Conduct of War 1789–1961* (London, 1961), *passim*. More specifically, D. E. Showalter, *Railroads and Rifles: Soldiers, Technology and the Unification of Germany* (Hamden, Conn., 1975).

7 For examples of this on the British side, see B. Bond, *The Victorian Army and the Staff College 1854–1914* (London, 1972); C. Barnett, *Britain and Her Army 1509–1970. A Military, Political and Social Survey* (London, 1970), pp. 299ff.; and, more generally, D. D. Irvine, 'The origin of capital staffs', *Journal of Modern History*, X, no. 2 (June 1938).

8 W. J. Reader, *Professional Men* (London, 1966); Z. S. Steiner, *The Foreign Office and Foreign Policy 1898–1914* (Cambridge, 1969); Sutherland (ed.), op. cit.

9 F. Fischer, *Germany's Aims in the First World War* (London, 1967), pp. 3–92; idem, *War of Illusions. German Policies from 1911 to 1914* (London, 1975), *passim*; J. Röhl, *1914: Delusion or Design?* (London, 1973); V. R. Berghann, *Germany and the Approach of War in 1914* (London, 1973); I. Geiss, *July 1914* (London, 1967).

10 G. Ritter, *The Sword and the Sceptre. The Problem of Militarism in Germany*, Vol. II, *The European Powers and the Wilhelminian Empire 1890–1914* (London, 1972); and especially, L. C. F. Turner, *Origins of the First World War* (London, 1970); idem, 'The role of the General Staffs in July 1914', *Australian Journal of Politics and History*, XI, no. 3 (December 1965), 305–23.

11 The first published book using these records was probably W. R. Braisted's *The United States Navy in the Pacific, 1897–1909* (Austin, Texas, 1958), a study of wider significance than its title at first suggests.

12 Apart from Chapter 2 in this book, see also Braisted's second study, *The United States Navy in the Pacific, 1909–22* (Austin, Texas, 1971); and R. D. Challener, *Admirals, Generals, and American Foreign Policy 1898–1914* (Princeton, New Jersey, 1973).

13 See also P. M. Kennedy, *The Samoan Tangle; A Study in Anglo-German–American Relations 1878–1914* (Dublin/New York/Queensland, 1974), pp. 290–3; and Herwig's latest study, *The Politics of Frustration. The United States as a Factor in German Planning 1888–1941* (Boston, Mass., 1976).

14 F. A. Johnson, *Defence by Committee* (London, 1961); N. H. Gibbs, *The Origins of Imperial Defence* (Oxford, 1955); J. P. Mackintosh, 'The role of the Committee of Imperial Defence before 1914', *English Historical Review*, LXXVII (July, 1962), 490–503.

15 Johnson, op. cit.

16 D. C. Gordon, *The Dominion Partnership in Imperial Defence 1870–1914* (Baltimore, 1965); J. E. Kendle, *The Colonial and Imperial Conferences 1887–1911* (London, 1967); R. A. Preston, *Canada and 'Imperial Defense'*

(Durham, North Carolina, 1967); J. Gooch, *The Plans of War. The General Staff and British Military Strategy c. 1900–16* (London, 1974), Chapter 5.

17 Apart from the works by Mackintosh and Gooch cited above, see also: N. d'Ombrain, *War Machinery and High Policy. Defence Administration in Peacetime Britain 1902–14* (Oxford, 1973); S. R. Williamson, *The Politics of Grand Strategy: Britain and France Prepare for War, 1904–14* (Cambridge, Mass., 1969); N. W. Summerton, 'The Development of the British Military Planning for a War against Germany 1904–14', 2 vols (PhD thesis, University of London, 1970); B. Bond, *The Victorian Army and the Staff College*, pp. 212ff.

18 On which, see M. Howard, *The Continental Commitment* (London, 1972); and P. M. Kennedy, *The Rise and Fall of British Naval Mastery* (London, 1976), Chapters 9–11.

19 Gooch, op. cit., pp. 289ff.; Williamson, op. cit., pp. 167ff.; d'Ombrain, op. cit., pp. 103ff. The best recent survey of Fisher's attitude is R. F. Mackay, *Fisher of Kilverstone* (Oxford, 1973), pp. 330ff.

20 Williamson, *passim*; P. G. Halpern, *The Mediterranean Naval Situation 1908–14* (Cambridge, Mass., 1971), especially Chapters III–V; H. I. Lee, 'Mediterranean strategy and Anglo-French relations 1908–12', *Mariner's Mirror*, 57 (1971), 267–85.

21 P. M. Kennedy, 'Maritime Strategieprobleme der deutsch-englischen Flottenrivalität', in H. Schottelius and W. Deist (eds), *Marine und Marinepolitik im kaiserlichen Deutschland 1871–1914* (Düsseldorf, 1972); idem, 'Tirpitz, England and the second Navy Law of 1900: a strategical critique', *Militärgeschichtliche Mitteilungen*, Issue 2 (1970).

22 B. Vogel, *Deutsche Russlandpolitik. Das Scheitern der deutschen Weltpolitik unter Bulow 1900–6* (Düsseldorf, 1973), pp. 161ff.; Fischer, *War of Illusions* (London, 1973), pp. 54–7; A. Moritz, *Das Problem des Präventivkrieges in der deutschen Politik während der ersten Marokkokrise* (Frankfurt am Main, 1974).

23 Turner, *Origins of the First World War*, pp. 91–115.

24 Braisted, *The United States Navy in the Pacific, 1909–22, passim*.

25 Kennedy, *The Rise and Fall of British Naval Mastery, passim*; M. Howard, *The British Way in Warfare* (Neale Lecture, London, 1975).

26 See Stone, Chapter 11 below; and idem, 'Die Mobilmachung der österreichisch-ungarischen Armee 1914', *Militärgeschichtliche Mitteilungen*, Issue 2 (1974).

27 It is to the Second World War that one must look to see the US navy and army pursuing different strategic priorities, with the former eager to concentrate on the Pacific war (where it would have the greater scope and prestige) and the latter preferring the 'Germany first' strategy (for a similar reason).

28 However, it is difficult to understand how d'Ombrain can write, 'The military policy with which the Government found itself saddled in August 1914 had been settled on and evolved quite independently of the CID' (*War Machinery and High Policy*, p. 112), when it was at the special CID meeting of 23 August 1911 that the army's scheme found far greater favour than the navy's, and when the government itself confirmed that strategy on 5–6 August 1914. What is true is that the CID never developed 'joint' planning of amphibious assaults (Williamson, *The Politics of Grand Strategy*, p. 370), but that was precisely because such

assaults were regarded as part of the maritime rather than the continental strategy.

29 L. L. Farrar, *The Short-War Illusion* (Santa Barbara/Oxford, 1973), *passim*; McElwee, *The Art of War*, Chapter 9.

30 Searle, *The Quest for National Efficiency 1899–1914*, pp. 23–4.

31 Williamson, op. cit., pp. 367–72.

32 Turner, *Origins of the First World War*, p. 46; idem, 'The edge of the precipice: a comparison between November 1912 and July 1914', *RMC Historical Journal*, 3 (1974), *passim*.

33 Fischer, *War of Illusions*, pp. 491–4.

34 The title of A. J. P. Taylor's book on this subject, published London, 1969.

35 Quoted in Fuller, *The Conduct of War*, p. 152.

36 Williamson, op. cit., pp. 187–93; Summerton, *The Development of the British Military Planning* . . . Vol. 2, pp. 434–71.

37 In this connection, it is interesting to note the hostile reaction given to Bloch's theories about the course of future wars by German military experts: see R. Chickering, *Imperial Germany and a World without War* (Princeton, New Jersey, 1975), pp. 387ff.

I

Diplomacy and War Plans in the United States, 1890-1917[1]

J. A. S. GRENVILLE

In 1890 America was at peace, the golden age appeared to be at hand; unfettered by the miseries of European strife, in prosperous rather than splendid isolation, the American people confidently looked forward to an even more exciting furture. But a new age of danger was rapidly approaching; the nineteenth century conditions of American safety – geographical isolation, the British fleet, as it turned out, the 'hostage' of Canada in American hands, and the balance of power in Europe – were passing away. The era which had seen the new world fattening on the follies of the old was coming to an end; soon the follies of the old world impinged on the peace and prosperity of the new. Within three decades the contest for world power fought out in Europe, and the rise of the youngest of the great nations, Japan, were to endanger the safety of the United States. Yet few Americans recognised the full import of these changes and the need for fresh policies.

In the conduct of foreign affairs one of the most essential considerations must always be to adjust policy, sometimes rapidly, to changing conditions. Now we know that the American people remained overwhelmingly isolationist in sentiment long after Washington's admonition to avoid entangling alliances had lost its validity. What, however, of America's leaders? How well did they perceive the new configuration of power and politics which faced America in the twentieth century? Much study has been devoted to this subject; but the contribution to American foreign policy of those men, the generals and admirals, whose very business it was to consider in concrete terms the shifting balance of world power, is virtually an unknown chapter, although this contribution was an important one. From the recently opened records of the United States Army and Navy Departments we may now attempt to answer one vital question, namely, how far strategic advice was responsible for the new role played by the United States in world affairs during the first two decades of the twentieth century. In the search for what Kennan has called 'the realities' of American policy a few weeks spent examining the military records are worth many years of theorising.[2]

Until the 1890s the American armed forces were considered not so much as the country's first line of defence against outside aggression, but as a police force to subdue troublesome Indians and Mexicans. In 1890, the same year as the Kaiser sensed the coming age of *Weltpolitik,* a number of men in America tried simultaneously to awaken the American people to the dangers. The intellectual giant among them was Captain Alfred Thayer Mahan.

When he published, in 1890, his *Influence of Sea Power upon History,* Mahan was a lecturer at the Naval War College. He believed that the American continent was threatened both from the West and from the East. Germany with her expanding population and boundless energy, he thought, would sooner or later attempt to colonise South America, while the teeming millions of China and Japan might burst across the barrier of the Pacific Ocean. With the construction of the isthmian canal across Central America, the Caribbean, he also prophesied, would become one of the great life-lines of trade and consequently a region of intense international rivalry. He warned that, unless the United States possessed a dominant fleet when the canal was built, the canal would prove a source of danger rather than of safety and welfare. The United States must therefore not rest content until she controlled the canal itself, and guarded the approaches to it with a powerful fleet of battleships.[3] Behind the advocacy of the annexation of Cuba and Hawaii lay not so much a growing American imperialism as a concern for the safety of the isthmian canal and the American continent.

The same conclusion had been reached in the same year (1890) by a group of naval officers called together by Secretary of the Navy Benjamin Tracy. They advocated an ocean-going battleship fleet in place of the floating coastal batteries, which the American battleships of those days virtually were. In the years which immediately followed, Mahan's ideas were translated into political action by a number of younger politicians, of whom the most prominent were Theodore Roosevelt and Henry Cabot Lodge. Before 1898 these proponents of the so-called 'large policy' did not so much seek to lay the basis of an American empire overseas as to provide for the safety of the American continents in the new realities of power and politics as revealed to them by Mahan.

Theodore Roosevelt's opportunity to shape policy came when Cabot Lodge and his supporters persuaded President McKinley to appoint him Assistant Secretary of the Navy. In the Navy Department 'T. R.' had, as he would have put it, a 'bully time' – but according to an entry in the private diary of Secretary of the Navy Long, Teddy went about his business like 'a bull in a china shop'.

Hitherto, in the absence of other evidence from the naval archives, it has been customary to credit Roosevelt with a large share of responsibility for the war with Spain and especially for the involvement of the United States in the Far East through the acquisition of the Philippines. Was it not Roosevelt who on 25 February 1898 sent the famous telegram to

Commodore Dewey to prepare for an attack on the Philippines? This decision has rightly been regarded by historians as a momentous step in United States policy, and it was therefore tempting to look on it as part of a great expansion of America overseas, brought about, or plotted, as some would have it, by Roosevelt, the supporters of the 'large policy' and Commodore Dewey.

This view, as I have already tried to show, does not fit in with the actual objective which the proponents of the large policy had in mind – the defence of the American continents. Nor does it fit in with the evidence discovered in the Navy Department archives. Incredible as it may seem, the attack on the Philippines was a secondary consideration, a by-product of the war with Spain.

The idea of attacking the Philippines was neither Roosevelt's nor Dewey's but the brain-child of a young naval lieutenant, William Warren Kimball, whose name ought to have, but certainly has not yet, found its way into the history books. In 1896, that is, before Roosevelt had joined the Navy Department, Kimball had drawn up a war plan providing, in the event of a conflict with Spain, for a simultaneous attack on the Spanish possessions in the Caribbean and in the Pacific. The main theatre of war was designated as Cuban waters. An attack on the Philippines was intended as a secondary, almost incidental, operation, to be undertaken merely to humiliate and embarrass Spain. In 1898 Kimball's general plan, in the absence of another, won Navy Secretary Long's and Roosevelt's approval. Here then is a most striking example of how a war plan, drawn up by a young naval officer, altered the course of history.[4]

It was Kimball's plan which Roosevelt set in motion on 25 February 1898. Only after Dewey's victory at Manila Bay on the glorious first of May did the exponents of the 'large policy' suddenly become converts to the 'larger policy' of carrying the American flag across the Pacific. In the decision to retain the Philippines they played an important role, but strategic considerations and a number of officers, members of a newly created Strategy Board, played the greater part.

Shortly before the outbreak of hostilities, Long had recognised that the organisation of the Navy Department made it difficult to conduct war operations efficiently. The hydra-headed administration consisted of six boards, over each of which presided a naval officer, jealously guarding the power of his own department. It was not always easy to move a ship in time of peace, as the commanding captain was liable to receive quite contradictory orders from more than one bureau chief. Such a division of command would have proved disastrous in wartime. But Secretary Long despaired of reforming the system radically, and so, in March 1898, he created instead a special Strategy or War Board, composed at first of Roosevelt and three bureau chiefs, Captains Crowninshield and Barker, and Commander Clover. After Roosevelt's departure Mahan and Admiral Sicard joined the Board, replacing Captain Barker and Commander Clover. The Board's task was to act in a purely advisory capacity. Yet from this modest beginning developed the General Board, whose members exerted a decisive influence on the overall American strategic planning, down to the American entry into the First World War.

In May 1898 the Board sought to strengthen Dewey's position at Manila. After the news had reached them that Admiral Camara was collecting the remnants of the Spanish fleet, whose destination, they feared, might be the Philippine Islands, the Board advised Secretary Long to secure Dewey's lines of communication by the acquisition of the island of Guam. In May 1898 McKinley ordered troop transports to Manila and to Guam to support Dewey. Thus the exigencies of war drove America into a deeper Far Eastern commitment. When eventually the armistice of 12 August 1898 brought the war to an end, the United States found herself in occupation of Cuba, Puerto Rico, Guam and the Philippines. But whereas the military situation in the Caribbean reinforced a concept of American policy long cherished, the state of affairs in the Pacific was brought about largely by the adoption of Kimball's war plan and the strategic advice of the War Board during the course of the conflict. No concept of American diplomacy lay behind the occupation of a part of the Philippine archipelago and the consequent American involvement in Far Eastern rivalries.

President McKinley now faced the entirely new and unexpected problem of what to do with the Spanish possessions in the Pacific. The American Commissioners sailing for Paris to negotiate a peace were given clear instructions to implement American policy in the Caribbean as stated before the war, that is, to secure Spain's renunciation of sovereignty over her Caribbean possessions, but their instructions concerning the Philippines were vague. The War Board had warned that their occupation constituted a major burden for the United States, and McKinley was reluctant to assume it. Nevertheless, other considerations besides strategic ones led McKinley in the succeeding months to insist on the acquisition of the whole of the Philippine archipelago.

By an extraordinary coincidence the Far East had become the cockpit of European rivalries just at about the same time as the Cuban-Spanish-American war. Germany, not content with a gradual growth of economic influence in China, had proceeded to rob the Manchu Empire of Kiaochow. This greed ushered in a new era of European imperialism in China. Russia grabbed Port Arthur, and Britain, to restore the balance, took over Wei-hai-Wei from the Japanese. By the summer of 1898 the partition of China seemed probable. Special American business interests were much alarmed by the development and from the winter of 1897 onwards bombarded the State Department with petitions. America's great market of the future, they believed, lay in China. The possession of the Philippines appeared to them a providential base, from which America might make her influence felt on the mainland of Asia.

Then the exponents of the 'large policy' added their voice to the general clamour. Less than a week after the battle of Manila Bay, Cabot Lodge hailed Dewey's victory as giving the United States 'a foothold in the East', and as offering vaster possibilities 'than anything that has happened to this country since the annexation of Louisiana';[5] while Roosevelt enthusiastically replied from the troopship that was carrying him to Cuba that the war must not be concluded before Cuba, Puerto Rico and the Philippines were taken from Spain. Another influential member of the group, Cushman K. Davis, Chairman of the Senate Foreign Relations Committee, ardently desired to see the United States keep the Philippines, and was anxious lest a weak President and the Peace Commissioners in Paris, surrounded by 'sexless cosmopolites' and engaged in 'guzzling' and 'guttling', as he put it, might lose sight of America's real interests.[6]

McKinley spent his time earnestly praying for an answer to the puzzling problem of the Pacific, while Cabot Lodge went in and out of the White House talking hard at him. As the President saw it, the United States had assumed responsibility for the Philippines and could neither escape the white man's burden nor hand the rebels over to the vengeance of Spain. Moreover, if the United States withdrew from the Philippines, the islands would no longer remain in the hands of a weak power. The presence of Admiral Diederichs' German squadron, the ships of the other European powers, and of Japan, served notice that, if America gave them up, one of these countries would try to grab them. At first McKinley was inclined to limit American demands to the island of Luzon, but in the end, having first convinced himself that the Almighty and the American public demanded that the United States flag should remain there, he gave way to these various pressures and instructed the Peace Commissioners to demand the whole of the Philippines. When on 6 February 1899 the Senate, by a narrow margin, confirmed the treaty of peace, the United States became a Far Eastern power.

During the next five years, that is from 1899 to 1903, the administration endeavoured to adjust American policy to the entirely new state of affairs brought about by the war with Spain. An army was dispatched to suppress the Philippine rising, and Cuba became a protectorate at the same time. With consummate skill Secretary of State John Hay sought to strengthen America's position by diplomatic means. The only European power with possessions and naval forces in the Caribbean was now Great Britain. Fortunately it so happened that Britain, hard pressed by Russia and France, was just at this time trying to concentrate her military and naval forces; and the British Cadinet was thus ready to lend a more sympathetic ear to American aspirations. By the Hay-Pauncefote treaty of January 1902, Hay not only secured British assent to the exclusive American control over the projected isthmian canal but also in reality the British recognition of American predominance in the Caribbean. The treaty paved the way for Roosevelt's coup in Panama a year later.[7]

The problem confronting Hay in the Pacific and in China was infinitely more grave. In this vast region the United States not only faced a friendly Britain but also other European great powers as well as Japan, each one of them powerful enough to dispatch America's weak military forces to the bottom of the ocean. Hay's well-known Open Door Notes of 1899 and 1900 thus were intended to preserve America's interests in China by purely diplomatic means. By enunciating as the two principles of United States policy the support of equal commercial opportunity and the maintenance of the integrity of China, and by seeking to give these principles some international sanctions, Hay, like President Monroe before him, had announced to the world the United States' intentions without possessing the necessary military force to implement them. But whereas America's military power caught up with President Monroe's doctrine, the same was not true of the Hay doctrine. The acquisition of the Philippines and Hay's notes in effect led the United States into a Far Eastern quandary, from which there seemed no escape until some four decades later America's China policy lay in ruins.

The great need to build up America's military might in this new era of American policy was not lost on the more far-seeing men of McKinley's generation, but only when a president acutely conscious of the realities of force that underlie diplomacy entered the White House did the executive provide real leadership to the nation. That moment came when Roosevelt succeeded to the presidency in 1901. Roosevelt never ceased to strive to convince Congress and the nation that the defence of America's interests required above all a large fighting fleet, and that the determination and ability to go to war was the best guarantee of peace.

The younger naval and army officers also did battle against a military machine that seemed totally inadequate for modern needs. The war with Spain had underlined the need for adequate staff work and the success of the War Board had pointed the way for the future. Among the most persistent advocates of a general staff for the navy was Captain H. C. Taylor. He had first laid plans for such a staff before Roosevelt in May 1897; now in 1900 he brought the idea once more to the attention of Secretary Long. Long, however, was reluctant to risk a fight with his entrenched bureau chiefs, hesitant about allowing the professional officers wide powers outside civilian control, and rightly dubious whether Congress could be brought to approve the scheme. Consequently he compromised, and in March 1900 created a board, known as the General Board, which possessed no executive functions, but was to serve as a purely advisory council which was constitutionally confined to considering such problems of strategy as the Secretary of the Navy might refer to it.[8] Under the dynamic leadership of Admiral Dewey, its first president, the Board, whose other members were the President of the Naval War College, the Chief of the Bureau of Navigation and the Chief of Naval Intelligence, soon outgrew these limitations. It became the chief military council of the nation, advising successive presidents on the grand strategy which the country must follow to preserve her present interests and to provide for her expanding needs in the challenging future. The influence of the Board on America's foreign policy was profound. Just as Mahan had dominated strategic thought in the 1890s, so Dewey was the intellectual giant who bestrode the years from 1900 until, in 1914, a stroke curtailed his effectiveness. His service to the nation during the war of 1898 is well known and was lavishly rewarded by his countrymen, but his infinitely more important contribution to national policy in later years still remains to be recognised by the historian.

The army was until the outbreak of the First World War very much the weak sister of the services. The defence of the United States was regarded primarily as a naval problem, yet the garrisoning of the outlying American possessions involved the army also in new responsibilities. Weak in numbers, the army had hitherto coped successfully with Mexicans and Indians, but had been caught woefully unprepared by the war with Spain. With no strategy board to co-ordinate their efforts, the chiefs of the army bureaux at the War Department had proved quite unequal to the crisis.

Just as in the navy, however, a few able and young army officers were alive to the need to reorganise the War Department. Elihu Root, appointed Secretary of War in 1899 to still their complains and to meet the criticisms of Congress investigating the scandals of 1898, was finally responsible in 1903 for the creation of a General Staff. His staff borrowed the prestige of the Prussian name without allowing it to enjoy any of its power. Indeed he leant rather more heavily on the ideas of an Oxford professor, Spenser Wilkinson, who in 1890 had written a remarkable book, *The Brain of an Army*. The influence of the army General Staff on American strategic and foreign policy before the First World War was in fact very slight. Yet it became obvious that some degree of army co-operation would be necessary if the navy was to play its role, since the defence of naval bases was a problem requiring the help of soldiers. To meet this need the year 1903 also saw the creation of the Joint Army and Navy Board, presided over by the indomitable Dewey. As if an omen for the future, the first years of inter-service co-operation proved a lamentable failure.

These three staff organisations were charged with the responsibility for formulating America's strategic policy in the new picture of power and politics. Their success would depend in large part on their ability to assess the probable development of international relations accurately. Unfortunately the cardinal truth escaped them. They failed to recognise that the growing rivalries of Europe in the Caribbean aided the United States in pursuing a policy of dominance, while in the Pacific it undermined United States security. The doctrine laid down by the strategists from first to last, on the other hand, declared that until the United States possessed a fleet powerful enough to be divided between the two oceans, the battle fleet would have to be stationed on the Atlantic seaboard ready to enforce the Monroe Doctrine and to meet any conceivable European threat of invasion.

Every naval officer had taken to heart Mahan's teaching that economic rivalries were the true cause of global conflict, and then, by a process of applying 'the precepts of history', it seemed a logical conclusion to regard Germany and England as the ultimate mortal foes of the United States. All naval war plans of the period were based on an application of Mahan's 'doctrines', however absurd the conclusion to which they led. Consequently this slavish imitation of Mahan's historical techniques helped to warp American strategic thought.

Roosevelt was an outstanding *Realpolitiker*, regarding as worthless a policy which was not backed by force to maintain it and if necessary by threat of war. His estimate of the Kaiser's ambitions made it appear likely to him that one day Germany would attempt to colonise portions of South America. Consequently he approved of the policy of retaining the undivided battle fleet in the Atlantic Ocean. His diplomacy, moreover, sought in a more forceful way than Hay's to secure for the United States every strategic vantage point in the Caribbean. With this end in view he took advantage of a revolution in Colombia to occupy the territory through which the Panama Canal was destined to run. At the same time he seconded with great vigour and considerable success the policy of the General Board for a large battleship fleet.

During the first three years of his office, Roosevelt, strangely enough, paid scant attention to the Far East. He was content to leave the Philippine difficulties to his Secretary of War, Taft, and the Chinese question to Hay. Russia rather than Japan appeared to be menacing the open door in China, and the conclusion of the Anglo-Japanese alliance in 1902, an alliance which ultimately proved disastrous to Anglo-American interests in the Far East, was welcomed in Washington as tending to uphold the integrity of the Manchu Empire. The strategists, moreover, took a decidedly unrealistic and rosy view of America's Far Eastern position. The early war plans of 1903 and 1904 providing for the defence of the Philippines were intended to meet a European foe rather than Japan. The General Board had then decided on the establishment of a first-class naval base in the Philippines, and selected Olongapo in Subic Bay as the most suitable site, and the Joint Board added its agreement.[9] The fact that Olongapo could not be defended from the land side did not perturb the strategists at this time, as the probable enemy, Germany, could only operate with naval forces. The General Board also looked forward to the establishment of a naval base on the coast of China, so that in the event of a partition, America would be able to make her weight felt. The policy of the strategists, however, ran counter to Hay's diplomatic efforts, and although Hay in the winter of 1900 did inquire about the possibilities of leasing Samsa Bay, he was happy enough to allow the matter to drop on learning of Japanese objections. But marines were nevertheless stationed in the Philippines for several years in readiness for the seizure of a Chinese base. Hypnotised by the prospects of America's future needs in China, the General Board, incredible as it may seem, was still pressing for an American coaling-station on the Chinese coast as late as November 1905.[10]

While the strategists advocated a policy in the Far East outdated by rapidly changing events there, Roosevelt speedily recognised that American interests in China were deeply affected by the outbreak of the Russo-Japanese war. Just as in the Caribbean, where America's safety depended on the divisions in Europe, so in the Pacific, American security had in reality been founded on the balance of power which the rivalry of Japan and Russia had provided. During the early stages of the war Roosevelt favoured and admired Japanese prowess, David fighting Goliath. Japan's smashing naval victories and the efficiency of her army soon led him to view the situation differently. His decision to accept the role of mediator and to bring about peace was certainly founded on the belief that America's interests required the maintenance of the balance of power in the Far East. It could not, however, be done; military realities and the growing antagonisms of the European powers had permitted Japan to gain a predominant position. Britain, hoping to save her Yangtze interests by placing them under Japanese protection, renewed the Anglo-Japanese alliance in 1905 and 1911, while Russia turned her attention once more to the Balkans and was content to sign secret treaties with Japan at China's expense, which allowed Japan the lion's share of the bargain. Consequently the United States was powerless to alter the course of events on the Asiatic mainland. Yet Hay's notes had committed the United States to the policy of maintaining Chinese integrity. This was a dilemma which no amount of diplomatic skill and finesse could solve. Worse still, any insistence on the part of the United States that Japan desist from spreading her co-prosperity sphere might lead to a Japanese attack on America's Pacific possessions.

Soon after the conclusion of the Russo-Japanese war, the strategists took a hard new look at the strategic probelms of the Pacific. The result of their deliberations was hardly encouraging. Gone were the days when they thought America might share in the partition of China. Indeed, now it appeared that the Philippines could hardly be held in the face of a Japanese attack. Yet it took another four years before strategic policy was adjusted to the new military realities. From 1905 until 1909, it was Roosevelt who led the strategists rather than the strategists who guided the administration.

The navy in the Philippines had selected Olongapo as the site for a naval base, but the army now declared that they could not defend it. The reduction of Port Arthur had shown that without adequate land defence a naval base was useless. The army therefore suggested Manila and its bay with Corregidor Island as the most suitable site for a naval base capable of defence. Dewey, however, stubbornly rejected Manila Bay as impracticable from a naval point of view. Not even Roosevelt's personal intervention ended the inter-service bickering.[11] The General Board and the Joint Board had fallen on evil days. In the end, in 1909, the navy declared that no suitable site for a first-class naval base could be found in the Philippines and that accordingly Pearl Harbor in the Hawaiian Islands should be developed. Clearly the strategists had come to the conclusion that the Philippines were virtually impossible to defend.[12]

Roosevelt had, however, already anticipated this result of the discussion two years earlier, when he referred to them as America's heel of Achilles. While the sailors despaired, the diplomats were left with the thankless task of trying to appease Japan without sacrificing China. From 1905 to 1917 they negotiated a number of interesting agreements with Japan, which in substance allowed Japan a free hand on the mainland, while in phraseology they paid lip-service to the 'open door' and 'Chinese integrity'. The Taft-Katsura conversation of 1905 was the first of these; it was followed by the Root-Takahira agreement of 1908, and finally by the controversial Lansing-Ishii agreement of 1917. In truth these agreements were of little value. The Japanese government had no intention of precipitating a conflict with the United States by attacking the Philippines as long as the United States did not impede their programme on the Asian mainland. They were ready, moreover, to give every conceivable paper assurance on the 'open door' and Chinese independence, but this did not restrain them one iota from furthering their own aggressive aims. However laudable or cynical the intentions of American diplomats may have been, American policy in the Far East made very little impression on international developments there in the years from 1906 to 1917.

Roosevelt and the strategists were nevertheless rightly perturbed by the defenceless position of America's possessions in the Pacific Ocean. In such a situation it seemed the height of folly to injure sensitive Japanese pride by humiliating Japanese immigrants on the western seaboard. Roosevelt did his best to smooth over the crisis in American-Japanese relations caused by the problem of oriental immigrants, but not before, for the first time in their history, a Japanese war scare swept over the American people.

Theodore Roosevelt, whose grasp of the strategic realities underlying diplomacy was better than that of any president before the outbreak of the Second World War, believed that only a large navy could guarantee the safety of America's insular possessions in the Far East and gain respect for the country among the great nations of the world all arming to the teeth. He now redoubled his efforts to win Congressional approval for new naval construction. He got two new battleships a year, having asked for four, and in February 1907 secured Congressional approval for the construction of the first American Dreadnought. In battleship strength, with sixteen first-class battleships, America had already gained a safe margin of superiority over Japan. He sent the fleet around the world to show the American flag in the Pacific (December 1907 to February 1909) and he dealt with American-Japanese differences in a conciliatory but firm way. These were the elements of Roosevelt's Far Eastern policy from 1906 until he left the White House in 1909.

His successor, Taft, sought to meet the problem by the new expedient of substituting the dollar for guns in the Far East, and law for brute force in the world at large, while Wilson was forced during his first five years of office to focus his attention on the European catastrophe.

The two great war plans, worked out by the strategists during these years, were entirely defensive in character. They were denoted by a colour to represent a possible enemy, orange for Japan, black for Germany. While the Orange Plan is chiefly of academic interest and showed just how defenceless the United States' position in the Pacific was, the Black War Plan with its subsequent amendments proved a vital influence on America's defence policy during the years which preceded the American entry into the First World War. Together they represent a tremendous advance in American strategic planning and are in fact the first modern war plans in American history.

War Plan Orange was completed in 1914.[13] It showed a realistic grasp of the Pacific situation. Logistics dominated the problem as the naval strategists saw it. If the means were lacking to ensure the arrival of the full naval strength in the area where the decisive battle of the war would be

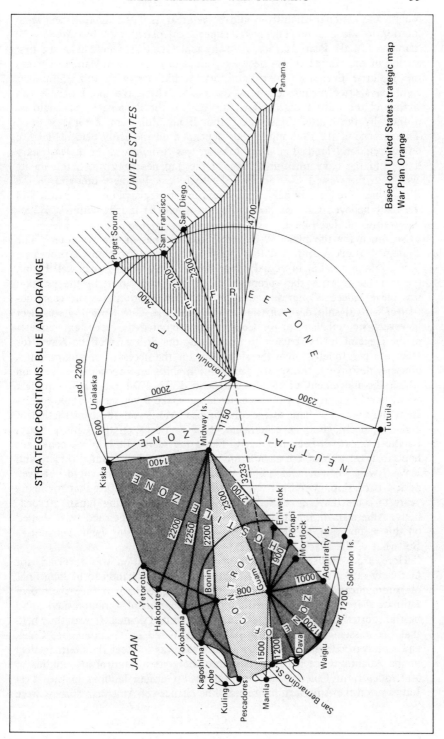

STRATEGIC POSITIONS. BLUE AND ORANGE

Based on United States strategic map
War Plan Orange

fought, the national calamity would be as great as if the fighting fleet were inferior to the enemy. The naval experts calculated that by way of the 'Panama Canal', Pearl Harbor, Midway and Guam, it would take the first section of the United States fleet sixty-eight days to reach Manila, whereas the Japanese fleet and troop transports would arrive in the Philippines eight days after having left Japanese ports. This gave the Japanese full control of the western Pacific for sixty days if the Panama Canal could be utilised by the United States fleet and, if not, full control for 104 days. The defence of the Philippines thus depended on the army plan of defence on Corregidor Island. The army mission was to hold out for at least sixty days, and the navy mission to engage the Japanese navy in battle on its arrival in the western Pacific, in order to relieve Japanese pressure on the Philippines. Guam was held to be the vital strategic point of control, and the navy believed that the decisive battle would be fought within a 1,200-mile radius of that island.

So much for the plans. What were the realities of the situation? The strategists frankly confessed that the plan departed from usual procedure in not taking account of actual conditions but in assessing that well before the war the reforms they proposed were instituted. In 1914 the position was bleak indeed. Congress had approved appropriations for the construction of a battleship fleet superior to the Japanese. The United States fleet however, was unbalanced, for Congress had ignored the persistent requests of the General Board, passed on to them by the Secretary of the Navy, for adequate personnel to man the ships and for the necessary auxiliary ships, cruisers, destroyers, transports, ammunition ships and above all colliers on which the movement of the fleet depended. In 1914 the battleship fleet could hardly reach San Francisco, let alone make a voyage of 10,000 miles from their Atlantic base to the Philippines. Moreover, the construction of defences, docks, and the establishment of garrisons on the United States Pacific islands had been neglected. The army in the Philippines could not hope to resist a Japanese assault for sixty days, while Guam, Midway and Hawaii were virtually defenceless and Pearl Harbor as yet could not even dock a battleship. War Plan Orange thus underlined the fact that for many years to come the United States was incapable of fighting Japan. Accordingly, American diplomacy during this period had to be, and was, shaped on this assumption, as illustrated by the famous Lansing-Ishii Agreement. But what of the Black War Plan?[14]

Here, from the strategic point of view the situation was reversed, for Germany rather than the United States suffered the handicap of long lines of communication. As against this, the strategists had to face their own estimate that a large German army of three-quarters of a million men could be transported to the West Indies and the United States. It was thus held that the mission of the United States fleet, based on Guantanamo, Cuba, and its advanced base, Culebra, Puerto Rico, was to meet the German fleet in the Atlantic, once it had passed into the zone of control at a radius of 500 miles from Culebra, and to prevent a German landing in the West Indies or on the American mainland. The chances of American success were rather gloomily rated about even. Clearly the strategists failed to recognise the enormous problems involved in endeavouring to send an army with all its supplies across the Atlantic Ocean. As yet geographical isolation still provided the North American mainland with a considerable degree of protection.

These two great war plans, Orange and Black, were completed before the outbreak of the First World War, and the historian approaches the 1914–17 period with some very interesting questions. We would like to know how far the war modified prewar plans, at what stage in the war the strategists drew up plans to co-operate with the allies, when precisely were the first army and navy plans drawn up to enable the United States to fight in Europe, what were the long-term objectives of the strategic planners, and to sum up, how far the nation had been brought to a state of preparedness before entering the war. The most important naval and army records for the period of the Wilson administration are now open to some historians and provide the answers to these fascinating problems.

As it turned out, when Congress in their investigation of 1920 addressed themselves to the problem of discovering how far the nation was prepared for 1917, they were asking the wrong question, and the answers they received from naval officers carefully hid the fact. From 1914 until February 1917 the General Board and the General Staff of the army were preparing not for the First World War but for the war which would follow it. The revision of the Black War Plan on 1 January 1915 recognised, it is true, that as long as the Central Powers and the *entente* were locked in battle, there was no threat to the Monroe Doctrine, and that in defence of American citizens maltreated by the Central Powers America might be forced to fight Germany.[15] But there was no thought of joining in the allied war effort; in effect the United States' war effort was limited to meeting any hostile German cruisers in the Atlantic. 'No other objective exists for the American fleet', in the words of the war plan, 'unless an expeditionary force is sent against German South Africa'! The Black War Plan was amended from time to time during 1916 and 1917 to provide for a variety of emergencies against a German fleet operating in the West Indies, and the purchase of the Danish West Indies was recommended by the Board in August 1916 to complete the defensive American position in the Caribbean.

Wilson pursued a lonely policy of trying to preserve America's neutral rights and of bringing the war to a close before the balance of power in Europe was destroyed. As late as February 1917 he shocked his Secretary of State, Lansing, by refusing to agree that an allied victory was necessarily a good thing. The Secretary of the Navy, Josephus Daniels, was deeply in sympathy with these pacific views, and while building up the United States navy, looked forward to a general disarmament after the European war was over.

In the summer and autumn of 1915 the General Board examined American naval needs in the light of the world war. Their views were adopted by Wilson. The General Board called for a navy second to none and recommended a building programme of battleship and auxiliary ships over a five-year period which would realise this aim. The great naval Act of 1916 gave this plan congressional sanction. But it is of cardinal importance to recognise that neither Wilson nor the strategists had recommended the construction of such a fleet in order to prepare the nation for intervention in the European war. In their memorandum of 6 August 1915 the General Board gave as their reason for the need of a large navy the problems that would face the United States when the war in Europe was concluded. 'History shows', the General Board wrote,

> that wars are chiefly caused by economic pressure and competition between nations and races . . . At the close of the present war it is not improbable that the defeated belligerents, with the connivance and perhaps participation of the victors, may seek to recoup their war losses and to expand at the expense of the new world. On the other hand, perhaps soon, the victor may challenge the United States . . . The naval policy should therefore make the United States secure in Western Atlantic, the Caribbean and the Pacific Oceans at the earliest possible moment.[16]

Even in August 1917 the Board could still write: 'A new alignment of powers after the present war must not find our fleet . . . unprepared to meet possible enemies . . . to act singly or jointly with all their naval powers against us.'[17] In the eyes of the strategists the United States had no friends in the world, only jealous rivals.

Perhaps the cardinal error of the strategists during the First World War was their failure to recognise the submarine menace. According to the General Board memorandum of 9 November 1915,

> The deeds of the submarines have been so spectacular that in default of engagements between the main fleets undue weight has been attached to them . . . Yet at the present time, when the allies have learned in great measure to protect their commerce, as they learnt a few months earlier to protect their cruisers from the submarine menace, it is apparent that the submarine is not an instrument fitted to dominate naval warfare.[18]

By 1917 they belatedly recognised that the issue of war hung on the success with which the allies could cope with German submarines. Every destroyer had to be pressed into service to convoy the allied supplies and the United States had less than fifty in commission at the outbreak of war.

And so it was that Wilson's passionate desire for peace, a mediated peace which he held was necessary to save 'white civilisation', and a grave strategic error on the significance of the submarine led the nation in 1916 to make a great military effort which was peculiarly ill-suited to the needs of 1917. Until February 1917 no thought whatever had been given to co-operating with the allies on land or on the high seas. Not even a rough plan existed to provide for the eventuality of sending an American expeditionary force to Europe. The war plans held in readiness by the army included an American invasion of Canada (1912–13) and also envisaged such possibilities as an attack on New York by Great Britain (March 1915) and the defence of the Pacific coast from a Japanese invasion (February 1915–March 1917).[19] The first plans for an American expeditionary force to Europe, not drawn up until February 1917, were based on the possibility of invading Bulgaria through Greece, and of invading France in the rear of the German armies in alliance with Holland.[20] All these plans were only fit for the waste-paper baskets of the War Department. Consequently the full impact of American intervention was delayed for many months. Wilson had not provided the leadership to prepare the nation effectively for a war which until the very last he regarded as disastrous, while the strategists had failed to consider eventualities which their president virtually refused to envisage.

I have attempted to provide a general and brief survey of the interaction of war plans, strategic planning and diplomacy for the momentous period in American history from 1890 to 1917. Looked at as a whole, these years witnessed a great change in diplomatic and strategic thought. Strategic concepts had virtually influenced American foreign policy in time of peace. But it is curious that practically the only offensive war plan to be found, Lieutenant Kimball's, coincided with the period when American power was only beginning to entitle the United States to be considered as a great power. The most striking characteristic of American war planning from 1903 until 1917 is that it was conceived in terms of defence, and also that the possibility of an alliance with Britain or any other power was given no consideration whatever. The military men continued to regard as absolutely axiomatic Washington's admonition against entangling alliances. But for a brief period their outlook remained entirely isolationist. Isolationism indeed was to most Americans not a 'policy' but a part of the American way of life.

NOTES

1 The research for this paper was undertaken while I was a member of the research seminar of Professor Samuel Flagg Bemis at the University of Yale during the session 1958–9 under the auspices of the Harkness Fund of the Commonwealth Fund. I wish to express my indebtedness to the Fund, to Professor Bemis for his wise counsel, and to the historical sections of the United States Army and Navy Departments, especially to Admiral E. M. Eller for his courtesy in enabling me to examine hitherto security-classified records.

2 The first book to do this, although not all the essential documents were available to the author, is William R. Braisted's scholarly and excellent study, *The United States in the Pacific, 1897–1909* (University of Texas Press, 1958). W. Schilling's 'Admirals and Foreign Policy, 1913–19' (unpublished Yale University PhD, thesis 1956), is also useful.

3 For Mahan's views on these points see especially his *The Interest of America in Sea Power Present and Future* (Boston, 1897).

4 War with Spain 1896. General consideration of the war, the results desired, and the consequent kind of operations to be undertaken. Plan by W. W. Kimball, Lt US Navy, Staff Intelligence Officer, 1 June 1896.

Navy Department, National Archives, Washington. See also Braisted, op. cit.

5 John A. Garraty, *Henry Cabot Lodge* (New York, Knopf, 1953), p. 197.
6 Garraty, op. cit., p. 199.
7 See J. A. S. Grenville, 'Great Britain and the isthmian canal, 1898–1901', *American Historical Review*, LXI (1955).
8 Harold and Margaret Sprout, *The Rise of American Naval Power* (Princeton University Press, 1946), p. 247.
9 Records of the Joint Army and Navy Board, National Archives, Washington, 9 December 1903, 19 December 1903.
10 General Board Correspondence, United States Navy Department, 25 November 1905, for a summary of strategic policy on this point and for the reaction of the State Department to naval demands.
11 Joint Army and Navy Board, 6 November 1907, 29 January 1908, 31 January 1908, 19 February 1908.
12 General Board Correspondence, 24 February 1909. Joint Army and Navy Board, 5 March 1908, 8 November 1909.
13 War Plan Orange, War Portfolios, United States Navy Department.
14 War Plan Black, War Portfolios, United States Navy Department.
15 War Plan Black, War Portfolios, United States Navy Department.
16 General Board Correspondence, 6 August 1915.
17 ibid., 29 August 1917.
18 ibid., memorandum on General Policy, 9 November 1915, Josephus Daniels Papers, National Archives, Washington.
19 Army War Plans, National Archives, Washington, reference to folios Canada, Great Britain and Japan.
20 Army War Plans, reference to folio Germany, memorandum, 3 February 1917.

2

Naval Operations Plans between Germany and the USA, 1898–1913. A Study of Strategic Planning in the Age of Imperialism[1]

H. H. HERWIG AND D. F. TRASK

In recent years historians on both sides of the Atlantic have been most eager to analyse the effect, on both internal and external affairs, of the creation of a large German battle fleet by the Imperial Naval Office ('Reichsmarineamt').[2] A number of scholars have gone one step further and investigated the actual tasks assigned to this force by the Admiralty Staff ('Admiralstab').[3] However, the existence of both German and American naval plans against each other has received little or no attention from historians of German-American relations. When such plans are mentioned, confusion, lack of precise data and heated sentiments all too often preclude sober discussion. After the First World War, William II denied to his blood relative George Sylvester Viereck the existence of any plans against the United States. 'Never was any plan for military or naval action against the United States prepared or even contemplated.'[4] The Kaiser's memory had obviously faded. The first discussion of such German naval plans appeared in two articles by the German-American scholar Alfred Vagts in the *Political Science Quarterly* (1939 and 1940). In the 1930s, during a visit to the Foreign Office in the Wilhelmstraße, Vagts examined copies of reports by the German naval attaché in Washington, Kapitänleutnant Hubert v. Rebeur-Paschwitz, to the State Secretary of the Naval Office, Kontreadmiral Alfred v. Tirpitz.[5] In 1958 Walther Hubatsch revealed an *Immediatvortrag* of 26 February 1900 by the Chief of the Admiralty Staff, Vizeadmiral Otto v. Diederichs, that recommended an attack on the coast of New England in the event of war between Germany and the United States. Hubatsch dismissed the plan as emblematic of 'der in allen Admiralstäben üblichen routinemäßigen Uberlegungen . . . Sie [the study] ist niemals zu einem Operationsplan ausgereift, sondern lediglich im März 1899 als Denkschrift aufgesetzt, die in ihrer Art ein Unikum geblieben sein dürfte.'[6] 'The American plan likewise has received little mention. It is best discussed in an unpublished Yale University dissertation of 1954 written by Warner Roller Schilling. Schilling's work was limited because he lacked information concerning the German plans; in a footnote he drew attention to a plan from 1901 by 'a Lieutenant on the German General Staff'.[7] A later study of American diplomacy and war plans by J. A. S. Grenville did not exhaustively treat the Black War Plan.[8] The following article is based primarily on document collections deposited at the Bundesarchiv-Militärarchiv in Freiburg, and at the US Naval History Division, Washington, DC.[9] Its purpose is to revise earlier treatments of these plans and to clear away some of the myths and misapprehensions still surrounding this topic.

I

The German naval documents do point up one *Unikum*, to use Hubatsch's term. There exists a study dated 13 March 1889 which first dealt with the possibility of a German-American war. It is certainly conceivable that the dispute between these two countries over possession of the Samoan Islands in that same year lead the Admiralty ('Admiralität') to turn its attention to the possibility of a future German-American naval encounter.[10] On 23 February 1889, the Acting Chief of the Admiralty, Vizeadmiral Freiherr v. d. Goltz, requested *Promemoria* on the subject 'Wie ist der Krieg mit Nordamerika zu führen und was ist dazu in die Wege zu leiten'. Kontreadmiral Guido Karcher, Chief of Staff of the Admiralty, replied to the request on 13 March, recommending 'die feindliche Kriegsflotte zu vernichten, die Handelsflotte durch Vernichtung und Vertreibung von den Meeren zu zerstören und endlich durch Bombardement . . . das Land zu schädigen und einen Druck auf die Bevölkerung auszuüben.' Karcher recognised that the German fleet was still too small effectively to carry out an invasion of American territory, and therefore concluded that the fleet would have to limit itself to 'Bekämpfung der Kriegsflotte und Störung des Handels durch Kreuzerkrieg.' The plan allowed for isolated cruiser raids, in order to interrupt maritime trade on the east coast of the United States, but stated quite clearly: 'Der Krieg wird sich hauptsächlich als ein Kreuzerkrieg abspielen.'[11] Germany's naval impotence against the United States in the Samoa question did not go unnoticed by her political leaders. A decade later, when German and American business interests once again clashed over the Samoan Islands, Bernhard v. Bülow, State Secretary of the Foreign Office, commented: 'Der Vorfall auf Samoa ist ein neuer Beweis dafür, daß sich überseeische Politik nur mit einer ausreichenden Flottenmacht führen läßt.'[12]

On 10 April 1898, Germany took the first step towards creating just such a *Flottenmacht* by passing the first Naval Law calling for 17 ships of the line, 8 *Küstenpanzer*, 9 large and 26 small cruisers, to be backed by a material reserve of 2 ships of the line and 7 cruisers. The passage of the bill was facilitated by a most clever naval propaganda directed by Tirpitz's Naval Office.[13] No stone was left unturned, no path untried, in this masterful manipulation of public opinion. The most prominent academicians in Germany joined the Tirpitz bandwagon,[14] providing a scaffold of cultural, economic, political, military and vulgar Darwinistic timber for the new structure.[15] This naval propaganda became 'ein höchst wirksames Kampfinstrument . . . Sie wurde Funktion eines nicht nominell, aber faktisch bestehenden Propagadaministeriums'[16] Few bothered to examine more closely the likely repercussions that such a measure would ultimately exert on Germany's relations with her European neighbours. It is perhaps profitable at this stage briefly to discuss past interpretations of Germany's naval policy under Admiral v. Tirpitz.

For Tirpitz and, to a lesser extent, for Bülow, the construction of a mammoth battle fleet was a clear either/or situation: 'Entweder Weltgeltung oder Niedergang.' Tirpitz formulated this position in his initial Reichstag speech on behalf of the first Naval Law on 6 December 1897: 'Ihre [Deutschlands Seeinteressen] Erhaltung ist zu einer Lebensfrage Deutschlands geworden. Werden diese Interessen Deutschlands in Zukunft unterbunden und ernstlich geschädigt, so muß Deutschland erst einen wirtschaftlichen und dann einen politischen Niedergang erleiden.' In the same session Bülow defended the Bill with the following words: 'Die Zeiten, wo der Deutsche dem einen seiner Nachbarn die Erde überließ, dem anderen das Meer, und sich selbst den Himmel reservierte, wo die reine Doktrin thront – [Heiterkeit – Bravo!] – diese Zeiten sind vorüber.' And further: 'Wir wollen niemand in den Schatten stellen, aber wir verlangen auch unseren Platz an der Sonne.'[17] Under the guidance of these two men Germany entered into a truly New Course, that of *Weltpolitik* and navalism.[18]

The creation of the fleet was justified by the *Risikogedanke* behind it; its ultimate strength would deter any naval opponent from risking an all-out naval encounter with Germany, to be left, even after a victorious outcome, at the mercy of a strong third naval power or coalition. In addition, it was hoped that the fleet would boost Germany's *Bündnisfähigkeit*, especially to relatively minor powers also in search of *Weltgeltung*. Gerhard Ritter has described the *Risikogedanke* as 'einen grausamen Irrtum' and the entire German naval policy as 'gigantische Fehlspekulation.'[19] Certainly the fleet contributed heavily to the growing antagonism between Germany and England; Ludwig Dehio has described Tirpitz's naval policy as 'eine Art von kaltem Krieg gegen die englische Weltstellung.'[20] There can also be no doubt that the fleet was constructed and developed primarily with England in mind.[21] And finally, it must be mentioned that this fleet was basically an offensive weapon.[22] It, and it alone, was to secure for Germany that cherished place in the sun:

> Es kam für uns also nicht darauf an, durch die Seerüstung zu verteidigen, was wir besaßen, sondern mit ihrer Hilfe friedlich zu erringen was wir besitzen wollten: Weltmacht. Dieser offensive Wille allein bietet die zureichende Erklärung für unseren Flottenbau. Er ist seit der Jahrhundertwende immer wieder formuliert worden.[23]

In 1898 the Spanish-American war provided German naval enthusiasts, flushed with their recent victory in the Reichstag, with an example of the importance of naval power for *Weltpolitik*. As early as 24 October, 1897, the *Münchner Allgemeine Zeitung* had published a statement by a member of the Centre Party supporting the pending naval Bill in the Reichstag. The anonymous writer assigned the future navy the task of abolishing the Monroe Doctrine by actively assisting Catholic Spain in the impending war with the United States. The American Secretary of State, John Sherman, was informed of this point of view by his envoy to Denmark.[24] In the same year Admiral George Dewey announced: 'It is indecent to fight Spain anyhow. Now, if France could come in too, we could save our faces, but best of all if Germany would come in. If only Germany could be persuaded to come in.'[25] The confrontation in the summer of 1898 in Manila Bay between Vice Admiral Dewey and Vizeadmiral v. Diederichs fanned the flames of navalism; war fever ran high in both countries.[26] The United States emerged anew as a dangerous rival for Germany in the pursuit of colonial possessions. The Republic pointed the way to a place in the sun by annexing the Hawaiian Islands, the Philippines, Guam and Puerto Rico in the aftermath of the erstwhile struggle for Cuban liberty.[27] Overnight the United States appeared as a serious factor in German naval planning.

On 22 November 1899 William II had told the British statesman Arthur James Balfour: 'Whenever war occurs in any part of the world, we in Germany sit down, and we make a plan.'[28] And indeed, during the winter of 1898 a young lieutenant in the Supreme Command of the navy ('Oberkommando der Marine'), the future naval historian Eberhard v. Mantey, had turned his attention to the formulation of a theoretical war plan against the United States. The assignment of these *Winterarbeiten* in 1897–8 reflected the growing German-American naval rivalry; the first five topics listed all dealt with aspects of American policy.[29] The *Winterarbeiten*, generally assigned either to test the theoretical planning capabilities of certain officers, or to shed light on current naval problems, have all too often been dismissed as insignificant *essais* by junior staff officers anxious for recognition and promotion. On the contrary, they often formed the basis for, and reflected the direction of, Admiralty Staff planning.[30] This is especially true if one keeps in mind that the senior Admiralty Staff officers did not take an active role in at least the initial and formative stages of planning, preferring instead to save their talent and energy for the *Immediatvorträge*, in which they had to present and defend these plans before the Supreme War Lord.[31]

In stark contrast to the study from 1889 by Kontreadmiral Karcher, a staunch supporter of cruiser warfare, Mantey recommended a naval assault on the area between Portland, Maine and Norfolk, Virginia.[32] 'Heir ist der Kern des Amerikanischen Landes, und hier können die Vereinigten Staaten [am] empfindlichsten getroffen und am leichtesten zum Frieden gezwungen werden.' Since the United States could not be blockaded into surrender due to its unlimited natural resources, the war would have to be won 'durch Erfolge auf dem Festlande der Vereinigten Staaten selbst'. In short, Mantey suggested a joint naval-military occupation of Norfolk, Hampton Roads and Newport News (later on also Gloucester, Massachusetts), to be followed up by operations up the Chesapeake Bay in the direction of Washington and Baltimore. Mantey noted particularly the dire condition of the American navy. Congress seemed extremely niggardly with its funds, thereby forcing the navy to copy existing, and hence antiquated, European designs. American democracy further hampered development: 'Ein großer Ubelstand für die Marine ist der, daß jeder freie Bürger mitreden darf und daß er, falls seine Meinung abgelehnt wird, rücksichtslos in der Presse den größten Lärm macht.' Finally, armoured plates still had to be purchased abroad since the local industries did not yet possess 'die genügenden Erfahrungen und ausreichende Leistungsfähigkeiten'. The American army was also pretty much of a 'quantité négligeable'. The only reliable troops available were some cavalry regiments that had been kept in combat readiness fighting the Indians! The militia was not even on a level with the German reserve: 'Der Dienst der Milizen ist die reine Spielerei.' And finally, morale in the armed forces was far below German standards. 'Man macht den Soldaten das Leben so leicht wie möglich, sorgt für gute Unterbringung, gute Verpflegung, gibt ihm fast keinen Dienst. Die Folge davon ist sehr gelockerte Disziplin, jammervolles Exerziren und viele Desertionen.'[33] Admiral Hans v. Koester, Chief of the Baltic Naval Station and designated Inspector-General of the navy, noted: 'Einverstanden. Eine fleißige Arbeit, die in übersichtlicher Weise einen allgemeinen Uberblick über die Küstenverhältnisse der Vereinigten Staaten gibt und im gegebenen Moment daher besonders interessirt.'[34] From the latter part of this verdict, it can safely be deduced that the possibility of a war with the United States was very much in the minds of some of Germany's leading naval officers. Was one already looking towards greater horizons than England and the North Sea?

In the United States such a daring scheme was not thought possible. In 1898 Commodore G. W. Melville, Chief of the Navy Department's Bureau of Engineering, estimated that in order for an enemy to risk operations in American waters, he would need a fleet twice the size of the American navy.[35] This could only mean the British navy; even on paper the German fleet did not qualify.

On 14 March 1899 the German Supreme Command of the Navy was dissolved by *Allerhöchste Kabinettsordre* and the Kaiser personally assumed the 'Oberbefehl der Marine'. Kontreadmiral Felix Bendemann was appointed first Chief of the newly created Admiralty Staff. The same month the ambitious Mantey submitted a second *Winterarbeit*, probably ordered by Kontreadmiral Oldekop or Koester,[36] which formed the basis for all later work on the operations plan against the United States. It far outdid the 1898 work in both boldness of scope and daring of execution. No less a target than New York City was selected. Mantey expected the United States to spread its troops in a thin line between Newport and Norfolk, with either New York or Norfolk serving as the navy's mobilisation centre. He dismissed Cape Cod, Nantucket Island, Martha's Vineyard, Block Island and Cape May as *Stützpunkte,* deciding instead on Norfolk. The success of this bold plan lay in the speed of its execution. Already in time of peace the requisite supplies and materials would have to be stored in German ports so that both men and material could be shipped to the eastern seaboard of the United States immediately following the declaration of war. Due to the unexpectedness of such a lightning strike 'kann man hoffen, die Minensperre noch nicht vollendet, das Personal zum Sprengen noch nicht hinlänglich ausgebildet, die Küstenbefestigungen noch nicht völlig armirt und mit genügender Munition versehen vorzufinden'. The Spanish-American war served to support these plans. 'Man erinnere sich nur der Zustände in Havana und in den Amerikanischen Häfen nach Ausbruch des vorjährigen Krieges, wie lange es dauerte um die Häfen nur einigermaßen verteidigungsfähig zu machen.' As examples of successful naval initiative Mantey cited Nelson's seizure of Copenhagen in 1801, the storming of New Orleans in 1862, and Admiral Farragut's 'damn the torpedoes' entry into Mobile harbour in 1864. Last, but not least, civilian panic would assist naval operations. 'In New York wird die größte Panik bei dem Gedanken an ein mögliches Bombardement ausgebrochen [sein].'

In this second study Mantey estimated that by 1900 the United States navy would consist of 7 ships of the line, 14 cruisers and 14 Küstenpanzer. Therefore Germany would need 17 ships of the line, 33 cruisers and 4 auxiliary cruisers for successful operations on the eastern seaboard. Three thousand tons of coal would be needed daily. By cruising for 25 days at an average speed of 8 to 9 sea-miles, it was estimated that 75,000 tons of coal, to be transported in 40 to 60 freighters, would be required. The problem of supplying this force with coal, ammunition, medical supplies, food etc., for an extended period in American waters was not discussed. Mantey's greatest worry remained the possibility that the American navy might refuse a decisive naval encounter. Basing his intelligence reports upon information received by the General Staff of the Army from Captain Count G. Adolf v. Götzen, Germany's military attaché in Washington, Mantey decided upon the deployment of two separate naval units. A blockade fleet would be stationed at the exit of Long Island Sound and a main fleet, for the storming of the New York fortifications, would arrive in New York at the same time. Entry into the harbour would be forced on the very day of arrival. If army troops ('2–3 Bataillone Infanterie und 1 Bataillon Pionire scheinen vollig ausreichend') were to be taken along, which Mantey did not think particularly necessary, they would be landed on Long Island and the main attack postponed until the morning following arrival. Once entry into the Lower Bay was forced, Forts Tompkins and Hamilton would be engaged and, if possible, grenades hurled into New York City. If this frontal attack failed, the force could withdraw and occupy Block Island, which afforded good telegraph connections with Germany. Mantey estimated that in order to overwhelm both the American navy and the coastal defences of New York, Germany would need 33⅓ per cent naval superiority.[37]

This daring plan was submitted to Vizeadmiral August Thomsen, Chief of the First Battle Squadron. Thus the 'Winterarbeit vom grünen Tische' progressed through the offices of the Naval Academy, Baltic Naval Station and Admiralty Staff to the highest-ranking, active commanding Front-Officer. Thomsen recognised the merits of the plan but discounted Mantey's emphasis on the element of surprise. New York could not simply be over-run and the long trip could not escape the attention of American intelligence forces. Applying a reverse *Risiko* thesis, Thomsen concluded:

> Der vorgeschlagene direkte Angriff auf New York wird daher für uns voraussichtlich nicht möglich sein, solange die Flotte der Vereinigten Staaten von Nordamerika noch existirt, und wenn sit nicht mehr existirt, wird auch die unsere so geschwächt sein, daß wir den Angriff auf die Befestigungen schwerlich unternehmen können.

The Admiral had an alternative plan. Instead of seizing Norfolk as a *Stützpunkt,* he suggested 'Perteriko', the seizure of which 'würde nur geringe Schwierigkeit machen'. If the American fleet engaged the German forces here, this would be to Germany's advantage since the enemy would then also be far removed from his home bases. From Puerto Rico operations against the mainland of the United States could be carried out at any time – especially against Newport and Hampton Roads. Thomsen was not certain that the seizure of New York, Washington, Baltimore and Phila-delphia would force the country between the east and west coasts – 'ist mir seiner Größe nach nicht bekannt' – to conclude peace. 'Ich möchte aber glauben, daß immerhin schon Vieles erreicht wäre, wenn der Osten Nordamerikas besetzt und in unseren Händen wäre.' And finally, Thomsen acknowledged the timeliness of this plan, 'weil augenblicklich jeder urtheil-ende deutsche Seeoffizier sich mit den Folgen eines kriegerischen Konflikts zwischen Deutschland und den Vereinigten Staaten von Nordamerika . . . beschäftigt.'[38] Two interesting points emerge from Vizeadmiral Thomsen's criticism. First, like Admiral v. Koester the previous year, Thomsen clearly revealed that a naval conflict between Germany and the United States was a definite possibility and not merely wishful thinking by junior officers, not mere 'Routine-Uberlegungen'. It is revealing to note that in this 'age of navalism' as Professor Langer has labelled the period, colonial disputes in far distant Samoa and Manila sufficed to turn the serious attention of Germany's leading naval officers to the likelihood of naval operations against the United States. Secondly, it argues little for the thesis, expounded by former leading naval officers and accepted at face value by many historians, that Germany's naval officers were especially 'weltoffen und weltgewandt', that Vizeadmiral Thomsen was not even informed, or bothered to inform himself, of the size and the industrial-military capa-bility of his potential opponent.[39]

Nevertheless, the new Admiralty Staff proceeded full steam on an operations plan against the United States. By utilising the two studies by Mantey, it was possible to set to paper the first detailed *Marschplan* during the same month as Mantey's second study, March 1899. In its basic execution it remained the model for a German assault on the east coast of the United States; later versions merely revised and streamlined the plan. The planners concluded that if Germany did not want to lose her overseas trade at the outset of the war, 'so muß unsere Flotte so schnell wie möglich offensiv gegen die amerikanische Küste vorgehen mit dem Zweck, die feindliche Flotte zum Schlagen zu bringen und zu vernichten'. The route of attack was to be as follows:

Der Marsch muß beim Aktionsradius unserer heutigen Schiffe eine Etappe zum Kohlen vorsehen. Als solche ist die westliche Azoren – Tope-Flores – in Aussicht zu nehmen. Der Marsch wird sich während der schlechten Jahreszeit, d. h. im Winter über Flores nach den nordöstlichen Antillen und von hier aus erst gegen die Ostküste der Vereinigten Staaten zu richten haben, im Sommer, also während der guten Jahreszeit von Flores fort in gerader Linie nach der amerikanischen Küste.

Puerto Rico was dismissed as a *Stützpunkt* because it was too far from the main theatre of the war; Frenchman Bay, Maine and Long Bay, South Carolina were suggested instead. The enemy fleet was expected to gather at Hampton Roads or Long Island Sound. Good supply depots could be established in the Cape Cod-Nantucket Island area. The main German fleet would be ready to sail on the 7th Mobilisation Day (*Ms-Tag*) while the train would be ready by the 9th *Ms-Tag*, and would join the main fleet on the 12th *Ms-Tag*. The entire convoy would proceed from Wilhelm-shaven to Flores (Azores) at 9 sea-miles. The older ships of the *Siegfried* class – SMSS *Siegfried, Boewulf, Hildebrand* etc. – would initially steam ahead at 12 sea-miles and recoal on the northern coast of either France or Spain. If this proved to be impossible, they would be towed the rest of the way to Flores. This leg of the trip would take ten to eleven days. Recoaling in the Azores would last one or two days. The Flores-Frenchman Bay journey would be undertaken at 7 sea-miles and, weather permitting, the *Siegfried* class ships towed. Travel time was estimated to be between eleven and twelve days. On the other hand, a Flores-Puerto Rico trip would require thirteen to fourteen days, with a further five to six days needed to reach Long Bay, in this case at an average speed of 9 sea-miles. The coal stop at Frenchman Bay or Long Bay would only last one day. Therefore the decisive fleet engagement would take place either between the 31st and 34th, or the 39th and 44th *Ms-Tag*, depending upon which route was selected.[40]

In December 1899 the man who had carried out the seizure of Kiaochow and who had confronted Dewey in Manila Bay was appointed Chief of the Admiralty Staff. He was immediately involved in the development of the operations plan against the United States. On 3 December 1899 Tirpitz asked Vizeadmiral v. Diederichs to supply the Naval Office with information on this subject:

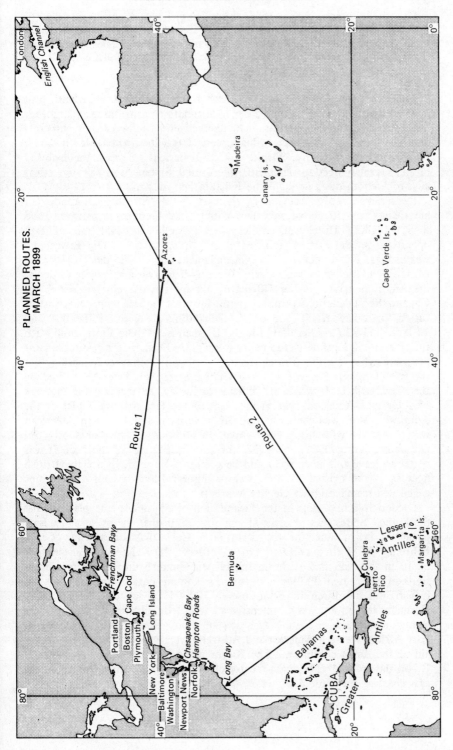

Um die Notwendigkeit unserer beabsichtigten Neuforderungen für die Schlachtflotte überzeugend nachzuweisen, werde ich mich bei den Verhandlungen in der Budgetkommission genötigt sehen, eine ausführliche Darlegung zu geben, wie sich die Situation fürs uns im Falle eines Krieges mit England oder Amerika gestalten würde.

Tirpitz did not want 'eine wissenschaftliche Admiralstabsarbeit', but stressed that he required a reply, 'der in laienhafter Form, für die Mitglieder der Budgetkommission verständlich, überzeugend nachweist, wie außerordentlich ungünstig ja aussichtslos unsere Lage in einem solchen Krieg sein würde'. Particularly, Tirpitz asked Diederichs to prove the inability of the German fleet to deal with the United States, 'weil wir um etwas auszurichten an die amerikanische Küste gehen müssen.'[41]

Diederichs's reply came on 20 January 1900. 'Effective Blockade der amerikanischen Küste ist mit den Mitteln des Flottengesetzes von 1898 nicht Möglich.' Instead, Diederichs urged combined naval and military operations on the eastern seaboard of the United States: 'Die Erwerbung werthvoller Küstenstädte der Neuenglandstaaten wäre das wirksamste Mittel, den Frieden zu erzwingen.' For this it was necessary first to defeat the American navy. 'In der Offensive liegt für uns das einzige Mittel der Gegenwehr.' Diederichs complied with Tirpitz's request to provide justification for a new naval increase by demanding 38 ships of the line and 12 large and 32 small cruisers for the German navy. 'Die Flotte muß auch für diesen Kriegsfall verdoppelt werden.'[42] Diederichs's estimate was precisely what Tirpitz himself hoped to obtain from the Reichstag, but the considerations for war with the United States could not be utilised by the Naval Office. It would be difficult to justify the increase for the case of a German-American war in the light of the fact that the Chief of the Admiralty Staff was contemplating offensive naval operations in American waters already with his present force. In addition, Tirpitz obviously did not want to set a final number (38) for the ultimate size of the fleet. It was better to leave this issue open and he preferred, instead, to use the British fleet as a comparison, 'da der Ausbau unserer Flotte darauf abzielt, uns gegen den seemächtigsten Gegner wehrhaft zu machen'.[43]

Diederichs's first step in the formulation of the operations plan against the United States was to make absolutely certain that the overseas cruisers possessed instructions for the event of a German-American war. On 1 February 1900 they received official orders: 'Das Kreuzer-Geschwader bleibt in Ostasien und sucht so schnell wie thunlich die feindlichen Seestreitkräfte bei den Philippinen auf. Es kommt darauf an, sie dort zu fesseln, um hierdurch indirekt unseren Handel zu schützen.' Here, also, Germany had to assume an offensive stance. 'Jede günstige Gelegenheit ist wahrzunehmen, dem Feinde Abbruch zu thun.' The cruisers deployed in East Africa, Western America and Australia were instructed to come to the aid of the Asian contingent. The Kaiser noted 'Einverstanden. Wilhelm I. R.' on the orders.[44] The main theatre of operations, however, was to be the east coast of the United States.

The offensive-oriented stance of the Admiralty Staff was stiffened by reports from the German naval attaché in Washington. On 26 January 1900 Kapitänleutnant v. Rebeur-Paschwitz submitted a lengthy memo to Tirpitz, wherein he concluded that operations into the interior of the United States would be hopeless and that 'ein Besetzen der nominellen Hauptstadt Washington würde gar keinen Eindruck machen, da weder Handel noch Industrie irgend wie von Bedeutung sind'. Instead, the naval attaché recommended 'schonungs- und rücksichtsloses Vorgehen gegen die im Nordosten gelegenen Handels- und Industriecentren', especially against Boston and New York, with Provincetown serving as 'Stützpunkt'.[45] Rebeur-Paschwitz had personally inspected the areas around Cape Cod and his report greatly facilitated Admiralty Staff planning against the United States.[46]

On 26 February 1900 Diederichs held his first *Immediatvortrag* on the subject of naval operation plans against the United States.[47] 'Um den Feind nicht die Seeherrschaft freiwillig zu überlassen, und unseren Handel und seine Flotte nicht der Vernichtung preiszugeben', the Chief of the Admiralty Staff recommended offensive naval operations on the east coast of the United States. The entire German fleet, included the ships of the *Siegfried* and *Baden* classes, as well as the old armoured frigates *König Wilhelm, Friedrich Karl, Preußen* and *Friedrich der Große* would participate, thus giving Germany numerical superiority over the American fleet. Such an expedition would not avoid difficulty. 'Diese Schiffe modernen Panzerschiffen mit Schnelladekanonen gegenüberzustellen im Kampf 3000 Meilen von den heimatlichen Stützpunkten ist mehr als "gewagt".' Still, it was calculated that enough initial, as well as subsequent, supplies and coals could be delivered. The route of attack remained: 'Etappe zur Ergänzung der Kohlenvorräthe auf den Azoren, Weitermarsch im Winter nach amerikanisch-Westindien, im Sommer direkt auf den Neuenglandstaaten.' Diederichs harboured strong doubts regarding the feasibility of such an undertaking at the present time, but expressed confidence for the future. 'Das Stärkeverhältniss der Linienschiffe ändert sich in den Jahren 1901 und 1902 zu unserem Gunsten derart, daß vom Herbst 1902 ab eine offensive Kriegführung durchgeführt werden kann.'[48]

Diederichs still held back from drawing up a final operations plan against the United States, to be submitted to the Kaiser, 'weil erst nach Bewilligung des schwebenden Flottengesetzes mit der Möglichkeit gerechnet werden kann, daß die Marine für ein offensives Vorgehen gegen die Vereinigten Staaten die Mittel erlangen wird.'[49] On 14 June 1900 the second Naval Law approved a German fleet consisting of 38 ships of the line, 20 large and 38 small cruisers.[50] Tirpitz had planned just such an increase almost from the moment of the passage of the first Naval Law.[51] Such a dramatic increase, in fact doubling, of the fleet was easily explained as having been necessitated by the worsening of the international situation since 1898 (Spanish-American war and Boer war) and was vociferously supported by the 'Flottenverein' (founded 30 April 1898).[52] William II had complained: 'Bitter not tut uns eine starke deutsche Flotte.' And Bülow informed the Reichstag: 'Die Zeiten der Ohnmacht und Demut sind vorbei und sie sollen nicht wiederkommen . . . In dem kommenden Jahrhundert wird das deutsche Volk Hammer oder Amboß sein.'[53] Bülow could hardly have dreamed how prophetic this quotation from Goethe would be.

Diederichs had placed special emphasis on close co-operation between the Admiralty Staff and the General Staff of the Army in the formulation of the operations plan against the United States. The Kaiser's marginal instruction, 'Admiralstab-Generalstab gemeinsamer Vortrag', on Rebeur-Paschwitz's report of 26 January 1900, served as the official basis for joint talks.[54] On 1 December 1900 Count Alfred v. Schlieffen, Chief of the General Staff of the Army, requested joint consultations for the purpose of drawing up an operations plan against the United States. Throughout the remainder of 1900, both planning agencies turned their attention to this plan. Naval planning had been slowed down somewhat by Tirpitz's request for information on the operations plan against the United States, to be used to justify the desired naval expansion to the Reichstag, from December 1899. This delay was further compounded by the necessity of converting Mantey's theoretical, strategic planning into a detailed mobilisation plan for both fleet and train.

On 10 December 1900 Diederichs presented the results of these long months of planing in still another *Immediatvortrag* on the state of naval planning against the United States. He again recommended Boston and/or New York as the most desirable targets, with Provincetown serving as *Stützpunkt*. He estimated that by 1901, Germany would have 22 ships of the line against 18 for the United States, a total of 172,145 to 141,893 tons of floating warships, with a German advantage of 138 to 114 pieces of heavy artillery. 'Deutschlands gepanzerte Flotte ist derjenigen Nordamerikas zahlenmäßig überlegen.' In ships available and suitable for duty on the Atlantic Ocean, Germany also held a favourable balance: 15 to 11 in ships of the line, 136,088 to 113,634 in total tonnage, and 97 to 90 in heavy artillery pieces. Hence the offensive could only lie with Germany. 'Ganz erfolglos aber müßte eine amerikanische Expedition in die deutschen Gewässer verlaufen.'[55]

William II proved to be a more sober military planner. He did not accept the optimistic calculations of his naval planners, and instead ordered that 'mit Rücksicht auf die zu Beginn eines Krieges noch bestehende Unmöglichkeit, genügend Truppen auf dem amerikanischen Festlande zu transportiren, als vorläufiges Ziel eines Vorgehens gegen Nordamerika die Insel Cuba in Aussicht genommen werden soll'. Diederichs was hardly pleased with this turn of events. On 25 February 1901 he asked Schlieffen to calculate the number of troops needed for an occupation of Cuba, but at the same time he reminded the General that Cuba was not the final goal and that the General Staff should also figure out how many troops it required for land operations against Boston and New York. 'Es erscheint mir daher nach wie vor nothwendig, unabhängig von den Vorarbeiten für eine Besetzung von Cuba (und Portorico) die Vorarbeiten auf den Immediatvortrag in das Festlandsgebiet auszudehnen.'[56]

Schlieffen proceeded cautiously. He took the Kaiser's position as Supreme War Lord at face value; open disregard of an Imperial decision did not appeal to him. On 13 March 1901 he sent his calculations to Diederichs. This letter is a model study in vagueness. Schlieffen obviously did not want to commit himself in writing. He agreed to Cape Cod 'als Operationsbasis sowohl gegen Boston als auch gegen New York', but insisted that the troops would have to break out of this narrow peninsula, preferably to Plymouth, as soon as possible after landing. The strength of the American standing army was judged at 100,000 men, of which number between 30,000 and 40,000 might be available for duty on the east coast at the time of a German landing. Of the 11 million men eligible for military duty in the United States, Schlieffen estimated that 106,000 had received 'eine nothdürftige militärische Ausbildung' and that the United States could therefore have some 100,000 men – 'von denen $\frac{1}{3}$ gut, $\frac{2}{3}$ mangelhaft ausgebildet sind' – available at the point of attack. He was even more cautious in estimating the number of German troops required for the operation, guardedly stating that this number would depend on 'der zu erwartenden Machtentfaltung des Feindes'. 'Bestimmte Zahlen können nicht gegeben werden, da die Amerikaner keine planmäßige Mobilmachung kennen, ihre Landesvertheidigung vielmehr auf die Aufstellung großer Freiwilligen Heere basiren, die erst organisirt und militärisch ausgebildet werden sollen, wenn der Krieg erklärt ist.' In any case, he required one 'Armeekorps' to secure the landing site (Cape Cod) and even greater numbers to break out of the peninsula. 'Hieraus ergibt sich, daß gleich 100,000 Mann nach der Halbinsel der Cape Cod Bay transportirt werden müssen. Diese Zahl würde voraussichtlich auch für eine Unternehmung gegen Boston genügen.' Operations against New York would require an even larger force due to 'der bedeutend längeren Operationslinie und der inzwischen jedenfalls erfolgten Verstärkung der feindlichen Streitkräfte'. Schlieffen did not bother to discuss the relative merits of Puerto Rico or Cuba as *Stützpunkte*, 'nachdem Seine Majestät die Entscheidung getroffen haben, daß als vorläufiges Ziel eines Vorgehens gegen Nordamerika die Insel Cuba in Aussicht genommen werden soll'. He merely expressed concern that the inhabitants of Cuba might prove hostile. 'Aller Voraussicht nach werden sich diese für Amerika und gegen Deutschland erklären.' Consequently, 50,000 men would be needed to secure that island as *Stützpunkt*. One hundred thousand additional troops would be required for 'ein Ubergehen auf das Festland von Amerika und Festsetzen auf demselben . . . Für ein Vordringen in Amerika würde aber auch diese Zahl voraussichtlich in keiner Weise ausreichen.'[57]

Diederichs was furious. To Schlieffen's evasive reply that the requisite German force would depend on enemy resistance, the Admiral commented 'das ist sehr geistreich!' in the margin. At the foot of Schlieffen's letter Diederichs added: 'Da nach Ansicht des Generalstabs auf dem Festland nichts ausgerichtet werden kann mit den Truppen, die wir zu transportiren in der Lage sind, *müßten* wir doch gegen die *Inseln vorgehen,* oder wir erklären uns militärisch Bankrott den Vereinigten Staaten gegenüber.'[58]

Diederichs refused to abandon his plans for a direct landing on the eastern seaboard of the United States. Three days after Schlieffen's reply he stated anew: 'Die Landung in Cape Cod-Bay ist weiterhin im Auge zu behalten.' On 20 March 1901 he asked Rebeur-Paschwitz to inspect all possible landing sites in the Boston/New York area, informing the naval attaché that the General Staff had answered his queries regarding the possibility of a German landing in the Cape Cod area 'im Allgemeinen im günstigen Sinne.'[59] In particular, Diederichs asked Rebeur-Paschwitz to board SMS *Vineta*, which was coming up from South America, for an inspection tour of Boston under the guise of a routine repair stop. The Admiral obviously still cherished the direct invasion project, despite an official veto from the Kaiser and an unenthusiastic response from the General Staff.[60] In March 1901 Rebeur-Paschwitz and Rittmeister v. Kap-herr completed a survey of possible landing sites in the Boston area. Two sites north of this city, Rockport and Gloucester, were recommended.[61] The naval attaché did not fail to report on the climate of opinion in the United States, stressing

> daß wenigstens für die Marine alle Veranlassung vorliegt, die Notwendigkeit einer Operation gegen die Vereinigten Staaten klar ins Auge zu fassen. Ich habe verschiedentlich . . . darauf hingedeutet, wie Selbstbewußtsein und Siegeszuversicht derselben gegenüber dem gesamten Europa in einer Weise gestiegen sind und wie dem in Presse, in den Reden der Parlamentarier und allen Orten in einem Maß Ausdruck gegeben wird, von dem man sich, glaube ich, bei uns vielfach noch gar keine Vorstellung macht.

Rebeur-Paschwitz asked especially that the gentlemen of the General Staff be informed of this sentiment in the United States.[62]

In retrospect it can be seen that Schlieffen's letter of 13 March 1901 formed a turning point in the formulation of the operations plan against the United States – despite Diederich's continued efforts on behalf of the direct invasion project. It marked a return to sober military strategy and a turning away from what can only be termed the reckless offensive-oriented thinking that had characterised Admiralty Staff thinking and planning ever since Mantey's first *Winterarbeit* of 1898. It further constituted a return to Tirpitz's *Stützpunktpolitic* which, as we shall see later, found its most distinct expression in the planning of Vizeadmiral Büchsel.[63] And finally, the letter shows quite clearly that a German-American conflict was a distinct possibility, that serious planning was under way among Germany's highest naval as well as military planners, and that in line with the expansionist theories of the navalism and imperialism of the period, one did not shrink back from contemplating and planning a war 3,000 miles away from one's own shores for stakes (Samoa, Philippines etc.) that can at best be described as mediocre.

German-American relations underwent further deterioration in 1901 due to the publication of a book that pointed out the feasibility of German naval and military operations against the United States. The author, Freiherr v.

Edelsheim, was a 1st lieutenant in the 2. Garde-Ulanen Regiment, at the time serving on the General Staff. He clearly foresaw a successful landing on the eastern seaboard of the United States; the navy's role would primarily be limited to hit-and-run attacks against the main sea ports while the army fought the decisive battles on land. Edelsheim espied victory in the sorry condition of the American army, calculating that of its 65,000 men only some 20,000 could be deployed against the invading German forces; 10,000 men would have to be kept out west to guard against the Indians! The American militia was regarded as worthless. The author realised that operations in the interior of the country were quite hopeless, but he believed that the seizure of large parts of the east coast as *Pfando-bjekte* would suffice to make the United States come to terms with Germany.[64] Schlieffen was extremely upset over this untimely publication, officially denying that it had any connection whatsoever with the General Staff.[65] It can safely be imagined that it caused a veritable furore in the Admiralty Staff. Its impact on German-American relations proved utterly ruinous.

As early as 30 March 1901 Senator Henry Cabot Lodge of Massachusetts had written Vice President Theodore Roosevelt that he considered a German landing in Boston – part of his constituency – 'well within the range of possibilities, and the German Emperor has moments when he is wild enough to do anything'. However, Lodge regarded a German landing in South America, probably Brazil,[66] as a more likely prospect. Roosevelt, in turn, informed Lodge that Germany was the real menace to the United States, emphasising that the Germans 'count with absolute confidence upon our inability to assemble an army of thirty thousand men which would be in any way a match for a German army of the same size'.[67] American naval officers had returned from the German fall manoeuvres of 1900 'greatly impressed with the evident intention of the German military classes to take a fall out of us when the opportunity offers'.[68] The book by Edelsheim showed Americans where the danger lay. The existence of official German naval plans against the United States now seemed a fact of life to most American leaders. On 19 November 1901 Jules Cambon could report to the French Foreign Minister, Theophile Delcassé, that German-American relations

are not bad. They are worse . . . One is jealous, one knows that one fights on either side for the commercial supremacy of the world; there is no agreement possible in this field, and it suffices that some guard-lieutenant at Berlin occupies his leisure in organising on paper an invasion of American territory by German troops to give new strength of actuality to Admiral Dewey's saying that the first war of the United States would be with Germany.[69]

The American naval attaché in Berlin (Beehler) remained oblivious to this tide of anti-American sentiment, continuing to laud 'their remarkably competent Emperor' and the merits of 'one Commanding Officer endowed with supreme authority to successfully conduct combined operations.'[70]

In Germany both Admiralty Staff and General Staff continued their efforts towards discovering a mutually acceptable *point d'appui*. Schlieffen informed Diederichs of the drawbacks of Provincetown and Rockport, pointing out that intelligence sources available to him (Captain Train) suggested that the United States was expecting a German landing in the Boston area.[71] The German Embassy in Washington (Holleben) informed Chancellor Bülow that Admiral Dewey had long ago concluded that a German attack would be directed against the islands of St Thomas and St John.[72] These two reports, though conflicting in their estimates of possible landing sites, clearly showed that the United States was alive to the problem of a German attack and that its planners had clearly recognised the most likely German invasion routes. To solve this dilemma, Diederichs abandoned all previous calculations. On 6 January 1902 he requested information from Rebeur-Paschwitz in Washington regarding the defence works of Long Island. Diederichs was especially interested in Great Gull, Gardiner, Fisher, and Plum Islands. He further wanted to know if Block Island was fortified and if it was in the American *Verteidigungsnetz*. Diederichs openly asked the naval attaché for his opinion regarding a German landing in Gardiner's Bay, followed by a land attack on Brooklyn.[73] The immediate outcome of this correspondence was an Admiralty Staff *Denkschrift* on 15 January 1902, recommending an assault on Puerto Rico, followed by a blockade of American Atlantic and Gulf ports and eventual operations against the north-east trade centres, especially Boston and New York. 'Am wirkungsvollsten würde eine Landung auf Long Island sein (z. B. in der Gardiner Bucht), und ein gemeinsames Vorgehen zu Lande und zur See gegen Brooklyn und New York.'[74] Another *Denkschrift* from the same year for the first time flatly announced: 'Einmal in Besitz von Portorico werden wir die Insel nicht wieder herausgeben.[75]

This renewed interest in combined navy-army operations against New York was reflected in the assignment of *Winterarbeiten* in 1901–2. On 21 April 1902 Kapitänleutnant Magnus v. Levetzow submitted his study of the most suitable invasion route for Germany in the event of war with the United States. Levetzow recommended a direct assault on New York, culminating in the conquest of Fisher's Island and Fort Wright. The study must have found favour with the Admiralty Staff, for during September and October of that year Levetzow boarded SMS *Vineta* and personally inspected Haiti (report to the Kaiser 2 October 1902), Port au Prince and Puerto Cabello (reports to the Admiralty Staff 26 September and 14 October 1902) as possible 'Stützpunkte'. His reports reiterated an old theme: 'Die Operationen an der Nordamerikanischen Ostküste werden voraussichtlich nur von kurzer Dauer sein Können.' Therefore he suggested hit-and-run bombardments of the coast between Portland, Maine and Cape Cod (à la Edelsheim). But when Levetzow suggested that operations against the United States take the form of cruiser warfare in order to interrupt American shipping and communications, he was immediately relieved of his assignment – an obvious indication of the fate awaiting all who even indirectly came into opposition with Tirpitz's battle fleet concept.[76]

Early in 1902 the Admiralty Staff underwent another change in leadership. Rivalry between Diederichs and Tirpitz finally forced the Kaiser to choose between the two. As successor to Diederichs the choice fell on Vizeadmiral Willhelm Büchsel, until then Chief of the General Department of the Navy and a close aide of Tirpitz. Hardly had Büchsel taken over his new post than the Venezuela crisis once again brought Germany and the United States to the brink of open hostility.[77] The relatively small European naval units (Great Britain 28,750 tons, Italy 14,800 tons, and Germany 11,147 tons) blockading Venezuela were overshadowed by Admiral Dewey's Caribbean forces (129,822 tons) and, in fact, proved to be a threat neither to American security nor to the Monroe Doctrine.[78] And just as the Boer war had acted as the necessary catalyst for the passage of the second Naval Law in Germany, the Venezuelan crisis served to obtain for American naval enthusiasts the desired increase in the size of the American navy.

Public pressure for an increase in the navy had been steadily mounting in the United States. Nurtured by retired naval officers, prominent financiers, industrialists and corporation lawyers, this as yet unorganised propaganda helped the American navy obtain Congressional approval for the construction, by 1920, of a fleet consisting of forty-eight capital ships.[79] As in Germany, there were in the United States certain influential circles that spearheaded the new wave of navalism:

> Shipowners, exporters, producers of goods entering largely into foreign commerce, and citizens anxious to enhance the power and prestige of the United States, all had favored increasing the Navy. The same was true of shipbuilders, the metallurgical industries, and others who participated directly or indirectly in the profits of naval construction. Then there were the professional members of the Service who had a perfectly natural desire to see their institution grow and prosper. And finally, there were the politicians, for some of whom . . . liberal naval appropriations served as a means of political advancement at the polls.

To be sure, there was a small vociferous minority that fought the naval programme as 'imperialistic, militaristic, grossly expensive, a menace to our peaceful relations, and calculated to impoverish the country', but they could not stem the tide of navalism and imperialism that was sweeping the land.[80] And the spectre of German naval operations in the Western hemisphere served to provide military backing for the proposed naval increases.[81]

Captain C. D. Sigsbee, head of the Naval Intelligence Office, informed the Secretary of the Navy on 21 January 1903, of his certainty that any German attack would be directed against Washington rather than Boston or New York, with Annapolis serving as the German base of operations. 'No other objective point in the United States is now so inviting for attack as the city of Washington.' Reminding the Secretary of the British and

Canadian route in 1814, Sigsbee pointed out the obvious advantages of a German assault on this city. The national gun shop, the gold and silver of the Treasury, the government archives and national prestige all precluded a German attack elsewhere. Captain Sigsbee disagreed with Admiral Dewey's belief in a German invasion of the West Indies: 'In order to clearly perceive the exposed condition of the National Capitol, it is only necessary to conceive the United States fleet as having been sent to the West Indies through a feint in the latter region by a strong naval power.'[82] This point of view accurately reflected German thinking from the winter of 1898; since then German planners had abandoned historic-bureaucratic for economic-demographic factors. Sigsbee was further concerned with possible German espionage and infiltration. On 11 March 1903 he officially recommended a survey to discover whether American sailors with German names were 'native born or naturalized; how long in the service before naturalization; how long in this country; how long in the navy; whether their tattoo marks are emblematic of patriotism to Germany or to this country, etc.'. He fully believed that Germany 'has a spy system on board our ships, a system most easy of accomplishment' and he worried whether or not artillery officers with German names would purposely fire off the mark in the event of war with Germany.[83] In Berlin the month of March witnessed equal fervour, though along more serious lines.

On 21 March 1903 Büchsel held his first *Immediatvortrag* on the state of naval planning against the United States:

Für die Kriegführung Deutschlands giebt es nur *ein* Ziel, der direkte Druck auf die amerik. Ostküste und des volkreichen Teils, vor allem New York d. h. also die *rücksichtslose* Offensive mit dem Zweck durch Verbreitung von Schrecken und durch Schädigung des feindlichen Handels und Eigenthums die Lage für das amerikanische Volk zu einer *unerträglichen* zu machen.

Germany still maintained numerical superiority in ships. Culebra and Puerto Rico were singled out as the best *Stützpunkte,* especially since they would give Germany control over the eastern exit of the Panama Canal, when completed. Such a plan would force the American navy to give battle in the Caribbean and would, in any case, provide good 'Pfandobjekte für die schließliche Abrechnung'.[84] The *Immediatvortrag* was unique in one respect; for the first time the Admiralty Staff concerned itself with the political situation:

Nothwendige Vorbedingung für einen Krieg Deutschlands gegen die Ver. St. ist eine *politische Lage in Europa*, die dem deutschen Reich völlig freie Hand nach außen läßt. Jede Unsicherheit in Europa würde die erfolgreiche Durchführung eines Krieges gegen die Ver. St. ausschließen. Ein solcher Krieg wird deshalb von uns nicht gesucht, er kann uns aber aufgezwungen werden.

It is indicative of the spirit of the age that the United States, in 1913, as we shall see later, counted on precisely such a political constellation in Europe. Büchsel's realisation that politics and diplomacy were, of necessity, integral parts of the overall maritime policy resulted in the first formulation of German naval war aims. The permanent possession of Culebra and Puerto Rico would give Germany 'die erstrebenswerte strategische Position' for the final peace settlement, thereby assuring Germany a role for the future in this region. 'Ihr dauernder Besitz bedeutet für uns den Schutzwall gegen die Anmaßungen der Monroe Doctrine.' In short, Germany's aims were: 'Feste Position in Westindien. Freie Hand in Südamerika. Aufgabe der Monroe Doktrine.'[85] To achieve these goals Büchsel ruled out a direct assault on New York as too risky; 'dagegen erscheint eine Landung auf und Einnahme von Long Island und eine Bedrohung New Yorks vom Westende dieser Insel aus ausführbar'. The Kaiser agreed to the occupation of Culebra and asked both Admiralty Staff and General Staff to complete plans for the occupation of Puerto Rico.[86]

In many ways Büchsel's *Immediatvortrag* formed the climax of all the planning that went into the operations plan against the United States. Here, before the Kaiser, he gave practical expression to the aggregate thoughts of a generation of German proponents of *Weltpolitik*. The hopes and aims of the 'Flottenprofessoren', such as Gustav Schmoller, were to reach fruition in the German 'Freie Hand in Südamerika'. With 'Aufgabe der Monroe Doktrine' German industry could, with impunity, exploit economic concessions in Venezuela, Brazil, Argentina and other South American states. And 'Feste Position in Westindien', to be realised through permanent possession of Culebra and Puerto Rico, marked the return of Admiralty Staff thinking to Tirpitz's *Stützpunktpolitik*. Büchsel once and for all abandoned the direct, offensive-oriented strategy of Diederichs in favour of a more cautious *Etappenoffensive*. Yet whereas Diederichs had directed his efforts primarily towards the goal of forcing the United States to enter peace negotiations, Büchsel now committed Germany to a naval offensive designed to destroy the Monroe Doctrine and with it America's dominant position in the Western hemisphere. The *Schwerpunkt* of naval planning had thus shifted from an offensive military to an offensive military-political campaign.

The final calculations for the operations plan against the United States rapidly neared completion following the Imperial directive of 21 March 1903. On 25 April Büchsel informed Schlieffen that the navy could provide the necessary forces for the occupation of Culebra. Once the American fleet had been defeated, the requisite land forces would be transported to Puerto Rico by the ocean liners of the Norddeutsche Lloyd and the Hamburg-Amerika-Line.[87] On 14 May Schlieffen answered that the army required 12,000 men, 3,700 horses and 671 mechanised vehicles for the occupation of Puerto Rico, with its 6,600 man force. The Chief of the General Staff did not see any difficulty in transporting this quantity of men and horses:

Die China-Expedition hat bereits die Leistungsfähigkeit der beiden großen Rhedereien, des Norddeutschen Lloyd und der Hamburg-Amerika-Linie erwiesen, die ohne besondere Anstrengung im Stande sein werden, den Transport von ca. 14 000 Mann und 3700 Pferden mit dem nötigen Material usw. zu leisten.[88]

Schlieffen did not think any further work was needed on the plan by the German naval attaché in Washington, and from 27 November 1903 it was officially referred to as Operationsplan III (O. P. III)'.[89] An Admiralty Staff *Denkschrift* of the same day optimistically prophesied: 'Am Eingang zur caribischen See werden uns . . . nur das Atlantische Geschwader verstärkt durch höchstens 2 Linienschiffe . . . erwarten können.' Public opinion in the United States would force the American navy to leave part of its fleet at home in order to protect the major eastern sea ports.[90]

During the next two years the plan underwent only minor changes and clarifications. During the winter of 1904–5 the problem of supplying the initial invasion forces, both naval and military, was detailed in fourteen separate studies.[91] The central problem of supplying these forces over an extended period in American waters simply was avoided; the Admiralty Staff concerned itself only with the initial phases of the operation. It was calculated that the German forces would now be ready to leave Germany not before the 40th *Ms-Tag* and reach Puerto Rico on the 60th *Ms-Tag*.[92] The Naval Office lent support to this plan, informing the Admiralty Staff on 25 March 1905 that it could provide coal for a journey of 10,000 sea-miles. Its studies further revealed that at any given time at least 30 freighters of about 100,000 tons, for the train, could be found and requisitioned in Germany's North Sea ports alone.[93] On the same day the General Staff informed Büchsel that a study by Major Erich Ludendorff had revealed the harbour of Ponce as the best landing site on Puerto Rico.[94] The navy now estimated that it would need 1,750 men for the occupation of Culebra. The General Staff's estimates for Puerto Rico climbed to 793 officers, 14,780 men, 6,074 horses and 894 mechanised vehicles.[95]

A final point of interest is the German estimate regarding the calibre of the armed forces of the United States.[96] Throughout the early period two constant themes dominated German evaluations of American naval personnel: the detrimental 'Verschmelzung des Offizier- und Ingenieur-Korps' and 'das vielfach in der Anciennität springen.'[97] On 1 May 1906 the most comprehensive 'Besprechung der Seestreitkräfte der Ver. Staaten von Amerika' was recorded. The old themes were once again aired, but with a new emphasis:

Die große Vermehrung des Materials hat zu einem sehr empfindlichen Offiziersmangel geführt . . . Man ist sogar – neben der Vermehrung der Kadettenzahl – dazu übergegangen, die Schulzeit der Marineakademie für dieses Jahr von den zuletzt schon üblichen 3½ (anstatt 4) auf ca. 3 Jahre zu vermindern und hat sich nur sehr ungern aus Anlaß der schlechten Disciplin auf der Marineschule zu einer Entlassung bzw. Zurücksetzung der minderwertigen Elemente enschließen können.

In addition, it was calculated that active American officers were generally too old – flag officers were between the ages of 59 and 62, while in Germany they were between 51 and 56; captains in the American navy were between 55 and 61·5, while in Germany they were between 42 and 52. 'Der Geist im Seeoffizierskorps wird als gut bezeichnet, wenngleich Nepotismus und Protektion nicht selten sind.' A major obstacle to improvement in this respect was that 'man den Schöpfer des jetzigen Systems, den früheren Unterstaatssekretär der Marine, Roosevelt, nicht gern desavouieren möchte'. The sailors in the American navy 'sind nicht die besten Elemente . . . und selten treibt innerer Drang oder Begeisterung junge Leute zum Dienst bei der Flagge'. The high rate of desertion (10·7 per cent or 3,227 men in 1905) brought with it 'Unzuverlässigkeit eines großen Teils der übrigen Leute'. Further, of the 6,600 yearly discharges, excluding desertions, only about half were due to normal circumstances, the rest due to 'moralischer oder körperlicher Untauglichkeit'. Of the crew, 83·7 per cent were American born, 6·8 per cent naturalised citizens, and 9·5 per cent foreigners. Among the non-commissioned officers 74·8 per cent were natives, 20·9 per cent naturalised and 4·3 per cent aliens. It is interesting to note that the study did not mention any possibility of espionage or even benefit from German-born sailors serving in the American navy, as Captain Sigsbee had feared.[98]

There was an element of truth in this criticism. The American navy, as well as its English and German counterparts, throughout this period suffered from a shortage of naval officers. 'The personnel shortage bore directly on the problem of efficiency. With officers and crews overworked, training and discipline inevitably suffered.' Above all, gunnery was at a dismal level; practice was unpopular and often left to the discretion of the commanding officers, and the Navy Department was indifferent to the introduction of precision instruments for range-finding, gun-sighting, and gun-pointing. It was only through the special efforts of President Roosevelt and Lieutenant William S. Sims, destined to head the American naval staff in London during the First World War, that the American navy corrected this deficiency. By December 1906 Roosevelt could tell Congress that the navy's shooting accuracy had improved fully 100 per cent.[99]

The year 1906 also brought changes in German naval strategy; by the summer of that year the political constellation in Europe had changed to Germany's disadvantage. This is reflected in the Admiralstab alteration of the 1903 O-Plan, entitled 'Marsch nach Westen', worked out by Kapitän zur See Georg Hebbinghaus:

Eine Kriegserklärung Deutschlands gegen die Vereinigten Staaten ist nur möglich, wenn wir im Bunde stehen mit England und unsere Flanke gegen Frankreich durch Österreich, Italien und eventuell auch Rußland gedeckt ist.

Under such a political alignment German forces would land in Canada and commence land operations against the United States. However, since England could not be counted upon to show only *Mißgunst* and since

French neutrality was hardly likely, all Germany could do in case of war with the United States was to gain control of the sea 'und Pfandobjekte, fern vom amerikanischen Festlande zu gewinnen.'[100] Such fantastic preconditions could not justify the existence of a potentially explosive war plan and on 9 May 1906 Vizeadmiral Büchsel decided: 'O. P. III ist nicht wie bisher speziell gegen die Vereinigten Staaten von Nordamerika gerichtet.' Instead, the plan was transformed into a theoretical exercise because of the increase in the American fleet and especially because of the political situation in Europe.[101]

What is surprising is not that the plan was dropped after only two years, but that it should ever have been formulated and lasted even this long. Already in 1904, Germany had suffered the twin blows of the Anglo-French entente cordiale and the Russian refusal of the 31 October offer, by Bülow and Friedrich v. Holstein, of a military alliance. The first Moroccan crisis in 1905, though resulting in the dismissal of the French Foreign Minister Delcassé, revealed Italian and American opposition to German imperialist expansion. The naive Björkö agreement of 1905, between William II and Nicholas II, which was rejected by the respective governments, further compounded Germany's estrangement in Europe. Only Austria-Hungary remained solidly in the German camp. From 1904 to 1906 the central theme of German foreign policy had been the forging of a continental block, headed by Germany, against Great Britain. By 1905 this policy had failed; the New Course of Tirpitz and Bülow had suffered shipwreck. The navy had not increased German's Bündnisfähigkeit, but rather had brought France and Great Britain together. And with Russia making overtures to the entente partners, Germany's Weltpolitik was effectively checkmated. In addition, the English Dreadnought programme of 1905–6 effectively undermined Tirpitz's entire naval policy.[102] Under such conditions even the most militant and anti-American officials in the Reich could not fail to recognise the frivolity of a war plan calling for full-scale naval operations on the east coast of the United States, to be followed by land operations against several major cities. The obituary on the New Course, that was to lead Germany 'herrlichen Zeiten entgegen', was delivered by the General Staff; it was precisely at this juncture, in December 1905, and January 1906, that Schlieffen drafted the famous Denkschriften that bear his name.[103] With the realisation that Germany was now firmly committed to wage a two-front campaign in any future war in Europe, 'O. P. III' must have seemed more and more an apparition from a far distant past.[104]

II

The United States of America did not draw up an official war plan against Germany until 1913. The fleet of forty-eight capital ships created on paper in 1903 had not materialised rapidly enough to justify far-reaching planning by the General Board.[105] Obstacles appeared everywhere. On 13 February 1913 the General Board complained to the Secretary of the Navy about undue political interference: 'The fleet as it exists . . . is the growth of an inadequately expressed public opinion . . . and has followed the laws of expediency and of the temporary passing passion of non-understanding political parties.'[106] Yet the navy hardly behaved better. Until 1913 it had been content to muddle through on a day-to-day basis. 'War plans' were 'miscellaneous collections of information about foreign nations' and 'suggestions for the fleet commanders'. No systematic planning guided naval policy. 'Ten years passed between the time the General Board defined American naval needs to be a fleet equal or superior to Germany's and the time when the Board made a systematic study of the problem of a German-American war.' The main reason seems to have been the fact that the United States simply did not have officers with sufficient intellectual training or the staff experience required for systematic planning.[107] That it still deemed it necessary to draw up a war plan against Germany when these hurdles had been overcome shows the very seriousness with which the possibility of a German-American conflict was treated.[108]

In 1906 American naval planners had counted on 'passive, if not active assistance' from Great Britain in the event of a German attack on the Monroe Doctrine.[109] By 1913 the General Board viewed the situation much more pessimistically, deciding to rely only on its own strength and resources. In all probability the turbulence of international events since 1897 – the Spanish-American war in 1898, the Boer war 1899–1902, the invasion of China 1900, the Russo-Japanese war 1904–5, the first Moroccan crisis 1905, the British-French-Russian *entente* 1904–7, the second Moroccan crisis 1911, the first Balkan war 1913 – encouraged the decision of American planners not to rely on any aid or forces other than their own.

In Germany Vizeadmiral v. Diederichs had played a major role in the formulation of the German operations plan against the United States; in 1913 Admiral Dewey presided over the General Board that developed the Black War Plan against Germany.[110] The 'men of Manila' carried out their antagonism on the drawing boards of the Admiralty staffs. The American planners believed that Great Britain would look upon a German attack on the Monroe Doctrine with sympathy and offer passive support, basically because it stood to gain most from a war between its two main commercial rivals. Britain would 'effectually provide against the interference of other interested European powers', leaving Germany free to make war 'with the certainty that her rear is safe from attack'. There appeared no prospect of assistance from any European power:

The United States has already differences with Russia; the French criticise our methods freely and are in sympathy with British European policy; it is too soon after the Spanish-American war to expect sympathy from Spain; Italy is in accord with France and England upon certain international issues, and Austria with Germany.

The horizon was a deep black. 'The United States is therefore isolated and can count upon no active friend in Europe whose interests coincide with hers.' Despite the turn of events since 1898. American naval planners still thought in terms of an isolated German-American war. The key to this incredible point of view lies in the deep-rooted economic Darwinism that the officers had inherited from Admiral Alfred Thayer Mahan:

> The steady increase of Germany's population; harder conditions of life as the home population becomes denser; the steady expansion of German home industries which must find a *protected* market abroad; the desire of the Imperial Government for colonial expansion to satisfy imperial needs; and the pronounced distaste of the Imperialists for the absorption of German immigrants by other nations; – these factors in the situation all lead to the conclusion that when conditions at home are no longer considered bearable and Germany is strong enough, Germany will insist upon the occupation of Western Hemisphere territory under the German flag, and the United States will then have to defend her policy by force, or aquiesce in the occupation.

This document appears surrealistic to the modern reader: a German attack against the American east coast precipitated by economic rivalry and supported by Great Britain, with Europe remaining neutral due to past antagonisms with the United States or due to fear of Great Britain!

The American strategists from the start ruled out even a temporary landing in Germany because of the distance between the two nations and the strength of the German army. Furthermore, 'there can be no permanently successful occupation of *home* territory by either of the belligerents'. Nevertheless, it was estimated that Germany had enough cargo capacity to transport a military force of 200,000(!) men, in addition to its fleet.[111] This would occupy 80 per cent of her entire shipping just for fuelling the initial crossing. Thereafter, 37 per cent would be required for further fuel supplies. The difficulty of supplying such additional necessities as fresh water, food, ammunition, medical supplies etc. was not even raised by the American planners. In the final analysis, the General Board did not expect Germany to embark on such a bold project since the time required to ship a force of more than 25,000 men would give the United States time to mobilise its naval as well as military forces.

The Black War Plan did not mention the possibility of a direct German attack on the east coast of the United States. Such a maritime gamble was dismissed outright as having no possible chance of success. At best, if the American fleet were divided between the Atlantic, where Dewey had concentrated his entire battle fleet, and Pacific stations on the first day of mobilisation, Germany could seize most of the Caribbean area. If the fleet were stationed on the Atlantic coast in its entirety, Germany might at best occupy an island or two in the West Indies. It is necessary to keep in mind that the General Board thought only in terms of capital ships; cruisers and other lighter craft could remain in the Pacific in the event of war with Germany. Not for a moment did the planners consider leaving part of their forces behind to protect coastal cities, as had been envisaged by the German Admiralty Staff *Denkschrift* of 27 November 1903.

The General Board expected the German convoy of 25,000 men and fleet to pass the English Channel on the 7th *Ms-Tag*.[112] It was estimated that the force would coal either at the Azores of Cape Verde Islands and then proceed to the Margarite Islands off the coast of Venezuela. Upon defeating the American naval forces – according to the German plan – the convoy would head either for Samana Bay or Culebra. The latter could be reached by the 27th *Ms-Tag*. To meet such a threat the American naval planners proposed assembling all available capital ships in the Lower Chesapeake Bay by the 14th *Ms-Tag*, proceeding to Culebra on the following day. The American naval forces would assume battle formation and await the arrival of the German convoy at Culebra, attacking the approaching enemy well to the east of this island. The planners expected a German force consisting of 19 battleships, 4 battle cruisers and 18 pre-Dreadnoughts.[113] The assembled American strength would be 12 battleships and 21 pre-Dreadnoughts. Numerically the American force would be 18 per cent weaker in capital ships and 48 per cent weaker in Dreadnoughts. Yet the General Board felt confident that its fleet was enough of a *Risiko* to deter a German invasion of the Western hemisphere:

> It would be suicidal for Germany, with a fleet only approximately equal to that of the United States, and in addition handicapped by the presence of the heavy train necessary for such distant operations, to attempt a descent upon American possessions in the Caribbean in the presence of the full American fleet at Culebra with a moderate train, protected by the advance base armament, and with ample supplies in fortified ports nearby.[114]

The Black War Plan concluded: 'Thus will readiness for war serve to prevent war.'

III

A comparison of these two war plans at once contrasts the offensive spirit of the German planners with the strategic defensive recommended from the start by their American counterparts. The seven-year difference in time of formulation is not crucial in explaining this contrast. German naval plans steered away from offensive strategy not because of any doubts regarding the capability of their new weapon, but because deteriorating political conditions in Europe required a military war plan that committed German forces to lightning strikes first west and then east; in short, to a plan which robbed the navy of all initiative. The massing of American naval power at Culebra, the very spot chosen by Admiralty Staff, General Staff and the Kaiser as the most suitable German *point d'appui*, well in advance of the planned arrival of the German forces, almost certainly points to a naval disaster for Germany. The American navy was prepared to meet a German invasion flotilla by the 27th Mobilisation day. In fact, the cumbersome mobilisation envisioned in 'O. P. III' foresaw a landing on Culebra at the earliest between the 39th and 44th *Ms-Tag* (March 1899 study). Later German revisions called for an even later arrival at Culebra. Under such conditions the American navy could, in all probability, have even brought its Pacific units to the Caribbean theatre in time for the decisive encounter.

There was also in the German considerations a general lack of respect for American land as well as sea forces, other than for the highest ranking officers. Insufficient discipline, morale, training, technical-industrial capability, naval construction know-how, and Congress's niggardly allottment of funds all seemed to undermine the effectiveness of the American navy. Eberhard v. Mantey even saw in the democratic principle of free speech a curb on American naval development. Such sentiments were not expressed on the American side. The Kaiser might frequently become the object of ridicule, but his armed forces were accorded the highest respect.

A common element in the thinking of all planners was the preoccupation with economic imperialism as the probable cause of an impending war.[115] And a final comment must surely direct attention to the dangers inherent in such planning. It no longer suffices, as has all too often been the case, simply to dismiss such plans as the labour of junior staff officers eager for recognition and promotion. In Germany Emperor, General Staff, Admiralty Staff; men such as Schlieffen, Tirpitz, Ludendorff; in the United States men such as Dewey, Daniels, Lodge and Roosevelt all contributed to the formulation of war plans. It is all too easy to lay the blame on the professional soldiers alone:

> Blind to the power in the earth, as exemplified by trench warfare, and neglecting the whole subject of the defensive, comparatively, while embracing the theory of the offensive *à l'outrance*, these officers, naval and military, made preparations, on training grounds and in the plans of General Staffs, which were based on gross misconceptions of the actuality presented by modern war on land and sea.[116]

For where were the wiser counsels of the political leaders? And of the intellectuals? They were all too often at the side of the Roosevelts, Lodges, Bülows, Tirpitz's, as well as at the meetings of the various naval leagues. If man is ever to recognise the folly and the futility of war, then a first step must surely be the recognition of the potential danger inherent in the very act of drawing up plans of aggression. We are left once again with Bismarck's warning that by painting the devil on the wall, one makes him at last appear. There can be no doubt that this 'devil' did, in fact, appear and that he contributed in no small way to the worsening of international relations, which ultimately led to the catastrophe of 1914–18.

NOTES

1 This project was supported through the Klaus-Epstein-Gedächtnis-Stipendium of the Alexander von Humboldt-Stiftung.
2 See, for example, J. Steinberg, *Yesterday's Deterrent* (London, 1965); W. Hubatsch, *Die Ära Tirpitz* (Göttingen, 1955); and A. J. Marder, *From the Dreadnought to Scapa Flow*, Vol. 1 (London, 1961).

3 See especially G. Ritter, *Staatskunst und Kriegshandwerk*, Vol. 2, *Die Hauptmächte Europas und das wilhelminische Reich, 1890–1914* (Munich, 1968) (cit. Ritter); R. Stadelmann, 'Die Epoche der deutsch-englischen Flottenrivalität', in *Deutschland und Westeuropa. Drei Aufsätze* (Schloß Laupheim, 1948) (cit. Stadelmann); L. Dehio, *Deutschland und die Weltpolitik im 20. Jahrhundert*, Munich, 1955 (cit. Dehio); V. R. Berghahn, 'Zu den Zielen des deutschen Flottenbaus unter Wilhelm II. *Historische Zeitschrift*, 210 (1970), S. 34ff (cit. Berghahn).

4 Cit. in A. Vagts, 'Hopes and fears of an American-German war, 1870–1915', in *Political Science Quarterly* 55 (March 1940), part II, 74, fn. 93 (cit. Vagts).

5 ibid., II, 59, fn. 62. These copies carried the notation 'Original an S.M.' on the cover. Since the Foreign Office almost never made copies of the reports of military and naval attachés, Vagts at once realised the importance attributed to this topic.

6 W. Hubatsch, *Der Admiralstab und die Obersten Marinebehörden in Deutschland 1848–1945* (Frankfurt am Main, 1958, p. 92) (cit. Hubatsch).

7 W. R. Schilling, Admirals and Foreign Policy, 1913–19, unpublished Yale University dissertation, 1954 (cit. Schilling) University Microfilm (Ann Arbor, Michigan) No. 64–11, 383, 17, fn. 32. Schilling is probably referring to the plan drawn up by Leutnant zur See Eberhard v. Mantey in the winter of 1898, or perhaps the second plan in the spring of 1899.

8 See Chapter above. In contrast to Germany, which numbered its plans, the United States used colours to denote its operational plans: black for the German (1913) and orange for the Japanese Plan (1914).

9 The main German source is Bundesarchiv-Militärarchiv, Marinearchive, Fasz. 5174 b: *Acta betr. Vorbereitung der Operationspläne gegen Nord-Amerika*, 4 vols, with one vol. *Neben-Akten* (cit. BA-MA, F 5174 b). Three further collections used are: Admiralstab der Marine, Fasz. 2015 (PG 65 956), Vol. I, 3, No. 8: *Acta betr. Immediatvorträge; Nachlaß Büchsel* (N 168); *Nachlaß v. Levetzow* (N 239); as well as other less relevant collections which will be cited in the notes. The American plan is in US Department of the Navy, Naval History Division, Records of the General Board of the Navy, Operational Archives, Box 10, War Portfolios.

10 In the early spring of 1889 German and American business interests clashed over the Samoan Islands, almost leading to open hostilities. A conference in Berlin (17 April to 14 June 1889) resulted in joint German, American and British rule over the islands. See H.-U. Wehler, *Bismarck und der Imperialismus* (Cologne/Berlin, 1969), pp. 398ff. F. Fischer, *Krieg der Illusionen. Die deutsche Politik von 1911 bis 1914* (Düsseldorf, 1969), pp. 90f. (cit. Fischer), attributes the joint rule decision to the clever negotiations of the State Secretary of the Foreign Office, Herbert v. Bismarck, who forged a united German-British front against American interests.

11 BA-MA, F 5174 b, I, 2–13, 19 a.

12 Bülow to the Foreign Office, 1 April 1899. The Kaiser added: 'Was ich seit 10 Jahren den Ochsen von Reichstagsabgeordneten alle Tage gepredigt habe.' Cit in J. Meyer, *Die Propaganda der deutschen Flotten-bewegung 1897–1900* (Bern, 1967), Inauguraldiss., p. 19 (cit. Meyer).

13 See, for example, the critical evaluation in Meyer, p. 26: 'Sie muß als Einsatzpunkt einer modernen Propagandaära betrachtet werden, wie sie dann das 20. Jahrhundert zu höchster Vollkommenheit herausgebildet hat, in der zur Unterstützung und Legitimierung der Regierungspolitik die Massen durch umfassende und pausenlose staatliche Einwirkung umworben, gewonnen, fanatisiert wurden, wobei man jedoch den Vorgang gleichzeitig so darstellte, als werde diese Regierungstätigkeit von einer schon vorher bestehenden Volksmeinung gefordert, als sei sie von einem Massenwillen zwangsläufig getrieben.'

14 Among the most prominent *Flottenprofessoren* were Lujo Brentano, Hans Delbrück, Otto Hintze, Max Lenz, Erich Marcks, Hermann Oncken, Dietrich Schäfer, Gustav Schmoller, Werner Sombart and Max Weber. For an exhaustive list see W. Marienfeld, Wissenschaft und Schlachtflottenbau in Deutschland 1897–1906, in Beih. 2 der Marine-Rundschau (April 1957).

15 'Nauticus' often brought citations from the works of Heinrich v. Treitschke, whom Tirpitz described as his great mentor, in support of navalism and imperialism. For example, in 1899: 'Es ist sehr gut denkbar, daß einmal ein Land, das gar keine Kolonien hat, gar nicht mehr zu den europäischen Großmächten zählen wird, so mächtig es sonst sein mag . . . Heute sehen wir die Völker Europas drauf und dran, weit über den Erdkreis eine Massenaristokratie der weißen Rasse zu schaffen. Wer bei diesem gewaltigen Wettkampf nicht mitwirkt, wird später einmal keine glückliche Rolle spielen . . . Und es handelt sich doch um unser Dasein als Großstaat bei der Frage, ob wir auch jenseits der Meere eine Macht werden können.' (Meyer, p. 45.)

16 ibid., pp. 23f.

17 Verhandlungen des Reichstags. 9. Legislaturperiode. 5. Session 1897/98. 4. Sitzung. Dezember 6, 1897, 46 A, 60 B, 60 D.

18 See Berghahn, op. cit., p. 99. 'So scheint – betrachtet man die Bülow-Zeit – Weltpolitik eines auf jeden Fall nicht gewesen zu sein: ein vages, gefühlsbetontes Streben nach Geltung, Anerkennung, Gleichberechtigung . . . Weltpolitik war keine Schwärmerei – zumindest nicht in den Köpfen der entscheidenden Persönlichkeiten – sondern der bewußt vieldeutig gehaltene Schlüsselbegriff für eine ursprünglich in sich durchaus logische und durchdachte militärische und politische Strategie des Regiments Wilhelms II.'

19 Ritter, op. cit., p. 185.

20 Dehio, op. cit., p. 48. A harsher verdict is in Theodor Schieder (ed.), *Handbuch der Europäischen Geschichte*, Vol. 6 (Stuttgart, 1968), p. 218: 'Militärisches Machtdenken bestimmte auch die von Wilhelm II und von Admiral Tirpitz . . . forcierte Flottenpolitik. Diese politisch unheilvolle und obendrein militärisch verfehlte Flottenrüstung war die Hauptursache des deutsch-englischen Gegensatzes nach 1900' op. cit., Fischer, pp. 93–4, has set himself apart from this school: 'Dennoch war es nicht der deutsche Flottenbau, der jede Ausgleichsmöglichkeit mit England verschloß . . . Weit mehr waren es die übermächtigen Tendenzen zur politischen und wirtschaftlichen Autarkie, die Deutschland an einer kompromißbereiten Bündnispolitik hinderten.'

21 Stadelmann, op. cit., p. 101; Ritter, pp. 184ff.

22 Stadelmann, pp. 91, 106. See also Berghahn, p. 61: 'Das Bedeutsame an diesem Konzept war indessen die Rigorosität, mit der alles auf eine Karte

gesetzt wurde. Im Gegensatz zur Ermattungsstrategie des Kreuzerkriegs sollte die Hochseeschlacht in einem einzigen Waffengang über das maritime Sein oder Nichtsein entscheiden.'

23 Dehio, p. 29.

24 Vagts, op. cit., 54, Part I, 521, fn. 14.

25 ibid, 522.

26 In an Admiralty Staff *Immediatvortrag* on 4 May 1903, Büchsel declared: '. . . aber seit Manila besteht tatsächlich eine scharfe Abneigung gegen Deutschland im gesamten Offizierkorps der Vereinigten Staaten, besonders dem der Marine und bei vielen einflußreichen Persönlichkeiten.' BA-MA, F 2017 (PG 65 962), 210f.

27 D. F. Trask, *Victory Without Peace. American Foreign Relations in the Twentieth Century* (New York, 1968), pp. 25ff. The following perhaps best typifies the spirit of the imperialist age: '[President] McKinley himself had claimed that he could not have come within two thousand miles of locating the [Philippine] islands on a globe when they were first attacked by Dewey, but, in common with many Americans, his geography improved considerably by the fall in 1898' (ibid., p. 28).

28 Cit. in Blanche E. C. Dugdale, *Arthur James Balfour* (New York, 1937), Vol. I, p. 291.

29 See 'Themata für Winterarbeiten 1897-8', of which the first five dealt with Cuba, Philippines, Monroe Doctrine, Central America and the United States as factors in German naval policy. BA-MA, F 3677, Inspektion des Bildungswesens: *Winterarbeiten der Offiziere ausschl. Akademiker*. I, 1, Vol. I, April 1893-Dezember 1904.

30 This becomes evident in the case of the operations plan against the United States. In 1898-9 four questions were assigned on the subject of possible invasion sites in the United States (Chesapeake Bay and Long Island), the bombardment of New York City, etc. In 1901-2, Diederichs ordered *Winterarbeiten* for 'Betrachtungen über den strategischen und taktischen Wert des nordamerikanischen Flottenmaterials' and on *Militär-Geographie* of North America, West Indies and South America. In 1902-3 Vizeadmiral v. Büchsel asked for *Militär-Geographie* of the coast and islands in the Caribbean Sea and the Gulf of Mexico; the military value of American holdings in the West Indies; the value of the future Panama Canal for the United States; the calibre of the American navy; the Virgin Islands; and how a European naval power could best defeat the United States. In the following year Büchsel again asked for evaluations of the American navy, of the West Indies, and of the Virgin Islands as American naval bases. In 1904-5 only one question was assigned on the United States: the value of maritime commerce on the eastern seaboard. As will be shown later, these assignments reflected the current Admiralty Staff thinking on a German-American conflict (loc. cit.).

31 Thirty years after the formulation of his plan, Vizeadmiral v. Mantey reflected: 'Moltke, Schlieffen, auch Waldersee haben ihre großen O-Pläne ganz allein gemacht, bei uns machten die O-Pläne irgendwelche intelligente kleine Leute und der Admiralstabschef gab seinen Segen und trug den O-Plan dem Kaiser vor. Letter, Mantey to Vizeadmiral a. D. Karl Hollweg, 16 April 1929, F 7590, *Nachlaß Hollweg*, Vol. 4.

32 Unfortunately it was not possible to discover exactly who assigned this topic, which headed the list in 1897-8. Usually the commanders of the

North and Baltic Sea naval stations asked the 'Inspekteur des Bildungswesens der Marine', in this case Kontreadmiral Iwan Oldekop, who was
concurrently director of the naval academy, to suggest topics that could
then be passed out in Kiel and Wilhelmshaven. (See letter, commander
of the North Sea naval station to 'Inspekteur des Bildungswesens', 11
September 1899.) Only the best *Winterarbeiten* were utilised by the
Admiralty Staff: 'Von den Winterarbeiten sind nur diejenigen hier zur
Vorlage zu bringen, welche eine besonders gute Bearbeitung erhalten
haben, so daß sie sich zur Einreichung beim Oberkommando eignen.'
(9 March 1897, Vizeadmiral Karcher, commander of the North Sea naval
station, to Kontreadmiral Oldekop, BA-MA, F 3677, I, 1, Vol. 1.) Hence
it is highly probable that the topic was assigned by Oldekop, who also
graded it, passed it on to Karcher, who, in turn, sent it to Admiral v.
Knorr, 'Kommandierender Admiral des Oberkommandos der Marine'.

33 BA-MA, F 5174 b, I, *Neb.-Akte*, 30–50. It is interesting to note that
Mantey paid almost no attention to the vital problem of supplying such
an expeditionary force across three thousand miles of open sea. Such
considerations were left for later stages of planning.

34 BA-MA, Fasz. 4909, Kommando der Marine-Station der Ostsee: *Acta
betr. Winterarbeiten* (November 1895–August 1900), P. 17, Vol. 1.

35 H. and M. Sprout, *The Rise of American Naval Power* (Princeton,
1966), p. 240 (cit. Sprout).

36 See note 32.

37 BA-MA, F 5174 b, I, *Neb-Akte*, 68–92.

38 ibid., 100ff.

39 These theses, expounded especially by former naval officers such as
Admirals Tirpitz, Trotha, Scheer etc., have found their way into
Hubatsch, *Der Admiralstab*; Albert Röhr, *Handbuch der deutschen
Marinegeschichte* (Oldenburg, Hamburg, 1963); and especially W.
Drascher, 'Zur Soziologie des deutschen Seeoffizierkorps', *Wehrwissen-
schaftliche Rundschau*, 12 (1962). Mantey later complained that the
naval officers had thought too much in terms of '*kontinentale* Politik'
and that especially the officers of the Admiralty Staff were merely 'eine
ungeschickte Nachahmung des Generalstabs . . . die Stäbe bildeten sich
alle ein, sie wären Halbgötter'. 'Wir waren ein auf eisernen Kasernen
verpflanztes preußisches Armeekorps.' Letter, Mantey to Hollweg, 16
April 1929, BA-MA, F 7590, Vol. 4.

40 BA-MA, F 5174 b, I, *Neb.-Akte*, 27–42.

41 BA-MA, Fasz. 5656, Admiralstab der Marine: *Acta betr. Flottener-
weiterungsprogramm* (1899–1907), VI, 1, 3.

42 loc. cit. The original draft of Diederich's reply is in BA-MA, F 5174 b,
I, 59–69, and dated 12 January, 1900.

43 BA-MA, F 5656, VI, 1, 3.

44 BA-MA, Fasz. 7639, Admiralstab der Marine: *Operationspläne (Januar
1897–September 1899)*, Vol. 3.

45 BA-MA, F 5174 b, I, 77–82. Bericht des Marineattachés der Kaiserlichen
Botschaft zu Washington No. 16: *Rekognoszierung von Cape Cod Bay
und Provincetown als Stützpunkte für ein Vorgehen gegen Boston.* This
is the report that Vagts saw in the Foreign Office in the 1930s, with the
remark on the cover, 'Original an S.M.'; see note 5.

46 Unfortunately, the records of the German naval attaché in Washington
are not available before 1901, and hence it was impossible to find the

original order requesting this information. The report from 26 January 1900 was sent by Rebeur-Paschwitz directly to Tirpitz. Shortly hereafter the Naval Office granted the Admiralty Staff permission to correspond directly with the naval attaché and on 20 March 1901 Diederichs asked Rebeur-Paschwitz to make another inspection tour of Boston and New York in search of a suitable landing site. BA-MA, F 5174 b, I. 102.

47 An Admiralty Staff *Denkschrift* to the *Immediatvortrag* of 26 February 1900 stated: 'Am 1. Dezember 1899 wurde dem Chef des Admiralstabs nach gegebenen Direktiven eine Disposition für einen Operationsplan eingereicht. Es wurden derselben die Voraussetzungen der Denkschrift vom März zugrunde gelegt.' BA-MA, F 2015 (PG 65 956), Vol. 3, 290.

48 ibid., 288–91. This is the *Immediatvortrag* cit. by Hubatsch, p. 92. See note 6.

49 BA-MA, F 5174 b, I, 85. J. A. S. Grenville and G. B. Young, *Politics, Strategy and American Diplomacy: Studies in Foreign Policy, 1873–1917* (Yale, 1966), p. 305 (cit. Grenville and Young), state: 'In December 1899 the Kaiser personally instructed Admiral Otto von Diederichs . . . and the now legendary Count Alfred von Schlieffen . . . to prepare a war plan against the United States.'

50 Compare this to Diederichs' recommendation of 20 January 1900 that Germany needed 38 ships of the line, 12 large and 32 small cruisers. See p. 48 above.

51 Stadelmann, p. 108, claims of the naval bill from 1898: 'Aber das Gesetz war von vornherein als Etappe, als Übergang zu einem größeren Ziel gemeint.' See also the verdict by Berghahn, p. 53: 'Die dem Flottengesetz von 1898 folgenden Novellen sind nicht, wie sie seinerzeit der Öffentlichkeit gegenüber immer begründet wurden, ad hoc aufgrund neuer außen- und innenpolitischer Konstellationen geboren worden. Vielmehr waren sie von langer Hand systematisch geplant; die äußeren Konstellationen wurden lediglich für sie ausgenutzt. Schon bald nachdem das 1. Flottengesetz verabschiedet war, erklärte Tirpitz dem Kaiser, daß spätestens 1902 eine weitere Stufe genommen werden müßte, wollte man das Endziel einer Äternisierung erreichen.'

52 M. Stürmer, 'Machtgefüge und Verbandsentwicklung im wilhelminischen Deutschland', *Neue Politische Literatur*, 14 (1969), H. 4, 505, sees a 'Koppelung von innerer Stabilisierung und außenpolitischem Kraftmeiertum': 'Das wurde 1898 dokumentiert, als die deutschen Blätter vor lauter Burenbegeisterung wie auf Kommando jedes Eingehen auf englische Bündnisnäherungen zurückwiesen und die Richtung Bülow/ Tirpitz die Lage nutzte, um mit dem ersten großen Flottengesetz vernehmlich zu verkünden, daß Deutschlands Zukunft auf dem Wasser liege. Damit war eine neue Dimension des Wettrüstens eröffnet.' See E. Kehr, 'Schlachtflottenbau und Parteipolitik 1894–1901', *Historische Studien*, 197 (Berlin, 1930), for the influence of .the naval league upon German internal politics and the passage of the Naval Laws.

53 Cit. in E. v. Mantey, *Deutsche Marinegeschichte* (Charlottenburg, 1926), p. 186.

54 BA-MA, F 5174 b, I, 84–9. The Kaiser's comment on Rebeur-Paschwitz's report was: 'Adm. St. Gen. St. g. V.' On 28 November 1900 Diederichs first asked Schlieffen to initiate these joint talks as

requested by the Kaiser; on 1 December Schlieffen informed the
Admiralty Staff of his willingness to commence work on these plans.

55 ibid., I, 89ff.

56 ibid., 96.

57 ibid., 98ff.

58 ibid., 98ff.

59 ibid., 101f.

60 ibid., 104.

61 ibid., 119ff. Kap-herr was officially listed as 'Rittmeister kommandirt zur
Kaiserlichen Botschaft in Washington'.

62 ibid., 109.

63 Vizeadmiral Wilhelm Büchsel, who succeeded Diederichs as Chief of the
Admiralty Staff in 1902, was Tirpitz's closest aide as Chief of the
General Department of the Navy. Ritter, p. 177, has denounced Tirpitz's
Stützpunktpolitik as a failure: 'So blieb der Erwerb von Kiautschou
isoliert, führte zu mancherlei diplomatischen Reibungen, schuf einen
politisch unerwünschten Interessengagensatz zu der neuen Großmacht
Japan und war im Kriegsfall gegen diese und England niemals militärisch
zu behaupten.' For a critical discussion of Tirpitz's reasoning behind his
'Stützpunktpolitik' ('die Schaffung einer Kette von maritimen Stützpunkten im Auslande'), see Hubatsch, pp. 88ff.

64 Freiherr v. Edelsheim, *Operationen über See. Eine Studie von Freiherr
von Edelsheim* (Berlin, 1901). The book was reviewed quite favourably:
'Im großen Ganzen müssen wir festhalten, daß wir zur Zeit . . . gegen
einzelne Großstaaten, wie beispielsweise gegen Rußland und die
Vereinigten Staaten, genügend stark wären, um einen Waffengang zur
See zu wagen.' The reviewer found fault only with Edelsheim's failure
to solve the problem of supplying such a force over an extended period:
'Wie aber, wenn die Zufuhr an Kampfesmaterial und an Lebensmitteln
unterbunden wird, das Feindesland nichts mehr liefert, der Feind zähe
und die Regierung nicht habhaft bzw. zum Friedensschluß nicht geneigt
ist?' It was a fair question and one that was avoided not only by
Edelsheim but also by the Admiralty Staff. A second reviewer pointed
out that 'der in der Einleitung ausgesprochene Wunsch, "weitere Kreise
für diese Frage zu interessiren", ist zweifelsohne erreicht'. Both reviews
are in *Militärwochenblatt*, no. 72 (1901), 1917ff., and no. 77 (1901),
2045ff.

65 The impact of the book on Schlieffen is mentioned in Vagts, *Political
Science Quarterly*, Vol. 55, Part II, 63; Hubatsch, 108, fn. 33.

66 Compare with Gustav Schmoller's statement from 1900: 'Wir müssen
um jeden Preis wünschen, daß in Südbrasilien ein deutsches Land von
20–30 Millionen Deutschen im folgenden Jahrhundert entsteht . . . ohne
eine durch Kriegsschiffe stets gesicherte Verbindung, ohne die Möglichkeit eines nachdrücklichen Auftretens Deutschlands dort ist diese
Entwicklung bedroht.' Cit in *Marienfeld*, pp. 31–2.

67 Cit. in *Selections from the Correspondence of Theodore Roosevelt and
Henry Cabot Lodge, 1884–1918*, Vol. I (New York, 1925), pp. 485, 487.
Roosevelt had been Governor of New York from 1898 to 1900; in
January 1901 he became vice-president and in September of that year
assumed the presidency following the assassination of William
McKinley. There was no question concerning his feelings towards
Germany: 'The specter of German aggression in the Caribbean or else-

where in Latin America, became a veritable nightmare with him. He was absolutely convinced that the Kaiser would one day start trouble somewhere in this hemisphere . . . Roosevelt harped on this theme until it became almost an obsession.' Sprout, p. 253.

68 Vagts, op. cit., vol. 55, part II, 63.

69 ibid., 66.

70 ibid., 57.

71 BA-MA, F 5174 b, I, 129–30. Date of the letter is 14 December 1901.

72 ibid., 131. In 1902 the German ambassador in Washington (Holleben) opposed a German-American conflict while the naval attaché (Rebeur-Paschwitz) encouraged it; in 1917 the roles were exactly the same between Ambassador Count Bernstorff and naval attaché Boy-Ed. See Vagts, op. cit., vol. 55, part II, 61.

73 BA-MA, F 5174 b, I, 132.

74 ibid., 137f.

75 ibid., 154.

76 BA-MA, Nachlaß v. Levetzow (N 239), box 1, Vol. 3, Ost-Amerika 1902–3. During the naval battle at Skagerrak (Jutland) on 31 May, 1916, Levetzow was Chief of the Operational Division of the High Seas Fleet; from August to November 1918, he was Chief of Staff to Admiral Reinhard Scheer.

77 In 1902 the Venezuelan government defalcated on several German and British loans and the resulting threat to their property decided these two powers to blockade the coast of Venezuela. Italy joined the blockade as a third member. On 21 January 1903 the German vessel SMS *Vineta*, bombarded the Maracaibo fortress into surrender, an act seen in American circles as a flagrant violation of the Monroe Doctrine. See Hubatsch, pp. 111f.

78 Vagts, op. cit., vol 54, part I, 532, fn. 39,

79 There was no equivalent to the German 'Flottenverein' in the United States until 1903, when the US Navy League was founded. Its main function was the publication of a monthly journal dealing with naval affairs of public interest: from 1903 to 1906 *The Navy League Journal* and from 1907 until 1916 *The Navy*. See Sprout, pp. 258f.

80 ibid., pp. 259–60. Some of the minority leaders were Representatives Claude Kitschin (North Carolina), T. E. Burton (Ohio), J. G. Cannon (Illinois), Chairman of the Committee on Appropriations and Senator Eugene Hale (Maine), Chairman of the Senate Naval Committee.

81 This was recognised by the Admiralty Staff in its *Immediatvortrag* on 4 May 1903: 'Die Vorspiegelung von der deutschen Bedrohung der Monroe Doktrin und deutschen Annexionsgelüsten in Südamerika ist wohl hauptsächlich zur Erzielung bedeutender Geldbewilligungen für die Marine aufgebracht und ausgebeutet worden.' BA-MA, F 2017 (PG 65 962), 209–11.

82 Cit. in Vagts, op. cit., vol. 55, part II, 68ff.

83 ibid., 69, fn. 80.

84 BA-MA, *Nachlaß Büchsel* (N 168), Vol. 8, 12–14.

85 loc. cit. At the last moment Büchsel decided not to present these war aims in the *Immediatvortrag*. Grenville and Young, op. cit., p. 306, attribute these words to the Kaiser.

86 BA-MA, F 5174 b, I, 163–7.

87 ibid., 180–3.

88 ibid., 190–1. The force was to be modelled on the expeditionary corps sent to China in 1900:

'12 Bataillone zu 750 Mann	= 9,000 Mann
1 Regiment Kavallerie	660 Mann
1 Regiment Feldartillerie	1,100 Mann
2 Königl. schwere Feld-Haubitzen	528 Mann
1 Pionir Bataillon zu 3 Kompagnien	650 Mann
	12,000 Mann'

in addition to various railroad, telegraph, etc., crews.

89 ibid., 43. On 18 September 1899, the Chief of the Admiralty Staff, Kontreadmiral Felix Bendemann, had ordered the following operations plans drawn up: 'I. (Krieg gegen Frankreich); II. (Krieg gegen Frankreich und Rußland); III. (Krieg gegen England); IV. (Krieg gegen Nordamerika).' It is likely that the Anglo-French *rapprochement*, that ultimately led to the *entente* (1904), caused the Admiralty Staff to drop its operations plan I (war against France), thereby advancing the other plans a case higher, Unfortunately, it was not possible to document this claim; the naval records contain only sparing information on the priority and numerical classification of the various plans.

90 See the 'Denkschrift zu O-Plan III', ibid., II, 1–5.

91 The train contained 'Wasserschiffe, Kohlenschiffe, Kabeldampfer, Munitionsschiff, Werkstattschiff, Pumpendampfer, Krankentransportschiff' etc. 'Vorarbeit 4, Zusammensetzung des Trosses' of 1904–5 introduced 14 further studies, listing in minute detail every phase of the operation from scouting the Azores to 'Kohlenergänzung' and 'Nachrichtenübermittlung', ibid., II, 205–17.

92 loc. cit.

93 ibid., I, 193. This communication from the Naval Office to the Admiralty Staff of 25 March 1905 also did not raise the key issue of supplying this force after the initial crossing.

94 ibid., III, 95. Schlieffen had earlier mentioned Mayaguez Bay, Aguadilla Bay and Port Guanica as possible landing sites on Puerto Rico.

95 ibid., 76–89, 103.

96 After World War I Tirpitz wrote: 'Die amerikanische Marine als Passivum für sich genommen, war so wenig ein gefährlicher Gegner wie die französische; sie beobachtete mit einer gewissen Eifersucht, einen wieviel höheren Kriegswert die deutsche Marine erlangte, obwohl ihre Baukosten um Milliarden geringer waren.' A. v. Tirpitz, *Erinnerungen* (Leipzig, 1919), p. 160, fn. 2.

97 BA-MA, F 5174 b, II, Admiralty Staff memo of 1 October 1905. It might be remembered that the 'Organisatorischen Bestimmungen für das Personal des Soldatenstandes der Kaiserlichen Marine' of 26 June 1899 had regulated advancement in the German navy along the lines of strict *Anciennität*, thereby excluding the possibility of rapid advancement beyond and ahead of one's classmates. See 'Untersuchungen zur Geschichte des Offizierkorps. Anciennität und Beförderung nach Leistung' in *Beiträge zur Militär- und Kriegsgeschichte* (Stuttgart, 1962), pp. 126f. (ed. by the *Militärgeschichtliches Forschungsamt*, Freiburg i. Br., vol. 4).

98 BA-MA, F 5174 b, III, 139–67.

99 Sprout, pp. 272ff. See also Büchsel's statement in the *Immediatvortrag* of 4 May 1903, 'Feindselige Stimmung in USA gegen Deutschland': 'Zwar mögen die erwiesene Unzuverlässigkeit des Schiffs- und Artilleriematerials einzelner Vereinigten Staaten Linienschiffe . . . die Kriegslust drüben Zanächst etwas dämpfen, der Zwangsfall, die Anmaßung der Vereinigten Staaten mit Waffengewalt zurückweisen zu müssen, bleibt aber für uns bestehen und gehört zu den näherliegenden Möglichkeiten, gegen welche gerüstet zu sein Pflicht ist.' BA-MA, F 2017 (PG 65962), 211.

100 BA-MA, F 5174 b, III, 7–12.

101 ibid., III, 3, 168. Admiralty Staff memo of 10 September 1906. By 1908 the American navy was second only to the British in first-class battleships and third in the world in total tonnage built and building. Sprout, pp. 272ff.

102 Berghahn, pp. 86ff., claims that the British Dreadnought programme destroyed 'sämtliche Berechnungen und Projektionen des Reichs-Marine-Amts'. For this pioneering revision of the Dreadnought programme interpretation, he presents the following arguments: 'Tirpitz hatte . . . sehr genaue Berechnungen darüber angestellt, daß es England, z.T. aus Personalmangel, auf die Dauer nicht möglich sein werde, Deutschland die für die Sicherung der britischen Vormachtstellung nötige Quantität an Schiffen gegenüberzustellen, und daß die Kaiserliche Marine infolgedessen bei einer besseren Ausbildung und Taktik eine für einen Defensivkrieg leichte Überlegenheit gewinnen konnte . . . Er hatte sein ganzes Vertrauen in die politische Zukunft des Deutschen Reiches auf ein hochentwickeltes militärisch-technisches Instrument gesetzt, an das er eine langfristige machtpolitische Strategie band. Mochten sich seine Berechnungen in den ersten Jahren nach der Jahrhundertwende auch scheinbar bewahrheiten, die unvermeidlichen, aber finanziell nicht tragbaren technischen Verbesserungen an diesem Instrument führten zu einem Wettrüsten, in dessen Verlauf der ursprüngliche Plan allmählich zerschlagen wurde' (ibid., pp. 90ff.)

103 See G. Ritter, *Der Schlieffenplan. Kritik eines Mythos* (Munich, 1956), pp. 47ff.

104 Leading army officers had long viewed the navy with growing suspicion. In 1896 Count Waldersee, Chief of the General Staff, stated: 'Der Kaiser scheint sich völlig in den Gedanken der Marinevermehrung verrannt zu haben.' By 1898 Waldersee commented bitterly: 'In der Marine wird die Idee immer mehr kultiviert, daß die Zukunftskriege auf der See entschieden würden. Was gedenkt wohl die Marine zu unternehmen, wenn die Armee geschlagen würde, sei es im Osten oder im Westen? Soweit lieben die guten Herren aber nicht zu denken.' Cit. in Meyer, op. cit., p. 189. Precisely such a situation was to arise in October 1918!

105 The General Board was founded in 1900, after the Spanish-American war, and it remained the only American naval planning agency until 1917. Its function was to prepare strategic and operational war plans, and to recommend size, composition and distribution of the fleet – in short, a combined Naval Office and Admiralty Staff. Admiral George Dewey was Chairman of the General Board from 1900 until his death in January 1917.

106 Cit. in Schilling, op. cit., p. 43.

107 ibid., p. 29, fn. 46.

108 This delay by American planners also seems to indicate that its war plan against Germany was not merely the result of 'der in allen Admiralstäben üblichen routinemäßigen Überlegungen', as the German plans have been described by Hubatsch, p. 92. A routine plan would have been comprehensible in 1898, or shortly thereafter; by 1913, fifteen years after the Manila Bay confrontation, such reasoning simply does not suffice.

109 Schilling, p. 20, fn. 35.

110 The following excerpts are from the Black War Plan submitted by the General Board, and accepted by the Secretary of the Navy, Josephus Daniels, probably in July 1913. The technical aspects of the plan, highlighted by a number of extremely complicated mobilisation timetables, had been carried out by the Naval War College. The Black War Plan is in US Department of the Navy, Naval History Division, Records of the General Board of the Navy, Operational Archives, Box 10, War Portfolios. A detailed discussion of the plan is in Schilling, pp. 1–49. The present authors wish to express their indebtedness to this earlier work, much of which forms the basis for the following discussion.

111 Grenville, p. 17, and Grenville and Young, p. 319, claim that the Board estimated the German strength at 750,000 troops.

112 Here, as in all their calculations, the American naval planners had left themselves a sufficient margin of error. Compare this estimate with Schlieffen's calculation on 14 May, 1903 of 12,000 (subsequently raised to 14,000) men. See p. 57 above.

113 There is an evident error in these American figures. Germany possessed 17, and not 19, battleships in 1913. In all probability, the American planners mistook two German battle cruisers for battleships. The American selection of Culebra appears to have been the result of good guessing; the documents contain no reference to a possible intelligence leak.

114 Grenville, p. 17, claims: 'The chances of American success were rather gloomily rated about even by the General Board.' This claim is repeated in Grenville and Young, p. 319.

115 The officers of the General Board were so steeped in Admiral Mahan's teachings that they feared that a German attack against only Panama or the Monroe Doctrine, and not against the continental United States, would, as in 1812, result in a division of war sentiment at home: 'The fear of financial loss by the influencial wealthy classes in the United States . . . will tend to force a peace after early successes, and before the United States can be placed upon an adequate war footing.' Cit. in Schilling, p. 46.

116 Vagts, op. cit., vol. 55, part II, 76.

3

Imperial Cable Communications and Strategy, 1870–1914[1]

P. M. KENNEDY

At the end of the nineteenth century, Britons could claim with some pride and reason that their empire was one upon which the sun never set. It was indeed the only *world* power, in the fullest sense of that word, possessing colonies and having interests in every ocean and continent of the globe. As far apart as the Cape and Malaya, New Zealand and Gibraltar, Aden and the West Indies, her dominions lay. Yet this impressive display of imperial might also carried with it certain grave and inherent disadvantages, notably in the realm of defence. In time of imminent or actual war, for example, it would be difficult for London to put this widely scattered chain of territories and naval bases swiftly on the alert, or to give instructions to the warships patrolling the various overseas stations. Nor was it easy to see how a remote colony, threatened by an enemy force, could make known its plight to the British government. Moreover, in an age of imperial disputes, early knowledge of developments upon the other side of the globe was of prime importance, particularly if rival nations did not possess this information or only acquired it later.[2] Even in less dramatic times, there was clearly a need for some rapid and efficient and secure means of communication between the component parts of the empire if local crises were to be dealt with, or policies requiring swift decisions were to be made.

Such a means was provided by the telegraphic cable. Invented by Morse in 1837, this instrument was quickly utilised to develop a regular international communications network by people appreciative of its great potential. It was, moreover, a safe form of passing messages since the information therein was exclusive to those connected to the wires; and this appealed to individuals and governments who wished to transmit information of a confidential nature. Cable communications were not absolutely secure, though, if constructed as part of a *land* telegraphic system. They could be tapped; they could also be easily cut or interrupted, particularly in wartime. Therefore, while providing a means of drastically shortening the length of time required to send a message across the world, the use of trans-continental lines for such purposes was anathema to the military strategists and the government. As one of the committees specifically formed to consider this question put it:

> The greater the number of states through which a land telegraph passes, the greater is the probability that one or more of them, at some supreme and critical moment, when telegraphic intercommunication between the United Kingdom and its dependencies or its allies is of the highest importance, may exercise its power of interrupting communication; and, unless we maintain our own more secure alternative routes, may thereby imperil our most serious interests, the safety of our dependencies, or even our existence as a nation.[3]

A *submarine* telegraph cable was a different proposition, however, provided that the line was direct or that the intermediate cable-stations were in the hands of the imperial power. It could not be tapped or censored, or even cut, unless special equipment was used. A widely developed system was seen to provide the empire with an efficient and secure means of communication, and to be a vital part of the network of imperial defence.[4] It is therefore not surprising to find that, after Britain had created such a system, the Colonial Defence Committee believed that 'the maintenance of submarine cable communications throughout the world in time of war is of the highest importance to the strategic and commercial interests of every portion of the British Empire'.[5]

This is not to say, however, that the submarine cable was conceived of exclusively or even primarily for strategic purposes, at least in the early stages of its development. To the mid-Victorian mind, the electromagnetic telegraph was regarded as the latest of a long series of technological inventions and developments, which had assisted progress and contributed to the growth of trade and prosperity; stockbrokers, businessmen, journalists and diplomats were seen to be the chief beneficiaries of this marvellous new contrivance. The first submarine cables of any international importance, those laid across the Channel in the early 1850s, were financed solely by private telegraphic companies for strictly commercial reasons; and, although the Atlantic cable which was laid in 1858 received some backing from the United States and British governments, little thought was given to its uses in the military sphere. On the contrary, President Buchanan replied to Queen Victoria's greetings on this occasion with the words:

> May the Atlantic telegraph, under the blessing of heaven, prove to be a bond of perpetual peace and friendship between the kindred nations, and an instrument destined by Divine Providence to diffuse religion, liberty, and law throughout the world.
> In this view will not all the nations of Christendom spontaneously unite in the declaration that it shall be for ever neutral, and that its communication shall be held sacred in passing to the place of their destination, even in the midst of hostilities?[6]

However, a system of communications as efficient and revolutionary as this inevitably attracted the attention of the military and naval departments of government, and of those who were concerned with the unity and security of the empire, who could perceive advantages in it entirely unconnected with business and commerce. In 1855 a cable had been laid from Varna to Balaklava for the use of the British army during the Crimean War; and even the Treasury was impressed when, following the collapse of the Indian mutiny, the rapid transmission of this news halted the embarkation of regiments in Canada and saved over £50,000.[7]

Nevertheless, it was not until 1870 that strategic factors were seen to affect the laying and control of telegraphic cables; and, predictably enough, it was the question of the all-important communications with India which provoked this change.[8] Before then, an ever-growing network of commercial lines had been established throughout Europe, and several companies were beginning to erect extensions through south-east Europe and the Near East to the Indian subcontinent. In 1865 contact with India was established by a land line from Constantinople to Fao (El Fáw) in the Persian Gulf, which was linked by a submarine cable to Karachi. Later, the Indian government itself erected a line from the Persian Gulf to Teheran, a terminal point in the trans-Russian system of the Indo-European Telegraph Company. However, the British government could hardly be expected to look with enthusiasm upon a system in which the link with their most vital possession passed through several foreign countries, and they therefore warmly welcomed the laying by the Eastern Telegraph Company of a submarine cable which virtually avoided all contact with Europe: indeed, so pleased was Whitehall that it agreed to pay the firm a subsidy for the twenty years following. This line, laid chiefly by the famous *Great Eastern* in early 1870, ran from London to Lisbon, thence to Gibraltar, Malta and Alexandria before going overland to Suez; from there, it ran to Aden and across to Bombay. The only weak points in this chain were in Egypt (partially eliminated after the 1882 occupation of that territory) and Lisbon, the capital of a traditional friend and ally of the British. Later, a second cable was laid to Gibraltar, via Vigo in Spain. Yet by 1891 concern for security had become so great that the Committee on Telegraphic Communication with India recommended that a further line be created to link Gibraltar and Land's End directly.[9]

Despite these weak points, the Eastern Telegraph Company's line was from the very beginning of the greatest strategical importance and was the first link in an intended 'all red' system, that is, a cable network which linked all parts of the empire without ever touching foreign soil. From India, extensions were laid to Singapore, and thence to Hong Kong; and from Singapore, too, a branch line was laid to Australia and New Zealand. Aden, a most important station, provided connections with Zanzibar, Mozambique and Durban, whence land lines ran to the Cape. The possession by the British of widely scattered colonies and coaling-stations was an obvious advantage for the creation of this system and, as the cable network was widened, more and more relatively obscure islands acquired an added importance.[10]

Yet the very existence of these strategic cables, and the heavy dependence of the British government upon them, placed an extra burden upon her defence forces and necessitated a careful appraisal of how best these lines could be protected in time of war. Some incidental protection would be offered, the Colonial Defence Committee felt, by the fact that the cables took the normal shipping routes, which were patrolled by the Royal Navy's cruisers; in addition, the deployment of a few guns near cable landing-stations would deter raids upon those lines lying in shallow water.[11] Nevertheless, the navy would not always be on hand and a later body of experts recognised that

> The continuous maintenance of cable communications cannot be relied upon during war, and no measures of protection can be taken which would render such communication absolutely secure in the presence of the efforts of a powerful and active naval enemy. The danger will arise especially at the outset of war, since preparations for cable-cutting would doubtless be made in advance . . .[12]

Thus the cable communications system appeared to the strategists to be particularly vulnerable, almost tempting hostile powers to interrupt it. It was true that the 1884 International Telegraph Convention had formulated rules concerning the protection of cables in peacetime, but it had also expressly stated that 'it is understood that the stipulations of the present Convention do not in any way restrict the freedom of belligerents'.[13] In fact, the Russian Admiralty had made preparations to cut British lines at several points during the Penjdeh crisis of 1885 : Britain, in contrast, was powerless to interupt the Russian internal telegraph system. She was also somewhat at the mercy of minor naval powers, which could 'at small cost and risk inflict heavy loss'. Since unrestricted cable-cutting would be on balance 'a severe loss to the Empire, which would suffer mostly from this type of attack', the Colonial Defence Committee recorded

> their strong opinion that no opportunity should be lost in defining the position of the cables of neutrals, and in taking any steps likely to lead to the eventual neutralization of all cables by promoting an international sentiment in favour of them . . . Nearly the whole of the existing cables touch British soil at one or more points, and none could be cut without causing direct injury to British interests. Any degree of immunity, however small, which could be secured by Treaty, or by international sentiment, would therefore be a definite gain to the Empire.[14]

Over the years, however, this pessimistic and defensively-minded attitude slowly changed. For a start, it was soon realised that it would be impossible to persuade other powers, particularly France and Russia, to accede to an international neutralisation agreement. Secondly, neutralisation did not provide a satisfactory answer to the problem of maintaining a secure link with the colonies and with India in particular; for while it was virtually inconceivable that all the lines to the East would be cut or interrupted, since it would take an impossible coalition of European governments against

Britain to achieve this, there was always the fear that neutral governments would censor cable messages during the period of hostilities. Although there was no international agreement upon cables or their neutrality in wartime, the Law Officers of the Crown held that government messages by a belligerent would be regarded as 'contraband of war' and therefore refused transmission by neutral operators. Properly coded messages would, of course, be declined by any neutral government's censors. One suggestion of the Colonial Defence Committee to meet this problem was that messages be subtly coded so that they were 'couched in terms which appeared to refer to commercial or personal business'.[15] Nevertheless, security would not be guaranteed by this method nor, for that matter, would celerity; and this idea was later abandoned 'owing to the practical difficulties which . . . stand in the way of giving effect to it'.[16]

As a result, the British turned more and more to the idea of establishing a network which would be absolutely independent of foreign countries. Gradually, the many weak points in the British cable system were eradicated by laying lines to by-pass them, or establishing completely different routes. This strengthening of the imperial communications system was chiefly due to the persistent pressure of the army, the navy and the Colonial Defence Committee in the next few years for 'all red' routes, about which these three bodies developed a virtual fetish. The greatest concern was for the routes to India and the Orient, which, as mentioned before, had been made reasonably safe by the duplication of the lines to Gibraltar via Vigo and Lisbon, and later by a direct Land's End-Gibraltar cable, as well as by the occupation of Egypt. Yet the strategists still remained suspicious of the latter country as a weak point in this chain. It was less alarming during the period of the Anglo-French dispute over the Nile valley, for British troops then guarded the Alexandria-Suez land line; but after 1904, when the colonial agreements with France provided at last for a form of neutralisation of the Suez Canal region and the withdrawal of those troops, the Colonial Defence Committee again began to worry. They therefore issued instructions for a military force to be alerted, if war ever threatened, to protect the telegraph; and in 1914 the cable was indeed guarded in this manner.[17]

Yet the Mediterranean line itself was very suspect to the experts, who were deeply conscious of their naval weakness in that area.[18] The naval bases of southern France and later that at Bizerta, and the threat of a Russian entry into the Mediterranean, alarmed the Colonial Defence Committee, particularly since the waters there were relatively shallow and did not present many obstacles in the way of grappling and cutting a cable. As early as 1887, the War Office was stressing that the importance of a direct West African cable to the Cape, and that route in general, 'can scarcely be exaggerated', and this was re-emphasised by the inter-departmental commission of 1898.[19] Three years later, therefore, a second major line was laid to South Africa and the East. Leaving Land's End, it swung directly southwards via Madeira, St Vincent (Cape Verde Islands), Ascension and St Helena to the Cape. From there, it ran overland to Durban, which was connected by submarine cable via Aden to Bombay.

In addition, a line was laid from Madeira to the British West African colonies of Gambia, Sierra Leone, Gold Coast and Nigeria, and thence southwards along the coast to South Africa. So vital had been the Cape cable (especially with the Boer war in progress) that the Western Telegraph Company was persuaded by the government to stop work on all its cables and to manufacture solely for the Eastern Telegraph Company, which was laying this line.[20]

However, even this route had its weak points in that it touched twice upon Portuguese colonial territory. With the future of her possessions in some doubt by the turn of the century, and with rumours abounding of the future disposal of the Madeira and Cape Verde Islands, the British felt unable to take any chances. Even the expectation that Portugal would be 'benevolently neutral' in time of war, and the knowledge that these stations were worked by British operators, was not enough to dispel all fears. Thus it was hoped that an 'all red' line would be laid from Gibraltar to Sierra Leone direct, while Ascension Island would be connected via South America with the West Indies network to provide an alternative route between the Cape and London.[21]

Despite the laying of the important Cape line in 1901, an inter-departmental committee which met in the following year announced: 'We do not consider that the cable communications between Great Britain and India are strategically satisfactory . . .' They would be much improved, it was suggested, by adding a spur to the new and extensive link between the Cape and Australia, which the Eastern Telegraph Company was laying via Mauritius, Rodriguez and the Cocos Islands. Such a spur could be laid either from Rodriguez to Ceylon, or from Cocos to Ceylon or Singapore: in any event, another secure line to India, which avoided further dependence upon the Aden-Bombay connection, would be assured.[22] Eventually, it was decided to lay a Cocos-Singapore line and a Mauritius-Seychelles-Ceylon line, a move which not only provided further links with India but also circumvented the insecure cable-stations at Zanzibar and Mozambique.[23]

Even before this secondary network around Africa and across the Indian Ocean was laid, the strategists were advocating the establishment of a completely new line – across the Pacific between Canada and Australasia, which would also indirectly provide a fresh link between Britain and India. As the Colonial Office put it,

> The risk of war incident to the present route would be avoided by a cable in the opposite direction. It would be throughout at a comparatively remote distance from any foreign naval stronghold; whereas all the present cables to Africa and the East and Australia pass close to the naval fortresses of Cherbourg, Brest, and in the Mediterranean to Bizerta, and generally along commercial routes which foreign cruisers would presumably select. They are also to a large extent laid in shallow seas, where they can easily be cut.[24]

Since this proposed line would be entirely between British territories, the empire 'would be able to communicate without having to rely on the sufferance of foreign Powers. In the case of war, this system would not be exposed to the regulations enforced by neutral Powers against belligerent messages'.[25]

It would be unfair, however, to conclude that the construction of the Pacific cable was motivated exclusively by the strategic advisers keen to eliminate weak points in their communications network, for the concept had been widely aired in Canada and Australasia during the previous two decades although financial reasons had always provided the stumbling-block. But by the turn of the century the concern for security in a decidedly hostile world, and the movement for closer imperial unity, prompted the governments of Britain, Canada, Australia and New Zealand to lay a trans-Pacific cable, despite the initial cost of £2,000,000. In 1902 this was duly done, the line being extended from the terminals of the Canadian Pacific Company's telegraph at Vancouver to the remote Fanning Island, 3,450 miles to the south-west; which remains, in fact, the longest stretch of submarine cable in the world. From Fanning Island, the connection was extended to Fiji and to Norfolk Island, where it bifurcated with one line going to New Zealand and another to Queensland. Moreover, strategic considerations also predominated during the selection of landing-places for the cable. For example, although it was recognised that a Pacific line via Hawaii would be shorter, cheaper and provide a faster service than one via Fanning, the Colonial Defence Committee pointed out that such a route 'would involve a departure from the principle of using only British territory for landing-stations'.[26] The suggestion was thereupon vetoed.

The strategic situation in the West Indies was also under consideration in this period. There a cable laid in 1870 had established a connection between London and Jamaica and the other islands, but this ran through New York, Florida and Havanna. As early as 1880, the Royal Commission on the Defence of British Possessions and Colonies declared that

on military grounds, the present telegraphic communication with the West Indies is open to one grave objection: messages between England or the Dominion of Canada and the West Indies must pass either through the United States and Cuba, or (as soon as the communication between Demarara and Para is completed) through Portugal, Madeira, the Cape Verdes and Brazil.[27]

The Commission therefore recommended that a cable be laid direct from Halifax to the West Indies, and that the telegraph company concerned be subsidised by the imperial government, both of which suggestions were carried out. Several years late, the Colonial Defence Committee felt that a cable connecting Halifax with Bermuda 'would materially enhance the effectiveness of Her Majesty's ships on the North America station, and contribute to the defence of the fortress'.[28] This, too, was achieved by means of an imperial subsidy to a private British company, but it was not many years before the Committee pleaded for a further extension of the West

Indies cable to St Lucia, 'which would be of considerable Imperial importance in a war with either France or the United States'. The government also accepted this advice.[29]

One final example of this 'all red' fetish was provided by the discussion over Far Eastern cables in 1899. The newly acquired possession of Weihaiwei needed to be linked to the imperial network, so that the diplomatic and naval moves of the other powers in the Gulf of Pechili could be followed. Weihaiwei was already connected by cable, first with the Great Northern Telegraph which ran across Russia and Siberia to Port Arthur; and secondly, with Hong Kong itself by a land line via Shanghai. However, neither of these provided the direct and secure link which the Admiralty desired. The navy wanted British staff to man the Shanghai telegraph station, and also pressed for a submarine cable to Weihaiwei, the Director of Naval Intelligence insisting that 'direct reliable telegraphic communication with Weihaiwei which in their Lordships' opinion is of supreme strategical importance, cannot be insured until the above two points are settled and an *all British* route thus completed'.[30]

As a result, the Admiralty opposed the German government's idea of a joint sea cable from Hong Kong to the Gulf of Pechili, splitting there to Weihaiwei, Tsingtao and Port Arthur. Instead, they supported the application of the Eastern Telegraph Company that it be allowed to lay an extension from Hong Kong to Weihaiwei, and be given the monopoly of landing rights in both harbours, an idea which the Post Office, the Board of Trade and the Colonial Office deplored. But it was rather the costs involved, and the Admiralty's tacit admission that they did not intend to establish a permanent advanced base at Weihaiwei, which killed this project for a while.[31] During the Far Eastern crisis which arose out of the Boxer rebellion, however, the government did sign an agreement with the company for the laying of a submarine cable between Shanghai and Weihaiwei, with only British staff working in each office. Though it was not the direct 'all red' line which was the navy's ideal solution, it was at least a swifter and more secure arrangement than that which had hitherto existed.[32]

Despite certain setbacks and postponements, the strategists had clearly achieved a dominating say in the selection of cable routes by the turn of the century. The Post Office and Board of Trade were rather dubious about this development, but were repeatedly forced to bow to the demands of the army, the navy, the Colonial Defence Committee and the various colonies. By this time, however, the costs involved in subsidising these imperial cables had become very heavy indeed. Most of these telegraph companies received an annual subsidy for twenty years, such as the £19,000 per annum given to the Africa Direct Telegraph Company for their West African line. In another case, a lump sum of £1,100,000 was granted to the Eastern Telegraph Company for laying their important cable down the East African coast. In fact, the Inter-Departmental Committee on Cable Communications calculated that up to the end of 1900 the imperial, colonial and Indian governments had paid out the staggering sum of £2,912,924 in cable subsidies.[33] Yet with the Cape cable and the all-governmental Pacific line under contemplation, an even greater expenditure was inevitable. This fact was noticed by the Treasury, which already in 1899 showed positive signs of alarm. In a strongly worded memorandum, the Chancellor, Hicks Beach, attacked those who considered

> that no communication of the kind is satisfactory which touches foreign soil, though that soil may belong to a nation with which we are not likely to be at war, or even to a nation who would almost certainly be our ally in the event of a war. And, further, existing cables are distrusted which are laid in shallow water, or landed in undefended places. If these views are to be accepted, I see no limit to the demands which may be initiated by a body like the Colonial Defence Committee . . . which is not likely to have the slightest regard to the cost.[34]

On these grounds, Hicks Beach attacked the plans for the Pacific, Cape and West Indies cables. As regards the Weihaiwei line, he scornfully reminded the rest of the Cabinet that in the 1885 (Penjdeh) war scare the Admiralty had spent £85,000 upon laying a cable from Woosung to Port Hamilton: two years later, the cable broke and was sold to a private dealer for £15,000.

Although the Chancellor's views were over-ruled by a Cabinet uneasy at the many potential threats to the security of the empire, he had pointed out an interesting development; for the deliberate creation of 'all red' telegraphs operated directly against the early idea and practice of laying lines along commercial routes to foreign capitals, weaving the cables of the world into one international system, with many countries sponsoring the projects and enjoying the benefits, as President Buchanan had hoped. Moreover, this commercial network, which was primarily financed and built by British companies, had become centred upon London and increased that city's predominance in banking, insurance, business and press agency matters: it was an advantage not lightly to be thrown away. Therefore, the Inter-Departmental Committee on Cable Communications of 1902 warned that a balance between the strategic and commercial advantages in cable-laying must be struck: naturally, cables which avoided non-British shores delighted the strategists but could not gain income from foreign governmental and business traffic, and stimulated other nations into laying their own lines. 'In view of these conflicting considerations,' the Committee concluded,

> we have not found it easy to formulate a general rule. We think, however, that appreciable but not paramount value must be attached to all-British routes; and we regard it as desirable that every important colony or naval base should possess one cable to this country which touches only on British territory or on the territory of some friendly neutral. We think that, after this, there should be as many alternative cables as possible, but that these should be allowed to follow the normal routes suggested by commercial considerations.[35]

There were, in fact, two types of cable being operated in the empire by the early twentieth century. The greater part of the British lines were the non-strategic, commercial ones, connecting London to the capitals of the world and totalling some 140,000 miles in length; they were rarely subsidised and often of comparatively short length. In addition, there existed those long-distance cables whose existence had been motivated to a large extent by political and strategic factors; they were government owned, like the Pacific cable and two of the Atlantic lines, or controlled by favoured and subsidised British companies and providing an 'all red' route. Of course, this difference was only one of degree, for the subsidised companies relied for a great deal of their revenue upon commercial and foreign messages; while the non-strategic cables in their turn dealt with government messages, say, to the British embassy in Vienna. All the cable companies had to give priority to official communications, which were prefaced by the authoritative words, 'Clear the line, clear the line'.[36]

The fact that the strategic cables received a governmental subsidy, and that the companies operating such lines were often granted a monopoly of landing rights in certain ports, aroused criticism from rival firms and from those who advocated 'free trade' and open competition with regard to all telegraphic communications. This the government refused to accept, arguing that the subsidised companies, particularly the Associated Companies which ran most of the 'all red' lines to India and beyond, had rendered great service to British interests; 'and through their efforts submarine telegraphy remained, for the first thirty years of its existence, almost exclusively in British hands'. Admittedly, these firms had made a good profit – the Eastern Telegraph Company's real dividend never fell below 6·75 per cent in the years 1873–1901 – but it was felt that their past services entitled them to 'a certain consideration' in the matter of landing rights. After all, several essential strategic lines would not have been laid at all had it not been for the government's appeal to, and subsidising of, the Eastern Telegraph Company. As far as Whitehall was concerned, there was no inconsistency in their assisting certain companies and not others:

> The normal course is that cables should be laid where they are required for commercial reasons, and should be left to pay their own way; but when the Imperial or Colonial Governments have required, for strategic or other reasons, cables which were unlikely to be self-supporting, they have naturally been obliged to pay the Companies for them by offering annual subsidies for a term of years. As a general rule the Imperial Government have given such subsidies only on strategic grounds . . .[37]

By 1911, a subcommittee of the Committee of Imperial Defence was able to conclude that, save for a line between Gibraltar and Sierra Leone, no more 'all red' cables were needed: even this suggested link was not urgent since they now believed that 'in view of the relations between this country and Portugal, it is improbable that any difficulty would be raised by that country as regards the use of the stations at Madeira and St

Vincent'. The system was, in fact, complete.[38] Furthermore, this creation of a worldwide strategic cables network had considerably eased the anxieties of the government's advisers. The earlier fears about the vulnerability of their own communications, and the hopes for a neutralisation in time of war, were gradually altered when it was realised that Britain had so many advantages in this field that her own weaknesses were outweighed. It was she, and not foreign powers, who held the trumps and as early as 1898 it was felt that the telegraphic communications systems of hostile powers should be attacked as soon as war had commenced:

> bearing in mind the superior resources possessed by Great Britain for carrying out this nature of attack, the Committee, after full discussion, have come to the conclusion that we ought to cut an enemy's cables wherever necessary for strategic purposes.[39]

These resources, admittedly, were very considerable. At that time, the British owned over 60 per cent of the world's cables, which reflected both their need and their financial ability to create a world wide system. But this also meant that they knew more than anyone else about cable-laying or cable-cutting, had more ships, and kept more spare cable. In 1904, for example, there were 28 British cable-ships; in contrast, there were 5 French vessels, 2 American, 2 Danish, 1 German, 1 Japanese, 1 Italian and 1 Chinese. Other countries relied to a large extent upon British help in laying or repairing: a British cable-ship had been sent to repair the Peru cable after it had been cut and separated during the Peru-Chile war, and breaks had been repaired by British vessels at depths of 2,700 fathoms. Furthermore, there was nearly always a British ship within call at any point if an emergency line was needed, since these were stationed all over the world and carried a reserve of cable. Thus, when Egypt was occupied, the spare cable from one of the Eastern Telegraph Company's vessels at Alexandria was used to lay a line to Suakin in the Red Sea: earlier, at the time of the Zulu war, a cable had been quickly laid from Aden to Durban. Another very important benefit was that Britain possessed a virtual monopoly of the vital gutta-percha, which was used to insulate the wires. Finally, there were the advantages automatically accruing to the world's greatest colonial and naval power, particularly in time of war:

> The numerous stations on British territory, and belonging to British Companies, which we possess on main lines of communication to foreign extra-European possessions, gives us special facilities (for censoring foreign messages). Further, the preponderating naval power, which we may safely anticipate in most parts of the world, will make it possible for us to occupy foreign places, and utilize their cable communications, which will, as a rule, be more advantageous than destroying buildings and apparatus, and damaging cable ends at landing-places.[40]

Once their deep oceanic lines had been laid, and a complex network of cables created, therefore, the British strategists' fears eased. In 1911 they worked out the following reassuring list of how many cable cuttings would be required to isolate the United Kingdom and various major colonies:

Country	Number of cable cuttings required to isolate it
United Kingdom	49
South Africa	5
Mauritius	5
Aden	9
Egypt	10
Straits Settlements	7
Australia	7
Gibraltar	9
Canada and Newfoundland	15
Malta	10

It has to be remembered that countries such as India, South Africa and Canada had many land-line connections as well; but, in any case, it was difficult to conceive of all the cables to any one of these colonies being cut, given the extent of British naval power at that time. Furthermore, even though the approximate positions of the British lines were known to foreign powers, the latter were believed to lack the special appliances and trained experts for grappling and cutting a deep cable. Since such experts might be obtained from Britain, however, the Law Officers of the Crown were persuaded to declare that it would be 'treason' for a subject to assist an unfriendly country in such a way.[41]

The planning of the Colonial Defence Committe for a time of war was most thorough and detailed, and constantly scrutinised to allow improvements. Having decided by 1898 that they 'ought to cut an enemy's cables wherever necessary for strategic purposes', it merely remained to work out the specific actions needed to isolate any hostile power, bearing in mind the simple fact that 'where one end of a foreign cable is landed on British territory it would not be necessary to cut it, as the control would remain in our hands'. All the alternative routes on British and foreign cables in case of hostilities were listed, with all feasible permutations regarding belligerents and neutrals, and the number of cutting operations required to isolate each country. If Britain were ever at war with France, her most likely foe at that time, the chief task would be to sever that country's seven cables to North Africa. Such an operation would be of doubtful value until British naval supremacy was established in the Mediterranean, however, for not only was there a grave risk that the cutting-vessel might be lost but the French would still be able to send messages to Algiers and Bizerta by boat. The cutting of these cables, and also the four lines to Corsica, would not necessarily be undertaken at the outbreak of war, although of course if a chance presented itself they should be cut. The French West African cables would be severed immediately, and so would the various lines in the West Indies, together with the new Brest-Cape Cod telegraph. In many cases (French Congo, Madagascar, Djibuti, Indo-China, New Caledonia) French colonies were solely dependent upon British cables and could be isolated easily, while the Committee also felt that the capture of the island of St Pierre would be more useful than severing the important French cable touching it on the way to New York.

Of the other potential enemy powers, only Russia, Japan and the United States were considered, an interesting reflection upon the state of British defence and foreign policy in 1898, although there were not many other powers who possessed cables at that time. Russia, the Colonial Defence Committee recognised, was invulnerable to cable-cutting operations and only if she was in alliance with France would Britain be justified in severing the Calais-Fanöe (Denmark) line of the Danish-controlled Great Northern Telegraph Company, which the Paris and St Petersburg governments used in order to avoid dependence upon the land telegraph through Germany. Neither Japan nor the United States possessed submarine cables worth cutting, unless they were allied with another power against Britain. In all these cases, the Committee was careful to point out, a combination of cable-cutting and the introduction of censors in British telegraph routes would be far less expensive and hazardous than direct assault upon enemy stations.[42]

By 1911, many of these recommendations were revised, it being recognised by the cable experts that the earlier report

> has become obsolete largely by reason of changes in the international situation . . . and for the present they have accordingly only considered the steps to be taken in the event of war with Germany or with the Triple Alliance, with or without Turkey. The possibility of France and Russia joining with the British Empire has been kept in view.[43]

This being the case, the schemes for the interruption of an enemy's cable communications were now much simpler, since only Germany had to be considered: 'The Austrian and Italian cables are unimportant from a strategic point of view', and only the Italian lines to Turkey and Sardinia need be severed. By this date, the Germans had built up a considerable cable network to their overseas possessions, even though the naval experts in Berlin recognised that they could not create their own secure 'all red' system without the acquisition of further colonies.[44] On the other hand, Germany had laid her lines chiefly between neutral stations, not only to avoid dependence upon the British but also to preserve the cables in time of war. International law did not restrict the action of belligerents in this matter, but it was generally accepted that lines between two neutral points should not be severed. Thus, while the subcommittee recommended the interruption of the German cables from Emden to Vigo and the Azores, they felt that 'it is probable that the cutting of the German cable between the Azores and New York would be strongly resented in the United States'. Similarly, it was feared that if the joint German-Dutch cable to Yap or the German-owned Monrovia-Pernambuco cable were cut, the Dutch and Brazilian governments might retaliate against British telegraph companies operating on their territory. It would be better to occupy the Yap station rather than provoke the Dutch into interrupting the Singapore-Australia cable, which touched at Batavia and Banjuwangi in Java. Nevertheless, the German line between Tenerife and Monrovia would be cut, since the Spanish and Liberian governments could be disregarded; while the colonies of South-West Africa, Kamerun and German East Africa were dependent upon British cables, and could easily be isolated. Berlin relied upon Russian lines to Tsingtao and French lines to Togoland, and if France was neutral would still be in telegraphic communication with the United States. But if Britain was allied with France and Russia, and action were taken at Yap and with the Emden cables, 'it would be possible to isolate Germany from practically the whole world, outside Europe . . .'.[45]

One of the more remarkable suggestions put forward by the British defence experts in 1898 was the 'cutting out' of several of their own cable-stations if the latter were indefensible and might be used by potential enemies who occupied a strong neighbouring position.[46] Thus the small undefended colony of Turks Island, a stopping-point on the Bermuda-Jamaica line, was to be cut out in the event of a war with France or the United States; and, in the former case, the same fate would befall Mahé in the Seychelles Islands, which would be cut out of the Zanzibar-Mauritius cable because of its predominantly French population. The biggest headache was the station at Bathurst (Gambia), which would almost certainly be over-run in the first few days of a war with France: yet the enemy naval squadron in nearby Dakar would make a cutting out operation such a risky venture that the inter-departmental committee recommended that this step should be taken forthwith, in peacetime, with the cable running directly to the defended port of Freetown in Sierra Leone instead. But by 1911 the strategic situation had altered so clearly in Britain's favour that the Colonial Defence Committee felt that these measures were now unnecessary, apart from directing the station at Walfisch Bay to disconnect itself from the Mossamedes-Cape Town line in the event of a war with Germany, in order to isolate South-West Africa. The same confidence was expressed over the earlier schemes to cut out foreign stations from British-owned lines. In 1898 it had been thought advisable, despite the risk of repercussions with neutrals to be ready to cut out the stations of Mozambique and Lourenço Marques on the East African line; Foochow and Woosung on the projected Hong Kong-Weihaiwei line; Java on the Singapore-Australia line; and several small stations in the West Indies and West Africa. As a result of Britain's *ententes* with France and Russia, and the virtual perfection of an 'all red' system, these steps were also judged to be no longer necessary.[47]

Many of these planned emergency measures to protect British cables and to interrupt enemy ones would be impossible without the close co-operation of certain telegraph companies, particularly the 'Eastern' group: hence the government's blind eye to the privileges which these firms obtained from their favourable position. The special ships of the Eastern Telegraph Company, together with those of the various cable construction firms in the United Kingdom, were essential for the cutting out of British or foreign stations, for destroying enemy lines, and for repairing cuts in the British system. The 1898 inter-departmental committee therefore proposed that the cable vessels of these companies, supplemented by others chartered locally by the Admiralty, be stationed near eighteen of the most important overseas bases. In the event of war, they would be put under the command of the local naval officer, and instructed to carry out the various tasks planned by the committee. Thus,

> the Eastern Telegraph Company's cable ship in the Mediterranean will proceed to Malta, and the one in the Red Sea to Aden. The Eastern and South African Company's ship on the West Coast of Africa will go to Sierra Leone, and the one on the East Coast of Africa to Mombasa. The Eastern Extension Company's ship, generally stationed at Singapore, will be transferred to Hong Kong, while the other ship of that Company will go to Port Darwin.[48]

It would also be necessary to ensure that adequate stocks of spare cable, and of cutting and repairing equipment, were kept in the companies' various depots, and supplemented by governmental stocks. The committee also hoped privately to persuade these firms to maintain on board their vessels extra trained cable personnel, who could be directed to take over other ships chartered and improvised for service at the outbreak of war. Generally speaking, the telegraph companies were to be responsible for the administration of their own vessels, the government providing only the strategic control and the funds for these extraordinary requirements. By 1911, many of the committee's more detailed instructions had been dropped, the government preferring a looser arrangement with the companies for the cutting and repairing of cables; but the close liaison between the two, and the strategical importance of this confidential co-operation, remained.

Much thought was given to the defence of British cable-stations. Ideally, the Colonial Defence Committee recommended, all cables should be landed under the guns of the fortress of the colony, which was a satisfactory arrangement for Bermuda or Gibraltar but less so when there was no fortress. As a substitute, they advocated that landing-places be defended with field-guns, machine-guns, or even rifles. All landing-points, from Capetown to Fiji, were examined, and improvements ordered. For example, finding it impossible to provide defences for the Zanzibar station, apparently due to some local difficulty, they recommended that the cables be taken from this weak spot and landed at Mombasa, where nearby troops could guard them. They also suggested that one of the cables from India which landed in the undefended harbour of Penang be transferred to Singapore. Other regions, too, caused difficulty: the fact that the cables across Canada lay for 3,000 miles only a short distance from the American border worried the Colonial Defence Committee and the Admiralty for decades, but they could no nothing about it. The open and undefended Newfoundland coast, where most of the Atlantic cables landed, was a problem which they also never satisfactorily solved.[49]

The position of the landing-point for the Pacific cable at Vancouver was considered for a long time. Some members of the Colonial Defence Committee wanted the cable landed under the guns of the fortress of Esquimault rather than on the west coast of Vancouver Island; but this meant an additional 55 miles of cable in shallow water, which made it, in the Admiralty's opinion, accessible to even the simplest cutting equipment. 'One of the main objects to be kept in view,' the Director of Naval Intelligence pointed out, 'is to get the cable in deep water as soon after leaving the landing-places as possible.' Thus, the line was not extended to Esquimault, but various ingenious precautions were taken to protect the isolated coastal cable-station. At first, the committee were worried about an attack by what they called 'ill-disposed persons from Seattle or San Francisco who might evade United States police forces' – a probable reference to the earlier Fenian raids. They therefore ordered an armed guard, and that barbed-wire fences be built around the station. Later, more sophisticated measures were ordered to baffle or frustrate landing-parties from a raiding enemy warship, such as having reserve instruments and cable stored secretly nearby. This became the practice for all cable-stations, especially the smaller ones, so that repairs could be effected as soon as the raiders had departed. Another cunning measure at Esquimault was the laying of numerous dummy cables for a few miles out to sea to baffle an attempt at in-shore cutting.[50]

Fiji proved to be another weak spot, where the committee could not sanction fixed defences, and therefore placed some hopes in a local militia force to hold the cable-station against a landing-party. When this scheme collapsed after a few years, they could only suggest the secret storage of spare cable and instruments, and assume that the navy's maintenance of the command of the sea in those waters would suffice. As for little Fanning Island, the strategists hoped that the atoll's inaccessibility was 'its chief protection against attack by a European enemy'.[51] It was impossible to cut out this station because of the great length of the Pacific line, and it was later suggested that the cable staff there should be provided with certain 'measures of defence'. The same recommendation was made in the Indian Ocean for Rodriguez and Cocos Island, and for Norfolk Island in the Pacific. The 1911 committee considered cutting out Norfolk Island and working a direct cable between Fiji and Brisbane before realising that this would also cut out New Zealand![52]

A very important and delicate aspect of the Colonial Defence Committee's consideration of the control of submarine communications in time of war was the establishment of some form of censorship over all telegrams. No legislative approval was sought for this, since it would be 'disadvantageous from a military point of view as calling attention to arrangements which it is desirable to keep secret'.[53] The censorship plans not only concerned the prevention of communication between a hostile country and its colonies and allies, but also measures to stop reports from enemy spies being sent out of British territory and to prevent the publication in Britain and the empire 'of true or false information which might exercise a prejudical effect on their civil population'. This withholding of correct but bad news was admittedly 'antagonistic to the Anglo-Saxon spirit' but might be necessary in Egypt or India. Basically, the government intended to check upon all telegrams leaving or entering the United Kingdom by the installation of censors at all telegraph offices, British or foreign. This work would be co-ordinated by a Chief Censor and his staff, based at the Central Telegraph Office in London. Even at the threat of hostilities, plans were made to insert a secret listening device in commercial lines running to a potential belligerent's capital to check for messages giving away vital information. The subsidised companies were taken into the government's confidence, and their operators had special instructions regarding suspicious telegrams. The same measures were to be carried out in the colonies, and it was hoped thereby to effect a stranglehold over all cabled information useful to an enemy or embarrassing to the British government. All these censors (officers on the reserve list) were to be appointed and controlled by the military authorities, and given every technical assistance by the Post Office. Apart from the use of the secret listening device at London if war seemed imminent, censorship would not be imposed until the Cabinet had given mobilisation orders for the armed services.[54]

It would be beyond the scope of this article to attempt to cover the strategic cable policies of the other great powers, but it should be mentioned that the advantages accruing to the British government through the careful fostering of 'all red' lines did not escape the attention of foreigners. Indeed, the *raison d'être* behind much of their own cable-laying was to challenge this British monopoly. The United States had become well aware of her dependence upon the Eastern Telegraph Company's goodwill in allowing messages to pass to and from Dewey's squadron during the Spanish-American war; and the islands of Guam and Midway were annexed for the specific purpose of providing cable-stations on their direct American line to the Philippines, which was completed in 1903.[55] The Germans, too, were struggling desperately to break the British cable monopoly, particularly to North America, and they laid their own cables via the Azores in 1900; but these cable-stations, and those of all their other lines, employed too many British staff to be considered a reliable means of communication.[56] The French, although laying independent cables to the United States, were also heavily dependent upon the British network for the rest of the globe, and visibly fretted at the insecurity of their own communications. Paris was roused to drastic action when, on account of the Boer war, the British installed a military censor in their Aden station in October 1899 to check upon traffic with South Africa, the east coast and Madagascar, and to turn back all coded telegrams. As a result, the French government embarked upon an intensive cable-laying programme, specifically noting in the draft of their telegraph bill of November 1900: 'England owes her influence in the world perhaps more to her cable communications than to her navy. She controls the news, and makes it serve her policy and commerce in a marvellous manner.'[57]

Yet the British dominance of world cable communications remained unchanged even in 1914, and other powers were by then turning eagerly to the newly developed wireless-telegraph to free themselves from their dependence. Experiments with this form of transmitting information had been carried out in the late nineteenth century, and in 1899 Marconi was able to send a message across the Channel. Two years later, his station at Cornwall could pick up a signal sent from Newfoundland, over 3,000 miles away, and in 1903 he successfully carried out long-distance ship-to-shore transmissions. So impressed were the Germans by this new invention that the government decided to build a chain of powerful W/T stations in all the major German colonies so that they could be swiftly alerted in times of crisis without using British-controlled cables. By 1914, Berlin was in wireless contact with Togoland, whence it was hoped to relay messages to German East Africa and South-West Africa. Stations had also been built at Kiaochow, Yap and Rabaul, and were being erected at Nauru and Samoa; and negotiations were taking place with the Dutch government for the construction of a German station in Sumatra, in order to link the Pacific colonies with East Africa. The Americans, too, had begun to erect W/T stations in the Philippines, Hawaii and Panama, and the French were considering a network for their colonial empire.[58]

Great interest was displayed in Britain for Marconi's invention, and an Act of 1904 put the wireless under government control.[59] By 1911 Whitehall had decided to create an imperial wireless system, with stations in Britain, Cyprus, Aden, Bombay, the Straits Settlements and Australia to supplement the cable communications; and the strategists urged that Hong Kong, West Africa and the Cape be included in this new network. They also pressed for a short-wave system of wireless communication with the Continent, particularly with France, in case the Channel and North Sea cables were cut by the Germans at the outset of a war; and the Admiralty strongly wished to be able to communicate with their ships at sea. Finally, many simply felt that the British Empire should automatically have the latest and most advanced form of communications system.[60]

Nevertheless, although the plans for erecting an imperial W/T chain went ahead and the Committee of Imperial Defence wrestled with the new censorship problems involved in it, the strategists remained quite clear in their minds that the wireless must only be seen as 'a valuable reserve in addition to cable communication'.[61] It could not be fully relied upon to send and receive messages, because the enemy could interfere with the transmissions. Moreover, the submarine cables were clearly a more secure way of transmitting vital information, for the simple reason that a wireless message could be picked up by any receiving-set within range: even coded transmissions did not guarantee absolute security since such codes could be broken, as the German naval ones were during the First World War and the Japanese diplomatic ones during the Second World War. It seems clear that Whitehall's steps to promote the formation of Cable and Wireless Ltd in 1928 were motivated precisely by the fear that the cheaper wireless services might force the more strategically valuable cable companies out of business.[62] Once again, the government had revealed its concern for security in its imperial communications and openly acknowledged the importance of the 'all red' cable system which its predecessors had so carefully built up.

It remains to be discovered whether the creation of this secure submarine cable network actually furthered the political unity and coherence of the empire as well. At first sight, the fact that an exchange of views between London and the self-governing colonies could take place within a day seemed to offer a solution to the British government's problem of wishing to present a united imperial front in world affairs whilst allowing for full consultation with the Dominion premiers; and no doubt the advocates of imperial federation welcomed the cable as a means of drawing the empire closer together to meet the challenges of the twentieth century.[63] But while the process of consultation was made much swifter, there is little evidence to suggest that differences of opinion between British and colonial politicians were in any way eased, let alone removed, by the use of the telegraph. When negotiating with the Germans over the partition of the Samoan Islands in 1899, for example, Chamberlain's ability repeatedly to wire reasoned explanations of British policy to the New Zealand government did not sway the tough-minded Seddon from protesting bitterly against any surrender of territory.[64] The cable certainly enabled the Dominions to press their point of view in London with greater force and celerity than before, but this is not to say that it resulted in a growing imperial cohesiveness.

It would also be of interest to know to what extent the administration of the empire was facilitated by the cable network, and in particular whether the 'man on the spot' was restrained from taking hasty and ill-judged actions by being placed on the end of a telegraph line. There is no doubt that the government in London thought that this would be so and looked forward to possessing a tighter control over certain consuls in the tropics whose zeal in dealing with native regimes and foreign representatives was a source of embarrassment.[65] Salisbury felt that the only way to put an end to the *furor consularis* in Samoa was to lay a cable from Auckland to that group.[66] Curzon chafed at the control over his Indian policy which this new method of communication gave to the British government, and Sir Robert Sandeman once remarked: 'I might have been a great man, but for the telegraph.'[67] Nevertheless, this was not always the case: the Aden-Durban cable, which had been laid amongst other reasons in order to supervise Sir Bartle Frere's activities at the Cape, proved fairly ineffective in restraining Sir Alfred Milner. Indeed, a recent study of the Colonial Office has concluded that, far from increasing London's control of overseas events, the telegraph gave local officials the chance to exaggerate any crisis.[68]

Yet, whatever the relative disappointments in the political and administrative spheres, the creation of a worldwide submarine cable system in the period 1870–1914 gave the British clear strategical advantages. By the eve of war, the success of the government's methodical policy had been widely recognised, not least by such imperialist pressure groups as were represented by the *Army and Navy Illustrated*, which candidly admitted:

The strength of our position is due to the past policy of fostering a system of British-owned cables, spread like a net all over the world, and constituting a monopoly which has grown stronger and stronger with each succeeding year. While that network was incomplete, and consisted of a few cables liable to be cut at any moment, the system was naturally a dangerous one to rely on in war. Now that it has been multiplied many times over . . . the telegraph may be expected to confer its greatest benefits from the strategical point of view.[69]

This forecast proved very true when war did come. Although several isolated cable-stations (Cocos, Fanning) were put out of action for a while by German cruisers, all lines were so complementary to each other that communication was never lost between the various parts of the empire. On the other hand, the Admiralty showed extraordinary speed in cutting the German cables: on the morning after the British ultimatum to Berlin had expired, for example, the two ends of the German Atlantic cable had been cut and were later taken into the harbours of Falmouth and Halifax. Other lines were similarly dealt with, and the German cables, like their colonies, were divided amongst the victorious allies in the Versailles settlement.[70] Moreover, the political advantages which Britain (and to a lesser extent, France) gained from the virtual control of war news to the United States and to the rest of the neutral world confirmed the value of this system of communication.[71]

In retrospect, one cannot help but be impressed by the efficiency of the strategic advisory bodies, and particularly of the Colonial Defence Committee, in this matter of submarine telegraph communications. While vast shake-ups were needed in almost all branches of the navy and the army between 1870 and 1914 to bring them into line with the realities of modern warfare, those concerned with the cables policy appear to have been extremely professional and competent. Naturally, they possessed many advantages, such as a great navy, an abundance of overseas possessions, and immense financial and technical resources within the nation itself; but credit for the skilful utilisation of all these factors cannot be denied. In their persistent striving for an effective cable communications system, in their rooting out of all the weak links in the chain, and in their detailed defensive and offensive preparations, those strategists had not only helped to strengthen the military bonds of empire in peacetime but also prepared that body better to meet the hazards and shocks which a worldwide war could present to it.

NOTES

1 This article has been read to, and benefitted from the comments of, Professor J. Gallagher's Commonwealth History Seminar (Oxford) and Professor M. Howard's War Studies Seminar (London).
2 A case in point is the Fashoda crisis of 1898, where Marchand was unable to refer to Paris for instructions, whereas Kitchener appears to have been

in regular contact with London. (One presumes that a telegraph line had been built along the railway which the British engineers constructed up the Nile valley.) Marchand's withdrawal to Cairo, caused by his need to communicate with the French government, weakened France's claim to have a say in the disposal of the Sudan and Delcassé furiously ordered him to return. See G. N. Sanderson, *England, Europe and the Upper Nile, 1882–99* (Edinburgh, 1965), pp. 332–62.

3 Cd 1056 (1902), Report of the Inter-Departmental Committee on Cable Communications, 26 March 1902, p. 22. See also the insistence of Sir Charles Dilke and Spenser Wilkinson upon this point in their *Imperial Defence*, 2nd edn (London, 1897), pp. 60–1.

4 'From an imperial point of view, and from the supreme right of self-preservation, intercommunication between the scattered units which form in their aggregate the British Empire, should as far as possible be in British hands, and should not be dependent upon the friendship or the caprice of other nations . . . there appears to us to be no safeguard so reliable as the maintenance and further development in the future of the British submarine cables which have served us so well in the past.' Cd 1056 (1902), p. 22.

5 Cabinet Papers, Public Record Office, London (hereafter Cab.) 11/118/15, Colonial Defence Committee memorandum 417M, secret, 7 July 1910. (This body was at this time one of the permanent subcommittees of the Committee of Imperial Defence.)

6 S. A. Garnham and R. L. Hadfield, *The Submarine Cable* (London, c. 1935), p. 31; B. Dibner, *The Atlantic Cable* (New York, 1964).

7 Garnham and Hadfield, p. 32; Dibner, p. 5.

8 Enough has been written in recent years upon the importance of India (e.g. R. Robinson and J. Gallagher, with A. Denny, *Africa and the Victorians: The Official Mind of Imperialism*, London, 1961; R. L. Greaves, *Persia and the Defence of India, 1884–92*, London, 1959), to convince the reader without further elaboration on my part that secure communication with that possession was regarded as vital by the British government. Details of earlier attempts to link India by cable have recently been given in J. W. Cell, *British Colonial Administration in the Mid-Nineteenth Century: The Policy-making process* (1970), pp. 224–34, 249–51. The various schemes put forward in the 1850s and early 1860s, all of which foundered upon Treasury objections and financial difficulties, had of course an underlying strategic motive as well as the more obvious commercial ones. But there does not appear to have been much Admiralty or War Office pressure for these lines, and there was certainly no discussion at that time of an 'all red' system.

9 Cab. 18/16/2, Inter-Departmental Committee report, 19 March 1891; Garnham and Hadfield, pp. 200–1; D. H. Cole, *Imperial Military Geography*, 10th edn (London, 1950), pp. 199–200.

10 Ascension, St Helena, Norfolk, Rodriguez, Fanning and Cocos Islands are good examples of this.

11 Cab. 8/1/12M, 'Protection of telegraph cables in time of war', 5 August 1885. At this stage, the Colonial Defence Committee, which prepared this paper, was a forerunner of the CID and not a subcommittee of it.

12 Cab. 18/16/2, report of 19 March 1891.

13 Commercial no. 8 (1885) France. International Convention for the Protection of Submarine Telegraph Cables, signed at Paris, 14 March

1884 (C.4384). The main problem for the delegates appears to have been to protect the cables from trawlers, which were continually breaking the lines laid in the shallow waters of the North Sea and English Channel.

14 Cab. 8/1/22M, 'Neutralisation of telegraphic cables in time of war', 19 July 1886.

15 Cab. 16/18/4, Report of Commission on the Control of Communications by Submarine Telegraph in Time of War, 22 October 1898. This code was to be prepared and communicated to all colonial governors and naval commanders. Messages would be sent to them under names 'previously registered secretly at the stations of British Companies'.

16 Cab. 16/14, CID Standing Sub-Committee report on Submarine Cable Connections in Time of War, 11 December 1911.

17 Cab. 16/18/4, report of 22 October 1898 already cited. Not content with this, the 1911 subcommittee recommended the erection of wireless telegraph stations at Suez and Alexandria, in order to duplicate the land lines. Both stations were to be provided with a garrison.

18 On this, see A. J. Marder, *The Anatomy of British Sea Power: A History of British Naval Policy in the Pre-Dreadnought Era, 1880–1905* (London/ New York, 1940), pp. 144–240, 393–416.

19 Colonial Office Records, Public Record Office, London (hereafter CO) 537/229, secret memo enclosed in War Office to Colonial Office, 20 May 1887; Cab. 18/16/4, report of 22 October 1898.

20 Cab. 18/16/5, memo of 26 March 1902. (This is the uncensored version of Cd 1056.)

21 Goschen to Hicks Beach, 13 December 1898, PPC 38, in Hicks Beach Papers, Gloucester County Record Office.

22 Cd 1056 (1902), pp. 18–19.

23 A chart showing British submarine cables can be found opposite page 204 of Cole's book. The map is not complete, however, and is far less detailed than the splendid one attached to the report by the CID subcommittee on Empire Wireless Telegraph Communications, 1914, Cab. 16/32.

24 Cab. 37/49/15, memo on the Pacific cable by Joseph Chamberlain, 18 February 1899. It was, of course, strongly supported by the Admiralty and the War Office.

25 ibid.

26 Cab. 18/16/3, report on the Pacific cable.

27 Cab. 8/1/4M, letter to Colonial Office of 13 February 1880.

28 Cab. 8/2/141M, CDC memo of 23 June 1898, enc. 1.

29 ibid., and minute of 29 December 1898 thereon. But Cd 1056 (1902), p. 20, mentions that the demand from the West India and Panama Company for an increased subsidy, together with the complications which had developed in the West Indies system as a whole, caused the government to postpone a decision on this matter.

30 Admiralty Records, Public Record Office, London (hereafter Adm.) 1/7424, Adm. to Foreign Office, 11 October 1899.

31 Cab. 37/50/37, Admiralty memo of 7 June 1899; L. K. Young, *British Policy in China, 1895–1902* (Oxford, 1970), p. 74.

32 Cd 1056 (1902), p. 56, gives a synopsis of this agreement. The British government gave the company a small subsidy, the Chinese government a far larger one.

33 ibid., pp. 78–9.

34 Cab. 37/49/15, Hicks Beach memo of 6 May 1899.

35 Cd 1056 (1902), pp. 15–16.
36 Cab. 18/16/4, report of 22 October 1898. See also CO 537/386.
37 Cd 1056 (1902), pp. 26–33.
38 Cab. 16/14, Report of 11 December 1911.
39 Cab. 18/16/4, report of 22 October 1898.
40 Cab. 18/16/2, report of 19 March 1891.
41 Cab. 16/14, report of 11 December 1911. These are the best examples: smaller colonies often possessed only one cable link to the rest of the world.
42 Cab. 18/16/4, report of 22 October 1898. This long report, and the later one of 1911, provide the essential details about the control of cable communications in time of war. Both were compiled by inter-departmental committees, which included representatives from the Admiralty, Army, Colonial Office, Post Office, and later the Foreign Office, India Office and Committee of Imperial Defence. (Esher was a signatory of the second report.) Naturally, none of the findings and recommendations could be presented to parliament, as was the case with the 1902 report.
43 Cab. 16/14, report of 11 December 1911.
44 For a hypothetical (?) scheme of the extra territories that would be needed to establish an all-German world cable system, see BA-MA (Bundesarchiv-Militararchiv, Freiburg), Fach 5174 a, *Ueberseeische Flottenstützpunkte – Ganz Geheim*, Vol. 2, Schröder memo of 15 April 1903.
45 Cab. 16/14, report of 11 December 1911. An exception would be the neutral line from Scandinavia to the United States, along which the famous Zimmermann Telegram was sent.
46 'The expression "cutting out" . . . means the joining up, in deep water outside a station, of the cables which run into it, so that communication will no longer run through that station or be easily interrupted by hostile action at or close to it.' Cab. 18/16/4, report of 22 October 1898.
47 ibid; cf. Cab. 16/14, report of 11 December 1911.
48 Cab. 18/16/4, report of 22 October 1898. Pages 17–18 of this report contain a convenient summary of all these cable-ships, together with their intended stations and duties.
49 On these various local defence schemes for cables, see Cab. 8/2/206M (Newfoundland); Cab. 8/3/303M (Mombasa); Cab. 8/3/295M and 317M (Australia); Cab. 8/3/324M (New Zealand); Cab. 8/3/248M (Penang and Malacca).
50 Cab. 8/3/267M, memo of 20 June 1901; Cab. 8/3/284M, memo of 29 November 1901.
51 Cab. 8/3/325M, memo of 5 August 1904 (Fanning Island); Cab. 8/3/303M, memo of March 1902 (Fiji).
52 Cab. 16/14, report of 11 December 1911. New Zealand was, of course, connected directly by cable to Australia, but the Wellington government would not have taken kindly to being cut out of the famous Pacific cable, which they had helped to pay for and maintain.
53 Cab. 18/16/4, report of 22 October 1898.
54 Cab. 17/92, 'Cable and Wireless Communication and Censorship', secret memo on the censorship of submarine cables in time of war, n. d.
55 On this, see W. R. Braisted, *The United States Navy in the Pacific, 1897–1909* (Austin, Texas, 1958), pp. 32–3.
56 BA-MA, Fach 5488, *Post- und Telegraphangelegenheiten – Ganz Geiheim*, Reichsmarineamt to Admiralstab, 10 March 1906, with encl. and marginal

comments thereon; ibid., Fach 5064, *Post- und Telegraphangelegenheiten*, Vol. 1, C-in-C *Hausa* (Azores) to the Kaiser, 7 October 1912.

57 Quoted in R. Hennig, 'Die deutsche Seekabelpolitik zur Befreiung vom englischen Weltmonopol', in *Meereskunde*, 6. Jahrgang, Heft 4.

58 BA (Bundesarchiv, Koblenz), Auswärtiges Amt, Abt. IIE, R85/777, *Akten betr. die drahtlose (Funken-) Telegraphie in Australien und Polynesien*, report of the *Hamburger Nachrichten* of 7 January 1914.

59 H. Robinson, *Carrying British Mails Overseas* (London, 1964), pp. 273–5.

60 Cab. 16/14, report of 11 December 1911; Cab. 16/32, 'CID sub-committee on Empire Wireless Telegraph Communications 1914', Admiralty memo of 14 July 1914; Cab. 17/92, Clarke memo B of 14 September 1906.

61 ibid. The erection of the W/T stations was postponed by the outbreak of war in 1914.

62 Cole, *Imperial Military Geography*, pp. 198–9. In 1950, the Post Office took complete control of Cable and Wireless Ltd.

63 On these hopes of imperial federation, see M. Beloff, *Imperial Sunset*, Vol. 1, *Britain's Liberal Empire* (London, 1969), pp. 26–159. Kipling, with his twin interests in empire and technology, was moved to write a poem called 'Deep-Sea Cables', of which the following sentence is of interest:

> Hush! Men talk today o'er the waste of the ultimate slime,
> And a new Word runs between: whispering, 'Let us be one!'

(Quoted in J. Morris, *Pax Britannica* (London, 1968), p. 61.)

64 A. Ross, *New Zealand Aspirations in the Pacific in the Nineteenth Century* (Oxford, 1964), pp. 249–52; P. M. Kennedy, 'The Partition of the Samoan Islands, 1898–9' (Oxford DPhil thesis, 1970), pp. 322–4.

65 On the role of the 'man on the spot' in imperial expansion, see W. D. McIntyre, *The Imperial Frontier in the Tropics, 1865–75* (London, 1967), especially pp. 372–85. For a good example of where the cable was greatly desired by the home governments, see P. M. Kennedy, 'The Royal Navy and the Samoan civil war 1898–9', in *Canadian Journal of History*, V, I (1970), pp. 57–72.

66 G. Cecil, *Life of Robert Marquess of Salisbury*, Vol. 4 (London, 1932), pp. 127–8.

67 R. L. Greaves, *Persia and the Defence of India, 1884–92*, pp. 42, 202.

68 R. V. Kubicek, *The Administration of Imperialism: Joseph Chamberlain at the Colonial Office* (Durham, NC, 1969), pp. 30–3.

69 Copy of *Army and Navy Illustrated* in BA-MA, Fach 5518, volume entitled *Wasserverkehrswege, Kabelverbindungen in England, Juli 1886–Januar 1919*.

70 Britain obtained one of Germany's North Atlantic cables, France the other. The French also obtained the German line to South America, while the Pacific cable was divided between the Americans and the Japanese.

71 As the Germans were well aware. See BA-MA, Fach 5065, *Post- und Telegraph- angelegenheiten – Ganz Geheim*, Vol. 3 (?) Rodewaldt and Weber to Reichsmarineamt, 11 November 1914, with memo.

4

The Revolution in British Military Thinking from the Boer War to the Moroccan Crisis

J. McDERMOTT

While it has been accepted that Austrian, French and German army officers acted in the interests of their services and played important roles in the making of their respective countries' external policies before 1914,[1] the role of their British counterparts has received insufficient attention. The idea of an England which was fundamentally anti-militarist and in which the civil arm always dominated the military has been accepted by most critics. This acceptance has led to a relative neglect of British military history in the crucial period of the early twentieth century. Until recently, works by J. K. Dunlop, Hampton Gordon and John E. Tyler[2] – all written in the 1930s – shared the field. Lately, however, new works have appeared by, among others, Samuel R. Williamson, Corelli Barnet, W. S. Hamer and Michael Howard, who have used evidence which was unavailable to their predecessors.[3] But important gaps remain in assessing both the motivations within military circles and the influence of the needs and strategic thinking of the army on Britain's external policy.

This paper examines the abrupt change that occurred in British military strategy between the Boer war and 1906 – a period of transition in British foreign relations – taking account of both the course of foreign policy and the ambitions of the army's bureaucracy. The change in the army's thinking whereby Germany replaced the Dual Alliance as the most likely enemy in any future war has traditionally been explained by a growing awareness of the German threat. While the political situation after 1902 must be considered, this paper contends that the turn against Germany was coincident with the establishment of the General Staff at the War Office in 1904 and was, in part, undertaken to serve the army's interests. In developing this thesis, the influence of Asian factors and the Committee of Imperial Defence on military policy making is taken into account. Finally, the period under scrutiny is significant because it sees the beginning of a trend toward increasing dependence of the 'expert' in strategic planning. Past failures and the increasing complexity of war planning brought into existence both the General Staff and the CID, and it is to the influence of these bodies that we turn our attention.

Attempts at War Office reform before 1899 failed because of the conservatism of senior officers, Gladstonian parsimony and anti-militarism in the government. When the Hartington Royal Commission recommended in 1890 the establishment of a general staff the Liberal member, Henry Campbell-Bannerman, denied the need for a ' "general military policy" in the larger and more ambitious sense of the phrase'. Indeed, he foresaw a positive danger in a 'body of officers . . . who sit apart and cogitate' about war. If such a body could not find 'an adequate field in the circumstances of this country', he warned, '[t]here might indeed be a temptation *to create a field for itself* . . .'[4] Thus was expressed a basic prejudice: distrust of the soldier and preference for improvisation in military planning. Though Campbell-Bannerman's warning would prove prophetic during his own administration, no action was taken on the commission's recommendation throughout the 1890s.

On the eve of the South African war, therefore, Britain's small professional army was in the doldrums, shot through with apathy and snobbery, trailing continental armies in size and intelligence facilities, and the Royal Navy in prestige. Although the Stanhope Memorandum of 1891 had defined the army's principal task as home defence and had stressed the unlikelihood of Continental action,[5] this definition was considered too limiting by reform-minded officers at the War Office.[6] Yet, since the Military Intelligence Branch was deplorably weak,[7] change could not be instituted from within the military department. Division of military opinion remained, therefore, coupled with inadequate preparation, the results of which were evident in the early course of the war in South Africa.

The defeats of 1899 and 1900 further diminished the army's status and raised serious doubts about its future. Hugh Oakley Arnold-Forster, a future Secretary of State for War, charged in 1900 'that our present military organization is seriously defective, and that its continued existence in its present form constitutes a serious danger to the Empire'. He criticised the lack of any clear, accepted statement of the army's role. It is true, he wrote, '*to say that our existing military organisation is based upon no known and accepted principle* . . . No one knows what the army is really intended to do, or on what principle, if any, its numbers are regulated . . .'[8] No progress had been made three years later when he took charge of the War Office: 'I do not find that any definite instruction exists as to what is the exact purpose for which the Army exists, and what duties it is supposed to perform.'[9] Indeed, Arthur Balfour, on becoming prime minister in July 1902, considered the War Office neglected and forlorn, 'the Ciderella of Departments'.[10]

Hence at the beginning of the twentieth century the British army lacked both status and a role without which it could neither justify its existence nor compete for funds with the august Royal Navy. Criticism and uncertainty were causing a crisis of identity at the War Office which the lack of a general staff aggravated. These problems demanded solution by 1901 as Russia, taking advantage of Britain's entanglement in South Africa, undertook military moves in the vicinity of India.

Possible invasion of India by Russia had long concerned British statesmen and strategists. It had been assumed, however, that in case of trouble the navy could force the Straits to attack and land troops in southern Russia, thus deterring an attack on India. But events in the 1890s – the formation of the Dual Alliance and increasing Turkish hostility towards Britain – made the Crimean strategy obsolete.[11] Henceforward, India would have to be defended by land across the North-West Frontier where naval power counted for little. By accident Britain had acquired in Asia the military responsibility of a continental power, a responsibility for which the army was ill equipped. This fact profoundly affected British strategic thinking from the 1890s.

The new situation caused anxiety in political and military circles. The search for an ally – unsuccessful in Germany, successful in Japan – was an attempt to enlist foreign manpower to help stem the tide of Russian expansion in Central Asia and the Far East. Within the Cabinet, Balfour voiced pessimism about the defence of India in case of a determined Russian assault.[12] At the War Office, the able and intelligent Sir Henry Brackenbury minuted that 'we are attempting to maintain the largest Empire the world has ever seen with armaments and reserves that would be insufficient for a third class military power'.[13]

The new situation was also reflected during 1901 and 1902 in the thinking of the army's strategic planners. Deprived of their traditional policy toward Russia, dependent on the fleet, and confronted by their own meagre resources, they displayed an abject pessimism, verging on despair, regarding Indian defence. Their attitude was based upon assumptions of the numerical superiority of the Russian army, its continuous land communications with the heartland of Russia (soon to be improved by the completion of the Orenburg to Tashkent railway), and the inferiority in manpower and organisation of the British army. The first full-scale attempt by army intelligence to deal with the problem warned that Russia could 'at any time, place 50,000 to 60,000 men in Afghanistan, as the mere heads of their columns . . . with countless numbers to follow, limited only by the total the theatre will support'.[14] Even without the new railway, Colonel William R. Robertson warned in January 1902 that Russia could mobilise 150,000 to 200,000 men for action in Afghanistan with reinforcements to follow at the rate of 20,000 a month.[15] Colonel E. A. Altham later pointed out that in the battle for India the British army of 292,864 men would be facing a potential Russian force of 3,600,000.[16] Not only was Russia strong in manpower, she was seen to be unassailable by a naval power with a small army. No offensive action by Britain was possible on the North-West Frontier, in the Far East (even with Japanese aid), the Caucasus, or Black Sea areas,[17] an opinion later supported by the First Sea Lord of the Admiralty.[18] Moreover, and perhaps most serious of all, the War Office planners doubted that the army could ever take responsibility for Indian defence without fundamental reorganisation. The inability to supply manpower for Indian defence was a constant theme, especially since Britain had commitments elsewhere. Hence, to defend India, army intelligence was forced to suggest conscription or alliance with Germany,[19] neither of which was a practical possibility.

The preceding assessments accurately represent the Military Intelligence Division's thought concerning Russia; they were no idle experiments in military planning. Indeed, the weakness of MID precluded such speculation. Moreover, since systematic war planning was a new weapon in the army's arsenal, intelligence officers had to be concerned with dangers which they believed to be immediate and practical. There is no doubt, however, that they overestimated the danger from Russia. When they studied maps in London, they failed to appreciate the immense difficulties involved in moving men and supplies across the rivers and mountains which separated Russia and India and negated much of Russia's apparent military superiority. But the soldiers were no more guilty than their civilian masters. Both Salisbury's and Balfour's Cabinets believed the most serious problem in imperial defence to be the Russian threat to India. Soldiers and politicians took it very seriously.

Thus it matters little how accurate MID's assessment was; it is how men perceive the situation at the time that is important. The problem of Indian defence produced division, confusion and an overall sense of weakness and futility in British policy. The director of military intelligence advocated alliance with Germany; Lord Roberts, the Commander-in-Chief, preferred isolation. The War and India Offices called for a permanent increase in the garrison of India, but from where were the troops to come? Military organisation was notoriously inefficient, manpower resources were strained, and the army's reputation was low. Consequently foreign policy was hamstrung and limited.[20] The Cabinet eschewed the use of force in Central Asia and sought, without success, agreement with Russia. Clearly, new initiatives were necessary, and to these we now turn – the establishment of the secretariat of the Committee of Imperial Defence and the General Staff at the War Office.

The secretariat and the General Staff came into being simultaneously as the result of the recommendations of the War Office (Reconstitution), or Esher, Committee. Both bodies were part of the same grand design of Lord Esher to improve the government's facilities for strategic planning and war preparation. This vital link has been overlooked by historians of both bodies, but the relation between the two bureaucracies was a significant factor in the evolution of British military policy from 1904.

Indeed, from its inception at the end of 1902 the Committee of Imperial Defence had important ramifications for the civil-military balance in the making of external policy. It greatly augmented the strength of military intelligence, whose membership increased by 50 per cent, and enhanced the importance of the director of military intelligence who sat regularly on the committee.[21] For the first time in British history a special body, including both Cabinet members and the prime minister on the one hand, and service officers on the other, convened regularly and kept minutes of their deliberations. Hence, the military expert acquired the potential to influence governmental thinking about foreign and defence policy. The CID was part of a new, tough-minded approach to problems stemming from appreciation of continental war planning, especially the German General Staff, and an overall disillusionment with the British penchant for muddling through. Moreover, those who advocated more participation by the experts in policy making were willing to bend constitutional practice to achieve their goal.[22]

The CID was established by Arthur Balfour who, by November 1903, believed that it required a permanent secretariat to draw up agenda and keep records.[23] The question of a more effective organisation for the CID became linked with the perennial issue of War Office reform. Esher, asked by Edward VII to become Secretary for War, refused but requested permission from Balfour to reorganise the War Office as head of an independent committee.[24] As a result, the War Office (Reconstitution) Committee, made up of Esher, Colonel Sir George S. Clarke and Admiral John Fisher, began deliberations with the assurance that whatever was recommended would be put into effect.

Before examining the fruits of their labours, let us examine the views of the committee. All three believed in an authoritarian empire held together by 'adequate physical force'. Though Britain had 'hitherto "muddled through" successfully',[25] they warned that this could not indefinitely be the case in a competitive world which strained British resources to the utmost. Better organisation of resources could be achieved by the application of scientific methods to problems of defence; thus they favoured giving the expert more say in policy making. Esher was the most influential of the three, and most of the committee's work was done by him. A man whose influence derived more from his personal connections than from any office which he held – he was on intimate terms with the King, a friend of Balfour, and a confidant of generals and admirals – Esher became a grey eminence behind the scenes in the making of foreign and defence policy. As early as February 1903 he had written to the King demanding a stronger CID to set out 'the *main lines* of Imperial Military policy'.[26] The committee, he believed, 'contains within itself the source of *political and practical initiative*' to decide national strategy, great issues of external policy involving both military and political factors.[27] Clarke was Esher's protégé, but himself no insignificant figure. A colonel in the Royal Engineers, he had held a string of important positions in the field of defence planning and organisation. As representative of the Admiralty, Fisher possessed the military mind, par excellence, and enjoyed putting army witnesses through their paces.

Part One of the Esher Report appeared in January 1904 and advocated a permanent secretariat for the CID to co-ordinate foreign policy with actual military power by collating military advice with information from other departments of state and, in turn, ensuring that the Cabinet appreciated such advice.[28] Thus the report considered the secretariat essential to the recommendations on War Office reform.

The two remaining parts of the Esher Report laid down the changes which were to go into effect at the War Office. Part Two called for the immediate establishment of a general staff to deal with 'military problems in the widest sense'. Headed by an officer freed from all other duties, 'educated for its special duties, drawing to itself the pick of the brains of the Army, and working continuously to improve . . . preparations for war', the general staff was to work in close association with the CID's secretariat.[29] This association was emphasised in the third part of the report, which stressed the duty of both agencies to anticipate contingencies which might arise in the field of military policy.[30]

Accordingly, on 6 February 1904 the General Staff was established as the War Office's department for strategic planning. The Chief of the General Staff, Sir Neville Lyttelton, became the sole adviser of the Secretary for War on strategy and military operations.[31] Major-General Sir James M. Grierson was appointed to the new post of director of military operations (DMO) in charge of both intelligence and mobilisation. Both officers sat on the CID, thereby forming the direct link between the military policy makers and the Cabinet. In subordinate posts were Colonels William R. Robertson and Charles E. Callwell, talented younger officers, whose duties were to acquaint themselves with any potential enemy, know Britain's military resources, and draw up contingency war plans. All military advice which was submitted to the CID after February 1904 originated in the General Staff.

The members of the Esher Committee shared the hope of the Secretary of State that the new department would make the War Office 'more fully aware of the part which the Army is expected to play in time of war'[32] They also conceived it as an elitist body to lead the army out of the wilderness, the rock upon which a reorganised, reinvigorated army could be built. By becoming an 'educating influence permeating the whole army',[33] and by unifying opinion as to the purpose of the army, the General Staff was expected to produce a corporate military interest and eliminate controversy which had instilled 'a baneful uncertainty and instability into our whole military policy'.[34] Thus the Esher Committee was concerned with, and worked consciously to promote, the interests of the army as the War Office acquired the policy-making organ possessed by continental armies. What is more, the potential existed for the Staff to use the CID to influence governmental policies.

This potential was enhanced by Sir George Clarke's appointment as secretary to the CID and by the close relationship between the War Office and committee. Esher worked assiduously to exalt Clarke's importance: all else, he wrote Fisher, was 'of secondary importance'.[35] Clarke responded by exercising initiative, largely determining the subjects which were considered by the CID and writing numerous memoranda for the Prime Minister.[36] Moreover, he became Balfour's close adviser on strategy and foreign policy. Hence under Clarke the secretariat became indispensable to the Prime

Minister, influential in its own right and possessed of significant initatory powers. Since according to Clarke himself military organisation was the subject most discussed at the CID,[37] War Office representation was strong and most memoranda for discussion came from that department.

It follows then that the CID, with Balfour as president in constant attendance, had enough civilian and military 'horsepower' to act as the inner cabinet that Esher desired to decide national strategy. From 1904 the General Staff realised the value of this link with the civilian authorities and because the Admiralty (for various reasons) remained aloof,[38] managed to dominate the CID and promote its strategic ideas through it.

Important problems concerning the army's role were unsolved as the General Staff began to function. A study by the defence committee had indicated by November 1903 that, as Balfour wrote to Kitchener, Commander-in-Chief in India,

> our Regular Army does not exist principally for the defence of Great Britain, but almost entirely (1) for the defence of India, (2) the retention of South Africa, (3) conceivably (but only barely conceivably) for the defence of Canada, and (4) for the purpose of small expeditions against the Naval Stations and Colonies of other Powers. Of these objects, the defence of India is undoubtedly the most formidable, and the one which throws the greatest strain upon the Mother Country . . .[39]

The army had fought tenaciously to retain its role in home defence, but the Stanhope Memorandum was superseded and the army stripped of its primary task.[40] The War Office did not relish the new significance of Indian defence, for, as even Balfour admitted, 'Perhaps the most fundamental fact [of the situation on the North-West Frontier] . . . is that the troops at our disposal are relatively few, [while] the troops of Russia [are] practically unlimited'.[41] Thus Balfour's dictum of November 1903 threatened at once to give the army an impossible task and to turn it into a supplier of reinforcements for India.

Before proceeding to the issue of reinforcements, there was another problem which bedevilled military, as well as political relations between London and Delhi. Division of effort between the two capitals frustrated Balfour. 'For many purposes,' he wrote Kitchener, 'we seem to be, not so much integral elements in one Empire, as allied States, one of which though no doubt more or less subordinate to the other has yet sufficient independence to make effective common action a great difficulty.'[42] Though the Prime Minister urged upon Kitchener a single military system to unite India and the Mother Country, nothing was done. Fundamental differences in outlook and goals remained, therefore, between the military departments of Britain and India.

One of the greatest of these concerned reinforcements in case of war with Russia. Already, before the dual creations of 1904, the subject had caused confusion and rancour. In July 1903 the pre-Clarke CID had endorsed the minimum number of reinforcements, 100,000 which the India Council considered necessary,[43] a figure 30,000 higher than that of the War Office.[44] News arriving early in 1904 that the Orenburg to Tashkent railway was to be extended to the Afghan frontier, thus increasing Russia's military potential in Central Asia, produced gloomy predictions from both India and the War Office. When the matter came before the CID, St John Brodrick, Secretary of State for India, reminded the members of the pledge to send 100,000 troops in case of trouble.[45] Lord Roberts, however, demurred, stating that the War Office, because of important deficiencies, could provide only 48,000.[46] But the CID refused to accept the Commander-in-Chief's advice and remained committed to send 52,000 non-existent reinforcements to India in case of war with Russia. This happened because Balfour was unwilling to provoke a clash with Curzon, the Viceroy, and Kitchener. Also to have conceded the correctness of Roberts' figure would have been tantamount to admitting that India could not be held against a determined attack by Russia. Thus the discrepancy between the number of reinforcements which India demanded and the number which the War Office could supply frustrated strategic planning in India as the CID's secretariat and the General Staff began their contributions to strategic thinking.

It is striking that, as Indian demands for reinforcements rose – to a maximum of 158,000 in November 1904 – the General Staff quickly used the CID to question the primacy of India in military planning. As early as May 1904, the Chief of the Staff argued against a single-minded concentration on India. In any case, stated Lyttelton, India could not be defended without conscription.[47] Grierson, the DMO, continued the attack by criticising Kitchener's penchant for overestimating the immediate danger from Russia.[48] The new approach was supported by the Secretary for War, Arnold-Forster, who pointed out, again at the CID, that the number of troops which could be supplied had a definite limit: it was no use talking about what India wanted; rather, it was a question of what the War Office could supply.[49] He later mentioned a figure of 91,000. Even this modest figure would absorb all reserves, leaving only twenty line batallions in England.[50]

This theme was pursued by the General Staff at a meeting of the CID on 16 November in response to Kitchener's demand for 158,000 reinforcements. It was opposed by a strong delegation from the War Office, comprising Arnold-Forster, Lyttelton, Grierson and Major-General C. W. H. Douglas, the Adjutant-General. The latter stated that compliance with the demand 'practically amounts to a sacrifice of our organisation, as well as our troops'.[51] Even if only 100,000 troops went to India, 'there will be no troops left for any other Imperial purpose'.[52] The message was, of course, that any British government approving such demands would have to face a military situation comparable to that which existed during the Boer war. Balfour got the message, but was unwilling to say no to Kitchener.[53]

From May 1904, therefore, the War Office attacked the supremacy of India in British strategic thinking through the CID. The officers feared that military policy would be tied inexorably to Indian defence, thus stripping the Staff of any function other than supplying reinforcements to Kitchener's army. What is more, there was no guarantee of success in India, where, if war broke out, numbers of reinforcements would be required beyond the capacity of the military system to supply without conscription. In seeking change, the soldiers encountered Arthur Balfour's inflexibility but found an ally in Sir George Clarke.

From July 1904 Clarke began to question the Asian military strategy. He criticised Indian officials for failing to take into account the mauling that Russia was taking from Japan in the Far Eastern war.[54] In November, when the issue of reinforcements was being thrashed out at the CID, he communicated to Kitchener on the need for flexibility in military planning.[55] Soon his criticisms acquired a mordant tone and sounded much like those of the General Staff. Further, he did not hesitate to impart them to Balfour, warning him that compliance with Indian demands would make India 'the predominant partner in Imperial defence' and encourage the ambitions of Indian officials.[56] In this way Clarke, who had close links with the General Staff, promoted its views to the Prime Minister. As a result, a split developed between the War Office and the secretary (supported by the Treasury), on the one hand, and Balfour, on the other, over strategy in Central Asia.

It was the General Staff, however, which took the initiative to break out of this increasingly frustrating situation. At the CID in December, Grierson advocated the establishment of a 'striking force' for attack overseas in conjunction with the navy.[57] Balfour objected on the ground that the demands of Indian defence precluded the use of British troops for any other purpose.[58] Grierson thereupon shifted his ground to the Army Staff College at Camberley, where a conference was held early in 1905 to review imperial defence as it affected the army. Clearly, the soldiers were moving, taking matters into their own hands. Addressing the conference the DMO attacked the predominance of India in military thinking. The army needed flexibility. Specifically, it should be able to attack nearby centres of military power.[59] The General Staff was shifting its attention from Asia to Europe, and the centre of military power that Grierson had in mind was Germany.

This action was revolutionary in two ways. First, before the Moroccan crisis began at the end of March 1905, Balfour's government did not seriously consider Germany as a future enemy. He and his Foreign Secretary, Lansdowne, viewed the *entente cordiale* as strictly a colonial settlement with France and were oblivious of its European ramifications. Russia, to them, was the enemy, as the Unionists continued to think imperially, rather than of the European balance of power, to the end of their term. Second, the General Staff abruptly reoriented British military thinking. Previously, the War Office had clung to the traditional view that France and Russia were Britain's most likely enemies. In February 1903, for example, a study by military intelligence had concluded that an Anglo-German war was not a practical possibility.[60] On the other hand, the War Office had opposed the *entente* with France on strategic grounds and, in early 1904, had advocated war, if necessary, with the Dual Alliance to support Britain's ally, Japan.[61] By the end of February 1904, however, the General Staff had begun to consider a European role for the British army.

Why did the Staff begin to consider a Eurocentric policy at this time? Indeed, in 1904 'talk of the inevitability of an Anglo-German war was in the air'.[62] The War Office trailed the Foreign Office and Admiralty in adopting anti-German prejudices. It was perhaps inevitable that the War Office should have followed other departments of state into the anti-German camp to protect Britain's interests. But there is yet another reason why the General Staff began to rethink military policy, one which, while secondary to the above, must be noted. This motive related to the army's internal needs. The CID's studies had shown Russia to be an extremely difficult foe for Britain in the long run. The problems which the North-West Frontier presented to the strategic planners – problems of distance, terrain, supply and, especially, of manpower – were staggering. Moreover, the military authorities doubted that Russia's defeat by Japan would result in any long-term alleviation of the problem. Thus they concluded that India could not be defended successfully without either conscription or alliance with Germany, both impossible conditions. Under existing conditions, therefore, Britain could not hope to defeat Russia in war. Against Germany, on the other hand, a small expeditionary force could be used with effect, particularly if Britain were allied to a first-class military power. Thus in military terms, Germany was a more 'practical' opponent for the British army, since traditional maritime strategy could be used against her. Hence, besides preparing the country for a European war, an anti-German strategy could provide the army with the role it lacked and, in turn, break the monopoly of India in military thinking.

The General Staff's subsequent activities indicate the new course at the War Office. Directly upon his return from Camberley, Grierson ordered a war game which postulated that Germany, invading France through Belgium, would encounter united Anglo-French opposition. The results, worked out during March and April, showed 'that there would be little chance of stopping the German turning movement [through Belgium to turn the French positions on the Meuse] unless the British forces arrived on the scene quickly and in considerable strength'.[63] The Staff's initiative cannot be passed off as an experiment in war planning which was not meant to influence the government. Indeed, it was consistent with Grierson's stated opinions on Indian defence and army organisation and with his subsequent actions. He visited Paris in the middle of March and went so far as to assure French officials that Britain would fight alongside France in the event of a Franco-German war.[64] Well before the German Kaiser set foot on Moroccan soil 31 March to precipitate a great European crisis, the General Staff had emerged on an anti-German course.

Though the redirection of British military policy had commenced before Germany challenged the *entente cordiale,* the Moroccan crisis had decisive effect. During it, Clarke and Esher involved themselves in matters of high policy and brought the advice of the General Staff to important civilian authorities. Consequently, by early 1906 members of the Staff were meeting regularly with their French counterparts to plan war against Germany.

British contingency planning for war against Germany began in July 1905 and followed traditional lines. The Admiralty proposed a special subcommittee of the CID to co-ordinate army and naval planning for a diversionary attack on the German coast to relieve pressure on the French army which would be bearing the full brunt of the German attack.[65] Hence the army would be a projectile fired by the navy, playing its usual secondary role in a dubious expedition to Schleswig or Pomerania. As has been seen, this was not the role which was favoured by Grierson and the General Staff.

Their view was brought to the attention of the Prime Minister by Sir George Clarke. When asked by Balfour towards the end of July to give his opinion about the course of a possible Franco-German war, the secretary gave his opinion (which was also the Staff's) that Germany would march through Belgium and that Britain must go to war with Germany because of the treaty of 1839.[66] This opinion was contained in a letter to Balfour, dated 17 August, in which Clarke stressed the likelihood of Germany being the aggressor in Belgium. 'I think, therefore,' he continued in a passage which Balfour thought significant enough to underscore as he read

> that it would be well that the G[eneral] S[taff] should be asked to prepare a paper discussing (1) the military advantages (if any) which Germany or France might expect to obtain by a violation of Belgian territory, and (2) the measure of resistance which Belgium, if backed by us, would be able to offer to such a violation. Possibly also (3) the time we should require to put two Army Corps, or the equivalent, into Antwerp.

'A study of this kind,' continued Clarke, 'is just what the G[eneral] S[taff] would like, and they might (perhaps) be able to achieve more success than in dealing with the Indian frontier.'[67]

The preceding statement is exceedingly interesting. It indicates not only that the General Staff was using the secretary to bring its new strategic ideas to the attention of the Prime Minister, but also that staff officers were anxious to be relieved of the intractable problems of Indian defence. The soldiers had an ally in Clarke who used his influence with Balfour in their interest.

Not until 19 September, however, after two further proddings from Clarke,[68] did Balfour request the Staff, in terms of Clarke's letter of 17 August, to undertake a study of Belgian neutrality in case of a Franco-German war.[69] Balfour's hesitancy resulted from advice from Sir Thomas Sanderson, permanent under-secretary at the Foreign Office, and Lord Roberts – both of whom urged caution[70] – and from his own ideas about defence priorities. In any case, the initiative for the Staff's study came not from the Prime Minister but from the secretary of the CID, probably, although this cannot be proved conclusively, with the connivance of the Staff itself. What is clear, however, is that Balfour gave his assent with great reluctance, since more than a month passed between Clarke's original request and Balfour's approval.

The General Staff's deliberations in the autumn of 1905 have been investigated in detail elsewhere.[71] They resulted in the recommendation that in case Germany violated Belgian neutrality, 'two British army corps should be landed at Antwerp within twenty-three days'.[72] Unanimous support for this policy within the Staff was not achieved until October when Callwell, who previously had favoured the Admiralty's scheme for an amphibious landing in Schleswig, joined his fellow assistant DMO, Robertson, and Grierson in the opinion that 'the most useful purpose to which [the army] could be put would be to give support to the French Armies in the field'.[73] There remained the necessity to have the continental policy accepted by the government of the day. Again, we will see the influence of Clarke and Esher at work.

Rumours of impending war between France and Germany were reaching London in December 1905 when Sir Henry Campbell-Bannerman (the dissenting member of the Hartington Commission) was forming a Liberal government upon the resignation of Balfour. Balfour, who continued to the end of his term to believe that the army's chief task was Indian defence, had appointed Esher *ex officio* member of the CID to help ensure its survival under a Liberal Cabinet. Thus Esher and Clarke, acting as the permanent nucleus of the CID at a time of governmental change, were in a position to influence events in a crisis when a power vacuum existed at the centre of the British government.

Also in December 1905 the General Staff's new European policy had reached full development. Grierson, in a *tour d'horizon* of British military requirements, placed European commitments at the top of a list of priorities. '[A] war with France against Germany,' he argued, '. . . is an eventuality to be seriously considered', and in such a war 'British aid to the French field force must come at once'. The DMO, moreover, made a definite policy recommendation to the incoming Liberal ministry: 'It is submitted that . . . we should be prepared to despatch [to France], as soon as transports could be collected, a force of at least four Cavalry brigades and three Army-Corps, which would amount to . . . about 120,000 men . . .'[74]

Nor did Grierson stop here. On the 18th he met Colonel Huguet, the French military attaché in London, and repeated to him his personal assurance of the previous March that Britain would aid France in a war with Germany.

Connected with these activities was the establishment by Clarke and Esher, without consulting any civil authority, of a CID subcommittee to co-ordinate war planning against Germany.[75] Both men were convinced that Germany had become Britain's most likely enemy, Esher since September 1904[76] and Clarke as a result of the Moroccan crisis. In the course of four meetings at the CID, 2 Whitehall Gardens, they put into practice their ideas about the initiatory powers of the committee, and, in turn, involved themselves in matters of high policy. Their activities were properly those of the Cabinet and went beyond Britain's commitment to France, which was limited to diplomatic support for the settlement in Morocco. At the first of these meetings (19 December), rival schemes for intervention in a Franco-German war were presented by representatives of the General Staff and Admiralty. At the second meeting (6 January), the army's strategy, prepared by Grierson and presented by Sir John French, was tentatively accepted. Also at this meeting the idea of joint planning with the French was raised. The third meeting (12 January) received a communication from Paris favouring intervention on the French frontier. The Admiralty consequently sent no representative to the fourth meeting: the CID was now the creature of the General Staff. Grierson and French, along with Esher and Clarke, considered a plan calling for a British expeditionary force to entrain at French Channel ports on the twelfth day of mobilisation.[77] On the same day (19 January), the DMO entered into his 'unofficial' conversations with Colonel Huguet.

Samuel R. Williamson, in his recent book on Anglo-French military planning before 1914, is unable to account for the CID's approval of the General Staff's strategy over the Admiralty's.[78] Indeed, in view of the Admiralty's traditional dominance over the army in strategic thought, the CID's action is surprising; but it can be explained by the close ties between the committee and the General Staff, ties written into the Esher Report. Both Clarke and Esher had worked consistently in the army's interest. Clarke considered efforts to plan strategy for Indian defence futile[79] and from August 1905 supported the shift to a Eurocentric strategy. As for Esher, Sir John French, who as future commander of the British Expeditionary Force in France had reason to be grateful, wrote that army officers 'all fully appreciated him as a man who devoted his great talents and splendid skill and brains *for the benefit of the officers of the Army, and to improve the position of the Army, and he had succeeded'.*[80]

The anti-German, Eurocentric military strategy which was adopted by January 1906 did improve the position of the army: it had found a role it could play without drastic reorganisation and it established a strategic dominance over the Admiralty which was to last throughout the First World War. Though doubts must remain, more light is cast upon the question raised by Williamson if the record of co-operation between the CID and General Staff is taken into account. Then one sees that the permanent nucleus of the committee was predisposed in the army's favour. The meetings of December and January were, therefore, the culmination of co-operation between the two bureaucracies.

In the course of these meetings, Clarke again carried military advice to an important Cabinet member, this time apprising the new Foreign Secretary, Sir Edward Grey, on 8 January of the plan for military conversations with the French. Grey, unlike Balfour, was only too happy to approve war planning against Germany because he feared war over Moroccan issues.[81] Military planning and foreign policy met on 10 January when Grey 'did not dissent' from the French ambassador's suggestion of 'unofficial communications' between military authorities of the two countries.[82] Of course, Grey did not inform either Parliament or the full Cabinet of this undertaking. But the plans of the General Staff were approved by those ministers – Grey, Haldane and Campbell-Bannerman – who knew of their existence.

While it is not suggested that the British General Staff operated from 1904 to 1906 principally to serve the army's interests there seems to be enough evidence to suggest that this factor must be taken into account as a significant part of the total picture. Bureaucracies habitually act not only for reasons of abstract national interest, but also to fulfil their own ambitions. The General Staff was no exception. When Balfour's strategic ideas threatened to subordinate the regular army to Indian defence, the Staff acted to retrieve its own and the army's future as an independent service arm. The evidence is strengthened when one considers the connection between the Staff and the CID. Esher conceived the secretariat as instrumental in improving the army's status; Clarke admitted that '[a] great army must justify its existence',[83] and his and Esher's actions helped it to justify its existence as the left wing of the French field armies in a possible European war. No doubt, as the Moroccan crisis dragged on, the times were propitious for the change, but the change was propitious for the army. Planning could henceforth be undertaken against Germany in conjunction with France without significant reorganisation. Moreover, though the army became an adjunct of the French army, strategic independence was won not only from Delhi, but from the Admiralty. British Staff officers embarked upon war planning against Germany, therefore, with a zeal which was nowhere in evidence when they were dealing with the North-West Frontier. Ironically, the change was accepted during the administration of Campbell-Bannerman, whose fears that a General Staff might 'create a field for itself' were partially realised, with important ramifications for the future of British foreign policy.

NOTES

1 On Austria, see Chapter 10 below; and G. A. Craig, *War, Politics, and Diplomacy* (New York, 1966). On Germany, see the same author's *The Politics of the Prussian Army 1640–1945* (Oxford, 1955); also M. Kitchen, *The German Officer Corps 1890–1914* (Oxford, 1968). On France, see P. M. de la Gorce, *The French Army. A Military Political History* (New York, 1963); and J. C. Cairns, 'International politics and the military mind: the case of the French Republic, 1911–14', *Journal of Modern History*, XXV (1953), 273–86.

2 J. K. Dunlop, *The Development of the British Army, 1899–1914* (London, 1938); H. Gordon, *The War Office* (London, 1935); and J. E. Tyler *The British Army and the Continent 1904–14* (London, 1938).

3 S. R. Williamson, Jr., *The Politics of Grand Strategy* (Harvard, 1969); C. Barnett, *Britain and Her Army 1409–1970* (New York, 1970); W. S. Hamer, *The British Army, Civil-Military Relations 1885–1905* (Oxford, 1970); Michael Howard, *The Continental Commitment* (London, 1972). Among periodical literature see A. Tucker, 'The issue of army reform in

the Unionist government 1803–1905', *Historical Journal*, IX, 1 (1966); and B. J. Williams, 'The strategic background to the Anglo-Russian entente of August 1907', *Historical Journal*, IX, 3 (1966).

4 *Hartington Report*, Part Two, Cmd 5979, xxix–xxx. (Italics mine.)

5 *Paper by the Secretary of State, laying down the Requirements for our Army*, dated 1 June 1891, Cmd 607.

6 William R. Robertson, who joined the Military Intelligence Branch in 1899, blamed the Stanhope Memorandum for the fact that 'broad military plans essential for the defence of the Empire as a whole received no adequate treatment in the War Office of the Period'. W. R. Robertson, *From Private to Field Marshal* (Boston, 1921), p. 92.

7 Before the Elgin Commission, Robertson testified that the staff of army intelligence numbered but nine permanent and one attached officer, whereas the corresponding organ in the German army numbered thirty-eight permanent and an equal number of attached officers. *Minutes of Evidence, Royal Commission on the War in South Africa*, I, Cmd 1789, 28.

8 H. O. Arnold-Forster, *The War Office, the Army, and the Empire* (London, 1900), pp. 42–3. (Italics in original.)

9 Arnold-Forster to Balfour, 27 October 1903, British Museum (hereafter BM), Balfour MSS, Add MSS 49722.

10 B. E. Dugdale, *Arthur James Balfour* (London, 1936), Vol 1, p. 365.

11 See J. A. S. Grenville, *Lord Salisbury and Foreign Policy* (London, 1964), pp. 24–7, 50–1. Also see M. M. Jefferson, 'Lord Salisbury and the eastern question 1890–8, *Slavonic and East European Review*, XXXIX, 92 (1960), 44–60.

12 At the end of 1901, Balfour argued eloquently and cogently in favour of British membership in the Triple Alliance, for reasons to do with Indian defence. See G. W. Monger, *The End of Isolation* (London, 1964), p. 64.

13 Minute by Brackenbury, 15 December 1899, cited in the report of the Royal Commission on the War in South Africa. App. E, Cmd 1789, 279.

14 Memo by Major E. A. Altham, DAAG, 'Military Needs of the Empire in a War with France and Russia', 12 August 1901, with an appendix by Major E. Peach, 31 May 1901. Public Record Office (hereafter PRO), WO 106/48, E3/2.

15 Memo by Col. W. R. Robertson, AQMG, 'The Military Resources of Russia and Probable Method of their Employment in a War between Russia and England', 17 January 1902, PRO, WO 106/48, G 3–1.

16 ibid., memo by Altham, 'Proposed Conference between Naval and Military Representatives of Great Britain and Japan as to Joint Action in the Event of War', no date, but before the conference which was held on 7 July 1902.

17 Memo by Altham, 'Military Needs of the Empire', 12 August 1901, PRO, WO 106/48, E3/2.

18 Kerr to Selborne, 2 April 1904, BM, Balfour MSS, Add. MSS 49707.

19 Memo by Robertson, 4 October 1902, PRO, Cab. 38/4/10; ibid., Altham to Nicholson (DMI), 14 October 1902.

20 An interesting example of the effect of the deficiency of manpower in Central Asia on strategic planning was the scheme hatched by Lords Curzon and Kitchener in India. They suggested the construction of a dam across the River Helmund 'to control the entire water supply alike of Persia and Afghan Seistan, developing either or both districts to unheard of wealth and prosperity, or reducing them to irretrievable ruin . . .' (Memo by Curzon and Kitchener, 7 August 1903, PRO, Cab. 6/1/30D.) Flood

waters from the Helmund were, apparently, supposed to fill the vacuum caused by the absence of British troops. In London, the scheme came to nought. Balfour sniffed that 'There are some remedies so powerful that they can never be applied'. He decided simply to leave southern Persia undeveloped, as a buffer area between Russia in the north and Britain in the Gulf. ('Draft Reply to Memorandum . . . of August 7 1903,' by Balfour, 24 November 1903, PRO, Cab. 6/1/32D.)

21 *Minutes of Evidence, Royal Commission on the War in South Africa*, 1 May 1903, Cmd 1791, 547–648.

22 Paul Guinn, in the prologue of his book *British Strategy and Politics 1914–18* (Oxford, 1965), has called attention to a trend in this period in which 'the older Liberal idea of an England governed by parliament, inefficient though it might be, was challenged by the new dynamic imperialist view of an authoritarian Empire administered with impartial efficiency by an elite military and civil bureaucracy composed of men of the British race'. The members of the Esher Committee, the CID and the General Staff were products of this trend.

23 Balfour to Arnold-Forster, 28 October 1903, BM, Balfour MSS, Add. MSS 49722.

24 Sir Philip Magnus, *King Edward the Seventh* (London, 1964), p. 326.

25 Lord Esher, 'National Strategy', BM, Balfour MSS, Add. MSS 49718.

26 Esher to the King, 4 February 1903, M. V. Brett (ed.), *Journals and Letters of Reginald Viscount Esher* (London, 1934), Vol. I, pp. 376–7 (hereafter *Esher Journals*).

27 Esher, 'National Strategy', BM, Balfour MSS, Add. MSS 49718.

28 *Report of the War Office (Reconstitution) Committee*, Part One, 11 January 1904, Cmd 1932, PRO, Cab. 17/13B.

29 ibid., Part Two, 24 February 1904, 'The Chief of the General Staff', Section IV. Cmd 1968.

30 ibid., Part Three, 7 March 1904, Cmd 2002.

31 Arnold-Forster on conclusions by the Army Council regarding the General Staff, no date, BM, Balfour MSS, Add. MSS 49723.

32 Memo by Arnold-Foster, 'Views of the Army Council with Respect to the War Office (Reconstitution) Committee', 28 May 1904, PRO, Cab. 37/71/72.

33 Clarke to Kitchener, 13 April 1905, Kitchener MSS, PRO 30/57/34, DD/5.

34 Memo by Esher, Clarke and Fisher, 'The General Staff', 28 April 1905, PRO, Cab. 37/78/115.

35 Esher to Fisher, 3 August 1904, in A. J. Marder (ed.), *Fear God and Dread Nought* (London, 1952), Vol. I, p. 322. At first, Esher was concerned about Clarke's performance as secretary. He wrote Fisher that 'at the Defence Committee, Clarke sits at a separate table in a far corner of the room . . . I have written to Clarke on the subject, and told him that he must sit on the left hand of the President of the Committee, and *assert* himself! He has not enough drive in him,' (ibid., Vol. I, p. 367 fn.). Clarke soon gained confidence and made up the deficiency.

36 Clarke, 'Note on the Imperial Defence Committee', enclosed in Clarke to Esher, 11 October 1905, BM, Balfour MSS, Add. MSS 49719; also in BM, Sydenham MSS, Add. MSS 50836.

36 Sir George Clarke (Lord Sydenham), *My Working Life* (London, 1927), p. 178.

38 Traditionally, the Admiralty displayed autonomy and little willingness to co-operate with the War Office in matters of strategic planning. The Admiralty, moreover, saw little need to co-operate with the CID since the Royal Navy had high status – the senior service – and a well-defined role in home and imperial defence. Indeed, Balfour's paper on invasion of November 1903 confirmed the navy's dominant role in home defence at the army's expense. Another reason for the Admiralty's aloofness was the personality of Sir John Fisher who became First Sea Lord in October 1904. The autocratic Fisher refused to share responsibility with or divulge strategic plans to the Committee of Imperial Defence.

39 Balfour to Kitchener, 3 December 1903, BM, Balfour MSS, Add. MSS 49726.

40 'Draft Report on the possibility of Serious Invasion', by Balfour, 11 November 1903, PRO, Cab. 3/1/18A. Balfour's paper did not, of course, settle the debate. Controversy continued as to Britain's security from invasion even after the outbreak of World War I. His paper was, however, the first authoritative assessment of the problem.

41 Memo by Balfour, 30 April 1903, PRO, Cab. 6/1/12D.

42 Balfour to Kitchener, 3 December 1903, BM, Balfour MSS, Add. MSS 49726.

43 Memo by Balfour to Curzon and Kitchener, 2 July 1903, PRO, Cab. 6/1/28D.

44 Memo by MID, 13 June 1903, PRO, Cab. 6/1/22D.

45 Minutes 32nd Meeting CID, 2 March 1904, PRO. Cab. 2/1.

46 ibid., minutes 33rd meeting CID, 4 March 1904; memo by Roberts, 23 March 1904, PRO, Cab. 6/1/41D.

47 Lyttelton did not explicitly recommend conscription, but the idea was implicit in the statement '. . . the maximum will not be reached until every able-bodied man has been trained, so far as financial conditions and public opinion in this country permit'. Memo by Lyttelton, 'The strength of the Regular Army and Auxiliary Forces, having regard to Peace and War Requirements', 1 May 1904, PRO, WO 106/44, E.1.6. (CID paper 22A.)

48 Memo by Grierson, 5 May 1904, PRO, Cab. 6/1/50D.

49 Arnold-Forster Diary, 3 May 1904, BM, Arnold-Forster MSS, Add. MSS 50338.

50 Minutes 54th meeting CID, 15 August 1904, PRO. Cab. 2/1.

51 Statement by Douglas, contained in a memo by the General Staff, 'Despatch of Reinforcements to India', November 1904, PRO, Cab. 6/2/72D.

52 Minutes 57th meeting CID, 16 November 1904, PRO, Cab. 2/1.

53 ibid., minutes 58th meeting CID, 22 November 1904.

54 Clarke to Balfour, 9 and 23 July 1904, BM, Sydenham MSS, Add. MSS 50836.

55 Clark to Kitchener, 18 November 1904, Kitchener MSS, PRO, 30/57/34, DD/2.

56 Memo by Clarke, 'Note on the Discussion of the 22nd [November 1904], Indian Reinforcements', BM, Sydenham MSS, Add. MSS 50836. Also found in BM, Balfour MSS, Add. MSS 49700.

57 Minutes 62nd meeting CID, 17 December 1904, PRO, Cab. 2/1.

58 Supplementary Note by the Prime Minister, 'Military needs of the Empire', 19 December 1904, PRO, Cab. 2/2/28A.

59 Maj.-Gen. Sir George Aston, 'The Entente Cordiale and the military conversations', The Quarterly Review, CCXLIII (1932), 367.

60 Memo by Altham, 'The Military Resources of Germany . . .', 10 February 1903, PRO, Cab. 3/1/20A.

61 See the author's unpublished PhD dissertation, 'British Strategic Planning and the Committee of Imperial Defence 1871–1907' (University of Toronto, 1971), p. 178.

62 A. J. Marder, *From the Dreadnought to Scapa Flow* (London, 1961), Vol. I, p. 110.

63 W. R. Robertson, *Soldiers and Statesmen 1914–18* (London, 1926), Vol. I, pp. 24–5. This represented a change of opinion for Robertson, for in January 1902 he had written a memorandum on Britain's treaty obligations in which he had stated that any military force that we could land [in defence of the Low Countries] would only be swamped by the vast armies of the Continent'. ('Memorandum on our Military responsibilities with regard to Belgium, Holland, Norway, Sweden, and Portugal', 30 January 1902, PRO, WO 106/44, E.1.6.)

64 C. Andrew, *Theophile Delcassé and the Making of the Entente Cordiale* (London, 1968), p. 286.

65 See Williamson, *Politics of Grand Strategy*, pp. 43–5. Williamson claims that this subcommittee never met. In fact it met, albeit in different form, in December and January 1905–6. See p. 175.

66 Memo by Clarke, 'Treaty Guarantees and the Obligations of Guaranteeing Powers', 1 August 1905, PRO, Cab. 4/1/64B.

67 Clarke to Balfour, 17 August 1905, BM, Balfour MSS, Add. MSS 49702. (Underlined heavily in pencil in the original.)

68 ibid., 26 August 1904 (underlined heavily in blue pencil in original), and 17-September 1905.

69 Balfour to General Staff, 19 September 1905, PRO, Cab. 17/69.

70 Sanderson had written to Balfour on 13 August to express scepticism about Clarke's views that Germany would violate Belgian neutrality. (Sanderson to Balfour, 13 August 1905, BM, Balfour MSS, Add. MSS 49739.) Roberts informed Balfour on 28 August that the army was no better prepared for a war in Europe than it had been in 1899–1900. (Roberts to Balfour, 28 August 1905, BM, Balfour MSS, Add. MSS 49725.)

71 See Williamson, *Politics of Grand Strategy*, pp. 47–52. Also see the author's 'British Strategic Planning and the Committee of Imperial Defence 1871 to 1907', pp. 239–41.

72 'Summary of Replies by the General Staff', 23 September 1905, PRO, Cab. 4/1/65B.

73 Memo by Callwell, 'British Military action in case of War with Germany', 3 October 1905, PRO, WO 106/46, D.F.e. 2/6. Previously, Robertson had found it necessary to squelch dissent by junior officers who were against continental operations. (Minute by Robertson, 29 September 1905, ibid.)

74 'Memorandum upon the military forces required for oversea warfare', by Grierson, 4 January 1906, PRO, WO 106/44, E 1/7.

75 For detailed discussion of these meetings, see Williamson, *Politics of Grand Strategy*, pp. 66–80; Monger, *End of Isolation* (London, 1963), pp. 240–56.

76 In that month, Esher had predicted a war between Germany and an Anglo-French combination. Esher to MVB, 9 September 1904, *Esher Journals*, Vol. II, pp. 62–3.

77 'Notes of Conferences held at 2 Whitehall Gardens, December 19, 1905 . . . January 19 1906', probably by Clarke, 18 January 1906, PRO, Cab. 18/24.

78 Williamson, *Politics of Grand Strategy*, p. 72.

79 Memo by Clarke, 'The Question of Seistan', 26 March 1906, PRO, Cab. 17/3.
80 G. French, *The Life of Field-Marshal Sir John French* (London 1931), p. 158. (Italics mine.)
81 See Grey to Haldane, 8 January 1906, National Library of Scotland, Haldane MSS 5907. Also, Grey to Campbell-Bannerman, 9 January 1906, cited in Sir Edward Grey, *Twenty-five Years* (London, 1925), Vol. I, pp. 114–15.
82 Grey to Bertie, 10 January 1906, cited in Grey, *Twenty-five Years*, Vol. I, pp. 70–1.
83 'Note on Threatened Invasions of India and Their Effect on British Policy', by Clarke, 3 April 1905, PRO, Cab. 6/3/100D.

5

The Royal Navy and War Planning in the Fisher Era

P. HAGGIE

When John Arbuthnot Fisher returned to the Admiralty as First Sea Lord on Trafalgar Eve, 1904, it was obvious to all who followed naval affairs that a period of major reform would ensue. Apart from Lord Charles Beresford, Fisher was the best-known naval personality in the land. As Commander-in-Chief Mediterranean he had greatly improved the speed, gunnery and tactical efficiency of the Fleet, while as Second Sea Lord and subsequently C-in-C Portsmouth he had already, by his control over the appointments of service personnel, laid the groundwork for reform. The *Daily Express*, later to become one of his most bitter Fleet Street critics, captured the optimism with which Fisher's return to Whitehall was greeted in a famous cartoon. In it, Nelson is seen clambering back onto his column at the sight of Fisher entering the Admiralty; the caption reads: 'I was on my way down to lend them a hand myself, but if Jacky Fisher's taking on the job there's no need for me to be nervous, I'll get back on my pedestal.' The feeling was well founded. In his years as First Sea Lord almost every corner of the Admiralty was rigorously examined and overhauled. The pace was relentless, the constantly reiterated goal '*Instant* readiness for War!'.

In one vital respect, however, the naval preparation for war remained inadequate, for little progress was made towards the development of a War Staff during Fisher's tenure of office. In fact not only did he fail to support such a development, he maintained a fierce opposition to it which is at first sight surprising in view of his earlier pronouncements on the subject of war planning. It is a paradox that has often been noted, but never satisfactorily explained, that the same man who appeared to be conscious of this important deficiency in the navy's intellectual preparation for modern war when C-in-C Mediterranean should have stubbornly resisted attempts to remedy it when he became professional head of the service.[1] It is the purpose of this paper to examine the paradox more closely.

In February 1902, as C-in-C Mediterranean, Fisher had put together one of his more interesting epistles inquiring about the state of war planning at the Admiralty and emphasising that 'there can be no more appalling dictum than "Don't make any plans until you see what the enemy is going to do!" '. He sent these remarks to his Flag Captain, Captain Prince Louis of Battenburg, with a covering note explaining that they were prepared for dispatch to Rear-Admiral Wilmot Fawkes (the First Naval Lord's private secretary), and adding: 'I do this in view of your remark of yesterday, "Is there no means of opening Lord Selbourne's eyes?" '[2] Prince Louis was an officer with considerable staff experience, having served as an assistant in the Naval Intelligence Department (NID) and as Flag Captain to the C-in-C Channel Fleet at the time of the Fashoda crisis. In his reply the Prince stressed the potential of the Naval Intelligence Department, if its strategic scope were widened and some real power given to it.[3] He suggested further that possible operations should be worked out in detail by senior officers of the foreign stations working within broad lines of policy laid down by the Admiralty. The key to these developments lay in increasing the power of the Director of Naval Intelligence.

> The time has come when the Director of this department [NID] . . . should be given such a position that his views, or rather the well-digested focused opinion of the many and versatile brains at work in his 'shop' cannot be lightly brushed aside or ignored. He should be a member of the Board, second only to the First Sea Lord and that officer's first assistant.[4]

Fisher was enthusiastic about the idea of a 'War Lord' and wrote in characteristically emphatic terms to his second-in-command, none other than Lord Charles Beresford:

> What we want is an additional naval member of the Board of Admiralty absolutely dissociated from all administrative and executive work and solely concerned in the preparation of the Fleet for War . . . a von Moltke on the Board. All the other Lords have too much to do.[5]

Beresford was returning to England on completion of his Mediterranean term. Subsequently elected to Parliament as Member for Woolwich, he was able to agitate for a War Lord both in the press and in the Commons. His recurring theme was that 'the business part of the Admiralty' should be divorced from 'that part on which the fighting efficiency depended'. 'The administrative faculty should be absolutely separate from the executive faculty, but at present they are mixed up.'[6] Soon his former C-in-C was obliged to express his (dubiously sincere) regrets to Lord Selborne for Beresford's extravagances.

Fisher himself continued to urge action in the lectures to the Fleet which were such a notable feature of his Mediterranean command. Sometimes the terms he used were of a kind he would have found highly embarrassing had they been utilised by his opponents after he became First Sea Lord.

> And so we come to your fighting fleet being ready to fight; they must be looking for the enemy, not looking for reinforcements. And what does this mean? It wants a *big thinking department*. That's the first thing. You want to begin *ab ovo* (as the Latin grammar says).[7]

He was foremost among those who were urging the establishment of a Naval War College. He even wrote a memorandum in 1902 on 'The Increasing Necessity for a General Staff for the Navy to meet War Requirements'. Small wonder then that there was bewilderment and dismay among his friends when it became obvious that the swift development of a comprehensive thinking department which some of them had anticipated under Fisher's leadership was not going to take place. Lord Esher noted late in 1904: 'Two years ago he snapped his fingers at the Board of Admiralty and urged every C-in-C to do likewise. Now he pipes a very different tune.'[8] What did happen was that towards the end of 1906 Fisher formed a small ad hoc committee under the chairmanship of Captain George Ballard, who until July of that year had been Director of Naval Operations. Other members included Captain E. J. W. Slade, a former director of the War College, and Julian Corbett, who was a lecturer there; the secretary was the ubiquitous Maurice Hankey. The job of the Ballard Committee was to draft the Naval War Plans.

It is difficult to avoid the conclusion that the reason for this sudden burst of activity, coming a full two years after Fisher's return to the Admiralty, and lacking the stimulus of a crisis in international affairs, was the continuing agitation of Beresford and his supporters concerning the state of preparation for war at the Admiralty. This impression is heightened by the detail in which the plans are set out. As Commander Kemp has pointed out, it does seem odd that plans which the Admiralty claimed 'are not in any way to be considered as those definitely adopted but are valuable and instructive because illustrative of the variety of considerations governing the formation of War Plans', should detail the actual names of the vessels told off for various duties.[9] The plans which the Ballard Committee produced are worth detailed analysis both because they represent the first attempt by the Admiralty at comprehensive strategic planning, and also because of the light they throw on the direction – and the quality – of that planning.[10]

The introduction survives in handwritten form in one of the surviving copies, confirming that it is the work of Julian Corbett. It is a reasoned statement of what its author believes to be the principles behind the plans. The first point made is the necessity to decide the cause of the war, before deciding on the strategy to be adopted. The question to ask is whether the war is one of limited or unlimited objectives. Having laid this down as the basic consideration for deciding what type of strategy to adopt, Corbett proceeds to attack the current practice of making vague generalisations about the purpose of command of the sea and on the uses of particular classes of warships and calling this 'war planning'.

For the purpose of forming war plans it must always be remembered that when we state the maxim that command [of the sea] depends on the battle fleet, we are stating the conclusion of a logical argument, the initial steps of which are highly important and cannot be ignored. The habitual oblivion of them frequently leads to false strategical conclusions . . . Again when we say that the function of the battle fleet is to seek out and destroy the enemy's battle fleet, although we are stating what is usually true, we are not helping ourselves to a logical grasp of naval strategy.[11]

Here Corbett is rebelling against the Fisher approach to war planning, which Captain Herbert Richmond also stigmatized. 'He [Fisher] generalizes about war, saying that it is to be made terrible, the enemy is to be hit hard and often, and many other aphorisms. These are not difficult to frame. But a logical and scientific system of war is another matter.'[12] An idea of the Fisher style can be gained from the minutes of a meeting of the First Sea Lord with the staff of the NID the previous year.

> It was considered by those present at the meeting that in a future maritime war the first duty of the British fleets and squadrons will be to seek out the corresponding fleets and squadrons of the enemy with a view to bringing them to action and fighting for what is the only really decisive factor – the command of the sea. It was considered that this policy also affords the most effective protection that can be given to our ocean trade against attack by the regular men-of-war of the enemy.[13]

Along with his criticism of this kind of grandiose vagueness, Corbett describes what he sees as being the correct use of various types of warship, including a defence of the value of speed in capital ships, and also the theory of the intermediate type (i.e. an apologia for the battle-cruisers). Of particular note in view of Fisher's dreams of Baltic operations is the assertion that 'for reasons familiar to every naval officer, it is certain that in future wars open blockade must take the place of close blockade as the basis of naval strategy'.[14]

Following these general remarks comes a more specific introductory section dealing with possible causes of a war with Germany. These are seen as three, namely: German absorption of Holland and Belgium and their colonial possessions; a similar absorption of Austria and parts of Turkey following the death of the Emperor Franz Josef; or the formation of colonies in South America. Following the principle of limited-objective warfare set out in the general introduction, the main operations in the first case were to be confined to seizing a position on the Netherlands seaboard which would lie on the flank of any German advance (Borkum being seen as the most suitable), and to aiding northern Holland and Antwerp with troops. An attack on the German fleet in harbour, or on any of the German fortified harbours, is seen as irrelevant to the main aim. The German fleet could not affect the situation so long as it remained in harbour, and to risk losses in attacking it would be futile. Similarly in the case of Austria, the aim of the plans should be to force the German fleet to come out and fight on ground of British choosing, rather than taking the offensive regardless.

In all three cases the prime aims of strategy should be adjusted to the particular aims of the war, whether this is to prevent German control of the seaboard of the Low Countries, to prevent her from becoming a Mediterranean power, or to prevent her exerting force in South America. Operations against enemy trade are in all three cases seen as subordinate.

In order to increase the pressure on the enemy and to strike at him financially it is necessary to undertake secondary operations against his trade. *We must be careful to keep this in its proper place, and to remember that it is not the primary object of the war* . . . The capture of the German colonies may be considered as a secondary objective also, since attacks on them will not exercise any direct influence on the object of the war.[15]

The implication throughout the introductory section is that British power to exercise adequate blockading pressure was limited. By extension, unless land forces were raised in such numbers as to allow significant military intervention, Britain alone could not hope to impede German continental ambitions. A strong case is also made for the creation of a War Staff, which Corbett continued to urge on Fisher. The introduction dwells on the need to prepare plans for all possible causes of dispute, and ends with the forthright statement:

If we hope to be able to hold our own when the time comes, we must also have everything so arranged that nothing remains to be done but to set the machinery in motion; it will be too late then to attempt to work out our plan of campaign, and to collect the necessary material.

When the war plans which follow are studied, however, it becomes clear that a radically different assumption is being made from that expressed in the introduction.

It is considered that the German war fleet itself is not a true ultimate objective, although its destruction is in general eminently desirable as a first step. The Germans would doubtless regret its loss, but no immediate suffering would thereby be entailed upon the national commerce and industries, *such as would arrive from a stoppage of trade.*[16]

The German mercantile marine is evidently regarded as the prime objective by the writers of these plans, and blockade as the prime weapon.

There are four plans in all, each of them in two versions, depending on whether France is assumed to be neutral or in active alliance with Britain. The first plan assumes that the destruction or enforced idleness of German shipping might be sufficient to bring hostilities to an end. If this is unsuccessful, the second plan provides for an increase in pressure by rigorously blockading German ports and preventing all trade, whatever flag it is passing under, from reaching them. If still greater pressure proves necessary, it 'can be exerted by attacking and harrying the second objective, the German coast, towns and population. But then we shall have practically reached the extreme limit of our powers of aggression, unless the third objective of a German army dependent on seaborne supplies is available'. The final plan assumes that this third objective is available, due to German occupation of the chief islands of the Danish Archipelago, Siaelland and Fyen.

In order to implement the first plan, cordons were to be placed across the English Channel and the northern entrance to the North Sea, while cruisers were detailed on the various trade routes to hunt down any German shipping outside the cordon, or which succeeded in breaking through it. 'These arrangements for the attack on German trade would in large measure also afford protection to our own, should any of the enemy's vessels succeed in breaking out to open water.'[17] The second plan was to be carried out by means of a *close* commercial blockade, dependent for its feasibility on the blocking of the Elbe. The escalation required in the third plan was to be provided by the destruction of the defences and facilities of the Baltic ports and the seizure of the North Sea islands of Borkum and Sylt as destroyer bases. The occupation of Siaelland and Fyen by the Germans was to be dealt with by an immediate and close blockade of these islands.

The German coast cannot strictly be accepted as itself constituting a primary objective, as the plans state. The only objectives which are considered to be of sufficient importance to justify the risk of attacking German territory are to capture and destroy German naval forces, to seize a base for the British destroyers and torpedo craft, or to increase the efficiency of the commercial blockade. The major aim throughout the plans remains the destruction of the German merchant marine and the stoppage of German seaborne trade in neutral bottoms. This aim, and the advocacy of close blockade to achieve it in certain of the plans, represents an outlook very different from that of Corbett. Clearly no satisfactory war plans could be elaborated until this vital point at issue between the writer of the introduction and the authors of the plans themselves had been cleared up.

Besides the internal contradictions of the document, it is open to further criticism. Altogether inadequate notice is taken, for example, of modern developments in sea warfare, particularly the mine and the submarine. In the introduction mines receive only passing mention as having 'a potentiality that cannot be ignored and, if not barred by treaty, may profoundly modify naval warfare.'[18] In fact mines had already been utilised to good effect by both sides in the recent Russo-Japanese war, and the naivety of the statement is all the more extraordinary in view of the fact that the Admiralty knew this, and had moreover been deeply impressed by the number of casualties inflicted by the new weapon. In the proposals for the bombardment of the Baltic ports no mention is made of any possible threat to the bombarding forces from either mines or submarines. The idea that commercial pressure could prove decisive was reinforced by the British naval attaché in Berlin, Captain Philip Dumas, who transmitted the Germans' own fears on this matter; but no consideration is given in the plans to the effect which the proposed measures would have on Britain's own seaborne trade in terms of increased freight and insurance rates.[19]

Despite the fact that the seizure and tenure of the Danish islands would require troops as well as marines, there was none of that cordial co-operation between army, navy, and Foreign Office which the introduction laid down as being necessary. A German descent on Siaelland and Fyen, we are told, 'is considered probable by those who have had opportunities of studying the German military organisation for war, though it is difficult to understand what Germany would hope to gain from such a move'.[20] It would be interesting to know who these authorities were who saw this move as probable, since the plans were prepared without any contact with the War Office.

The shortcomings of the plans are no reflection on the men who compiled them. None of those concerned had received any training in strategic planning apart from what they had managed to pick up through service in the existing Intelligence Department, and as the NID in practice was limited to the preparation of fleet dispositions in the event of mobilisation, such gleanings were bound to be meagre. As for the War College, the standard of training given can be judged by the accounts of some of the war games played there; they betray an altogether too simple approach to the problems of waging war. The attack failed, however, because *by accident* the British fleet changed its night position on this particular night . . . [German troop transports] arrived off Barrow without being noticed, but two submarines *happened to be* leaving that morning for their station, having just been completed at the works. These vessels met them at the entrance to the river, and they were all torpedoed.[21] Such quotations need no gloss.

On completion the plans were sent for criticism to some of the commanders who would have to carry them out, but their alternative suggestions were based on an equal lack of strategic training and little better understanding of the problems involved. Sir Arthur Wilson's remarks (C-in-C Channel Fleet) do at least show a better understanding of the dangers of mine and torpedo, and he condemns close blockade: 'A continuous watch off all the German ports, in sufficient strength to prevent anything from coming out, would be very difficult and costly to maintain, and, if effective, would bring us no nearer the end.' To this Fisher minuted: 'This is Admiral Yamamoto's secretly expressed opinion, based on the Japanese naval study of the question of war between Germany and England.'[22] Wilson's own suggestion was a distant blockade, with one British fleet based on the south coast and the other on Ireland or the west coast of Scotland. In the event of France being an active ally he envisaged in addition amphibious raids on the German coast, accepting the mine and torpedo risk in view of the importance of making an effective diversion. Despite comments such as these, neither Fisher nor Wilson fully escaped from the idea that naval operations close to the enemy's coastline and harbours were still feasible, as witness the former's famous Pomeranian schemes and Wilson's defence of such schemes before the Committee of Imperial Defence (CID) at the time of the Agadir crisis.

In sum, the Ballard Committee's plans show clearly the lack of an agreed basis for strategic planning within the navy, and how little notice had been taken of the revolutionary developments in sea warfare that marked the latter half of the nineteenth century. Speed of execution may be to blame for some of the inconsistencies and omissions, but it cannot be held responsible for the fundamental confusion of thought revealed. Under pressure, Fisher's administration had produced war plans, and this in itself was undeniably an advance on the vague and woolly generalisations of the past; but the plans themselves serve only as proof of the distance the navy still had to go before it possessed a brain commensurate with the speed and sophistication of modern sea warfare.

Not only did opinions remain conflicting within the Admiralty; there was no co-ordination with any outside body, either the War Office, the CID or the French. The committee's plans made no practical proposals for co-operation with the French. In a modified version of the plans dated 1908, it is proposed to give the duty of commerce protection to the French in the event of an Anglo-French conflict with Germany because 'the French cruisers are more suitable than the British for the attack and protection of trade'.[23] The damaging nature of this admission was not seen by an Admiralty which still believed in everything being subordinate to the destruction of the enemy fleet, and it was not until 1912 that the British first approached the problem of joint planning with their continental allies. The official Admiralty line was set out in some 'Comments on the Building Programme of the British Navy', written to defend the prevailing level of construction in the light of the destruction of the Russian Baltic Fleet at Tsu-Shima. 'The Board of Admiralty, as the responsible naval advisers of the Government, cannot base their plans on the shifting sands of any temporary and unofficial international relationship . . . ententes may vanish. Battleships remain the surest pledge this country can give for the continued peace of the world.'[24]

Consequently it is not surprising to find a report of the DNI on German naval building dated January 1908 in which the calculations of strength still include a possible Franco-German combination. In the same year an Admiralty paper on the redistribution of the fleet stated that 'the purpose always kept in view and actuating the further policy of fleet distribution is to develop further the concentration against Germany (or Germany and France combined, if ever that most improbable contingency arises)'.[25] It illustrates the state of British defence co-ordination in 1908 that the navy could be considering, albeit only as an outside chance, the possibility of a Franco-German alliance against Britain, while at precisely the same time the War Office was consulting the French military as to the most effective way in which France could utilise British military aid in the event of an Anglo-French war with Germany.

Fisher himself only once entered into conversation – if it can be so called – with the French. At the beginning of January 1906 Captain Mercier de Lostende, the French naval attaché in London, called on Fisher with the diplomatic purpose of investing the Admiral with the Grand Cross of the Légion d'Honneur. He seems to have been surprised and not a little pleased at the frank nature of the ensuing conversation. Fisher spoke freely to him about dispositions, but the nearest the conversation came to a consultation was in the single sentence: 'Je suppose que, à votre côté en France, vous avez pris vos précautions.'[26] It was a confused account of this meeting which misled Sir Edward Grey into thinking that Anglo-French naval conversations had begun.[27] In fact what Fisher did not speak of at this meeting was more significant than what he revealed. No mention was made of naval co-operation or of Fisher's own plans for seaborne raids on Germany, and no further meetings of any kind took place.

An important point which must be borne in mind here is the action of the French in 1870, when sailors had been taken from the fleet to fight in the field against the Prussians. After such an act by a French government only thirty years previously, the general coolness of British naval officers towards consultations becomes more understandable, and it would be unfair to blame their absence solely on Fisher. Equally, it was a service tradition to be sceptical of alliances. Fisher summed up this attitude in one of his Mediterranean lectures: 'I was once told by a Cabinet minister that I quite overlooked the fact of our having allies. I don't quite see where they are at present, and as regards sea fighting they would be a damned nuisance.'[28] Even as regards the Japanese, with whom Britain had a formal alliance, the Admiralty were unwilling to do more than the absolute minimum demanded by courtesy in the way of consultations.[29]

Nor were the Admiralty any more forthcoming towards the Committee of Imperial Defence and the War Office. Fisher's own prejudice against politicians and contempt for the military were important factors here. It was his firm belief that the army should remain subordinate to the navy, 'a projectile to be fired by the navy', as he once put it to Selborne. 'We shall never get the army right until it is incorporated with the Navy and the soldiers all wear the same uniform like we do in the Navy! – they will all pull together then.'[30] As for the CID, his great fear was that it would develop into an 'Aulic Council' usurping the functions of the First Sea Lord in time of war. This suspicion remained even after Charles Ottley, a former DNI and a 'Fisherite', succeeded Sir George Clarke as secretary of the CID. The consequences for combined planning were disastrous.

The impact of the first Moroccan crisis in 1905 had for a time forced an appreciation of the need for inter-service consultation even on Fisher. On 24 June he asked the DNI, Ottley, for a statement apropos manning the existing war fleet in the event of sudden action being necessary in support of France, and also the dispositions of the fleet in the event of naval action against Germany. Ottley's reply pointed out the crushing superiority of the combined British and French navies even if Russia should join Germany, and advocated close blockade as the means of defeating the latter. When this was dispatched to the C-in-C Channel Fleet for his comments, the split within the navy over the wisdom of close blockade which was later enshrined in the Ballard Committee's plans, is revealed clearly in Wilson's reply. He sees blockade as ineffective and a descent on the German coast with as powerful a force as possible as the only way Britain could assist France: . . . the result [of an Anglo-French combination to resist Germany] would depend entirely on the military operations on the French frontier and we should be bound to devote the whole military forces of the country to endeavour to create a diversion on the coast of Germany in France's favour.[31]

Both Fisher and Clarke thereupon sought to bring the question of joint military and naval operations before the CID. Ottley wrote a memorandum on 'The Preparation of Plans for Combined Military and Naval Operations in time of War', in which he stressed the limitations of the Admiralty war planning apparatus.

> The consequence of this limitation of the powers of the intelligence departments to those of a 'thinking' rather than an 'executive' branch is that it can never be possible to carry the organisation and preparation of plans for a great joint military and naval expedition beyond a certain point . . . [they] must indeed be regarded as a basis on which executive orders and instructions would be formed rather than in themselves embodying such executive orders.[32]

At first sight this statement might seem to oppose Beresford's argument that the executive and thinking departments should be separate, but in fact there is no contradiction. Beresford's argument concerned the separation of executive and thinking *duties*; Ottley is concerned with obtaining executive *authority* for the NID.

Sir George Clarke took issue with Ottley's argument, minuting:

> But both Admiralty Council and Board of Admiralty can give any executive orders they desire; the flaws meant therefore, lie in the fact that *joint* action of the two departments is not directed by any outside authority except the Cabinet. The Cabinet in time of war would decide and give orders; but in peacetime this does not operate. Hence inadequate and improper measures of preparations.[33]

The importance of this exchange is that here we see an attempt being made to enable the Cabinet to take decisions, through the CID or its subcommittees, in time of peace. In this way the Admiralty and War Office would be furnished with the executive authority to back their opinions, rather than merely possessing advisory powers – exactly the result Ottley wanted for the NID within the navy. Clarke's exaggerated view of the power of the Admiralty is characteristic of those who saw in it a model for the War Office. In fact the shortcomings of both institutions were similar. Although the army had more experience in utilising staffs, neither service possessed an adequate staff effectively to utilise the information collected by their respective Intelligence Departments, and the requiremnts of both were dictated by the Treasury which lacked familiarity with defence requirements.[34]

Subsequent to this exchange, a proposal to establish a subcommittee to deal with combined operations was brought before the CID and adopted, with provisions for its proceedings to be kept most secret.[35] The fate of this proposal is instructive. It seems that Esher hoped this device might avoid a confrontation between Balfour and Field-Marshal Lord Roberts in the CID over conscription; he wrote to Balfour in September 1905 supporting the proposal. He had great hopes for its future also; he foresaw it 'fulfilling the highest functions of a General Staff, the only sort of General Staff suited to our requirements, i.e. a joint Military and Naval Staff'.[36] But despite such high hopes the subcommittee never met.[37]

Two possible reasons for this may be advanced. Fisher's own approach to the CID in June had been highly uncharacteristic, and was prompted by his firm belief in the likelihood of war. This threat of war receded after the French accepted the plan of a conference over Morocco, and Fisher in all probability had second thoughts over the wisdom of allowing the new subcommittee to become established. By the end of the year he had returned completely to character and withdrew the naval representative (Ottley again) from the unofficial conversations concerning British aid to France which had begun after the fall of Balfour's government. In addition to Fisher's second thoughts, one of the tasks which Esher saw the sub-committee as fulfilling disappeared in November 1905 when Lord Roberts resigned from the CID.

One result of Fisher's brief excursion into the realm of joint planning was that the War Office for the first time got wind of the Baltic schemes, some of which were later incorporated in the War Plans. The resultant memo fired across Whitehall from Colonel C. E. Callwell (Assistant Director of Military Operations) to Captain Ballard (at this time Assistant Director of Naval Operations) roundly condemned the schemes and put forward the War Office idea of assisting the French by a direct military commitment. The arguments used were substantially the same as at the later more famous confrontation between Admiralty and War Office in the CID at the time of the Agadir crisis.[38] The Admiralty ignored the criticism and retreated into isolated contemplation and elaboration of the Baltic schemes without even inquiring if the troops they planned to commit to Pomeranian landings and island garrisons would in fact be available.

Despite increasing criticism of this attitude, there were no major alterations in the methods of strategic planning during Fisher's term of office. The critics even managed to obtain an official inquiry into Admiralty policy which, in its conclusion, looked forward 'with much confidence to the further development of a Naval War Staff, from which the naval members of the Board and Flag officers and their staffs at sea may be expected to derive common benefit'.[39] The 'Navy War Council' which resulted was, however, a sham; like the earlier War Plans, the formation of the Council was a sop to the critics and the politicians rather than a genuine attempt to tackle the problem. The First Sea Lord presided over the new body, which included the assistant secretary of the Admiralty, the DNI, the Director of the Naval Mobilisation Department (which had taken over mobilisation planning from the NID), and the Rear-Admiral in command of the War College. The organisation was typical of Fisher – an advisory body working under himself – and since he was not in sympathy with the Council's aims it stood no chance of success. Captain Herbert Richmond summed up the Council as 'the most absurd bit of humbug that has been produced for a long time . . . the study of war forms no part of its work. The First Sea Lord remains supreme and imposes his crude strategical ideas on the nation.'[40]

In defence of Fisher it has been claimed that he simply did not have the time to devote to the creation of a War Staff in addition to his other reforming commitments. Such a claim is easily refuted by a glance at the Navy Records Society edition of his papers, where the editor gives just two examples of the vast range of interests which he continued to pursue as First Sea Lord. He has often been pictured as a man unwilling to consider the views of relatively junior officers, but although his receptiveness to the ideas of others waned as the number of his enemies increased, this charge is initially the complete reverse of the truth. Maurice Hankey served as a young Marines officer in the Mediterranean Fleet under Fisher, and competed for one of his essay prizes. He records:

> My essay was forwarded to the Admiralty but what gave me the greatest pleasure was that at least one of my ideas was tested at fleet manoeuvres and eventually adopted as part of Fisher's War Tactics. It was thus that the C-in-C picked the brains of the Fleet, stimulated his officers and applied the results to the practical problems with which he was faced.[41]

In fact Fisher would consult, talk and argue with anyone he considered had special knowledge or a novel point of view, regardless of his rank; it was the 'juniority' of many of the selections he made when Second Sea Lord and C-in-C Portsmouth that aroused resentment in some of the older officers.

What must be appreciated in seeking to explain Fisher's attitude towards the creation of a permanent War Staff is that his strategic gifts were limited. His undeniable brilliance as an administrative reformer did not extend to the fields of strategy and tactics. Despite the similarity of the terms they used, his concept of war planning was never as advanced as that of Beresford, for example, although the latter's presentation tended to be confused. Even his paper on 'The Increasing Necessity for a General Staff for the Navy' sounds much more exciting than it is; its content adds nothing to the published Fisher correspondence.[42] Fisher's concept of war planning remained old-fashioned; while a staff could be useful in preparing plans of mobilisation and disposition, strategic planning was to remain the sole prerogative of the First Sea Lord and was to be divulged to absolutely no one. His approach to Ottley during the first Moroccan crisis is significant in this connection, for his queries merely concerned the manning and dispositions of the fleet. He was to be his own 'Naval Moltke', to the dismay of those like Corbett and Esher who had looked to him for the creation of a genuine Naval Staff. The outlook which Fisher represented was more concerned with preparations for the outbreak of war than with plans for its prosecution. It took insufficient account of the problems of improvising strategy in an age when the scale of fleets and the speed of movement and communications set a greater premium than ever on forward planning. It was even more difficult to justify given the almost universal view that any future war would be short. It was thought that modern industrial states could not tolerate the disruption of a long conflict. In 1912 an outline scheme was drawn up for the most efficient employment of the country's shipbuilding resources in time of war. The duration was assumed to be six months, and few would have considered a longer war feasible.[43]

In practice, as we have seen, Fisher utilised various ad hoc devices in lieu of a proper Naval Staff, but his personality was such that he would never have been able to work with an established and responsible staff. There is a very close resemblance here to another great figure in Imperial Defence at this time, Lord Kitchener. Both were men of tremendous drive and effectiveness. Both worked largely outside established channels, centralising authority in their own persons and, having done so, 'performed miracles of improvisation, and extracted from subordinates whom [they] trusted and occasionally loved much more than they or anyone else believed that they had to give'.[44] Just as Kitchener, through these very qualities, was ill-suited for the post of Secretary of State for War, so was Fisher ill-equipped to work with a formally constituted War Staff. To be effective such a staff would have to possess a degree of executive power; this Fisher could never accept.

'He is a genius, and a genius may do things not within the compass of ordinary men: but his predecessors have not been nor may his successors be geniuses'.[45] This judgement of the generally acute observer Herbert Richmond has led to Fisher's own strategic gifts being consistently over-rated His genius was not strategic; even had it been, the task of preparing war plans in modern conditions was beyond the scope of a single mind. Fisher never appreciated this: as with all great men the fault was great.

NOTES

1 Fisher's most recent biographer, Richard Hough (*First Sea Lord*, London, 1969), although disposing convincingly of the views of Taprell Dorling (*Men O'War*, London 1929), is no more convincing than previous writers in seeking to answer this question. See pp. 273–7.

2 Fisher to Battenberg, 10 February 1902. A. J. Marder, *Fear God and Dread Nought* (London 1952), Vol. I, p. 225.

3 The NID had been established in 1886, largely through the prompting of Lord Charles Beresford, then Junior Naval Lord. Although its terms of reference were wide-ranging, its duties in practice were confined to matters of disposition and mobilisation. See Public Record Office (PRO), *Admiralty Memorandum on War Organisation* (Cabinet Papers), Cab. 37/18/45; *Hansard*, 12 March 1912; Geoffrey Bennett, *Charlie B* (London 1968), p. 137.

4 Battenberg to Fisher, 11 February 1902. M. Kerr, *Battenberg* (London, 1934), p. 165.

5 Fisher to Beresford, 27 February 1902. Marder, *Fear God*, Vol. I, p. 232.

6 *Hansard*, 20 June 1902.

7 R. Bacon, *Life of Lord Fisher of Kilverstone*, 2 vols. (London 1929), Vol. I, p. 177. Fisher's support of a War College can be followed in ibid., Vol.

I, p. 153, and Marder, op. cit., Vol. I, pp. 203–4, Vol. II, p. 101. The College came into existence in 1901 and was firmly established at Portsmouth five years later. Fisher's continued support of this institution is comprehensible for, unlike a War Staff, the College posed no threat to the authority of the First Sea Lord.

8 *The Journals and Letters of Viscount Esher*, ed. M. V. Brett, 4 vols. (London 1923), Vol. II, pp. 110–11.

9 Navy Records Society, Vol. 106, *The Fisher Papers*, Vol. II, ed. P. K. Kemp (London 1964), p. 317.

10 For ease of reference the version of the plans considered is that published by the Navy Records Society in their edition of Fisher's Papers edited by Commander Kemp (see preceding note). None of the versions preserved in the Admiralty Records (PRO, Adm. 116/866B) differs materially from this.

11 Kemp, op. cit., pp. 321–2.

12 A. J. Marder, *Portrait of an Admiral* (London 1952), p. 49. Richmond was one of the very few naval officers to see clearly the important role which staff work would play in future maritime warfare, and he served as one of Fisher's assistants at the Admiralty until his heretical views and forthright character caused him to be transferred.

13 PRO, Adm. 116/866B. Those present were Fisher, Ottley (DNI), Bacon, Inglefield and Ballard (Assistant DNIs), Commander Wilfred Henderson and W. F. Nicholson, Fisher's private secretary.

14 Kemp, op. cit., p. 331.

15 ibid., pp. 360–1. (My emphasis.)

16 ibid., pp. 362–3. (My emphasis.)

17 ibid., pp. 364, 382.

18 ibid., p. 337.

19 PRO, Adm. 116/1043B. Dumas' dispatch of 1 February 1907. In an earlier dispatch (12 November 1906, Adm. 116/942) he transmitted the criticism of the German Chief of the 'Admiral Staff', Büchsel, that the staffs of British Admirals were far too small.

20 Kemp, *The Fisher Papers*, p. 363.

21 ibid., pp. 451, 453. (My emphasis.)

22 PRO, Adm. 116/1043B. See also Kemp. op. cit., p. 455.

23 PRO, Adm. 116/942. For the beginning of Anglo-French naval conversations in 1912 see *British Documents on the Origins of the War*, ed. G. P. Gooch and H. Temperley (London 1922–32), Vol. X (ii), pp. 582–3; and Churchill to Grey, 23 August 1912, W. S. Churchill, *The World Crisis*, 6 vols. (London 1923), Vol I, pp. 112–3.

24 PRO, Adm. 116/866B.

25 Captain Slade's report in PRO, Cab. 37/91/2.

26 *Documents Diplomatiques Français*, 2nd ser., VIII, 308.

27 Gooch and Temperley, op. cit., Vol. III, p. 203; G. M. Trevelyan, *Grey of Falloden* (London 1937), p. 135.

28 Bacon, op. cit., Vol. I, p. 177.

29 P. C. Lowe, *Great Britain and Japan 1911–15* (London 1969), pp. 25–6.

30 PRO, memo to Selborne, 20 May 1904, Adm. 116/942.

31 A. J. Marder, *The Anatomy of British Sea Power* (London 1940), pp. 504–5.

32 PRO, Adm. 116/866B.

33 ibid.

34 The Army Staff College had been firmly established at Camberley in 1857,

yet in the navy as late as 1893 the C-in-C Mediterranean (Tryon) was able to give an order which resulted in the sinking of his flagship and his own death for want of a staff to advise him of its folly. Even in the 1930s as able a First Sea Lord as Chatfield could reduce the length of the Staff course from a year to six months, believing in the light of Invergordon that staff officers were 'out of touch' with the men. The course was later restored, but the incident shows the persistence of the Nelsonic dictum 'my Staff is my Captains'. See Sir O. Murray in *Mariner's Mirror* (1939), pp. 328–30.

35 PRO, minutes of 76th and 77th meetings of the CID, Cab. 38/9/61, 65.
36 *Esher Journals*, Vol. II, pp. 110, 117. See also George Monger, *The End of Isolation* (London 1963), pp. 228–9.
37 Lord Hankey, *Supreme Command*, 2 vols. (London 1961), Vol. I, p. 62.
38 PRO, Adm. 116/866B. CID Records, Cab. 38/16/7, 13; 19/47–9.
39 Cd 256 (1909). The conclusions of this report are reproduced in A. J. Marder, *From the Dreadnought to Scapa Flow*, 5 vols. (London 1961–9), Vol. I, pp. 198–200, and Hough, *First Sea Lord*, Appendix 3, pp. 368–9.
40 Marder, *Portrait of an Admiral*, p. 62.
41 Hankey, op. cit., Vol I, p. 18.
42 This document is now in the Fisher papers in the possession of the Duke of Hamilton (Lennoxlove MS, Ref. F.P. 90). I am grateful to Mr R. F. Mackay of St Andrews for this reference.
43 PRO, Adm. 116/1100B.
44 Philip Magnus, *Kitchener* (London, 1968 edn), p. 450.
45 Marder, *Portrait* . . ., p. 23.

6

Joffre Reshapes French Strategy, 1911–1913

S. R. WILLIAMSON

Joseph Jacques Césaire Joffre assumed command of the French army on 28 July 1911. At 59, Messimy's third choice for the new post of Chief of the General Staff possessed an undistinguished military record. The son of a Pyrenean barrel-maker, General Joffre had fought in the Franco-Prussian war while a student at the Ecole Polytechnique; subsequently, much of his army service had been in the French colonies. In 1904 he returned to France to become the Director of Engineers, a task he performed with credit. Then, after serving as a divisional and corps commander, he became Director of Support Services for metropolitan France in 1910. A trained and competent engineer, Joffre understood well the organisational and logistical requirements of the French army. The same could not be said for his appreciation of grand strategy: indeed, he had had no training or experience in this area, not having attended the Ecole Supérieure de Guerre or even commanded an army-size unit in the annual war games. Rather, he brought to his new post the proper political and religious credentials and a certain peasant capacity for making the right intuitive decision. These qualities had advanced him to the apex of the French military hierarchy; they would not be enough to ensure his success as France's chief strategic planner.[1]

Joffre shared most of the strong convictions and prejudices of the offensive school of military theorists. Confident that 'the offensive alone made it possible to break the will of the adversary', he agreed with de Grandmaison and Foch that the counter-offensive was outdated, useless and unworthy of the French army. No longer would the French wait for the first blow and attack only when certain of the enemy's location. Although Joffre's later actions suggest that he never quite understood the limits of the 'all-out offensive', his firm, zealous commitment to the doctrine influenced every facet of his strategic evaluations. Moreover, he could impose his views upon the army, since the elimination of the divided high command removed any organisational barriers to the establishment of an 'offensive' orthodoxy. Unlike his predecessors, Joffre bore responsibility for the preparation both of war plans and of the army to implement them.[2] Assisting him in this work was General de Curières de Castelnau, a staff officer well acquainted with the details of Plan XVI and equally anxious for offensive action.[3]

In their planning the two generals faced a pair of especially vexing questions: what deference to pay to Britain's attitude towards Belgian neutrality, and what value to place upon British military assistance. Their answers may usefully be examined within the context of Joffre's reshaping of French strategy.

Changes in the French high command had come at a perilous moment. The Moroccan crisis, fanned by Lloyd George and excessive German demands in the Congo, looked ominously like the occasion for war, a prospect Joffre regarded with no great confidence. The recent shake-up of the army's leadership, combined with the inadequacies of Plan XVI, suggested discretion rather than a rush for valour. The chances for victory were less than the 70 per cent established by Napoleon: to improve these odds became the General's overriding concern.

His first step was to review intelligence estimates on Germany's probable strategy in case of war. Detailed information about the German rail network near Aix-la-Chapelle and Moltke's alleged annotations on a recently acquired 1906 *Kriegsspiel* reaffirmed Joffre's fear that Germany might strike through Belgium. But these intelligence estimates, not nearly so precise as their 1904 counterparts, furnished the General with little guidance about the probable extent of a German sweep into Belgium.[4] Would such a drive be the major German attack in the west, or simply a secondary thrust to divert attention from the Alsace-Lorraine frontiers? How many German corps would be employed? Would reserve units be utilised? Would the Germans cross the Meuse into central Belgium? French intelligence, though confident the Germans would not use reserve troops or traverse the Meuse, offered only the vaguest answers to these questions. The paucity of intelligence placed Joffre in a difficult dilemma – he had to defend against a German flanking move, the extent of which remained unknown, yet not jeopardise his ability to wage offensive war. From both standpoints he disliked Plan XVI: it had insufficient provisions against a German attack through Belgium; it was, despite de Lacroix's provisions for a prompt counter-attack, too defensive for Joffre's tastes. On the other hand, Michel's proposed new plan for a defensive stance along the entire Belgian frontier struck Joffre as equally unsuitable. Of his situation in August 1911 he later wrote:

I thus found myself faced . . . with an approved plan which manifestly did not correspond to the hypothesis of the most likely manoeuvre on the part of the enemy, and . . . with a tentative plan which exaggerated the importance of this hypothesis and thereby incurred the most dangerous risks.[5]

Joffre decided upon a hurried revision of Plan XVI. Variation Number 1 (completed in September) was his attempt to bolster the defences along the Belgian frontier and at the same time prepare for offensive action elsewhere. The Fifth Army was shifted northward from Vouziers on the Aisne to Mézières, just six miles from the Belgian Ardennes. Supporting this force would be three cavalry corps, the XIX Corps from North Africa, and the BEF concentrated round Hirson and Maubeuge. In sum, nearly 350,000 men, or a fifth of the total military strength of the *entente,* would be deployed along the Franco-Belgian frontier. This composite force, Joffre was confident, could resist and repel any German move across southern Belgium. The changes prompted by Variation Number 1 along the Alsace-Lorraine borders were equally significant: de Lacroix's 'army of manoeuvre' now became simply another frontier army centred on Verdun. The other four armies retained their old alignments, though they were moved closer to the frontier. From these positions Joffre planned to launch an immediate offensive. The major attack would be directed between Metz and Strasbourg, with the French troops around Verdun taking offensive action against any German moves from Metz and Thionville.[6]

But Joffre was not content just to revise Plan XVI. He also strove to increase the effectiveness of possible military assistance from France's allies and friends. Before 1911 the Russians had, despite continual French pressure, refused to promise more than unspecified offensive action by the twentieth day of mobilisation. In late 1910 even this minimum expectation was shaken when St Petersburg withdrew several units from Russian Poland and the Tsar met with the Kaiser at Potsdam. Although General Sukhomlinov, the Russian Minister of War, assured Paris that Russia remained ready for military action, the French were apprehensive.[7] In an attempt to clarify things Joffre decided to send General Dubail to St Petersburg for new staff talks in late August. During his visit Dubail repeatedly stressed France's desperate need for effective Russian aid. All the evidence, he told the Russians, pointed to a massive German assault in the west coming through Lorraine, Luxembourg and Belgium. 'With the aid of the English army on its left wing', France planned to counter the German challenge with an immediate and vigorous offensive. But for this action to succeed the Russians had to strike simultaneously in the east. While insisting that the Russians needed four more years to recover from their Manchurian fiasco, General Zhilinskii, the Russian Chief of Staff, eventually agreed to undertake some offensive action by the sixteenth day in the hope of tying down at least five or six German corps otherwise employable on the western front. The vast expenditures and loans to the mercenary Russians seemed at last to have brought, and bought, results.[8]

With the British, or, more accurately, with Henry Wilson, the new French high command enjoyed increasingly intimate relations. Joffre paid far more attention to British assistance than had his predecessors. His revisions of Plan XVI contained detailed, elaborate provisions for the concentration of British troops. He was clearly confident of British help and ready to exploit it along the Belgian frontier. Again unlike his predecessors, Joffre was also more open and candid with the British officers. His discussions with Wilson, for example, about French intelligence reports and French plans for the employment of *entente* forces contrasted sharply with previous French reticence on such matters.[9]

Still, the new Anglo-French intimacy did not mean that there was genuine joint strategic planning. There was joint consultation and some joint discussion, but Britain's military weakness and the lack of a positive British commitment made London the junior partner in the planning process. And this relationship was reinforced by Henry Wilson's own conception of the problem. Rabidly Francophile, the DMO deferred far too frequently to French leadership, accepting almost without question French estimates on German intentions and French plans for the location of the BEF. Moreover, he failed to press for French candour about the overall nature of French strategy. Anxious to ensure British participation in a continental war, he was less concerned about the course such a war might take. But he never abandoned or compromised London's right to determine the employment of the Expeditionary Force once it had arrived in France. On this point there was, indeed, surprisingly little consultation among the *entente* partners – a fact which partly explains the confusion pervading British efforts in August 1914.

By late September 1911 Joffre's most immediate military problems appeared under control. A revision of Plan XVI was in effect, early Russian offensive action seemed assured, and British assistance appeared more certain than ever. As the Moroccan tension abated, the General began to consider the requirements for an entirely new war plan. The first prerequisite, he quickly decided, was an accurate statement of France's diplomatic commitments and understandings. It particularly rankled military planners to think that for seven years they had been ignorant of the 1902 secret convention with Italy; as a consequence two valuable French corps had been wastefully deployed along the Alps. Nor had the War Ministry ever received an official diplomatic appraisal of Anglo-French relations. In the General's opinion poor co-ordination between the Quai d'Orsay and rue St Dominique needlessly complicated and hampered French strategic planning. Adolphe Messimy readily agreed with Joffre's desire for political guidance, but found Caillaux unwilling to discuss the matter in late September.[10]

Messimy, however, refused to take no for an answer and continued to press Joffre's case for political guidance in the formation of a new war plan. Finally, on 11 October, Messimy and Joffre were allowed to plead for improved inter-departmental co-operation at a meeting of the Conseil Supérieur de la Défense Nationale, the lack-lustre French equivalent of the Committee of Imperial Defence. Citing the Italian example and emphasising the urgent need for information about Belgium's probable attitude in a conflict, the War Minister requested that the Council 'study all the questions' that might require or influence military operations. This sensible proposal was opposed by Foreign Minister Justin de Selves, who vehemently insisted that the army should first disclose the military considerations, then the

Quai d'Orsay would 'make known the diplomatic possibilities; it will say whether it is or is not in agreement with the War Department'.

Joffre strongly disagreed. The question of Belgium was, he declared, not simply a military one. Rather it was 'above all in the province of diplomacy. If we violate Belgian neutrality first, we will become *provocateurs*. England will not join us. Italy will be able to declare against us. We will consequently be stopped,' he emphasised, 'by political considerations. If only military considerations count, we would have, on the contrary, the greatest interest in taking the offensive through Belgium.' But de Selves remained unconvinced. He explained that during the Agadir crisis, when war seemed imminent, he and the General had agreed not to violate Belgium ahead of the Germans. Such departmental co-ordination was adequate; there was no need for any preliminary statement on the diplomatic situation. When Joffre and Messimy refused to abandon their demand for political assistance, the Foreign Minister grudgingly consented to informal conferences between representatives of the War Ministry and the Quai d'Orsay.[11]

On 15 October Joffre availed himself of the Foreign Minister's reluctant generosity: he sent the Quai d'Orsay a memorandum outlining a series of military problems with political overtones. Would the military convention with Russia, for example, 'have the force of a Treaty'? Was there 'complete agreement regarding the interdiction against our troops being the first to violate Belgian territory'? Given the predominance of German influence in Luxembourg, was that tiny country's neutrality also sacrosanct? And he raised the question of the *entente* relationship. He wanted to 'know whether the relations established between the general staffs are the consequence of a treaty or of a written or verbal agreement between the two Governments, or whether they are the result of a tacit consent between them. Can it be expected that *in all probability* Great Britain will support us in a war with Germany?'[12]

The Foreign Ministry, moving with unusual vigour, supplied the guidelines in five days. Taking Russian help for granted, the Quai d'Orsay paid special attention to the problem of Belgium: France, it warned, could not violate the terms of the 1839 guarantee treaty on Belgian neutrality. But it softened this admonition by observing that Germany seemed 'certain' to enter Belgium, and once that occurred France could take whatever measures were militarily desirable. Further, the diplomats placed no obstacles to preventive military action in Luxembourg, 'since Great Britain had not the same interest in the matter of Luxembourg's neutrality as she had in Belgium's'. On the question of British help the Quai d'Orsay refrained from advice; there was no attempt to gauge the probability of British participation.[13] Yet, as the position on Luxembourg indicated, French officials, both military and civilian, recognised that the prospect of British intervention was inescapably linked to the neutrality of Belgium. This became quite evident in early 1912.

On 12 January General Joffre again brought the Belgian issue before the Council of National Defence. Declaring that a German move through the Belgian Ardennes was certain, he requested permission to launch offensive action through Belgium at the first news of a German attack, and the Council approved. In the debate over this request Delcassé, now the Naval Minister, pressed for an even stronger policy. Claiming that Belgian neutrality had originally been a British device against the French, he argued that the cordiality of *entente* relations might induce London to abandon its scruples about the 1839 accord. France would then be able to launch immediate offensive action through Belgium. Both Caillaux and de Selves hotly contested this notion, insisting that the British would never alter their position. France, lamented the Foreign Minister, had to accept the limitations at hand.[14]

Joffre continued to consider the merits of an immediate offensive through Belgium, however. He was possibly encouraged in this by bits and pieces of information reaching him about an apparent change of attitude among the Belgians. For years the French attachés in Brussels had sent sceptical, sometimes scathing reports about the ruling Catholic party's determination to defend Belgian neutrality and about the value of Belgian military preparations. Now the situation seemed to be shifting. King Albert after Agadir had implemented certain military precautions, and there were new signs of Belgian apprehension about Germany. Brussels appeared more realistic about its unenviable location between two over-armed neighbours.[15] Furthermore, in late January the French attaché reported that General Jungbluth, the Belgian Chief of Staff, had expressed the idea that neutrality was a 'hindrance'. There was the possibility that Belgium under the new King would pursue a more active foreign policy. Captain Victor Duruy, though doubting that the Belgians would choose a French alliance over a German one, reported that the situation had possibilities for France. Similar comments and impressions reached Joffre from Henry Wilson: in a conversation with Foch the DMO repeated that General Jungbluth was pro-English and 'very much in sympathy with us [France]'.[16] These varied indications about a possible shift in Belgian sentiments may well have convinced Joffre that an offensive through Belgium might not only be feasible, but also politically acceptable – even to the British. At any rate, the fall of the Caillaux government in late January provided the General with still another opportunity to broach the possibility of an immediate attack through the Belgian Ardennes.

On 21 February Raymond Poincaré, the new Premier, summoned an informal group to the Quai d'Orsay for a review of France's defence posture. Those present included Admiral Marie-Jacques-Charles Aubert, the new Chief of the Naval Staff; Paléologue, the new Director of Political Affairs; Millerand, the new War Minister; Delcassé, held over as Naval Minister; and Joffre. At the meeting Joffre once more advocated a French offensive across lower Belgium. Assuming that Britain would agree and that France *'could come to an understanding with the Belgian government beforehand'*, the General outlined the military rationale for such an operation. If war came, the French army planned to launch immediate offensive action against Germany. The question was where – Lorraine, Alsace or the Belgian Ardennes? Rough terrain and the fortress system ruled against an attack through the 'lost provinces', leaving the Belgium-Luxembourg corridor the most attractive alternative for a French offensive. An assault in this area would not only counter any German flanking move, but would also gain swift passage to German territory. In addition, observed Joffre, such a manoeuvre 'would make it possible for the British army to participate more efficaciously in our operations, and the assistance of this army would bring us a marked superiority as compared with our adversaries'.[17] But to be successful the French attack through Belgium had to be immediate. It could not depend upon whether the Germans actually violated Belgium, for if the Germans did not do so the French forces would be hopelessly out of position. France must either plan to disregard Belgian neutrality or be content to accept an offensive on less favourable terms in Lorraine.

Joffre's appeal for action through Belgium again gained the support of Delcassé, this time joined by Millerand. But Poincaré refused to consider the possibility. He maintained that it would be difficult, if not impossible, to reach a prior agreement with the Belgians: diplomatic reports indicated that German influence within the Belgian government remained strong. Poincaré's principal opposition, however, stemmed not from the probable Belgian attitude but rather from the probable British reaction. Whatever the status of the *entente,* he feared that an offensive through Belgium would run the risk of alienating the unpredictable Anglo-Saxons.[18] Moreover, the Anglo-German talks then under way reinforced Poincaré's caution. He knew that in the negotiations Britain was demanding freedom to help France against any unprovoked German attack; yet this narrow definition of Britain's 'obligation' to France encouraged few hopes that London would sanction a French offensive across Belgium. Nor could the French Premier ignore the ramifications of losing British military and naval help, so carefully arranged by the staff talks, through an injudicious attack northward. Poincaré thus ruled against any French offensive via Belgium. The most he would concede was permission to attack should there be the 'positive menace' of German action. As Joffre later remarked: what was meant by a 'positive menace'?[19] Confronted with Poincaré's adamant position about the neighbouring kingdom, the General transferred his hopes for offensive action back to the area first envisaged in August 1911, that is, to Lorraine.

Poincaré, while rejecting Joffre's strategic desires, decided to probe the British position on Belgium. The Congo and the Anglo-German negotiations provided him with convenient excuses. On two separate occasions he had Paul Cambon emphasise to Arthur Nicolson the benefits which would accrue from British recognition of Belgium's 1908 annexation of the Congo: such action would end Anglo-Belgian bitterness, make the *entente* more attractive to Brussels, and reduce the German ability to cause trouble. Each time Cambon's pleas fell upon deaf ears; Nicolson would promise no immediate change in British policy.[20]

Poincaré's other approach to the Belgian issue involved the Anglo-German negotiations. In mid-March Paul Cambon casually mentioned to Nicolson that the mounting evidence of a German build-up near Aix-la-Chapelle 'could only be explained by the intention of violating Belgian neutrality'. If German scouts were on the verge of crossing into Belgium, 'must we,' Cambon asked him, 'await the occupation of Belgium by the German army in order to advance on our side?' Nicolson replied simply, 'C'est bien grave'.[21] Later, when the Anglo-German negotiations for a possible neutrality formula failed to collapse, the French revived the hypothesis of possible action in Belgium. Cambon told Grey on 29 March that if 'Germany concentrated troops upon Aix-la-Chapelle with the obvious intention of entering Belgium, France might be compelled to take the initiative'. The implications could not have been clearer: the French might have to violate Belgian neutrality and thus a 'neutrality formula' might deprive them of British assistance. But the Foreign Secretary, as usual, carefully avoided any comment upon Cambon's observation.[22] Much the same thing happened five days later when the chargé cautioned Nicolson that a neutrality agreement with Berlin would be difficult to interpret. Such an accord, for example, might prevent 'the entry of French troops into Belgian territory which the English and French Staffs considered as necessary in certain cases'. The Under Secretary again refused to be drawn, insisting instead that the chances for an Anglo-German agreement were slight.[23] Despite his trial balloons, Poincaré had learned precious little about the British attitude toward Belgium.

The Foreign Office's studied reticence on Belgian neutrality concealed a renewed British interest in the problem. At this very time both the Foreign Office and the CID were carefully examining Britain's probable relationship to Holland and Belgium in time of war. Eyre Crowe, in another of his thoughtful, lengthy memos, insisted in early March that Germany would almost certainly violate Belgium 'on the very outbreak of war' and that Belgium would resist. He thought that Britain was 'entitled, if so minded – not to say, bound – to come to the assistance of Belgium'. Yet, if war came, Britain should do nothing that might alienate the Belgians; Britain, he cautioned, should be careful not to 'place itself hopelessly in the wrong in the eyes of the world at the moment of entering on a life-and-death struggle'.[24]

The Senior Clerk's sensitivity to Belgian feelings was not entirely shared by members of the CID. In late April the Committee considered what action Britain should take if Belgium failed to resist German aggression. Haldane contended that Britain would under international law be justified in taking any action it so desired; Arthur Nicolson argued that Britain could take 'steps to enforce . . . neutrality, even were she [Belgium] unwilling that we should do so'. Churchill, on the other hand, thought 'it would be a great pity if we had to rescue Belgium against her will'. To avoid this unseemly development there was talk of discussing the matter with Brussels. Sir John French thought that 'the Belgians were disposed to favour [Britain] . . . and that proposals would not be unwelcome'. And he added that 'it would certainly make an immense difference to a British army employed on the Continent which attitude the Belgians were to adopt'.[25] When the CID adjourned on 25 April, several aspects of British policy were quite clear. First, if Germany attacked Belgium, Britain would uphold its strategic interests with or without Belgian permission. Second, to avert friction with Brussels, attempts would be made to establish better Anglo-Belgian relations. Finally, there was not the slightest hint or suggestion of any form of preventive action by Britain or the *entente* prior to a German violation of Belgian sovereignty. Had Paris decided to press London in less elliptical, ambiguous terms about a French offensive through Belgium, it would have received a decided rebuff.

While the CID was debating the need for closer ties with Brussels, Henry Wilson was hard at work on the same problem. In early March he had spent three days touring eastern Belgium – Stavelot, Liège and Ciney. The excursion strengthened both his conviction that the Germans would try a flanking move and his belief in the value of Belgian assistance. In early April, on his own initiative, the DMO attempted to revive the long-suspended Anglo-Belgian staff talks. On 5 April he crossed to Ostend to brief Lieutenant-Colonel Tom Bridges about a démarche: the attaché was 'to tell the Belgians that Britain could put 150,000 men "at the decisive point and time" . . . but that the Belgians must play their part by further strengthening Liège and Namur and by calling for help as soon as their country was invaded'.[26] If there was any mention of Anglo-French arrangements, Bridges was to plead ignorance.[27]

On 23 April Bridges attempted to carry out Wilson's mandate; the results were disastrous. Contrary to the DMO's expectations, General Jungbluth displayed not the slightest interest in Bridges's revelations about British capabilities. More importantly, Jungbluth took immediate umbrage at the attaché's imprudent assertion that Britain would intervene regardless of Belgian desires if Germany moved first. Bridges then compounded his *faux pas* by repeating the idea of unilateral intervention to General Michel, the War Minister. An angered, indeed enraged Michel declared that the Belgians could protect themselves and would fire upon any would-be British saviours.[28] His language was so violent in fact that Sir Francis Villiers sought out Davignon, the Foreign Minister, and assured him that Bridges's comments had no official sanction.[29] The damage, however, was done. Henry Wilson's ill-advised attempt to improve Anglo-Belgian ties had backfired.

The anger that greeted Bridges's remarks reflected a new stiffening of Belgium's attitude towards the *entente* powers. This toughness had begun in September 1911, coincidental with the Belgian military measures which had so impressed London and Paris. Thoroughly frightened by the Agadir crisis, Belgium's political and military leadership had undertaken a major re-evaluation of Belgian policy. Three questions in particular worried Brussels: how to devise a military strategy that would limit the destruction of Belgium, how to ensure that a guarantor nation did not force Belgium into a war against its will, and how to ensure that a protecting power, once invited, would leave. Slowly, over a period of months and after much debate, the answers emerged. Militarily the Belgian General Staff planned to oppose any violation of Belgium; at the same time they hoped to confine all the fighting to a small area, possibly to the province of Belgian Luxembourg. Simply stated, Belgium would resist, yet seek to avoid losing either its integrity or its neutrality.[30]

Among the possible guarantors of Belgian neutrality Great Britain got the most attention. The British military and naval preparations in 1911, the growing solidarity of the *entente*, and Britain's expressed interest in Antwerp and the Schelde convinced Brussels that London might rush, quite uninvited, to help Belgium;[31] this would virtually guarantee that all of Belgium would be exposed to the dangers of war. As a hindrance to any premature British action, the Belgian leadership secretly hoped the Dutch would fortify Flushing. Still, the Belgians could not altogether ignore the possibility that they might need external assistance. Anxious to avoid becoming the pawn of either a victorious Germany or France, Brussels decided to draft in advance a convention for any future protectors to sign; this, it was hoped, would guarantee the preservation of Belgian independence. From Belgian planning there emerged one unmistakable result: renewed determination to protect Belgium's neutral status, both politically and militarily. It was this prideful determination which Colonel Bridges's démarche aroused and alarmed. His mention of possible pre-emptive action simply reinforced Belgian fears about British intentions. By mid-1912 the chances for improved *entente* co-operation with Belgium were at an end, and during the remainder of that year the gulf grew wider.

In September and again in October General Michel, the Belgian War Minister, brutally rejected British suggestions that Germany contemplated a violation of Belgian neutrality. He made it quite clear, wrote Captain Howard Kelly, the naval attaché, 'that in his opinion the dangers of a breach of Belgian neutrality lay more from England than anywhere else'. Citing the British preparations in 1911, the General complained that Belgium now had to expect a British attack either at Antwerp or in conjunction with the French left. In the future the Belgians would have to defend against attacks from not one but three sides.[32] A few weeks later Michel expressed doubts to Colonel Bridges that Britain would act if the French violated Belgium, which meant that Great Britain was 'a potential enemy' and as such, had to be watched and could no longer be regarded as the Power to which Belgium could confidently appeal for help'. This dogmatism led Grey to comment curtly: 'If Germany does not violate the neutrality of Belgium no one else will do so.'[33] Michel's display of antagonism towards the *entente*, coupled with sharp attacks upon France in much of the Belgian press, stirred latent Anglo-French fears about Belgium's genuine willingness to defend its neutrality. This in turn increased apprehension about what Belgium might do if the *entente* were to resolve, unannounced and uninvited, to check a German attack.[34]

These unpleasant indications particularly worried Sir Edward Grey. So long as a weak and helpless Belgium resisted a German attack, Britain would unquestionably intervene on the Continent. But a German-Belgian détente would jeopardise all of this. Grey would find it difficult to win public support for British intervention if the Belgians permitted an invasion of their own country; moreover, the British would be deprived of Belgian military help, which Henry Wilson reckoned at 'twelve to sixteen divisions'. And even more dangerous to the chances for British intervention, given the new mood in Brussels, would be an impetuous French violation of the neutralised state. Such an attack would completely undermine one of the ostensible and most appealing justifications for Britain's continual strategy – the preservation of Belgian independence.

At the same time Grey faced a practical problem of how to communicate these fears to the ever-sensitive French government. On this point, however, he received unexpected help from Henry Wilson, who was equally disturbed by the trend of opinion in Brussels, so disturbed in fact that he wanted to reach an agreement with Paris on the treatment of a possibly hostile Belgium. These mutual concerns led the Foreign Secretary to authorise another Wilson trip to France.[35] The General could discuss his own problem and also caution the French Staff about an imprudent attack northward. Exactly eight months after Poincaré had first sounded London on preventive offensive action through Belgium, Henry Wilson brought the answer.

On 26 November Wilson bluntly warned General de Castelnau that if 'France violates Belgian neutrality first, the Belgian army will march with the Germans, and the English government, perhaps put in the position of respecting neutrality, could find itself in a very embarrasing situation. Thus', he admonished, 'the French army has no interest in being the first to violate Belgian neutrality.' The question of a hostile Belgium was an entirely different matter. 'Would not the Belgians,' the British General asked, 'then become the objective of the English army?' No, responded de Castelnau, 'les Allemands' would remain the object of the Anglo-French forces.[36] This view the DMO accepted.

Joffre later wrote that Wilson's unequivocal pronouncement about Belgium was 'of the very highest importance for it obliged me definitely to renounce all idea of a manoeuvre a priori through Belgium'.[37] This assessment vastly exaggerates the importance of Wilson's trip. In actuality his comments simply supplied the coup de grâce to any lingering plans Joffre might have had for an attack through Belgium – an early autumn staff study by Colonel Georges Demange had already turned down, on both military and political grounds, any such operation as a part of the new war plan.[38] But the fatal blow to Joffre's proposals had come much earlier, from the opposition of French politicians. Anxious to retain British friendship, with its military and naval potential, not to mention its economic resources, first Caillaux and then Poincaré blocked the demands for action in Belgium. In this sense the entente played an important, negative role in the formulation of French strategy. London's attitude constrained the French to settle for an offensive in Lorraine; ultimately this deployment would compound the errors and failures of French intelligence. A French attack through Belgium would have had little chance of success, but the concentration of forces for such an offensive might have placed France in a much stronger position to resist the eventual German onslaught. If Joffre bears the final responsibility for succumbing to the madness of the offensive à outrance, the elusive prospect of British help, or, more precisely, the ambiguous *entente*, shares the responsibility for creating the framework in which Plan XVII was elaborated.[39]

During 1912 Joffre and his staff laboured over a new war plan. Simultaneously the popular and professional press was also analysing the problems of French grand strategy. Most French commentators, like the French Staff, expected not only a German offensive along the Lorraine frontier, but also a flanking manoeuvre through Luxembourg-Belgium; but this thrust through Belgium would, they believed, stay below the Meuse.[40] For example, Lieutenant-Colonel A. Grouard, who predicted German attacks in the south aimed at Chaumont-Troyes and in the north at Verdun-Mézières, doubted that any German sweep would cross the Meuse. Only an occasional prophet warned that if the Germans came through Belgium they would do so in strength: General Gabriel Herment, writing in the *Journal des sciences militaires*, insisted that the Germans would over-run the Belgian forts along the Meuse and move to block British intervention by seizing the Channel ports. And General de Lacroix, the former Generalissimo, stressed the dangers implicit in a German attack through Belgium.[41] Nevertheless, public comment about German strategy generally stiffened Joffre's view that a German drive would stay in the Ardennes.

There was somewhat less agreement about how France should counter German strategy. The new 'offensive' orthodoxy within the high command was shared by many of the military essayists.[42] Still, there were some like Captain Sorb who tempered their enthusiasm for offensive action with a perception of the dangers involved. He, for instance, wanted the French commander to take the initiative in seeking a decisive battle; yet he also thought that circumstances (or defensive-offensive considerations) should dictate the direction of the French attack. He personally envisaged two arenas for offensive action, one in the Longuyon-Thionville area, the other in the Lunéville-Sarrebourg vicinity.[43]

A few other military analysts were even less enchanted by the idea of unconditional offensive action. General Bonnal, reviewing de Grandmaison's published lectures, ridiculed the Colonel's ideas as mere rhetoric and warned that sometimes a commander must assume the defensive. Emile Mayer, one-time officer turned military critic, repeatedly emphasised the defensive advantages conferred by the new artillery and fire-power. But perhaps the most incisive challenge to the offensive mania came from Colonel Grouard, a man whose criticisms of Napoleonic strategy had already labelled him as a heretic among French military writers. In *France et Allemagne: la guerre éventuelle* Grouard refuted assurances that only offensive action offered a safe, sure, feasible panacea for France's military situation. He called instead for a return to a defensive strategy with France waiting to counter-attack. Such a counter-attack could be launched through the Ardennes and thus disrupt if not stop a German flanking move. In sharp contrast to the offensive orthodoxy, he insisted that France at least avoid a decisive battle until Russian and British help was available.[44] Eventuallly Grouard's prognosis of France's military predicament proved accurate; in the short run his criticisms, like most external criticism of military policy, prompted no changes and perhaps even strengthened the hold of the offensive school – for Joffre's new war plan was the virtual incarnation of the *offensive à outrance*.

On 18 April 1913, after nearly twenty-one months of study, General Joffre presented the War Board with an outline of his new offensive plan (XVII). Manpower requirements, the probable nature of German strategy, and the proposed French response to that strategy formed the crux of his presentation. When the three-year service law was in operation, the General expected to have 710,000 men available in forty-six divisions. Every effort would be made to place the maximum number of troops in the north-east 'in order to gain a decisive result'; but, in keeping with the tenets of the offensive theorists, twenty-five reserve divisions were assigned to secondary functions.[45] By contrast, Joffre estimated that Berlin would have 880,000 men available by the end of 1913, most of whom would be deployed on the western front. He regarded a German advance from Alsace and Lorraine as a foregone conclusion, with a German drive across Belgium toward Mézières as highly probable. But Joffre doubted that such a drive would traverse the Meuse, or that it would even be a part of the initial German assault. Nevertheless, if the Germans crashed through the Ardennes, he was confident that the French forces, aided by the BEF, could check them.[46] And like his predecessors, he believed that the French advances in Lorraine would more than offset German gains elsewhere.[47]

This grossly inaccurate estimate of German intentions reflected the Second Bureau's continuing ineptness. Even when the final concentration orders for Plan XVII were issued in early 1914, it was stated as 'probable that a great part of the German forces will be concentrated on the common frontier'. Nancy, Verdun and Saint-Dié were regarded, in that order, as the probable objectives of a sudden German attack. And in May 1914 French intelligence still insisted that any German move through Belgium would stay below the Sambre and Meuse as it headed for Montmédy and Hirson.[48] In actuality the Schlieffen-Moltke Plan would send two German armies across the Meuse, swinging as wide as Brussels and Lille. Also, the Germans would employ, contrary to expectations, reserve divisions on an equal footing with regular units. It was this calculation about reserve troops, a miscalculation perhaps fortified by an alleged German staff memo on the subject, which was possibly the crucial intelligence error.[49] If the Germans were to utilise only regular divisions, then their ability to launch a major sweep through Belgium seemed reasonably out of the question; yet French intelligence did receive information in late 1913 which suggested that the Germans might employ reserve divisions and, moreover, there were new reports in 1913 of German rail construction around Luxembourg and Cologne.[50] None of this information, however, produced any significant revision of Joffre's strategic plans.

On French strategy, the General's comments to the War Board were terse and to the point. He gave his subordinate commanders only the vaguest hints about the French offensive. Unlike de Lacroix with Plan XVI in

1908, Joffre was not forced to explain or to defend his intentions. There were several reasons for his reticence: in the first place his fellow generals did not demand more information, in itself a reflection of his increasing domination of the high command, nor were there any cantankerous old men like General Duchesne on the War Board to pose the penetrating or embarrasing question. Joffre's associates, Michel excepted, shared his faith in the offensive and élan; and implicit in these noble virtues was a certain disdain for plans that were too detailed, and therefore too confining to the spirit of the French soldier. Finally, Joffre could not reveal his attack scheme for the simple reason that he had not yet decided definitely where to attack. Lorraine remained the most obvious area for action, but Joffre occasionally resurrected the idea of a Belgian manoeuvre.[51] Not until early 1914 would he irrevocably opt for Lorraine. In the meantime the War Board had his assurances that the offensive would bring France victory, and bring it quickly.

In the course of his presentation Joffre offered the War Board a candid, and realistic, assessment of the value of British help. British co-operation, he declared, remained uncertain because London 'wanted to make no engagament in writing'.[52] Nor was there any guarantee that if Britain did intervene all six divisions would immediately depart for France. Indeed, even Henry Wilson was worried about the chances of the entire BEF being available.[53] These uncertainties prompted Joffre to tell the War Board: 'We will thus act prudently in not depending upon English forces in our operational projects.'[54] On the other hand, the General made clear his expectation of British naval assistance, asserting that 'the interest of English commerce was too evident for Great Britain to hesitate to fight on our side'.[55] In sum, Joffre interpreted the military conversations for what they were: arrangements that facilitated British intervention but did not guarantee it. Yet this prudence should not obscure the point, already noted, that the lure of British help had forced him to renounce a possible Belgian operation. Certainly this limitation influenced France's grand strategy far more than the inclusion or non-inclusion of the BEF in Plan XVII.

In his strategic exposition Joffre said little about an essential prerequisite for a successful French offensive: Russian help. There was, on this count, no apparent cause for worry. Franco-Russian relations had never been more cordial or intimate. Poincaré's strong views on foreign policy and his trip to Russia in mid-1912 had eased Russian apprehensions about the Third Republic; and the rousingly successful visit of the Tsar's cousin (and future Commander-in-Chief of the Russian Army), Grand Duke Nicholas, to the French manoeuvres in September 1912 had also helped. It was on this occasion that Nicholas' impetuous, Montenegrin-born wife, Anastasia, had asked for a small piece of Lorraine soil to carry back to Russia and talked wildly of the reunification of the 'lost provinces' to France.[56] These public displays of goodwill were supported by the continuation of French-financed rail construction in Russia and by steady improvements in the Russian army. More importantly, General Zhilinskii pledged in the 1912 and 1913 staff talks that 800,000 soldiers would be deployed along the German front, with some action beginning after the fifteenth day. The Russian planners considered action in three different locations: toward Konigsberg, toward Allenstein in East Prussia, or across the Vistula past Thorn toward Berlin (the latter, which the French repeatedly encouraged, would have severed East Prussia from the Reich).[57] In 1914 the Russians actually did take the first two options, launching a double attack toward Konigsberg and Allenstein.

A comparison of the Franco-Russian military arrangements with those of the *entente* reveals several instructive differences. Staff consultations between Paris and London after 1910 were virtually uninterrupted; those between St Petersburg and Paris remained on an annual basis. The informality and frequency of the Anglo-French exchanges disabused each party of some illusions about the other; the Franco-Russian talks were always high level and formal, with appearances replacing realistic thinking. Furthermore, in spite of the ambiguity of the *entente*, the French displayed a trust in the British that was not repeated toward the Russians: Henry Wilson was not privy to every facet of French planning, but he knew far more than the Russians did. For their part the Russians were equally secretive with the French about their intentions, though the problems of a two-front war naturally caused some strategic ambivalence in St Petersburg. By the same token, geography necessitated closer Anglo-French planning if the two countries hoped to co-operate effectively in a common theatre of war. Another factor could not help but reinforce *entente* co-operation: when the British and French Staffs agreed upon something, action followed. Such was not often the case when the French and Russian experts settled upon a plan. Not surprisingly, as John Cairns has pointed out, 'the French army seemed to count almost more surely on the nation that refused an alliance than on the nation treaty-bound'.[58]

Joffre's presentation of the new plan in April 1913 provided the first and last opportunity for any significant modification in the call for offensive action. The War Board neither then nor later seriously considered the merits of the proposal. In early May Etienne, the War Minister, accepted the new scheme without change; immediately the staff bureaucracy began work on the logistical and strategical details. Ten months later, in February 1914, the army commanders finally received their respective plans of mobilisation and concentration. In May, two years and ten months after Joffre had assumed command, Plan XVII became operational.

The new plan covered every phase of French preparations: concentration assignments, border protection, transportation movements and intelligence instructions. Everywhere the impress of the offensive school was clear. The orders succinctly stated: 'Whatever the circumstances, it is the Commander-in-Chief's intention to advance with all forces united to attack the German armies.'[59] Unlike its German counterpart, Plan XVII did not, however, establish a precise schedule for offensive operations. In fact, the general orders permitted Joffre a remarkable degree of elasticity in taking the offensive. There were provisions for double offensives north and south of the Metz-Thionville complex; in addition, should the Germans violate

Belgium, Joffre retained sufficient flexibility to shift the northern offensive attack to the north-east, through Luxembourg and the Belgian Ardennes. Regardless of their ultimate location, these offensive assaults were expected to bring about the decisive battle so dear to the offensive theorists. Once that battle was won, victory would quickly follow elsewhere.

To achieve this victory Joffre divided French forces into five armies. Three would be located along the Alsace-Lorraine frontier from Verdun to Epinal. Another army, the Fifth, would be assigned to the Franco-Belgian border from Montmédy to Sedan to Mézières, roughly the same assignment it had had since 1911. Despite a consensus about the risks of a German operation south of the Meuse (and Joffre's later protests notwithstanding), Plan XVII brought no notable improvement of France's immediate frontier defences in the north. But Joffre did achieve new flexibility by reviving de Lacroix's idea of an 'army of manoeuvre' which could be employed as the circumstances dictated or the commander chose.[60] This Fourth Army at St Dizier, composed of three infantry corps and a cavalry division, could either join in the assault upon Thionville or shift northward to help the Fifth Army if the Germans came through the Ardennes. A semi-reserve force, it constituted Joffre's one concession to the counter offensive school of French strategy, his one concession to the realities of his strategic dilemma. Significantly, none of the orders for Plan XVII made any mention either of a British zone of concentration or of the possibility of British help.[61]

There is no need for still another analysis or critique of Plan XVII, for earlier critics have reconnoitred the available terrain.[62] Several points merit special emphasis, however. In the first place Plan XVII represented a fundamentally unsound compromise between the realities of France's military situation and the desires of its military leaders. French manpower resources were simply inadequate to meet both the requirements of security and the exigencies of offensive operations. In his determination to seize the offensive, Joffre neglected an equally important principle of warfare: security. Although uncertain about the extent of a German move through Belgium, he none the less concentrated his forces in Lorraine. Further, he completely exposed his left flank from Mézières to the sea with only the BEF, whose arrival he held as doubtful, available to protect part of this 110 mile sector. In August 1914 four British divisions would face the might of two German armies. Admittedly British sensitivity over Belgian neutrality prevented French offensive action in the one area where it might have stalled the German drive. Yet London's attitude did not force the General to plan an attack against the heavily fortified area of Lorraine, nor to neglect the elementary requirements of security. Nor did it cause him to relegate twenty-five reserve divisions to secondary functions. For these decisions the allure of the 'offensive' school remained the culprit.

In the second place, at no time did the British exercise a positive role in the formation of French strategy. Joffre and de Castelnau consulted and informed Wilson on certain issues, but in the main kept their own counsel. London's lack of influence upon French planning was in turn matched by

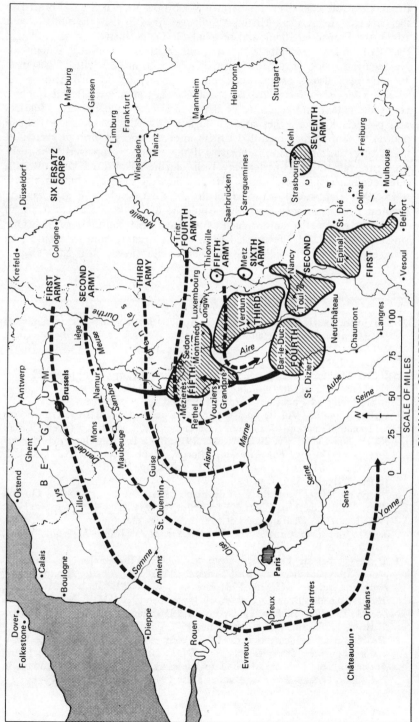

PLAN XVII: SCHLIEFFEN PLAN

the modest role conceived for 'Armée W' by the French Staff. Located in the triangle Le Cateau-Hirson-Maubeuge, the British divisions would adjoin the French left flank and be available for defensive action. Although the BEF might participate in a counter-offensive toward Dinant or Neufchàteau, none of Joffre's schemes envisaged active British assistance. In spite of Wilson's exhortations, Paris did not view British help as the so-called 'decisive' factor in the opening stages of a war. But if dubious about the extent and relability of British assistance, the French – soldiers and politicians alike – hesitated to forfeit this help by violating Belgian neutrality. The French regarded British intervention as a form of insurance, useful at a war's outbreak, imperative if the war was prolonged. The main problem was to get London involved on the Continent. Once Britain intervened, it would be committed to the cause of France, come what may.

In 1909 Henry Wilson asked Foch: ' "What would you say was the smallest British military force that would be of any practical assistance to you in the event of a contest such as we have been considering?" ' ' "One single private soldier," responded Foch on the instant, "and we would take good care that he was killed." '[63] French opinion never changed.

NOTES

1 On Joffre's early career, see Pierre Varillon, *Joffre* (Paris 1956), Chapters 1–2; General René Alexandre, *Avec Joffre d'Agadir à Verdun: souvenirs, 1911–16* (Paris 1932), pp. 7–12; Alistair Horne, *The Price of Glory: Verdun, 1916* (London, 1962), pp. 19–24.

2 Joffre, *Memoirs*, Vol. I, pp. 30, 26–35; Alexandre, op. cit., pp. 13–23. See also Ralston, *The Army of the Republic*, pp. 331–43.

3 Joffre preferred Foch, but Messimy blocked the appointment.

4 Joffre, *Memoirs*, Vol. I, pp. 18–19, 45–7; untitled French Staff memo on a German violation of Belgium, December 1909, Archives Guerre, 'Plan XVII', box 137; diary, 29 September 1911, in C. E. Callwell, *Field Marshal Sir Henry Wilson: His Life and Diaries*, 2 vols. (London 1927), Vol. I, p. 104; *Les armées françaises*, tome I, Vol. I, pp. 15–16.

5 Joffre, *Memoirs*, Vol. I, p. 18.

6 Memo by Joffre, 'Note du sujet du plan', 29 August 1911, Archives Guerre, 'Plan XVI', box 130; 'Plan XVI: ordre de bataille', [?] September 1911, ibid., box 132; 'Ordre aux 3e et 4e bureaux de l'état-major de l'armée', *Les armées françaises*, tome I, Vol. I: *Annexes*, no. 5; Joffre, *Memoirs*, Vol. I, pp. 22–3.

7 'Procès-verbal de l'entretien entre les Chefs d'Etat-major généraux des armées française et russe', 20–1 September 1910, *Documents Diplomatiques Français*, 2nd ser., XII, no. 573; Pichon to Brun, 7 December 1910, MAE, 'Russie', n.s. 40; Brun to Pichon, 14 December 1910, DDF, 2nd ser., XIII, no. 83; Louis to Pichon, 23 December 1910, ibid., nos. 101, 102; Matton to Brun, 17 February 1911, ibid., no. 157.

8 'Procès verbal de l'entretien du 18–31 août 1911, entre les Chefs de l'Etat major des armées française et russe', DDF, 2nd ser., XIV, no. 232; Joffre, *Memoirs*, Vol. I, p. 23; Dubail to Messimy, September 1911, quoted in J. Caillaux, *Mes mémoires*, 3 vols. (Paris 1942–7), Vol. II, pp. 143–4.

9 Memo by Joffre, 'Note du sujet du plan', 29 August 1911, Archives Guerre, 'Plan XVI', box 130; diary, 29 September 1911, in Callwell, *Wilson*, Vol. I, pp. 104–5.

10 Joffre, *Memoirs*, Vol. I, pp. 37–8.

11 'Procès-verbal de la séance du Conseil Supérieur de la Défense Nationale du 11 octobre 1911', *DDF*, 2nd ser., XIV, no. 424.

12 This memo is summarised as quoted here in Joffre, *Memoirs*, Vol. I, pp. 39–42; neither the French diplomatic nor military files contain a copy.

13 ibid., pp. 42–3.

14 'Note de présentation', 9 January 1912, Archives Marine, ES 23; Caillaux, *Mes mémoires*, Vol. I, pp. 213–4; Joffre, *Memoirs*, Vol. I, pp. 47–8.

15 Albert Duchesne, 'L'armée et la politique militaires belges de 1871 à 1920 jugées par les attachés militaires de France à Bruxelles', *Revue belge de philologie et d'histoire*, 39 (1961), 1092–1126.

16 Duruy to Alexandre Millerand, 25 January 1912, *DDF*, 3rd ser., I, no. 522; 'Conversation du général Foch avec le général Wilson . . . 4–5 février [1912]', Archives Guerre, 'Attachés militaires: Angleterre', box 11.

17 Joffre, *Memoirs*, Vol. I, pp. 50–1.

18 Raymond Poincaré, *Au service de la France: neuf années de souvenirs*, 10 vols. (Paris 1925–33), Vol. I, pp. 224–5; Antony Klobukowski to Poincaré, 12 February 1912, MAE, 'Belgique', n.s. 20.

19 Joffre, *Memoirs*, Vol. I, pp. 51–3. London regularly informed Paris about the Anglo-German negotiations; see e.g., P. Cambon to Poincaré (tel.), 13 February 1912, *DDF*, 3rd ser., II, no. 30.

20 Poincaré to P. Cambon, 23 March 1912, *DDF*, 3rd ser., II, no. 252; P. Cambon to Poincaré, 29 March (tel.), 2 May 1912, ibid., nos. 271, 406.

21 P. Cambon to Paléologue, 21 March 1912, ibid., no. 240.

22 Poincaré to P. Cambon, 28 March 1912, ibid., no. 269; Grey to Bertie, 29 March 1912; G. P. Gooch and H. Temperley (eds.), *British Documents on the Origins of the War, 1898–1914*, 11 vols. in 13 (London, 1926–38) (hereafter BD), Vol. VI, no. 559.

23 A. de Fleuriau to Poincaré, 4 April 1912, *DDF*, 3rd ser., II, no. 300.

24 Minute by Sir Eyre Crowe, 10 March 1912, *BD*, VIII, no. 321.

25 Minutes of the 116th meeting of the CID (25 April 1912), Cab. 2/2/3; see also 'The Attitude of Great Britain towards Belgium in the event of a violation of Belgian Territory by Germany in Time of War', 9 April 1912, Cab. 4/4/1.

26 B. Collier, *Brasshat: A Biography of Field Marshal Sid Henry Wilson* (London 1961), p. 128.

27 7 April 1912, Wilson Diaries; cf. Lt-General Sir Tom Bridges, *Alarms and Excursions* (London 1938), pp. 62–3.

28 Note by Léon van der Elst (Secretary General of Belgian Foreign Ministry), 24 April 1912, Great Britain, Foreign Office, *Collected Diplomatic Documents Relating to the Outbreak of the European War* (London 1915), 360–1. See also J. Wullus-Rudiger, *La Belgique et l'équilibre européen*, 2nd edn (Paris 1935), pp. 78–9, 321–2; Luigi Albertini, *The Origins of the War of 1914*, trans. and ed. Isabella M. Massey, 3 vols. (London 1952–7), Vol. III, pp. 430–2.

29 J. Helmreich, 'Belgian concern over neutrality and British intentions, 1906–1914', *Journal of Modern History*, Vol. 36 (December 1964), p. 424.

30 ibid., 421–5; memo by Arendt, 'En cas de guerre', November 1911, Belg. Arch., 'Indépendance neutralité', X.

31 See e.g., 'Note au Baron de Gaiffer du 6 août 1912 sur la situation qui serait faite à la Belgique en cas de guerre', Belg. Arch., 'Indépendance neutralité', XI.

32 Kelly to Villiers, 12 September 1912, *BD*, VIII, no 324, note by van der Elst, 7 October 1912, Belg. Arch., 'Indépendance neutralité', XI.

33 Bridges to Villiers, 8 October 1912, *BD*, VIII, no. 326; minute by Grey, ibid. Grey specifically assured the Belgians on this point in 1913; see Grey to Churchill, 11 April 1913, *BD*, X, pt. 2, no. 472.

34 Memo by Davignon, 21 November 1912, Belg. Arch., 'Indépendance neutralité', XI. Minutes of the 120th meeting of the CID (6 December 1912), Cab. 2/3/1; also see Nicolson to Villiers, 30 December 1912, quoted in *H. Nicholson, Sir Arthur Nicholson, Bart., First Lord Carnock: A Study in the Old Diplomacy* (London 1930).

35 Diary, 22 October 1912, in Callwell, *Wilson*, Vol. I, p. 118; 18–19, 26 November 1912, Wilson Diaries; Ritter, *The Schlieffen Plan* (Munich, 1956, English edn New York, 1958), p. 88; Villiers to Grey, 22 November 1912, FO 371/1300.

36 De Castelnau to Millerand, 27 November 1912, Archives Guerre, 'Plan XVII: Armée W', box 147b; Millerand to Poincaré, 12 December 1912, *DDF*, 3rd ser., V, no. 53.

37 Joffre, *Memoirs*, Vol. I, p. 54; also see entry for 10 February 1913, Maurice Paléologue, *Au Quai d'Orsay à la veille de la tourmente: journal, 1913–4* (Paris 1947), pp. 30–2.

38 Memo by Demange, 'Note relative au dispositif de réunion et au plan d'operations des armées du NE', n.d. [autumn 1912], Archives Guerre 'Plan XVII', box 137.

39 For a caustic French view on the British constraints, see L. Garros, *L'armée de grand-papa: de Gallifet à Gamelin, 1891–1939* (Paris, 1965).

40 See e.g., Captain Sorb [Charles Cormier], *La doctrine de défense nationale* (Paris 1912), pp. 38–81; and Col. Arthur Boucher, *La France victorieuse* (Paris 1911), pp. 50–6.

41 Lt.-Col. A. Grouard, *France et Allemagne: la guerre éventuelle*, 4th edn (Paris, 1913), pp. 83–110; General Herment, 'Considérations sur la défense de la frontière du nord', *Journal des sciences militaires*, 5 (15 October 1912), 384–8; General de Lacroix, 'Quelques mots au sujet de la neutralité de la Belgique', *Revue militaire générale*, 6 (September 1912), 273–6.

42 See e.g., Captain Altmayer, 'Je veux', *Revue militaire générale*, 6 (October 1912), 417–46.

43 Sorb, op. cit., pp. 82–101; cf. 'De 1870 à 1912: à propose de la doctrine de défense nationale du Captain Sorb', *Journal des sciences militaires*, 2 (1 April 1912), 278–300.

44 General Bonnal, 'Considérations sur la tactique actuelle', *Journal des sciences militaires*, 5 (15 October 1912), 380–1. On Mayer and Grouard see Liddell Hart, 'French military ideas before the First World War', in *A Century of Conflict 1850–1950* (London 1966), pp. 142–8; and A. Grouard, *France et Allemagne: la guerre éventuelle*, 4th edn (Paris 1913), pp. 69–73, 140–2, 198–201.

45 *Les armées françaises*, tome I, Vol. I, pp. 18–29; minutes of the War Board, 18 April 1913, Archives Guerre, 'Procès-verbaux du Conseil Supérieur de la Guerre', box J; 'Plan XVII: avant propos', ibid.; Joffre, *Memoirs*, Vol. I, pp. 66–98.

46 'Etude du plan d'opérations contre l'Allemagne, considérations d'ensemble', 18 April 1913, Archives Guerre, 'Plan XVII', box 137; diary, 19 April 1913; M. Paléologue, *Au quai d'Orsay à la veille de la tourmente: journal, 1913–1914* (Paris 1947), pp. 104–5.

47 See the testimony of Joffre and General Alexandre Percin before the Briey Commission, 23 May, 4 July 1919, France, Assemblée Nationale, Chambre des Deputés, session de 1919, *Procès-verbaux de la Commission d'Enquête sur le rôle et la situation de la métallurgie en France: défense du Bassin de Briey*, 2 vols. (Paris 1919), Vol. I, pp. 126–8; Vol. II, pp. 158–9.

48 'Directives pour la concentration', 7 February 1914, *Les armées françaises*, tome I, Vol. I: *Annexes*, no. 8, p. 21; 'Plan de renseignements', 28 March 1914, ibid., no. 10, p. 44; 'Analyse du plan de mobilisation pour l'armée allemande (édition 9 octobre 1913),', May 1914, Archives Guerre, 'Plan XVII', box 149.

49 In early 1913 the French obtained a staff memo, ostensibly written by Col. Ludendorff, which inferred that reserve troops would not be utilised initially; Pichon to P. Cambon, 5 April 1913, *DDF*, 3rd ser., VI, no. 210. However, in early 1914 the *Journal des sciences militaires* published an alleged German document, supposedly left in a train compartment, which outlined German war plans: in it reserve divisions were scheduled for employment but the German attack would remain south and east of the Belgian Meuse ('La concentration allemande', 16th ser., 7 (15 February 1914), 337–71).

50 L. Koeltz, *La guerre de 1914–18: les opérations militaires* (Paris 1966), 60–2; for reports of rail construction, see MAE, 'Allemagne', n.s. 95. When the French military archives are reopened during 1969, scholars should be able to evaluate more thoroughly the failures of French intelligence before 1914.

51 See L. Garros, 'Préludes aux invasions de la Belgique', *Revue historique de l'armée*, Vol. 5 (January–March 1949), pp. 36–7.

52 *Les armées françaises*, tome I, Vol. 1, p. 19; but see Captain Louis Le Merre's staff study (May 1912) which concluded that Britain would intervene on the Continent unless the Germans launched a surprise naval attack; Archives Guerre, 'Attachés militaires: Angleterre', box 11.

53 Artus Henri de La Panouse (French attaché in London) to Millerand, 11 December 1912, Archives Guerre, 'Plan XVII: Armée W'. box 147b; diary, 12 March, 1913, in Paléologue, *Journal, 1913–14*, pp. 75–6.

54 *Les armées françaises*, tome I, Vol. I, p. 19.

55 ibid.; cf. minutes of the War Board, 18 April 1913, Archives Guerre, 'Procès-verbaux du Conseil Supérieur de la Guerre', box K.

56 Louis Garros, 'En marge de l'alliance franco-russe, 1902–14', *Revue historique de l'armée*, 6 (January–March 1950), 29–30.

57 ibid., 32–42; Joffre, Memoirs, Vol. I, pp. 57–61; Poincaré, *Au service de la France*, Vol. I, pp. 110–11. The records of the staff talks are in *DDF*, 3rd ser., III, no. 200; ibid., VIII, no. 79.

58 J. C. Cairns, 'International politics and the military mind: the case of the French Republic, 1911–1914', *Journal of Modern History*, Vol. 25 (September 1953), p. 278.

59 Copies of these orders are in *Les armées françaises*, tome I, Vol. I: *Annexes*, no. 8.

60 Joffre did not apply this label, but the comparison is obvious.

61 On 4 July 1919, Joffre claimed that the secrecy of the conversations prevented any mention of British assistance in the orders. *Procès-verbaux . . . défense du Bassin de Briey*, Vol. II, p. 140.
62 Among them see General Selliers du Moranville, *Du haut de la tour de Babel* (Paris 1925), pp. 97–109; Sir Basil Liddell Hart, *Reputations* (London 1928), pp. 22–9; and General Charles Lanrezac, *Le plan de campagne français et le premier mois de la guerre (2 août–3 septembre 1914)* (Paris 1921), pp. 15–48. For critical defences of Joffre, see Duffour, *Joffre et la guerre de mouvement*, pp. 96–105; Varillon, *Joffre*, pp. 101–8.
63 Callwell, Wilson, Vol. I, pp. 78–9.

7

A German Plan for the Invasion of Holland and Belgium, 1897

J. STEINBERG

I

On 3 May 1897 the Commanding Admiral of the Imperial German Navy, Admiral Wilhem von Knorr, presented to Kaiser Wilhelm the High Command's operational plans in the event of a war against France.[1] During the course of his audience, Admiral von Knorr received instructions to prepare a similar operational study for a war against England. The project, entitled 'Memorandum: an Operation against Antwerp', which was developed by the Admiralty Staff in response to the Kaiser's order, was so remarkable and audacious that there was some question of presenting it at all. The scheme involved a simultaneous land-sea operation against the mouth of the river Schelde, the seizure of Antwerp and a series of forts on both the Belgian and Dutch banks of the Schelde by a *coup de main*, and the violation of the neutrality of both Belgium and Holland. It also required Germany to commence hostilities at least twenty-four hours before a formal declaration of war against England (or England and France together) had been made.[2] The details of the operation were worthy of Jules Verne. Before the outbreak of war, a German squadron, composed of seven steamers of about 5,000 tons and a small escort convoy, was to slip out of the estuaries of the Jade, Weser and Elbe. Twenty-four to thirty hours later, the convoy would assemble under cover of night in the mouth of the Schelde, and move to prearranged positions. An hour before daybreak, landing operations were to begin at seven points, and by noon Antwerp, the islands of Walcheren and South Beveland, and the most important coastal forts on both banks of the Schelde estuary would be in German hands. Simultaneously, the German VII and VIII Army Corps would have crossed the Belgian and Dutch frontiers and, in three swift striking columns, would have raced across Holand toward Breda and Antwerp. Once the Schelde estuary and Antwerp were firmly held, the invasion of England could be mounted.

Corvette Captain Schröder, the author of the plan, was the head of Section AIII*a* in the Admiralty Staff. When he completed his memorandum on 12 November 1897, he submitted it to Admiral von Knorr together with a historical study of the English expedition against Antwerp of 1809. Von Knorr circulated it among the other section chiefs for comments and criticism. The head of Section AI wrote, 'The entire plan seems to me so adventurous and impractical that I consider it entirely worthless to waste further effort on it'.[3] Schröder refused to accept that argument and replied: 'Every war is an adventure – so is a *coup de main* against the Schelde. AIII is quite aware of that, but we have not permitted ourselves to be deterred by that awareness from carrying out the All Highest's order – to study the matter seriously and to expend a good deal of effort on it.'[4]

Other objections were forthcoming. The head of Section AV, who was responsible for manoeuvres and technical questions, pointed out that there would never be as many as seven steamers in any one German harbour at a given time, that embarking 11,000 men was quite impossible without letting the whole world know that something was going on, that nocturnal navigation of the Schelde was not easy, and that the state of repair and fortifications of the forts St Marie, St Philippe and Perle were not sufficiently known. Indeed, the details of the plan would require a good deal of further study.[5] The head of AIV argued that the massing of the VIII Corps on the Dutch border and the assembling of units in German ports would soon be noticed and might have disastrous consequences for the success of the plan. Besides, if the experiences gained in loading 1,400 men for the China expedition were to be a guide, loading 11,000 men might take weeks. Finally, AIV disagreed that the nearest point to the English coast was necessarily the best point to launch an invasion.[6] On 7 December Schröder circulated his answers to all the various objections. He pointed out that an invasion of England would not be launched from one base only, but from several, of which Antwerp was undoubtedly the best. Moreover, the General Staff of the army, which had been consulted, agreed that Antwerp offered by far the best opportunities.[7] Obviously, secrecy was the main problem, but it would be reduced if the High Command and the army arranged annual embarkation exercises and the VII and VIII Corps manoeuvred often and publicly near the Dutch frontier. People would soon get used to the arrival of large forces in northern harbours. Finally, Schröder replied to his critics:

If the preparation and execution of this operation involves the same waste of time as in our recent troop-transports to China, the whole Antwerp affair is off. There is nothing left but to report to His Majesty that the Navy just cannot carry out a *coup de main* against Antwerp or support similar operations with land forces.[8]

The horror at such a confession of failure would seem to have been enough to silence the doubters, because the plan was permitted to move to the next stage.

During the month of December, the military attaché in Brussels was instructed to carry out discreet investigations along the Belgian coast, with particular attention to the condition and state of readiness of the crucial coastal forts. The attaché's report, dated 8 January 1898, was received and incorporated into the plan.[9] On 10 February Admiral von Knorr asked Count Schlieffen, Chief of the General Staff, to supply the Admiralty Staff with additional information.[10] By 21 February 1898 Admiral von Knorr was ready to report to the Kaiser in private audience. He began by requesting His Majesty to order SMS *Stein* to conduct secret observations along the Dutch and Belgian coasts in order to fill in certain missing bits of evidence. The operation would, Knorr continued, require complete control of the mouth of the Schelde. The navy would have to control Antwerp, the island of Walcheren, the port of Vlissingen and the town of Breskens. There were certain preconditions: the sea route from the German North Sea ports to the Schelde must be open; secrecy must be maintained; the execution must be speedy. Neither the Belgian nor Dutch governments must suspect anything. The *coup de main* depended on surprise. If the two governments were alerted, the forts would be manned and the operation would be a fiasco.

Lastly, Admiral von Knorr emphasised that only close co-operation between the army General Staff and the Admiralty Staff could assure success. Arrangements must be made for regular, full-scale practices in loading and unloading troops, and orders for the army's operations worked out. 'If your Imperial and Royal Majesty should see fit to approve my remarks, I should be very grateful for an order empowering me to make formal contact with the Chief of the General Staff to that end.'[11] The Kaiser approved the plan as presented, and issued the requisite orders to von Knorr, enabling him to order SMS *Stein* to prolong its stay in Antwerp by two days in order to carry out the required investigations. At the same time, he approved the suggestion that the Commanding Admiral and the Chief of the General Staff begin consultations on the implementation of the plan.[12]

On 4 March von Knorr forwarded a copy of the report made to the Kaiser to Count Schlieffen, and in the covering letter suggested the formation of a joint commission to work out the details of the plan. As soon as the strategic studies had been completed, Knorr suggested that the War Ministry and the Imperial Naval Office be asked to send representatives to the commission in order to work out the administrative and financial side of the plan.[13] While the High Command awaited a reply, Captain Schröder submitted a detailed report on the fortifications and strategy of the Dutch army, the quality of the equipment and personnel, the probable strategy of the Dutch navy, and descriptive material covering geography and water conditions in Holland. The report was ninety-eight pages long and examined every aspect of Dutch defence.[14]

Finally, on 17 June 1898, Count Schlieffen replied to von Knorr's letter.

In reply to your very kind letter of the 4th of March, permit me to express my full agreement with Your Excellency's view that the feasibility of a maritime undertaking against Antwerp is dependent on the existence of certain political preconditions. If, at the moment, the political situation hardly gives us a picture of the way in which such preconditions might develop, preparations and preliminary work can and must be carried out, which might be necessary for the various possible or intended operations. For the Army, such preparations would include the development of a plan for a ground attack on the fortresses, and the arrangement of practice embarkations and debarkations of troops and material.

Count Schlieffen concluded by suggesting that a representative of the War Ministry be included in the commission from the beginning, and named Colonel von Wittken as representative of the General Staff.[15]

Admiral von Knorr replied a few weeks later by posing a variety of practical questions. How many troops would be necessary for the embarkation manoeuvres? How many ships? Where ought they to take place? What equipment should the troops carry and how ought the transport ships to be fitted out?[16] At this point, the thread of the narrative snaps. A note in the file says that further correspondence was transferred to a separate folder, entitled 'Troop Transport', which is unfortunately missing.[17]

II

The function of a military staff is to make plans for the event of war. The fact that the General Staff or the Admiralty Staff had plans for a war against England as early as 1897 is interesting but not especially significant. What is significant, apart from the audacity of the conception, is the nonchalance with which the neutrality of both Belgium and Holland was tossed aside. Not one single comment was made on this aspect of the plan. Captain Schröder was criticised on every point except the crucial one: that the operation would necessarily make Germany the aggressor in a war against England. The staggering political and military consequencies of such a gross disregard for the rights of non-belligerents apparently never occurred to anyone. Schröder dismissed the question in two paragraphs. He may have thought that his arguments were so self-evident that no more was needed.

We must consider, first of all, that in a war between Germany and England our national wealth, the welfare of the German people, yes, perhaps, our very existence as a state, would be at stake. In the face of such considerations, clinging to artificially constructed clauses of international law would be far more reprehensible from an ethical point of view than merely bending the law because circumstances force us to do so. If the life of the nation is at stake, disregarding the neutrality of Belgium and the Netherlands need not dismay us. Besides, there is no question of the conquest of neutral territory, but merely the temporary occupation and use of certain areas, with full compensation and regard for the remaining rights of the owners . . . Even the greatest international lawyers are fully aware of the necessity of such actions against neutral states under certain circumstances. This has been expressed in the famous phrase, 'international law only protects the vital and virile states'.

No provision was made for consultation with the civilian authorities of the Reich. Diplomats, like generals and admirals, were to have sealed orders and could do nothing but obey them. German ministers in The Hague and Brussels were to drive to the foreign ministries, while the German army rolled across the borders and the navy seized the Schelde estuary. They were to deliver laconic Notes which would inform the two governments that

> political conditions oblige the German Empire to carry out a temporary occupation of the mouth of the Schelde and Antwerp. In order to maintain good relations between the Imperial German Government and the Governments of Belgium and the Netherlands, it is requested that Dutch and Belgian troops be temporarily withdrawn from the above-mentioned districts and places, and that a commission be entrusted with the surrender of all the war supplies and armaments in the occupied areas, against full compensation for the value thereof.

So much for diplomacy. The diplomats retired, one imagines, to await the victory. Schröder was not blind to the possibility that the operation might fail. In fact, he considered a failure possible, if an operation were mounted against the Low Countries by the army alone. He confined his remarks on that possibility to one brief sentence. 'No violation of the neutrality of another state,' he commented drily, 'is more dubious in its moral and practical consequences than one that ends in a failure.' The events of 1914 demonstrated the truth of that assertion, but Schröder seems not to have realised that the moral and practical consequences of a German success were equally dubious.

Can Schröder seriously have believed that the Belgians and Dutch would not fight? The very assumption that the railroad network would be intact as far as 's Hertogenbosch or Breda was unrealistic. Yet without the railroad, how could Schröder expect to have elements of the VIII Corps on the quay at Antwerp within forty-eight hours? A curious quirk of the German military mind always made it quite impossible for German generals and admirals to take their neighbours' nationalisms seriously. While it was obvious to them that German nationalism justified any aggression and that German nationalism was a holy cause, indeed a mission, it never really seemed credible that Belgians or Dutchmen or Norwegians or Poles could have national fervour too. Schröder's bland assumption of Belgian and Dutch pliability was never challenged by anyone in all the notes and comments. If the same inability to understand the mentality of the Dutch and Belgians had not been at the heart of the Schlieffen and Moltke plans, one might be tempted to believe that Schröder's naïveté was an isolated occurrence. Surely, the other members of the Admiralty Staff ought to have raised the question. Was it unreasonable to demand that Captain Schröder develop practical proposals to cover the case in which the Belgians and Dutch fought back bitterly? Nothing of the sort was done. von Knorr reported the plan as it stood without even mentioning the possibility. The great Schlieffen never really took the Belgian army seriously. After all, they were just Belgians. Why should they fight? For years, the General Staff seriously believed that Belgium would tamely submit to a temporary German occupation. The German government had the nerve to make such a proposal to the Belgians on 7 August 1914 and were genuinely surprised when the Belgians indignantly rejected it.[18] Ludwig Dehio, in his superb essay, 'Gedanken über die deutsche Sendung, 1900–1918', lists countless examples of this same awesome capacity for misunderstanding, which he draws from the works of the greatest German historians of the period.[19] If the great Max Lenz could seriously suggest in 1900 that the next war would be the war of all the Powers against England,[20] Captain Schröder can, perhaps, be excused for imagining that the Belgians and the Dutch would not fight.

The third 'Fehlrechnung' is less obvious, because it is a matter of degree and not kind – the assumption that all the Powers were as unscrupulous as Germany. Since 'violation of Belgian neutrality by either France or Germany will surely be unavoidable', Schröder argued that Germany would be well advised to act first. 'A helpful England would have a superb pretext to seize the Schelde itself, in agreement with Belgium. In our case it would be merely a question of preventing this little English pleasantry.' The difficulty here is that Schröder was quite right, or very nearly right. During the years between 1905 and 1914, the French General Staff had often to be restrained by their government or by the British General Staff from adopting 'preventive war' plans against Germany.[21] Most Germans sincerely believed that England was quite capable of sneaking into Wilhelmshaven one day and sinking Germany's fleet. Admiral Fisher was fond of making such bombastic hints. Schröder certainly thought so. 'The English government has never hesitated to disregard the rights of neutral nations when British interests were at stake. Is there a more flagrant example than the *coup de main* against Copenhagen in 1807?' This idea became in time such an obsession with the Kaiser and with naval officers that a verb, 'zu Kopenhagen', was created, and the naval and quasi-naval writings of the years before 1914 were filled with gloomy predictions that the English were about to 'Kopenhagen unsere Flotte'.

If England, France and Russia were as ruthless as Germany thought they were, there was no reason to trouble overmuch about violating Belgian and Dutch neutrality. The other Powers would regard it in the same realistic way as Germany did. Here we come back to the error of degree. The other Powers may well have been as ruthless as Germany in principle, but none was in practice. Russian weakness, English and French public opinion and political structures held them back. The difference may have been slight, but it was all important. Schröder offers a perfect example of this difference, when he supports his undertaking against Belgium and Holland by arguing, as the entire German government began to do after 1914, that these countries had never been neutral at all. The fact that Dutch and Belgian defences faced landward seemed to Schröder a clear indication that the two small countries were relying on England to defend their coasts. 'One gets the impression,' he wrote, that the Belgians are absolutely certain of the assistance of English war-ships. This assumption was decisive at the time when Antwerp was chosen as the central Belgian defensive position, although from a military and political point of view Brussels would have been preferable. It is not impossible that England and Belgium have made certain agreements with regard to Antwerp.

It was, of course, not impossible. It just happened not to be true. Schröder simply could not grasp that Belgium and Holland knew with certainty that England had no interest in attacking them and a great interest in defending them. No agreement was needed. Everyone understood this elementary principle of the balance of power except the Germans.

It is startling to recall that the plan we have been analysing was written, not in 1913, but in 1897. It is as if all the clichés, miscalculations and fallacies of Germany's conduct of war and behaviour in peace had sprung, miraculously summarised, from the brain of Captain Schröder. It is uncanny to find them all, nearly twenty years before the Great War. There are the same machiavellian suspicions and the same boastful assertions. As in the Schlieffen Plan of 1905, no consideration is given to the necessity for political and diplomatic preparation, nor even for consultation. The war plan is an automatic process, which demands the same subordination of civil to military considerations, which was to make the Schlieffen Plan so fateful and destructive for Germany. According to Captain Schröder, 'as soon as mutual relations [between Germany and England] have taken on a form which suggests that war is unavoidable, absolutely no hesitation must be permitted in the seizure and occupation of Antwerp'. Who would decide when that moment had been reached? The anguished days of July 1914, the hysterical scenes with the Kaiser, and Moltke's panic at the thought of calling off the machinery of the great *Aufmarsch,* are contained in embryo in Schröder's plan. If Gerhard Ritter is correct when he suggests that the development of the Schlieffen Plan was a more ominous and fateful occurrence than all the noise and dust of the naval rivalry,[22] can we not see in the 'Operation against Antwerp' the same terrible and inevitable consequences? This forgotten sheaf of papers, mouldering in the Admiralty files, and its forgotten author are, in a peculiar sense, as important as Schlieffen himself.

Schröder was, we may assume, not a prophet. He had no need to be. A plan with all the same inherent difficulties and risks, misunderstandings and self-delusions, was, in fact, fastened on the German army by Count Schlieffen and accepted as gospel by his successors. Thus whatever may have been wrong in Schröder's plan was also likely to be wrong in Schlieffen's. And yet it was adopted, worse, it was carried out. The attitudes, which Schröder reflected with more than ordinary brilliance in the 'Operation against Antwerp', must, therefore, have been very common; so common that a plan as risky as Schröder's could seriously be presented as the navy's mature and considered analysis of a crucial strategic problem; so common that an equally risky plan could be adopted by the army. It cannot be overemphasised that the ideas embodied in the Schlieffen and Schröder plans were felt to be so self-evident that they required no defence. Criticism of these ideas was not suppressed in the Admiralty Staff. There was none.

Secondly, these ideas had become dominant well before Germany's external position in the world had been threatened. Whether they were born of optimism and a sense of surging national power, as Professor Ritter believes,[23] or of a more complex mixture of assertiveness and anxiety, as I see it,[24] the fact remains that they were born and grew before, not after, the period of international tension had begun. German plans of attack were not a response to the ominous consolidation of hostile alliances. We now know that plans to settle with France by going around the French left flank, that is, by violating Belgian neutrality, were mentioned in the General Staff as early as 1891, and that in the summer of 1897, they became the central considerations in Germany's strategy for a war against the Dual Alliance.[25] There is no evidence in the naval archives that both plans were not conceived independently. Is it no more than a coincidence that the same ideas occurred at the same time in two separate planning staffs? It is far more probable that Schlieffen and Schröder formulated for the first time certain ideas which had been widely held in less precise form for years.

If that is so, Germany's attitude towards international relations was bound to change. The plans were, as we have seen, automatic. To succeed, they had to unfold without political interference. The possibilities open to German diplomacy were reduced by the paradoxical requirement that a defensive war open aggressively. Moreover, the acceptance of such plans by the political leadership of the Reich implied a degree of subordination of civilian judgement to military 'necessity', which was not a characteristic of any of the other Powers with the possible exception of Russia. There is evidence that this surrender by the civilians took place as early as 1900,[26] and was often repeated after that. Finally, even if the plans had never been made known beyond the walls of the High Command of the navy, they must have been the products of a peculiar mental and emotional climate. That climate could neither be confined to the military nor fail to influence civilian decisions. Germany in 1897 must have differed from the other Powers to the extent that the new militant atmosphere had begun to dominate men's thoughts. Captain Schröder's ideas were a symptom of that difference. Is it unfair to see in that difference, not a response to international tension, but one of its decisive causes?

APPENDIX
(Excerpts from a translation of the original handwritten draft)

Very Secret   Berlin, November 1897
Hand to Hand Only

Memorandum: An Operation against Antwerp
After the direct audience of 3rd May 1897, in which the basic lines of a German operation against England were presented,[27] His Excellency[28] ordered investigations to begin on the question of the way in which the Dutch and

Belgian coasts could best be used by us as a base for any operation. The investigations and the study of the available material have led to the following conclusions:

Above all, the position of the Netherlands and Belgium in a war between Germany and England must be considered first. The Kingdom of the Netherlands is, to begin with, a colonial Power; as far as one can see, there is no reason for that nation to take sides against either belligerent. Any tendency toward supporting England would immediately threaten the country with an invasion by Germany . . . In such an invasion, the Dutch territory would soon be over-run and be confined within the first few days of operations to the provinces of Utrecht and Holland. These two provinces may, however, be fairly described as '*Festung Holland*', one of the strongest defensive positions in Europe. The national leadership will under such circumstances hardly consider an active alliance with England. Equally doubtful from the standpoint of the Government of the Netherlands would be an open co-operation with Germany. The immediate occupation of the vast and very wealthy Dutch colonies by the English would be the consequence of such an alliance with Germany . . . We must, therefore, be prepared for the probability that in a war between Germany and England, the Netherlands would make every effort to observe strict neutrality.

The same applies to Belgium, indeed more so, since that nation, on the basis of its internationally regulated status, is not permitted to enter any alliance whatsoever and may only use its army for the defence of its own territory . . .

We must consider, first of all, that in a war between Germany and England our national wealth, the welfare of the German people, yes, perhaps our very existence as a state, would be at stake. In the face of such considerations, clinging to artificially constructed clauses of international law would be far more reprehensible from an ethical point of view than merely bending the law because circumstances force us to do so. If the life of the nation is at stake, disregarding the neutrality of Belgium and the Netherlands need not dismay us. Besides, there is no question of the conquest of neutral territory, but merely the temporary occupation and use of certain areas, with full compensation and regard for the remaining rights of the owners.

The history of war in every age shows us such examples. They will be repeated as long as wars are waged. England itself can serve as the best example. The English Government has never hesitated to disregard the rights of neutral nations when British interests were at stake. Is there a more flagrant example than the *coup de main* against Copenhagen in 1807? Even the greatest international lawyers are fully aware of the necessity of such actions against neutral states under certain circumstances. This has been expressed in the famous phrase, 'international law only protects the vital and virile states'.

The value which possession of the Dutch and Belgian coastal bases would have for us, if an invasion of England is involved, that is, if we wish to win the war at all, is clear from the mere fact of the distances. Such a victory over England cannot be won by the fleet alone. Thus, one must consider the difference between the distance from the German North Sea and that from the mouth of the Maas or the estuary of the Schelde to the English east coast. From Wilhelmshaven to the coast of Norfolk at Great Yarmouth, the distance is approximately 270 sea miles. A transport convoy, doing 10–12 knots per hour, would need at least 24 hours to make the journey. The

distance from Vlissingen to Dover or to Sheerness, both useful points for
large-scale troop landings, is approximately 80-85 sea miles; in other words,
less than one-third of the time would be required.

The distance from Ostend or Nieuwport is even less, only 60 sea miles, but
because of the military and hydrographic conditions at these ports, they
would be less suitable . . . The chances of launching a successful invasion
of England are improved by an increase in the number of jumping-off points
which are available. If in addition to the German harbours on the Elbe,
Weser and Jade, the estuary of the Schelde was also in our hands, the
chances of a successful tight blockade by the enemy would be far less
serious . . .

The estuary of the Schelde is ideal, providing Antwerp can be seized by a
coup de main. The possibility of such a *coup* exists and the operational plan
which follows will attempt to demonstrate that this is so. The operation
depends, however, on the choice of the time. The beginning must be set
sufficiently early to permit the *coup* to take place. If Belgium has mobilised,
and has had a chance to carry out the mobilisation plan for the defence of
the country in every particular, any hope of success disappears. Thus the
point in time at which we will have to seize control of the Schelde estuary
and the fortress of Antwerp must necessarily depend on the general circumstances and the state of the relationship between Germany and England. As
soon as mutual relations have taken on a form which suggests that war is
unavoidable, absolutely no hesitation must be permitted in the seizure and
occupation of Antwerp. If war has been declared and the freedom of movement of our shipping in the North Sea threatened, the chances for a *coup de
main* against Antwerp are lost, since an isolated undertaking by the Army
alone would probably be a failure. No violation of the neutrality of another
state is more dubious in its moral and practical consequences than one that
ends in a failure. There is, finally, an additional point to consider. The
stronger defences of Antwerp face inland. Those on the river itself are far
less impressive.

The Belgians, relying on the sea forces of the Guarantor Power, England,
seem to regard the sea front in its present form as entirely adequate. One gets
the impression that the Belgians are absolutely certain of the assistance of
English warships. This assumption was decisive at the time when Antwerp
was chosen as the central Belgian defensive position, although from a military
and political point of view Brussels would have been preferable. It is not
impossible that England and Belgium have made certain agreements with
regard to Antwerp. At the very least, one may reckon on the certainty that
the English will make every effort to occupy the mouth of the lower Schelde
before we can. The English will assuredly not repeat their mistakes of 1809,
but will carry out their expedition differently. If the English succeed in
occupying the estuary of the Schelde, with or without Antwerp, we shall be
as unable to drive them out of the position, as they would be to drive us out
if we were to get there first.

The operation outlined here is based on the assumption that the North
Sea has not yet been blockaded by an overwhelmingly strong English fleet
and on the assumption that Belgium has not mobilised to defend its
neutrality. There is no reason to expect serious military counter-measures
from the Netherlands, because the main strength of Dutch defences lies in
the provinces of Utrecht and Holland . . . The provinces which lie south of
the Maas, Nord, Brabant and Seeland, form the district of the 3rd Army

Division with headquarters at Breda. They are, however, entirely undefended. There is scarcely a single armed fortress, with the exception of the tiny fort at Terneuzen. The formerly well-defended places, Nijmegen, 's Hertogen-bosch, Breda, Bergen-op-Zoom, Middelburg and the formerly powerful sea-fortress of Vlissingen have not been in operation for years. This was to avoid a dangerous fragmentation of the Dutch Army which is, in any event, small. All the available Dutch forces are to be used in defence of the 'Festung Holland'. This circumstance favours the necessary planning and co-operation between German land and sea striking forces in an undertaking against Antwerp and the West Schelde.

The operations of the sea forces will be unfavourably affected, especially the necessity for unobserved preparation, by the transportation of large forces of troops. Thus, one is compelled to keep the amphibious force as small as possible. On the other hand, the occupation of the widely dispersed positions along the Schelde estuary and the seizure of Antwerp demands a considerable number of soldiers. For example, we estimate that the defence of Antwerp and environs will require a force of 40,000 men.

The nature of the topography in Nord and Brabant, as well as the existing railroad network, however, favour the easy transportation of the necessary troops and permit, once the Navy has successfully carried out the *coup*, the speedy deployment of the land forces to defend the entire position. Once we have Antwerp and the Schelde in our control, we can readily assemble the Army Corps needed for the invasion of Britain and easily prepare their embarkation. The invasion will require a separate operational study.

The following general ideas have been used as the basis of the operational plan for the occupation of Antwerp, the islands of Sud-Beveland and Walcheren, as well as the Dutch portion of the southern bank of the Schelde estuary:

(1) Before the outbreak of war, a German squadron will slip out to sea, composed of smaller transport convoys moving out of the Jade, Weser and Elbe. Within 24 hours, the convoy will assemble at the mouth of the Schelde and slip into the estuary under cover of night. Warships and transports will be so deployed that a simultaneous landing and attack on all the various forts can be made at the break of day.

(2) The troops transported for the *coup de main* are, of course, completely inadequate for the occupation and defence of the entire Antwerp position. As soon as the forts have been taken, the nearest Prussian Army Corps, the VIII and parts of the VII, must advance along the line Mosel-Boxtel-Breda-Roosendaal toward South Beveland and Walcheren, from which points they can be ferried across the Schelde by our squadron. Moreover, if we have the city, the outer forts have no value for the Belgians and it is reasonable to assume that they will speedily evacuate the entire area, without the necessity of heavy fighting.

Given these basic ideas, the details of the plan would be as follows:

A. *Naval Operations:* Using the excuse that the colonies must be supplied with troops and artillery, seven steamers will be loaded in Cuxhaven, Bremerhaven and Wilhelmshaven as unobtrusively as possible. The ships will have a carrying capacity of about 5,000 tons, and will be ready at the wharf . . . Each ship will carry 1,600 men and the total expeditionary force will comprise:

    9 Battalions Infantry
    6–7 Companies, Light Artillery
    4 Companies, Marine Artillery
    3–5 Companies, Sappers

The escort convoy will include 8 battleships, 'Siegfried' Class, the *Pelikan* with 400 mines aboard, 2–3 avisos, 3 torpedo boat divisions, 6 armoured gunboats and 4 coal tenders.

A further addition to the strength of the expeditionary force may be expected within 48 hours of the attack by the land forces. Up to that point, no counter-measures from the English or anyone else may be expected in such force as to threaten our initial successes. English undertakings may be safely discounted, because within the first 48 hours she will find it very difficult to collect enough ships with sufficiently shallow draught to navigate the Schelde. The Channel Fleet has few such vessels at the moment.

B. *Army Operations:* The operations of the land forces to secure our position on the Schelde and to occupy Antwerp can only be briefly treated here. The preparation of this side of the operation will take place in the General Staff. In general, the following outline will be used:

(1) The VII and VIII Corps have been exercising in brigades for some time now and have been practising troop transport by train. To this end, considerable amounts of rolling stock have been assembled in Düsseldorf on the Lower Rhine, in Cologne and along the Mosel. Night alarms and embarkations are being practised. The regiments have been brought to 'augmented peacetime strength' through calling up a portion of the active reserves.

(2) During the night when our fleet puts to sea, according to the plan outlined above, the Corps commanders of the VII and VIII Corps will receive final orders for the plan, and the troops in the Rhineland garrisons will be loaded during that same night. Shortly before dawn they will cross the border along three lines of attack: Kleve, Nijmegen, 's Hertogenbosch; Wesel, Hoch, Boxtel; Krefeld, Blerik, Eindhoven, Breda. The columns will assemble in the area Roosendaal /Bergen-op-Zoom, which will be the central staging area for the occupation of the islands of Walcheren and South Beveland. How far the railroad network will be used will depend on the behaviour of the garrisons in 's Hertogenbosch and Breda. There is no reason to expect serious resistance.

A fullscale mobilisation of the VIII Corps will not be involved, since the operation depends on speedy penetration of Holland . . . If Breda can be taken before the railroad has been damaged, the first Prussian troops will embark at Vlissingen or Vlakke (on the South Beveland Canal) or Bath; ships will be ready to transport them across the Schelde and they will debark on the quay at Antwerp. If all goes well, this stage can be reached in the first 48 hours. The remaining troops of the VII and VIII Corps will complete the defences of the islands of South Beveland and Walcheren, the Katzand district and the south bank of the Schelde.

On the morning of the day on which the fleet enters the Schelde and the Army crosses the borders, our Ministers in Brussels and The Hague will present identical Notes to the respective governments to the effect that 'political conditions oblige the German Empire to carry out a temporary occupation of the mouth of the Schelde and Antwerp. In order to maintain good relations between the Imperial German Government and the Governments of Belgium and the Netherlands, it is requested that the Dutch and Belgian troops be temporarily withdrawn from the above-mentioned districts and places and that a commission be entrusted with the surrender of all the war supplies and armaments in the occupied areas, against full compensation for the value thereof.'

Concluding Remarks:
The above represents a first stage in a larger operation against England. Even if an invasion should prove impractical as a result of the great difficulties involved, the possession of Antwerp and the Schelde estuary would be of enormous military value for Germany. The English would be compelled either to attack the Schelde with a very powerful force, or to carry out a very tight blockade. An English naval attack would hardly have a chance, because the navigable waters of the Schelde are not suitable for the heavy English battleships. The expulsion of our troops from their heavily fortified positions in Walcheren and South Beveland is also out of the question. It is fair to assume that the English would lose more than they would gain by a frontal attack on the Schelde. Above all, a German occupation of the mouth of the Schelde would absorb so much of the English fleet that far weaker units would be left to blockade our North Sea coast, and probably no forces at all for a blockade of the Baltic.

Finally, we may cast a glance at the operation against Antwerp in the event of a war between the Triple Alliance and the Dual Alliance. The operation under those circumstances seems to be even more promising, assuming England remains neutral at first. Perhaps, the occupation would be even more important for political reasons, since violation of Belgian neutrality by either France or Germany will surely be unavoidable and a helpful England would have a superb pretext to seize the Schelde itself, in agreement with Belgium. In our case it would be merely a question of preventing this little English pleasantry. How much the High Command of the Army would value the possession of Antwerp in their operations on the West Front cannot be judged here.

For the maintenance of our naval supremacy in the North Sea, the possession of the Schelde would be of decisive importance. As long as we lay within the mouth of the Schelde with a portion of our naval strength, it would be impossible for the French to maintain a serious blockade of the North Sea, even if the powerful Mediterranean Squadron was transferred to the operation.

The conclusion that the possession of Antwerp and the mouth of the Schelde would be enormously valuable for the German naval operations, whether in a war against England or against France or against both together, seems, therefore, to be entirely justified. It is, accordingly, recommended that further consideration be given, and additional plans be worked out, for the occupation of the fortress of Antwerp and the other necessary positions on both banks of the West Schelde.

For Section AIII (Initialled) Sch., 12.xi.1897.

NOTES

1 The documentary sources of this article come from the hitherto unpublished operational plans found in the German Naval Archive, the University of Cambridge. The archive includes 111 reels of microfilm, covering documents from the files of the Imperial Naval Cabinet, The Admiralty Staff of the Imperial Navy, Departments A and B, and the Imperial Naval Office. The documents were filmed at the Admiralty in London in 1959, as a joint project of the University of Cambridge and the University of Michigan. The plan discussed in this article, part of which is printed in the annex, was found in a file entitled 'Operations against Belgium and Holland, Very Secret, Hand to Hand only', and bearing the reference number, 'III, 3–18, Admiralty Staff'.

2 In his memoirs, Admiral von Tirpitz states categorically that 'the first official plan for an operation against England was worked out in the Admiralty Staff during the course of the twentieth century . . .' (Tirpitz, *Erinnerungen*, Leipzig, 1920, p. 59). The statement follows another categorical assertion that 'the plan for a German battlefleet was created without any thought of a war against England . . .' (ibid., p. 58). The discovery of the memorandum of 1897 certainly diminishes, if it does not destroy, the value of Tirpitz's attempts to justify himself in this way. Plans for a war against England were devised before the first Navy Law had been introduced, indeed, before Tirpitz became State Secretary of the Imperial Naval Office in June of 1897.

3 Adm. Archive, III, 3–18, pencil comment, dated 26 November 1897.

4 ibid. Reply to AI, 7 December 1897.

5 ibid. Comments of AV on Operational Plan, 23 November 1897.

6 ibid. Comments of AIV, 4 December 1897.

7 In a note of 15 November 1897 prepared by AIII*b*, a letter to the General Staff, reference AI 190 VII, is mentioned. At that time no reply had been received in the Admiralty Staff. The original letter from the General Staff was not in the files, but it is safe to assume from Captain Schröder's remark that a reply to the series of questions raised must have arrived between 15 November and 7 December.

8 ibid. Reply to AIV and a AV, 7 December 1897.

9 Attaché report, Brussels, no. 5, dated 8 January 1898.

10 III, 3–18. Letter, Admiral von Knorr to Count Schlieffen, 10 February 1898.

11 Direct Audience, original draft, marked 'Very Secret – From Hand to Hand Only', dated Berlin, 21 February 1898.

12 III, 3–18. Handwritten memorandum, 'Results of Audience of His Majesty', signed by von Knorr, dated 21 February 1898.

13 III, 3–18. Letter dated 4 March 1898, Admiral von Knorr to Count Schlieffen, original draft with corrections.

14 III, 3–18. 'Memorandum re: Carrying out an Operation against Holland – Very Secret. From Hand to Hand Only'. Drawn up by Captain Schröder, dated 15 March 1898.

15 II, 3–18. Letter, dated 17 June 1898, signed by Count Schlieffen, to Admiral von Knorr.

16 III, 3–18. Letter, original draft with corrections, from Admiral von Knorr to Count Schlieffen, dated 13 July 1898.

17 The ultimate fate of the plan is unknown. The records of the German army prior to 1914, which were stored in the Reichsarchiv in Potsdam until 1936, were then transferred to Berlin and, it is believed, destroyed during the Second World War. Professor Gerhard Ritter, who made use of these archives during the war while preparing his monumental history of militarism, *Staatskunst und Kreigshandwerk*, 2 vols. (Munich 1954 and 1960), noted several entries in the Secret Journal of the General Staff: '10.1.1899 Memorandum from Commanding Admiral of the Navy – re: War against England; 20.3.1900 Two General Staff officers sent to joint consultations on operational undertakings at sea, suggestion of Chief of Admiralty Staff' (Vol. II, p. 195, n. 51). Professor Ritter, relying on a recent study of the German Admiralty by Walther Hubatsch (W. Hubatsch, *Der Admiralstab und die obersten Marinebehörden in Deutschland 1848–1945*, Frankfurt am Main, 1958), suggests that these discussions were occasioned by naval plans for offensive striking attacks in the North Sea. Hubatsch would seem not to have known of the existence of the plan either. He writes of a plan against France which involved a strike at Le Havre by sea but seems to have confused correspondence with regard to the amphibious operations against Holland and Belgium with a separate study for naval support in a war against France alone (Hubatsch, ibid., p. 91). Hubatsch is certainly confusing the two plans when he argues that one reason for the abandonment of offensive operations against France was the lack of shipping space for the transportation of three army corps. There is nothing in his account to explain why a naval operation alone against the coast of France should have been dropped because troop transport space was not available.

18 Hans W. Gatzke, *Germany's Drive to the West* (Baltimore 1950), p. 8.

19 Ludwig Dehio, *Deutchland und die Weltpolitik im 20. Jahrhundert* (Fischer Ausgabe, Frankfurt, 1961), pp. 63ff.

20 ibid., p. 83.

21 Gerhard Ritter, *The Schlieffen Plan – Critique of a Myth* (London 1958), p. 8.

22 Gerhard Ritter, *Staatskunst und Kriegshandwerk*, 2 vols. (Munich 1954 and 1960), Vol. II, p. 240.

23 Ritter, op. cit., Vol. II, p. 246.

24 I cannot understand how plans which forced Germany to strike the first blow, a foul one at that, and which staked everything on one risky manoeuvre can be regarded as manifestations of optimism. Surely, Professor Ritter's own evidence belies this argument. When Germany really was militarily vastly superior to its enemies, as in the days of the elder Moltke, Germany's strategy was calm and defensive. Both Schlieffen and the younger Moltke were essentially pessimists, and the Schlieffen Plan was a counsel of despair. For Moltke's acute pessimism see Generaloberst Helmuth von Moltke, *Erinnerungen, Briefe, Dokumente* (Stuttgart 1922), pp. 153, 243, 288, 298, 301, 304ff., 337; for Schlieffen's gloomy estimate of Germany's chances, see Gerhard Ritter, *The Schlieffen Plan – Critique of a Myth*, foreword by B. Liddell Hart, p. 100, in which Professor Ritter quotes the following passage from Schlieffen's *Der Krieg in der Gegenwart*: 'An endeavour is afoot to bring all these Powers together for a concentrated attack on the Central Powers. At the given moment, the drawbridges are to be let down, the doors are to be opened and the million strong armies let loose, ravaging and destroying,

across the Vosges, the Meuse, the Konigsan, the Niemen, the Bug and even the Isonzo and the Tyrolean Alps. The danger seems gigantic.' Schlieffen's writings are filled with a almost paranoid preoccupation with 'the revengeful enemy' waiting 'in his lair for the best moment to break out. Attack is the best defence' (Schlieffen, *Gesammelte Schriften*, Vol. I, p. 18).

25 Ritter, op. cit., p. 247.

26 Cf. Bogdan Count Hutten-Czapski, *Sechzig Jahre Politik und Gesell-schaft*, 2 Vols. (Berlin 1935–6). Hutten-Czapski, who was Hohenlohe's private secretary, describes a dinner at which Schlieffen outlined his plan to Hohenlohe, as well as a meeting with Holstein, in which, at Schlieffen's request, Hutten-Czapski outlined the plan to violate Belgian neutrality (pp. 371ff). A note on one of Schlieffen's later drafts of the plan indicates that it had been discussed with Bülow (Ritter, *The Schlieffen Plan*, p. 92).

27 A marginal comment on the original document points out that there was a discrepancy between Schröder's statement and the Admiralty records, which indicated that at the audience of 3 May 1897 plans for an operation against France were presented and that the Kaiser then suggested that plans for an operation against England be developed.

28 Wilhelm von Knorr, Commanding Admiral of the Imperial Navy (1895–7).

8

The Development of German Naval Operations Plans against England, 1896–1914[1]

P. M. KENNEDY

In the years following the fall of Bismarck, the relations of the great powers fell into a state of relative flux as the statesmen and foreign ministries of Europe adjusted to a diplomatic scene no longer dominated by that amazingly ruthless and clever man.[2] The most noticeable of the consequent developments was the formation of the Dual Alliance, which restored the European political and military balance and in the first instance drove closer together Great Britain and the Central Powers, who felt distinctly uneasy at this incongruous yet undoubtedly powerful alliance between Tsarist Russia and republican France. Yet, while the links between St Petersburg and Paris were steadily strengthened, those between Britain and the three nations which comprised the Triple Alliance, Germany, Austria-Hungary and Italy, grew more distant. This itself was due to long-term factors – in particular, the traditional British distaste for continental commitments which might bind it to a certain action in some future crisis – but it can be seen quite clearly also as a direct consequence of the deterioration in Anglo-German relations in the mid-1890s.

The Heligoland-Zanzibar treaty of 1890, the high point of the so-called Anglo-German 'colonial marriage', had itself contained portents of future discord between the two signatories. The agreement was received with dismay by German colonial circles and led almost directly to the formation of the ultra-chauvinistic and anglophobic Pan-German League, which was thenceforward to maintain an unremitting pressure upon the imperial government to pay due regard to Germany's interests abroad. Moreover, the delight with which Wilhelm II, Caprivi and their advisers greeted the treaty was soon muted by the realisation that the British had no intention of committing themselves to the quadruple alliance upon which Berlin had pinned its hopes.[3] At the same time as Salisbury, and more especially Rosebery after him, annoyed the Wilhelmstrasse by declining to promise firm support in the Mediterranean to Germany's two weak and nervous alliance partners, colonial disputes in Africa and the South Seas between Britain and Germany re-emerged against a backcloth of rapidly growing public interest in overseas acquisitions.[4] The quarrels of 1893–4 over the Niger, Samoa and the Congo were very sharp and had repercussions elsewhere – with Rosebery threatening Berlin via Vienna with complete indifference to the Mediterranean situation whilst Caprivi hastily attempted to restore better relations with St Petersburg. The overall policy of the two powers was becoming rather similar: whether it was called 'splendid isolation' or 'the free hand', both indicated that they meant to work alone, realising that 'the basic comon interest which had been so strong up to 1894 had disappeared'.[5] Even the return of Salisbury to office in 1895 did little to check this trend, partly because of personal differences between him and the Kaiser, but chiefly because the various legacies in foreign affairs left by the Liberal administration (Mediterranean, Armenia, Far East) had once again resulted in the two powers taking up differing attitudes which could not easily be reconciled. The thorniest problem of all was that of the Transvaal, where the growing German interest in the Boer republic had already caused the Liberal foreign secretary, Kimberley, to warn that Britain would not even 'recoil from the spectre of war' to preserve her supremacy in southern Africa.[6] This did not check the German government, however, and when the news of the Jameson Raid reached Berlin at the end of 1895 the Kaiser became very excited; if the scanty evidence we possess of the scenes at the Wilhelmstrasse are accurate, the notorious Kruger Telegram dispatched on 3 January 1896 was the least of the actions contemplated by Wilhelm and his advisers. Yet this, in turn, provoked an even more dramatic response when the British announced the formation of a naval 'Flying Squadron', ready to go anywhere in the world.[7]

The reaction in Berlin to this gesture, which was possibly as much a move in the Venezuelan confrontation with the United States as in the Transvaal crisis with Germany, was even more serious: for the first time, the Germany navy realised that it could no longer exclude the possibility of future war with Great Britain and decided that it required a naval operations plan in the event of that dire contingency occurring.[8] Though war planning has often been dismissed as a somewhat artificial indication of the policy of a government at any given time, in that it is always to be expected that naval and military staffs will devote much of their energies to contingency planning and hypothetical war situations, this agrument is far less valid for the nineteenth century, when such activities were extremely limited. In any case, the decision to institute preparations for an operations plan against another power is much more a *political* one and almost invariably follows indications that that power's policies could be troublesome or threatening in the future.[9] If the plan fell into desuetude after a few years, as did Mahan's famous 1890 scheme for the US navy's operations in a war against Britain, one might agree that it was or had become unreal and academic; but if it is being constantly worked upon, and is subjected to occasional major changes which parallel more general developments in strategy and international relations, then it would be reasonable to assume that its significance is far greater and that a study of this topic could lead one to a better understanding of both the calculations and the policy of a government with regard to certain other powers. In the case of German naval planning against England in the two decades preceding the First World War, this is certainly true. This activity was the natural military corollary of the fluctuating relations between London and Berlin and it attracted the constant support and interest of Kaiser Wilhelm himself.

The preparation of operations plans was the responsibility of the High Command of the Navy, which in 1899 was to be dissolved and remoulded into the Admiralty Staff.[10] From the very beginning of their planning against Britain, the staff officers concerned realised that the task of evolving a reasonably successful strategy was extremely difficult, if not absolutely hopeless: the Royal Navy was far superior in strength to its German equivalent, which had sunk to being only the sixth largest in the world by 1897, following years of disorganisation and comparative neglect.[11] The Chief of Staff at the high command, Rear-Admiral von Diederichs, began the first of many memoranda on this topic on 5 March 1896 with a gloomy assessment of Germany's chances against such an overwhelmingly powerful opponent. The coastline of Germany would be blockaded in wartime and her overseas trade cut off, he suggested; and, although enemy operations in nearby waters gave opportunities for occasional small victories, these would in all probability be insufficient to tilt the naval balance. Then, throwing in a proposal which appears to have been born more out of desperation than anything else, Diederichs finally argued that one risky alternative remained – an offensive against the Thames estuary immediately upon the outset of war in the hope of surprising an unprepared British force and of gaining strategic control of the North Sea.[12] This daring proposal provoked a flurry of marginal comments and memoranda from almost every other officer in the department. All were aware that the greater part of the Royal Navy was deployed on overseas stations, particularly in the Mediterranean, and that only the Reserve Fleet, which consisted of second-class battleships, was based at the Nore. Here was an ideal – perhaps the only – chance for a swift and decisive strike by Germany's First Battleship Squadron. Not all the staff experts were convinced of the correctness of such a scheme, one of them tartly commenting:

It is equally to be considered that England will never declare war before she has collected a fleet of overwhelming superiority in the Channel or off the Thames. Under such conditions this sort of offensive thrust would be pointless.[13]

Nevertheless, the majority of the planners concurred with the overall conclusions in favour of an offensive operation which Diederichs drew together at the end of the following month.[14]

After a hiatus of almost one year, during which time the only document of note was a memorandum advocating an ingenious though impracticable scheme to bring Britain to her knees by strewing about a thousand mines off her ports, earnest consideration of an operations plan was resumed at the direction of Vice-Admiral von Knorr, Commanding Admiral of the Navy; and on 31 May 1897 the ideas of the planning section were presented by him in an audience to the Kaiser. Admitting that in existing circumstances a lasting success against the Royal Navy was impossible, Knorr nevertheless argued that energetic action by the German fleet was the better of the two courses open to them. Since Britain's aim would be 'the naval and commercial destruction of Germany', she would send forces to the German coast as soon after the outbreak of war as possible, but waiting for her in a defensive position would offer few benefits. On the other hand, a strike against the Thames before the British had recalled the Mediterranean Fleet would secure Germany's mobilisation at home, give her merchant vessels an opportunity to reach port, disrupt English coastal commerce and – most important of all – offer the only chance of bringing the enemy to its knees; for, if the Reserve Fleet could be annihilated in a swift action, it might conceivably be possible to rush an invasion force across the Channel before the Mediterranean Fleet arrived in home waters around the fifteenth day of the war. Since such a stroke probably required possession of the Schelde estuary as an advance base first of all, Knorr continued,

> the government of the Netherlands must be induced into an alliance by our political leadership, or possibly by military pressure by land. If this does not succeed, then we must establish ourselves there by force.[15]

The political difficulties of seizing either Dutch or Belgian territory as embarkation ports were not ignored, but the Kaiser agreed with the proposals outlined and ordered Knorr to initiate joint planning with the General Staff, where, as Diederichs noted in the margin, 'people are not yet thinking of fighting with England'.[16]

Although planning for an invasion of England was to continue for several years after Knorr's audience with the Kaiser, it still possessed, as a recent study has pointed out, a considerable amount of 'wishful and unanalytical thinking' in its early stages.[17] In his letter to Schlieffen of 2 June 1897, Knorr requested the co-operation of the General Staff in the matter of landing areas, transport facilities and troops, and then added, almost as an afterthought, the crucial question: 'Must the connection with Germany after the landing be maintained under all circumstances? The navy will probably not be in a position to do so.'[18] While waiting for the army's answer, however, many officers in the high command did at least cast doubts upon the possibility of seizing either the Netherlands or Belgium as a preliminary invasion move against England, indicating that more realistic views were beginning to make themselves felt. Occupation of, or alliance with, the first-named nation was felt to provide an ideal excuse for the British to seize the Dutch East Indies; the over-running of Belgium would break the 1839 treaty and almost certainly provoke a French reaction;

and the chances of achieving surprise against the British would be small.[19] Without a strong naval ally, as Knorr himself had suspected some time earlier, the prospects for a lone German strike against England were not good.

Schlieffen's answer, tardily sent on 14 December 1897, did not alter this trend. Agreeing to the assumption that the British Reserve Fleet would be defeated on the fifth day of the war and that there would be a ten-day gap before substantial enemy reinforcements arrived, the Chief of General Staff pointed out that it would take too long to over-run ports in the Low Countries and that the invading army destined for England should be assembled in Germany's North Sea harbours; the number of troops would depend on the number of transports available. As to Knorr's most important question, Schlieffen concluded philosophically that the army would have to press the British to surrender more energetically than ever if its own lines to the continent were broken; but in an earlier section he referred to the invading force as being a 'prisoner' without sea mastery and gloomily portrayed a collapse due to troop and ammunition shortages if it could not prevail upon the British government to order the surrender of the Royal Navy.[20]

Although the high command's reply to this letter was to encourage more detailed joint studies of the transportation problems involved, other factors caused further reservations to be expressed about the feasibility of this offensive operation. In the first place, the coming into office of Bülow in 1897 signified a turn to *Weltpolitik* and led to the dispatch of more warships to the Far East to the detriment of German naval strength in home waters. As one officer, Scheder, put it,

> The earlier plans, that is, to recall home all overseas vessels at the outbreak of war, will no longer be able to be maintained in view of the present policy of the German Emperor.[21]

At the same time, the British had greatly strengthened their Channel Fleet following the 1897 Jubilee review at Spithead, and the German navy would only have a chance of success in battle if that force was elsewhere; yet that would only occur if war broke out suddenly, a contingency so unlikely that the high command officers were increasingly reluctant to base any serious plans upon it. In any case, even preliminary investigations had shown that the German transport fleet on hand at any given time was totally inadequate to ship the six to eight Army corps which Schlieffen had deemed necessary to conquer England in as swift a time as possible. As early as December 1897, therefore, Knorr was forced to report to the Kaiser that an offensive operations plan would have to be given up.[22] Since this fact was not officially transmitted to the General Staff until 10 January 1899, further detailed work – narrowing down the landing zone to between Aldeburgh and Great Yarmouth – continued; yet it was clear to the high command that an invasion could only be launched if Germany possessed powerful naval allies, an unlikely event but one which allowed Knorr to give full reign to his fertile imagination. In a lengthy memorandum of 12

September 1898, he postulated various political combinations against Britain, including a Russo-German one, which would jointly invade India, take effective action in the Far East, try to block the Suez Canal and perhaps even attempt to send troops to seize the Cape of Good Hope! In view of Schlieffen's obsession with a two-fronted war against the Dual Alliance, and Bülow's determination to maintain a 'free hand' between Britain and Russia, it was clear that a sense of unreality continued to pervade early German naval thinking about a war against Britain.[23]

One further and very major development was to complete the collapse of these plans for an offensive strike against the Thames at the outset of war – the rise of Tirpitz to a position of dominance inside the fragmented command structure of the imperial navy. His crucial role in the enormous growth of the German fleet has been minutely examined in several studies and it is only necessary here to recall his major strategical ideas. Already by 1897 Tirpitz had eschewed any form of commerce raiding and had evolved instead a scheme to create a homogeneous force of battleships which would be able not only to defend German coasts but also to threaten the overall maritime superiority of the most powerful navy existing; thus the British, unable to concentrate their many battle squadrons in the North Sea owing to pressing commitments elsewhere in the world, would recognise the power of his 'risk fleet' and become more amenable to German aspirations, according Germany the *Gleichberechtigung* that the Kaiser craved. On the other hand, this risk theory would only become fully effective after the battle fleet had reached a considerable size and this required a period of years – 'the danger zone' – during which Germany's foreign and naval policy would have to be as cautious and undramatic as possible.[24] The first priority was to build up the home battle fleet quickly as a defensive force and Tirpitz therefore strongly opposed any ideas of risking it in some madcap invasion scheme proposed by his rival Knorr. Thus, as Chancellor Hohenlohe noted, he warned against such a plan, with or without allies, saying:

> The idea of an invasion of England is insane. Even if we succeeded in landing two army corps in England, it would not help us, for two corps would not be strong enough to hold their positions in England without support from home. Tirpitz concludes that all policy hostile to England must rest until we have a fleet which is as strong as the English. The alliance with Russia and France would not help us. The Russians cannot come over the mountains to India, they have enough to do to maintain their Far Eastern possessions.[25]

Moreover, Tirpitz also insisted that an invasion of England was impossible without lasting naval supremacy in the North Sea and when Captain Maltzahn, a proponent of such a strike, argued that Napoleon would have needed only one day in 1805 free from the interference of the Royal Navy to send his army across the Channel, he angrily noted:

That was Napoleon's error. If he had really succeeded in getting across and was later cut off, then both he and his army would have been lost – as in Egypt, where only flight and the premature conclusion of peace saved him from total defeat.[26]

It was probably no coincidence, therefore, that the newly formed Admiralty Staff formally presented its full arguments for 'The Defensive against England' in December 1899, the same month in which Tirpitz disclosed his risk theory for the first time publicly when explaining to the Reichstag the need to double the battle fleet from the size established under the first Navy Law of 1898.[27] In an audience with the Kaiser on the 12th of that month, the Chief of Admiralty Staff, Rear-Admiral Bendemann, explained the new strategy which had been evolved in the case of war with England alone, accepting that there was little prospect of Germany having naval allies. A reckless offensive against the Thames was rejected from the start, but so too was the passive policy of remaining in the Elbe, for this contradicted the very essence of a battle fleet, which was 'effective action'; it would lead to a slump in morale and it offered few strategic prospects, especially when the enemy brought home more squadrons and imposed a tight blockade of the German North Sea coastline. To prevent the German battle fleet from being bottled up in those harbours, it would be preferable to withdraw them to Kiel in the Baltic, where they would have a greater protection and freedom of action. However, the autumn 1899 manoeuvres had indicated that a successful defensive strategy in the Baltic would be most unlikely if the Royal Navy was allowed to steam through the Belts unhindered. Consequently, continued Bendemann,

> The execution of a vigorous defensive absolutely requires that we should compel Denmark voluntarily or with force to unite with us . . . It is of the highest importance that we obtain control of the coasts of the Belts immediately in the first days of war or even before Denmark can carry out its mobilisation.

With the Baltic entrances securely held by German troops, the British would be unwilling to send patrols into the Heligoland Bight lest they were surprised by a flank attack from the north; but it was even more likely that they would react strongly by seeking to force their way through the Belts, where their strength would be much reduced by torpedo-boat attacks, by mines and by hastily erected artillery, before they encountered the German fleet. Finally, if the British decided to divide their battle squadrons into two, this would present the intact German force, exploiting the inner line of the Kaiser-Wilhelm-Kanal, with an even more favourable opportunity for victory over a diminished enemy fleet.[28] Blithely opining that this proposed action was not to mean the political control of Denmark, but was rather to secure that country's independence, Bendemann also reported to the Kaiser that further co-operation would be necessary between army and navy in order to implement such a policy at the outset of war; to this Wilhelm readily gave his sanction. While inter-service studies of an invasion

of England petered to a halt, therefore,[29] those concerning an invasion of
Denmark were begun. Yet even in Schlieffen's first reply to the Admiralty
Staff's request, a hint emerges of what was to prove to be the Achilles'
heel in Bendemann's strategy if international relations between the Great
Powers underwent further change. The Chief of General Staff was willing
to consider an advance into Denmark in the case of war with Britain alone,
but added:

> If England has one or perhaps even two great powers as allies on the
> continent, then the parts of the German army capable of offensive actions
> would be completely tied to operations on the country's borders.[30]

Since Schlieffen did not include the Danish border in this category, the
implications were obvious: the army was being prepared almost exclusively
for the execution of the great two-fronted plan to which the Chief of
General Staff was to give his name, and any other operation was regarded
as a distraction. Offensives against Denmark were not part of this grand
scheme, as the navy should have known; in 1892, in replying to a high
command request for the occupation of Denmark in the event of war
against the Dual Alliance, Schlieffen had emphasised that all available
troops would be employed elsewhere, on the east and west fronts.[31] If
Britain were allied with a continental power against Germany, these same
conditions would apply; and even in the case of an Anglo-German war
alone, which Schlieffen clearly did not consider a likely contingency, he
did not wish to go further than an occupation of Fünen (Fyn) Island by
one division.

Despite this unpromising answer from the army, it was agreed by both
services that a small joint committee should be set up to consider operations
on Danish territory in more detail. For the navy, which regarded war with
Britain alone as the most likely possibility of all and had placed all its
hopes upon a defensive strategy in the Baltic, it was necessary to secure
many forms of military assistance, such as the establishment of gun emplace-
ments, observation posts and guarded anchorages, and for this reason
considerable importance was attached to these discussions; for Schlieffen,
the matter was an irritation and it was probably upon his account that,
although detailed investigations of the seizure of Danish islands continued
apace, no final decision over the implementation of this strategy was reached
in the years following.[32] This in turn worried the naval planners, who also
opposed Schlieffen's parallel refusal to increase the army's commitment to
the defence of the Frisian and other North Sea islands. The Admiralty
Staff reasoned in 1901.

> The negative attitude of the army is fully understandable when one realises
> that the strategical basis upon which the (Army-Navy) negotiations of
> 1896 rested was the case of a war between Triple and Dual Alliances, in
> which naturally the highest demands would be made upon the army.
> Today however the political situation is somewhat different. Following the
> vigorous expansion of our navy there is no need to fear the danger of a

successful offensive action by the fleets of the Dual Alliance or France alone against our coasts, provided that a considerable weakening of our home battleship force to the benefit of overseas stations does not take place.

On the other hand, the case of a war between Germany and England, which was earlier in the background, must be seriously brought into the circle of our operational preparations, and England's superiority is at present and in the foreseeable future so large that we must reckon under all circumstances with a swift, energetic and continuous offensive against our coasts, especially the North Sea ones. The same or similar naval relations will also occur in any alliance-war in which England stands against us as an enemy. Since, however, the case of a war between Germany alone against the Dual Alliance *and* England does not need to be considered, the result is that the present discussions over the defence of the Frisian Islands must proceed from a strategical basis which allows the army a far greater freedom of action than was the case upon the assumption of a war between Triple and Dual Alliances.[33]

The fact that Tirpitz, too, invariably opposed any extra expenditure upon fixed defences, preferring to devote funds to further surface vessels, precluded the possibility that these North Sea islands would be substantially reinforced;[34] but the army's reluctance to commit itself willingly to the proposed Denmark operation was more important and unnerved the Admiralty Staff. The latter considered an English alliance with France and Russia to be completely unrealistic but was becoming increasingly alarmed at the steady build-up of the Royal Navy's forces in home waters by 1902. Admiral von Koester, the Commander of the Training Fleet, had already pointed to the higher state of efficiency of Britain's reserve squadrons and to the joint manoeuvres of the Channel and Mediterranean Fleets, which meant that it was at least conceivable for the Royal Navy to have twenty-nine first-class battleships off Germany's North Sea harbours one day after the outset of war. Captain Souchon re-emphasised this later in the year:

England is in the position to deploy three times as many ships against us in our waters and in addition to keep back sufficient forces for its coasts and main trading routes . . . If this is accepted, then we ought not to reckon upon the favourable chance of deploying our entire fighting force against a weak part of the English naval forces. In the North Sea as in the Baltic the part of the English forces will be superior to our entire fleet.[35]

For this reason, the Admiralty Staff continued for the next two years to urge that any future military operations against Denmark in a war with Britain should be as thorough and extensive as possible, even including the seizure of Copenhagen. Yet Schlieffen was quick to point out that this would take approximately two full army corps, which he insisted could not be withdrawn from the major fronts; perhaps, he suggested in 1903, it would be better to leave Denmark alone altogether.[36] By the following year, moreover, the creation of the Anglo-French *entente* further weakened the Admiralty Staff's struggle to close the Baltic entrances. When Bendemann's successor, Büchsel, strove to be allowed to effect a separate mobilisation of the navy against Britain alone in case of need, Schlieffen protested furiously:

> One cannot reject the most earnest suspicion that in this case France will be England's ally. Should England declare war on Germany, then France would follow that example within the shortest time. The first declaration must therefore be the signal for Germany to mobilise its entire army and fleet, if need be to institute a preventive war against France ('nöthigenfalls Frankreich gegenüber das Prävenire zu spielen'). To prejudice the execution of this general mobilisation by a preceding partial one would be ruinous to a high degree.[37]

Although the reply to this from the Chancellor's office (drafted by Holstein) suggested that the dispute was 'purely academic', Büchsel took alarm at the army's attitude, fearing that the only possible offensive action the navy could undertake in a war against Britain was being excluded, and that at a time when the two nations appeared to be moving towards a state of hostilities. In the crisis period of the Russo-Japanese war, when the Dogger Bank incident had brought the Anglo-German naval rivalry into the open for the first time and provoked German fears of being 'Copenhagen-ed', this dispute came to a head. At a meeting between Wilhelm, Bülow, Schlieffen and Tirpitz on 18 November 1904, the decision appeared to go to the navy: the army was ordered to keep two army corps in readiness near the Danish border even though the possibility of France joining Britain against Germany could not be excluded.[38] According to Tirpitz, Schlieffen had been silent at that conference but the Chief of General Staff made his influence felt by the beginning of the next year. Moreover, he was joined by a very worried Bülow, whose policy of the 'free hand' had been greatly affected by the *entente cordiale*, the course of the Russo-Japanese war and the Anglo-German naval scare of 1904–5. Although Tirpitz had recently opposed the idea of an alliance with Russia, on the grounds that this would increase the risk of an English attack upon the still weak German fleet, the Chancellor felt compelled to treat the Russians with great care and feared that the occupation of the Belts would provoke a hostile reaction in St Petersburg.[39] Therefore, Büchsel's proposal for a swift operation to seize *both* sides of the channels, justifying this with the words 'In order to defend our Baltic coasts in the case of war between Germany and a sea power, certain encroachments upon the neutrality of Denmark and Sweden would be essential', fell upon deaf ears.[40] With both Bülow and Schlieffen against him, Büchsel was forced to give way, informing Tirpitz on 18 February 1905,

> His Majesty the Kaiser has recently ordered that the navy has *not* to count upon the assistance of the army in a strategical defensive in its operations in the Belts. His Majesty the Kaiser has arrived at this alteration in the previous basis for the deployment of his fleet because on the one hand the Chancellor has recently expressed important doubts from a political standpoint while on the other hand the army cannot provide the troops necessary for the occupation of Danish territory without making success in another place questionable.[41]

The final words quoted above indicate again that the quarrel between army and navy was not confined to military considerations of Denmark's position alone; in fact, there was an almost perfect corollary in their respective attitudes to small neutrals in the west, particularly Belgium. For Schlieffen, the two army corps desired by the Admiralty Staff for Denmark were of crucial importance to strengthen his planned great sweep through Belgium in time of war. To Büchsel, this was doubly disastrous, for the navy not only saw its Baltic scheme collapse but also earnestly desired that Belgium and the Netherlands should remain neutral.

Büchsel's regard for the neutrality of the Low Countries was as pragmatic and cold-blooded as Schlieffen's for Denmark and Sweden. The navy held that the first action of the British in a war with Germany would be to attempt a close blockade of her foe's maritime commerce, and in such a situation the Dutch and Belgian ports would acquire even more importance for German overseas trade than in peacetime. If the army over-ran those countries, the British would have little hesitation in blockading their harbours and in seizing their colonies. In terms of naval strategy and world opinion, Germany had nothing to gain by such an act. It might well be that the Royal Navy would disregard the accepted practice concerning neutral shipping in time of war and blockade the ports of the Low Countries in any case, but this could possibly lead to complications with the United States; and Büchsel disliked the idea that all prospects of Germany benefiting from this uncertain situation should be completely extinguished by Schlieffen's obsession with his army's right wing.[42]

The decision of February 1905 did not altogether prevent further questioning by the navy of Germany's actions against her small neighbouring states in the case of war with Britain, or with Britain and France.[43] As late as 1910 the Admiralty Staff was uncertain what exactly the army planned to do in the west and wished again to point out the benefits which might accrue to Germany from leaving the Low Countries alone; a hint from a General Staff officer, who intimated that Holland's neutrality would be respected but was 'very reserved' about Belgium, satisfied this curiosity for a while.[44] A further attempt to have the matter raised in 1912–13 was hindered by the army's reluctance to confer about it – especially with civilian authorities such as the Foreign Ministry and the Chancellery – and the Admiralty Staff was by then resigned to seeing both Belgium and the Netherlands over-run if the General Staff so wished.[45] In subsequent conversations and exchanges over Denmark the army was even more rigid. In March 1908, Moltke assured Baudissin, the new Chief of Admiralty Staff, that while he anticipated large-scale landings by the British on the Danish and German coasts in the event of war with the Triple Entente, this would not greatly affect the main area of operations; in November 1909, he further warned that, even if Denmark freely joined Germany as an ally, obligations to defend her should not be made 'at the cost of our major operations'; and in September 1911 Chief Quarter-Master Stein emphasised that 'even if Denmark under compulsion from the enemy could not completely fulfil its neutrality obligations towards us, we would not be able to retaliate against Denmark by active proceedings'.[46]

The General Staff's veto upon the use of troops in Denmark naturally caused the entire recasting of the Admiralty Staff's plans, and led to years of internal argument over the best strategy to adopt against a Britain which was concentrating more and more of her naval strength in the North Sea and which could now possibly count upon the support of the French navy too. Even without the collapse of the scheme to hold the Baltic entrances, the situation was worsening. During the crisis at the end of 1904 one officer at the Imperial Navy Office was reduced to proposing that an alliance with the United States might be bought at the cost of Germany's colonies in the Pacific and China. Bendemann more realistically suggested that a strictly defensive strategy would have to be implemented.[47] This latter policy was adopted by Büchsel early in 1905, in his first attempt to draft a new operational plan following the unsuccessful appeals to the Kaiser over Denmark. It would now be foolish, the Chief of Admiralty Staff argued, to make the Kattegat the main area for the deployment of the battle fleet, since without security from the land it would be impossible to establish the torpedo-boat bases and minefields there which were vital to reduce the enemy's overwhelming superiority. Moreover, 'in view of the threatening probability that the English will begin war with an assault upon one or more important points on our North Sea coast' they had no alternative but to keep the battle force near the Heligoland Bight if a conflict seemed about to break out. In the unlikely event of the Royal Navy entering the Baltic in force, a German fleet based on the Elbe would be able to disrupt its line of communications to Rosyth; but if the attacker sent only light forces through the Belts, then the German Third Battle Squadron (at Danzig) would be able to take care of them. It would be necessary to create better defences for the Elbe and its approaches against any form of English attack and to instruct the Commander-in-Chief, High Seas Fleet, to maintain a defensive strategy except where favourable opportunities offered themselves near the German coast; a full offensive should only be undertaken when the English superiority in numbers had been reduced by the rigours of blockade, and the Commander-in-Chief must be warned against senseless and risky sorties. Despite the risks to morale, this was the only possible strategy left to them.[48]

There were also political reasons for this defensive posture, unmentioned in Büchsel's memorandum but made explicit by him a year later: despite the suspicion that a war with Britain would also bring the Dual Alliance (or at least France) onto the side of Germany's enemy, a modified form of Tirpitz's risk theory still held sway. A reduction in the Royal Navy's strength by submarine and torpedo-boat attacks upon blockading forces might lead to a favourable opportunity for a decisive fleet action:

> Even if our fleet were to a great part destroyed in this action it is still possible that the total losses of the English fleet would be so great that it could no longer fully maintain naval mastery in the North Sea in relation to the attitude of powers friendly to us and to the rest of the warships remaining to us. But this regard for the political situation also argues

against a swift inducement of a decision at sea. So long as it is not finally established that Germany has to fight it out alone, the existence of the German fleet works as a power factor which can be of significant influence upon the decisions of other nations.[49]

Other influential bodies felt a similar interest in maintaining a 'fleet in being' for political reasons. In March 1907 Büchsel reported a conversation in which

the State Secretary for Foreign Affairs held it to be very necessary with regard to neutral powers in a German-French-English conflict to avoid our opponents having successes at sea at the outbreak of war. Every naval victory of Germany, especially near the enemy's coast, however small, would work extraordinarily favourably. The Chief of General Staff expressed the opinion that it would be unwelcome for the army if the English achieved unrestricted naval mastery in the North Sea soon after the start of the war and therewith the possibility of transporting troops in chosen directions.[50]

It was only a small consolation for the Chief of Admiralty Staff to feel that the British naval concentration in home waters which Tirpitz's fleet programme had provoked was weakening that power's influence in the rest of the world – for this was no help strategically to the High Seas Fleet and quite the reverse of the former argument that such overseas interests would keep the Royal Navy weak in the North Sea.[51]

One consequence of this change in the German operations plan was the greater attention paid to the defences of the North Sea coastline, especially around the Elbe estuary. In another lengthy memorandum of early 1906, Büchsel demonstrated that these defences would be totally inadequate in the event of a surprise English attack and not much improved if 24 hours' advance warning of such an attack were given: hence 'the pressing necessity that we must continually work for the improvement of the war-readiness of each point'. In particular, Cuxhaven should be turned into a first-class fortress now that the High Seas Fleet was to be based on the Elbe; Heligoland and other offshore islands required improved defences; fortifications, batteries, underwater defences, docks, information services were all required.[52] This even Tirpitz confessed would be a necessity, although he felt that money should only be allocated for defences in places such as Heligoland which could assist an offensive sortie by the battle fleet.[53] His agreement led to a mass of planning and preparations in the years following, and to a steady improvement in the defensive capabilities of certain points – developments which, though unknown to the Germans, were parallelled by the increasing realisation on the British side that assaults upon the German coastline during a purely Anglo-German war would be difficult tactically and useless strategically.[54]

A growing awareness upon the German side of this very point, that the British might act much more cautiously than had hitherto been assumed, was to have little effect upon Büchsel's new operations plan for some years.

Tirpitz's basic strategic tenets, developed in the late 1890s, still held sway although a number of Admiralty Staff officers had long been in some doubt about how the Royal Navy would act in time of war.[55] In early 1904 Büchsel himself had pressed for preparations for vigorous commerce raiding in time of war since 'through this one can force England to a close blockade, which perhaps it might otherwise avoid';[56] and in the revised operations plan drawn up for 1906 the possibility that the British might *not* undertake an offensive all along the German coast was mentioned although discounted. Even at the time of its formulation, the official plan came under attack from Admiral Koester, then Commander of the active battle fleet, who criticised it as being too defensive and restricted in its nature, arguing that a waiting policy was not the best way to defeat the British, who would be permitted by it to recall further vessels from overseas stations at leisure.[57] This caused Büchsel to rephrase his directives in the following two years, permitting the C-in-C, High Seas Fleet, to institute an offensive sortie if he was convinced that circumstances assured Germany of a certain victory; but even here the restrictions imposed by the Admiralty Staff upon vigorous action by the battle fleet were many. However, a real change in the German naval operations plans against England had to await the replacement of Büchsel by Vice-Admiral Baudissin at the beginning of 1908. One of his first moves was to inquire cautiously of the General Staff whether it still felt that the fleet should be held back at the outset of war and, upon receiving Moltke's reply that the army did not wish to restrict the navy's freedom of action, Baudissin was able to develop his ideas further with his colleagues.[58] At an audience of 12 March 1908, he argued before the Kaiser that the most recent British manoeuvres had shown that the Royal Navy would not send its battleships close to the German coast; it would therefore be necessary to attack the enemy's light blockading forces, possibly with the entire High Seas Fleet, in order to reduce his numerical superiority, and even a full fleet action should be risked if circumstances permitted it.[59]

This was only the beginning of Baudissin's campaign, however, and in the late autumn of that year he requested permission for the High Seas Fleet to be fully set free. Whether the Royal Navy instituted a close blockade or a more distant one, it would have succeeded in cutting off Germany's maritime commerce with the outside world and a waiting strategy on the part of the German navy would have little effect upon this; in any case, such a strategy was also prejudiced by the length of time it took for the main battle fleet to sortie from the entrance to the Elbe. The natural role of sea-going warships was the offensive and the sooner this was effected, the better. Baudissin's daring completey won over Wilhelm who remarked that 'the explicit offensive only corresponded with his wishes, though a similar strategy in the first years of our development had been impossible'.[60] The Chief of Admiralty Staff had also captured the imagination of Prince Henry of Prussia, the new C-in-C, High Seas Fleet, with 'the possibility of a sortie against the Scottish coast' and persuaded Admiral von Fischel, Commander of the North Sea Station, that 'to use a High Seas Fleet for the local defence of river mouths would be the same as if we allotted our

Field Army to defend our fortresses'.[61] As a result, although a defensive operations plan was still to be kept up to date in case circumstances compelled its use, the new directive to the C-in-C, High Seas Fleet, now read:

> Your task is to do the greatest possible damage to the enemy, risking all the forces at your disposal. To that end you should attack the enemy at sea with all available forces. If you do not encounter the foe during the first sortie, then some of his coastal areas (listed in the appendix) are to be strewn with mines and hostile shipping is also to be destroyed by other means as far as possible.[62]

By the following autumn, Baudissin had exchanged posts with Fischel but the new Chief of Admiralty Staff showed no inclination to alter his predecessor's strategy; in fact, he re-emphasised the importance of an offensive sortie in terms reminiscent of the doctrines of Mahan:

> In the final analysis we are fighting for access to the ocean, whose entrances on that side of the North sea are in England's hands. However the war may be fought, we are therefore basically the attacker, who is disputing the enemy's possession. The Navy Law allows for this, in that it has laid the main point of our sea power upon battleships. Thus both the aim of our strategy and the special nature of our naval development equally suggest to us that the decision be sought on the high seas.[63]

Unfortunately for the Admiralty Staff, however, the Nelsonic vigour implicit in this plan was already being undermined by a further aspect of Germany's 'naval development' – the launching of the first German Dreadnought-style battleships, the *Nassau* class, which were too large to pass through the Kaiser-Wilhelm-Kanal until the broadening operations upon the latter had been completed approximately six years later. Since all new German warships were worked up to full efficiency in the Baltic before joining the fleet, the *Nassau* battleships would be forced to reach the Elbe at or after the outset of war by means of the forty-hour journey around Denmark, thereby running the grave risk of being intercepted and overwhelmed by a superior enemy force. To avoid this, it would be necessary to dispatch the High Seas Fleet into the Baltic via the canal first of all to join up with the *Nassaus* for this trip. Yet the prospect of bringing the entire force back to the Elbe via the Belts, Kattegat and Skaggerak was not a pleasant one, although the Admiralty Staff insisted that it had to be done since the North Sea was the main operational area. The attitude of Denmark became more important than ever, but despite these considerations there was little hope of persuading the General Staff to alter its attitude about operations against Germany's northern neighbour. Most important of all, Baudissin's strategy of an immediate and energetic thrust against the Firth of Forth by the High Seas Fleet at the outbreak of war would be greatly prejudiced if that force were first of all required to assemble in the Baltic and then to pick its way through the Belts before emerging into the

North Sea: all surprise would be lost, as would a considerable amount of fuel.[64]

In addition, the Admiralty Staff's insistence upon a concentration of the fleet in the Elbe – a strategy which it was stated in 1906 was not to be deviated from even if an enemy force was wreaking havoc along the Baltic coastline – was coming under attack from other directions. An attempt at operational planning by officers in the Imperial Navy Office had led to a memorandum of May 1909 entitled 'Deployment off Heligoland or in the Kattegat?', in which the vote was only grudgingly given to the former region.[65] The arrival of Vice-Admiral von Holtzendorff as C-in-C, High Seas Fleet, late in 1909 led to further questioning of the offensive strategy. Holtzendorff at first declared himself willing to undertake an immediate sortie against the Firth at the outset of war during the high summer months but argued that his fleet would neither be fully prepared nor at full strength at any other time of the year; the winter months were especially bad in this respect. Since the local defences in the Heligoland Bight were in no way completed, he was reluctant to see the Elbe as his main base. Moreover, Holtzendorff did not like the odds against him and his opposition to an offensive in the winter months gradually extended to bring a more general objection. His battle fleet, even without the new Dreadnoughts, was the core of the German navy and should only be used under favourable circumstances. The latter would most probably come about, he insisted, if he could deploy his fleet in the Baltic. If it was fully prepared when war broke out, it should cruise in the Skaggerak and await the right moment for action; if it was not ready, it should only go as far as the Belts and then retreat upon encountering the enemy's battle fleet, tempting it into a situation where torpedo-boats, submarines and mines could be employed until a balance of forces was achieved. Even in 1909, he could argue that 'the history, national character and military purpose' of the British would cause them to force the Baltic entrances regardless of loss. Finally, Holtzendorff felt, Heligoland and the Elbe region should be left to look after itself.[66] The pendulum of the basic strategical argument was swinging again in favour of the defensive and a concentration in the Baltic.

The reaction in the Admiralty Staff to these arguments was at first very hostile, as their marginal comments upon Holtzendorff's submission clearly show;[67] but the state of the battle fleet that winter was admittedly very weak and Fischel's influence was not great – Tirpitz, ever suspicious of rival empire-builders, had seen to that. A compromise was arrived at on 12 November 1909, when a conference between the two sides agreed that while an energetic offensive would be implemented in wartime if a lucky chance (*Glücksfall*) occurred, Holtzendorff should be permitted to dispose and arrange the High Seas Fleet for a 'waiting offensive'. Nevertheless, Fischel only regarded that strategy, which he referred to more bluntly elsewhere as a 'defensive' one, as a temporary measure and was in no way inclined to agree that it should prevail when the readiness of the High Seas Fleet had improved. In a letter to Holtzendorff three days later, he restated his belief that an offensive in the North Sea was the ideal policy, which would only be substituted by a more cautious one if all prospects for success were excluded from the beginning. With regard to the newer Dreadnoughts which were too wide to pass through the Kaiser-Wilhelm-Kanal, the Admiralty Staff maintained that the best solution would be for them to join the Fleet at the Elbe as soon after trials as possible, to avoid being cut off in the Baltic if war occurred.[68]

This clash of opinion between the C-in-C, High Seas Fleet, and the Admiralty Staff continued for the two years following, even after Fischel had been succeeded by Vice-Admiral von Heeringen in March 1911; there is no indication that Holtzendorff ever accepted the opinions of the Admiralty Staff or that the latter was ever able to assert its claim to full supremacy in the field of strategic planning. Yet with the launching of further Dreadnoughts, the question of the deployment of the High Seas Fleet at the outset of war – and therewith the prospects of a swift offensive across the North Sea – had become very important by 1912. By this stage, Heeringen was subjecting Holtzendorff's views to strong attack: a sweep by the fleet from the Baltic would be sure to alert the enemy and allow him to adopt the better tactical position; it would waste more fuel; the long voyage would strain the accompanying torpedo-boats; and if contact with hostile warships was not made quickly, the fleet would soon have to retrace its lengthy route back to Kiel. The notion that the Dreadnoughts and pre-Dreadnoughts should only join up in the Skaggerak as one force after war had begun Heeringen dismissed as foolish: the High Seas Fleet could not afford to be caught piecemeal by a superior enemy. It was also foolish to maintain that the capital ships of the Royal Navy would be drawn into the Belts.[69]

That the Kaiser agreed to Heeringen's arguments early in 1912 was probably due to the support the latter was receiving at this time from Tirpitz. The State Secretary's arguments, as was often the case, touched upon political as well as strategical reasons. A planned concentration in Danish waters at the outbreak of war would mean that the fleet would normally be based at Kiel, a virtual acknowledgement to the world that it could not prevent a North Sea blockade by the enemy. A disappointed nation, continued Tirpitz, would with right query what their great financial sacrifices had been for and the navy's policy would appear as 'bankrupt'. Having scored very heavily on this point, he also argued that the German Bight was far superior to the Kattegat for the fleet whether an offensive or a defensive strategy were adopted against Britain.[70]

At this, the lengthy prewar debate over the merits of the North Sea or Baltic as the main operational area of the High Seas Fleet was concluded; but the decision was accompanied by a reversion from an offensive to a waiting strategy. Tirpitz had hinted in his memorandum that he favoured the latter by arguing that an assembly and sortie of the fleet from the Baltic would almost certainly lead to a decisive naval battle, which in some cases the German navy would do better to avoid; a fleet based on the Elbe was in a more favourable position to accept or reject battle. The Admiralty Staff was also becoming opposed to Baudissin's original scheme, although with more reluctance. In the days of growing tension before an Anglo-German war broke out, it was clear that the British Admiralty would direct its battle squadrons to 'before war positions'; a surprise raid by the High Seas Fleet was therefore impossible and the great size and efficiency of the Royal Navy made a toe-to-toe battle far from home a near-suicidal venture for the German navy. It would be a more sensible strategy to await the British attempts to blockade Germany's North Sea ports and to seek battle around Heligoland. The war directives to the C-in-C, High Seas Fleet, approved of by the Kaiser on 3 December 1912, were therefore once again changed, to the following:

1 The war is to be carried out from the German Bight.
2 The chief war task should be to damage the blockading forces of the enemy as far as possible through numerous and repeated attacks day and night, and *under favourable circumstances* to give battle with all the forces at your disposal . . .[71]

So much was this waiting policy adhered to that the idea of sending out the High Seas Fleet to interrupt the transport of British troops across the Channel to France and Belgium in the event of a European war was rejected in favour of U-boat attacks. War games and further memoranda in the years 1913–14, by which time Vice-Admiral von Pohl had taken over as Chief of Admiralty Staff, served only to confirm the official strategy. It is true that the British fleet manoeuvres in 1913 were clearly postulated upon the policy of a wide blockade and that this caused the Admiralty Staff to think of a 'distant offensive'; but this alternative appeared upon closer investigation to be far too risky whilst the High Seas Fleet was so numerically inferior. Only the U-boats and torpedo-boats should be deployed offensively, Pohl recommended in May 1914.[72] When war came, therefore, the directive to Vice-Admiral von Ingenohl of 30 July 1914 was cast in the same spirit if not words as those of the previous two years: the enemy's blockading squadrons would first of all be weakened until an approximate equalisation of forces existed, then the High Seas Fleet would emerge to give battle *provided* that the situation was favourable.

Even when it had become clear by the autumn of 1914 that the steady development of mines, torpedoes and submarines had compelled the Royal Navy to abandon the strategy of a close blockade, the German policy remained unchanged: the battle of the Dogger Bank confirmed the need to stay on the defensive and the material successes at Jutland did not alter this. In the final two years of the war, neither the British nor the German admiralty was willing to take risks which might lead to a worsening of its own strategical positions. A stalemate developed in which the British could not lose the surface war, even if they seemed to be unable to win it by means of a decisive fleet battle. In such circumstances, the Germans elected to preserve their battleships rather than to risk a full encounter, but this 'fleet in being' strategy caused a serious deterioration in morale and greatly reduced the effectiveness of the role Tirpitz had expected his navy to play in the struggle against England. Ironically, the decision in the final month of the war to adopt an energetic offensive by the High Seas Fleet was wrecked neither by the enemy nor by strategical factors but simply by the unrest among the crews.[73] It was difficult to expect the ordinary sailor, wearied by the war and aware that peace was in the offing, to accept the idea of a reckless offensive against a much larger enemy when his superiors had for so long eschewed such a policy.

Examined in strict chronological order, the German naval planning for a war against England in the years 1896–1914 appears to have been exceedingly erratic and confused. This is certainly true but it might be more accurate to say that it was also extremely susceptible to changes on the broader military and political fronts. The very early schemes for a reckless offensive against the Thames were based upon despair at opposing such a powerful maritime rival as Britain and upon the knowledge that the Royal Navy was weak in home waters, considerations which underwent change by the turn of the century, when Tirpitz's 'risk fleet' was being rapidly constructed. The substitution of a defensive policy in the Baltic entrances was much more realistic strategically, especially when the British assembled more and more of their warships in home waters; but the General Staff's absolute refusal to divert forces intended for a two-front war to the overrunning of Denmark had thrown this strategy into confusion by 1905. Nor was it resolved by the adoption of a strictly defensive policy for the battle fleet based upon the Elbe, and by 1908 Baudissin had broken completely free of these ideas, arguing that Germany's only chance of victory at sea lay in a surprise strike against the Firth. No sooner had his viewpoint triumphed, however, than it was undermined by the launching of the German Dreadnoughts and the opposition of Holtzendorff. The alternative strategy of deploying the High Seas Fleet in the Baltic was beaten off after much debate but only at the cost of the offensive plan itself. By 1914 the German navy was still anticipating a naval battle which would take place under circumstances favourable to it, and in the first few days of the war Pohl could agree that 'the "defensive" of the English fleet begins at the enemy's coast'.[74] Such a calculation was so obviously a reflection of the basic strategic concepts of Tirpitz that a summary of the Grand Admiral's role and influence in operational planning is probably worthwhile before bringing this study to a close. Ostensibly, this would be a difficult task on anthing other than a superficial level. Tirpitz had been much more of a tactical than a strategical thinker before he took over the Imperial Navy Office, where all his energies were needed to create and enlarge his battle fleet. Also, his later works are written with far too much hindsight and with the need to defend his former policies as reliable indications of his prewar thinking. Finally, the Admiralty Staff, although never able to exert its independence in planning, did exist as the department of the navy responsible for all the official operational drafts and plans. Nevertheless, sufficient material exists for a reasonably full picture of Tirpitz's connections with the planning. It is to be remembered here that Büchsel, Fischel, Heeringen and Pohl had all served under Tirpitz in the Imperial Navy

Office and regarded themselves as his men, even though their assumption of the post of Chief of Admiralty Staff presented them with different responsibilities and, occasionally, priorities. They kept him reasonably well informed of the changes in their operations plans by means of joint audiences with the Kaiser and inter-departmental correspondence and, especially during the navy scares with Britain after 1904, through confidential conversations with him. When, moreover, they were hostile to him, their period of office was short-lived: Diederichs and Baudissin are good examples of this.

In fact, merely to list Tirpitz's frequent appearances in the chronological narrative above is to answer the question about his influence upon strategic planning. It was he who insisted upon the creation of a battle fleet in the North Sea as the basic policy of the German navy, and who rejected all idea of commerce-raiding or of invading England; he who had control of decisions about fortifications for Heligoland and the North Sea naval bases, which so concerned the Admiralty Staff; he who was consulted over the question of Danish neutrality and who accepted Büchsel's revised plan when Schlieffen finally triumphed; he, more than anyone, who was aware of the consequences of building Dreadnoughts which could not pass through the existing Kaiser-Wilhelm-Kanal; he who criticised his own staff in 1909 for thinking that a simple 'fleet in being' strategy was the official policy then;[75] he who opposed Holtzendorff's arguments for concentration of the fleet in the Baltic; and finally he who advised upon a change from the offensive in 1912. This waiting policy, despite his later assertions to the contrary, he fully accepted at the outset of the war; even in 1915, when a change of policy was clearly necessary if the strategic stalemate in the North Sea was to be ended, Tirpitz felt that a reckless offensive would be unwise until the relative fleet strengths had altered in Germany's favour. Though he was not involved in the detailed day-to-day preparation of war plans, it seems fair to conclude that no major changes in strategic policy occurred without his knowledge and approval.

One aspect of his overall strategy in the event of war with England, the role of commerce-raiding and operations in the colonies, amply illustrates this control and influence. Although the ideas of the *jeune école* were attracting much interest in Germany in the 1890s and although Bülow's promotion as foreign minister symbolised the nation's turn to *Weltpolitik*, Tirpitz had insisted as early as 1897 that

> commerce-raiding and transatlantic war against England is so hopeless, because of the shortage of bases on our side and the superfluity on England's side, that we must ignore this type of war against England in our plans for the constitution of the fleet.[76]

This influence could be seen in the high command, where Knorr in early 1898 had been encouraging the Kaiser to take advantage of the entanglement of the United States in the Spanish-American war by securing the Danish and Dutch West Indies as prospective naval bases; three months later, in a second memorandum which touched upon acquisitions in the Pacific, he was compelled to remind Wilhelm that even an ideal overseas fleet base would be useless unless all energies were concentrated first upon building a fleet.[77] As Truppel, then in the Admiralty Staff, wrote: 'First the fleet, then the bases. That (the latter) has another 10 years' time.'[78] Despite the Kaiser's glee at the acquisitions of the Carolines and Samoa in 1899, the Admiralty Staff poured cold water upon the idea of developing them as fleet bases. Tirpitz himself was uneasy at the acquisition of Kiaochow, disapproved of the Venezuela actions, rather unwillingly assented to the operations against the Boxers and pressed for the return of those forces from the Far East as soon as possible. All warships sent overseas merely weakened his basic North Sea strategy. It is hardly a surprise to learn, therefore, that the German plans for commerce-raiding were far less advanced or controversial (despite occasional criticisms from naval writers such as Valois, Maltzahn and Galster) than those for the battle fleet. In fact, although the small cruiser detachments in the tropics did have operational instructions in the event of war with Britain, there was little attempt after 1897 to develop a more general scheme for this type of warfare. Moreover, it was often only advocated by the Admiralty Staff as a means of either drawing away British vessels from the crucial North Sea region or of forcing the enemy to institute a close blockade which he might otherwise be inclined to avoid. Thus, although by the approach of war the policy of commerce-raiding had become more properly organised, Tirpitz had ensured that it was never regarded as anything other than a side-affair, a strategic distraction.[79] As for the defences of the German colonies, he was insisting as late as July 1914 that that was not the responsibility of the navy.[80] Yet if German naval operations plans against Britain in the pre-1914 period bore the firm imprint of Tirpitz's own ideas, it is equally interesting to note the extent to which a number of experienced Admiralty Staff officers expressed doubts from time to time upon the validity of some of his basic strategical assumptions. Since these officers lacked Tirpitz's political influence and personal power, their viewpoints made little impression upon established strategy; but this does at least suggest that his calculations were not as obvious and 'natural' as his defenders have claimed. In particular, doubts were expressed upon two key aspects of Tirpitz's strategy towards England: that the Royal Navy would be able to deploy only part of its strength in the North Sea because of its other commitments, and that it would institute a close blockade of the German coast at the outset of war. From March 1896 onwards, certain officers had felt it necessary to point out that war was unlikely to break out with Britain before the Royal Navy had assembled a large fleet in home waters. Just after the turn of the century, Büchsel had expressed doubts about a close blockade by the Royal Navy, and the growing awareness that a waiting policy by the High Seas Fleet might turn out to be strategically useless was the chief reason for Baudissin's more offensive scheme in 1909; yet Tirpitz never altered his conviction that the British would come across the North Sea and present the High Seas Fleet with a favourable opportunity for victory.[81]

These are by no means the only criticisms which have been made of Tirpitz's naval policy: his financial calculations were unsound, his internal political ones too optimistic; his belief that Germany would achieve technical superiority in warships was questionable, as was his assumption that her favourable diplomatic position would remain unchanged; his hope that she would be able to pass safely through a 'danger zone' was simply naive in view of British sensitivity to any naval challenges. Yet such mistakes, grave though they were, pale in comparison with his miscalculations in the strategical field, where he should have been much more at home. For him not to have considered until it was too late that the British might neutralise his challenge by concentrating the Royal Navy in the North Sea and by adopting the policy of the distant blockade seems incredible until one realises that he had simply transferred his fixed and deterministic way of thinking in political terms into the strategical arena. He had only *one* strategy and was deeply reluctant to accept that the grounds upon which it was based might be erroneous. The British concentration in the North Sea was a surprise to him but he could not bring himself to believe that they would also adopt a distant blockade. Perhaps it was psychologically impossible for him to consider this before 1914, since it would have meant admitting the virtual failure of his long-term hope to achieve *Gleichberechtigung* with the British.

The Admiralty Staff, living in the shadow of Tirpitz who saw to it that its duties were circumscribed, frustrated by the unco-operativeness of the General Staff, frequently opposed by the C-in-C, High Seas Fleet, and often knocked off course by circumstances beyond its control, was never in a position to have absolute authority for naval operational planning against Britain;[82] but it did honestly attempt to grapple with the basic military problem facing the German navy – how to evolve a strategy which offered some prospect of success against an enemy in the North Sea when both the numercial and the geographical balance was tilted against Germany. Most of the time it adhered to a defensive strategy but it was willing to admit of an alternative. It is not difficult to see that Baudissin's offensive scheme was rooted in the same mixture of hope and despair that characterised the very early operations plans under Knorr, and that it had only an outside chance of succeeding against such a well-prepared and formidable foe; it was therefore easy for Tirpitz or Holtzendorff or the political leaders of Germany to convince the Kaiser that a waiting policy was the best one for the fleet. Yet at least the Admiralty Staff recognised the key strategical fact of the Anglo-German naval race – that since it was Germany that was challenging Britain's naval predominance, it was also up to the High Seas Fleet to go out and give battle if this aim were ever to be realised. Given the geographical situation and the balance of forces, only the Royal Navy could safely institute a waiting policy: Germany certainly could not, despite the risks involved in the alternative strategy, and the directive that an offensive should only be undertaken 'under favourable circumstances' was almost bound to prevent a decisive fleet battle from ever occurring. It is of interest to note that the two scholars who have studied the respective British and German naval plans in most detail have both arrived at the conclusion that only by offensive sorties by the High Seas Fleet early in the war was there a chance of breaking Britain's control of the North Sea and its exits to the wider world.[83] Such a strategy, although effectively squashed by the return to the defensive in 1912, was never fully given up by the Admiralty Staff, much to its credit. One might fittingly conclude this survey with one final expression of the view of this school of thought that victory in war could only be achieved by taking risks. In April 1919, as the general hopelessness of the German navy's waiting policy had been made plain and as the High Seas Fleet was resting in captivity in Scapa Flow, a staff officer looking through the earlier operational planning documents discovered Heeringen's 1912 phrase about 'under favourable circumstances' and angrily wrote in the margin:

> The mistake lies here! This restriction upon the freedom of action (of the fleet) existed until 1908, then we conquered it, now it is there again. The central point of the question is: one cannot know *beforehand* if the opportunity is favourable, Result: wait, wait, wait![84]

NOTES

1 As with my previous ventures into this field, I am obliged to certain close friends and colleagues for their comments and encouragement, in particular Professor A. J. Marder, Dr V. R. Berghahn and Dr W. Deist.

2 On great power rivalries in the 1890s, see W. L. Langer, *The Diplomacy of Imperialism*, 2nd edn (New York 1951), still the best survey; and A. J. P. Taylor, *The Struggle for Mastery in Europe 1848–1918* (Oxford 1954), pp. 325–71.

3 The deterioration in the Anglo-German relationship is explored in more detail in T. A. Bayer, *England und der neue Kurs* (Tübingen 1955).

4 G. N. Sanderson, 'The African Factor in Anglo-German Relations, 1892–95' (unpublished paper for the Commonwealth and Overseas Seminar of the University of Cambridge); P. M. Kennedy, 'Anglo-German relations in the Pacific and the partition of Samoa, 1885–1899', in *Australian Journal of Politics and History*, XVII, no. 1 (1971), pp. 59–63.

5 C. J. Lowe, *The Reluctant Imperialists: British Foreign Policy 1878–1902*, 2 vols. (London 1967), Vol. I, p. 196.

6 Cited in L. M. Penson, 'The new course in British foreign policy 1892–1902', *Transactions of the Royal Historical Society*, 4th ser., XXV (1943), p. 128.

7 N. Rich, *Friedrich von Holstein*, 2 vols. (Cambridge 1965), Vol II, pp. 466–70; A. J. Marder, *The Anatomy of British Sea Power: A History of British Naval Policy in the Pre-Dreadnought Era, 1880–1905* (Hamden, Conn., 1964 reprint), pp. 256–9.

8 W. Hubatsch, *Der Admiralstab und die obersten Marinebehörden in Deutschland 1848–1945* (Frankfurt 1958), p. 65. That the decision to prepare an operations plan was a result of the Transvaal crisis is mentioned specifically in BA-MA (Bundesarchiv-Militärarchiv, Freiburg), F 5587, III, 1–10, vol. 1, memorandum of 2 February 1898 by Grapow. The bundle (or 'Fach') numbers 5586 and 5587 contain nine large volumes of documents entitled *Operationspläne gegen England – Ganz Geheim*, which have formed the core of this present study.

9 This is certainly very true on the German side in this period, where the institution of operations plans by the navy against France and Russia (early 1890s), Great Britain (1896), USA (1898–9), and Britain and France (1904–5) was clearly linked to the state of international politics.

10 The organisation of the German navy in these years, which had significant consequences upon the decision-making process in general and also upon the effectiveness of matters such as operations plans, is discussed in Hubatsch, *Admiralstab*, pp. 49–161.

11 For the state of the German navy in the mid-1890s, and in the years following, two recent studies are invaluable: J. Steinberg, *Yesterday's Deterrent: Tirpitz and the Birth of the German Battle Fleet* (London 1965); and V. R. Berghahn, *Der Tirpitz-Plan: Genesis und Verfall einer innenpolitischen Krisenstrategie unter Wilhelm II* (Düsseldorf, 1971).

12 BA-MA, F 5587, III, 1–10, Vol. I, Diederichs memorandum, Top Secret, 'Gesichtspunkte für einen Operationsplan der feindlichen Streitkräfte beieinem Kriege Deutschlands allein gegen England allein', 3 March 1896.

13 Comment of AIII of 11 March 1896 on the Diederichs memorandum. (Staff officers often preferred to give their numbers rather than signatures under a memorandum or minute, as above.)

14 ibid., Diederichs memorandum, 23 April 1896.

15 ibid., Knorr memorandum, 'Immediatvortrag Betreffend Grundzüge für einen Operationsplan Deutschlands allein gegen England allein', 31 May 1897; and an earlier draft, with the same title, of 20 May 1897. It is quite possible that these May 1897 memoranda also fulfilled Knorr's *political* aim of a greater fleet programme: see Berghahn, *Der Tirpitz-Plan*, p. 103.

16 BA-MA, F 5587, III, 1–10, Vol. 1, comments on Immediatvortrag document of 31 May 1897 by Knorr and Diederichs.

17 Howard R. Moon, 'The invasion of the United Kingdom: Public Controversy and Official Planning 1888–1918', 2 vols. (unpublished London PhD thesis, London, 1968), Vol. II, p. 656. Appendix A of Dr Moon's thesis contains a succinct summary of 'German Staff Considerations of the Invasion of England' around the turn of the century, although the dates and titles of certain documents which he used on microfilm do not exactly coincide with those in the original files in Freiburg.

18 BA-MA, F 5587, III, 1–10, Vol. 1, Knorr to Schlieffen, 2 June 1897. (All of the documents and especially the inter-departmental correspondence in these files are liberally adorned with the description 'O.[perations]-matter, Top Secret! From Hand to Hand!'

19 See also in this connection Chapter 7 of this book.

20 BA-MA, F 5587, III, 1–10, Vol. 1, Schlieffen to Knorr, 14 December 1897. See also Friedrich-Christian Stahl, 'Der Grosse Generalstab, seine Beziehungen zum Admiralstab und seine Gedanken zu den Operationsplänen der Marine', *Wehrkunde*, XII Jg. (1963), Heft 1, 10–11; idem., 'Armee und Marine im kaiserlichen Deutschland', *Die Entwicklung des Flottenkommandos* (Bd. IV, Beiträge zur Wehrforschung, Darmstadt, 1964), pp. 40–1; Moon, *Invasion of the United Kingdom*, pp. 658–60.

21 BA-MA, F 5587, III 1–10, Vol. 1, AIII[a] note of 5 January 1898.

22 ibid., AIII[b] memoranda of 16 December 1897 and 15 February 1898; ibid., Knorr note of 15 May 1898.

23 ibid., Knorr memorandum, 'Kriegführung gegen England', 12 September 1898. It is interesting to note that German naval operations plans against

the United States were of an equally fantastic nature at this time. See also Chapter 2 of this book.

24 Tirpitz's strategy is examined in more detail in P. M. Kennedy, 'Tirpitz, England and the second Navy Law of 1900: a strategical critique', *Militärgeschichtliche Mitteilungen*, no. 2 (1970); idem., 'Maritime Strategieprobleme der deutschenglischen Flottenrivalität', *Marine und Marinepolitik im kaiserlichen Deutschland 1871–1914*, ed. H. Schottelius and W. Deist (Düsseldorf, 1972).

25 Fürst Chlodwig zu Hohenlohe-Schillingsfürst, *Denkwürdigkeiten der Reichskanzlerzeit*, ed. K. A. von Müller (Stuttgart, 1931), p. 464.

26 BA-MA, Tirpitz Papers, N253/164, 'Auszug aus der Schrift Maltzahn, mit Randbemerkungen des Staatssekretärs' (copy).

27 For details of the second Navy Law, see Berghahn, *Tirpitz-Plan*, pp. 205–48; and also his discussion on pp. 286ff. of the Admiralty Staff's political *need* to provide the Kaiser with operational schemes in these years in order to justify its own *raison d'être* and to gain more personnel.

28 BA-MA, F 5587, III, no. 10, Vol. I, Bendemann memorandum, 'Die Defensive gegen England', November 1899; BA-MA, F 7639, Vol. III, Immediatvortrag memorandum, 12 December 1899.

29 Moon, *Invasion of the United Kingdom*, pp. 672–7.

30 BA-MA, F 5587, III, no. 10, Vol. I, Schlieffen to Diederichs, 16 January 1900.

31 Stahl, 'Armee und Marine im kaiserlichen Deutschland', p. 39.

32 The detailed plans can be found in BA-MA, F 5586, III, 1.0.10, 2 vols.

33 BA-MA, F 2016, PG 65958, Admiralty Staff memorandum, 'Zum Immediatvortrag betreffend den Schutz der friesischen Inseln', 11 January 1901.

34 BA-MA, F 5587, III, no. 10, Vol. I, Tirpitz to the Commander, North Sea Naval Station, 1 September 1902.

35 ibid., Koester to Wilhelm, no. 72 of 26 February 1902; ibid., Souchon memorandum, 'Krieg mit England', 22 November 1902.

36 BA-MA, F 5586, III, 1.0.10, Vol. I, Schlieffen to Büchsel, 6 August 1903.

37 AA (Auswärtiges Amt Archiv, Bonn), Deutschland 138 Geheim, vol. 6, War Ministry to Chancellor, Secret, 17 October 1904. See also BA-MA, F 5627, IV. 2–1, Vol. I, Büchsel to Tirpitz, 18 May 1904; Hubatsch, *Admiralstab*, p. 114.

38 BA-MA, F 5586, III. 1.0.10, Vol. II, Büchsel memorandum, 19 November 1904. See also BA-MA, F 2017, PG 65964, Büchsel minute of 3 December 1904 on Immediatvortrag document.

39 German policy in this complex period of late 1904–early 1905 has been covered in Berghahn, *Der Tirpitz Plan*, pp. 376–415; Rich, *Holstein*, Vol. II, pp. 678–729; Hubatsch, *Admiralstab*, pp. 119–20; J. Steinberg, 'The Copenhagen complex', *Journal of Contemporary History*, I, no. 3 (1966), 31–40; idem., 'Germany and the Russo-Japanese war', *American Historical Review*, LXXV, no. 7 (1970).

40 As recounted by Kiderlin in a memorandum of 14 November 1905 in AA, Deutschland 138 Geheim, vol. 6.

41 Quoted in Hubatsch, *Admiralstab*, p. 120. See also Steinberg, 'Copenhagen Complex', 36–7.

42 BA-MA, F 2045, PG 66077, Admiralty Staff 'Denkschrift über die Kriegführung gegen England 1905', partly reproduced in Hubatsch, *Admiralstab*, pp. 247–50.

43 See, e.g., BA-MA, F 5587, III. 1.N.10, Vol. 3, Admiralty Staff memorandum, 'Auszug aus einem vorläufigen Exposé über Blockadewirkungen bei einem Kriege Englands-Deutschlands', March 1906.

44 ibid., Vol. 5, Admiralty Staff memorandum, 'Unser Verhalten gegenüber Holland und Belgien in einem Kriege gegen England allein, und gegen England und Frankreich', 8 February 1910; ibid., memorandum by A. R. (Captain Rieve?), 24 February, 1910.

45 ibid., Vol. 6, Admiralty Staff to Chancellor (draft), 2 March 1912, with Behncke minute thereon, and Admiral Staff to General Staff (draft), 24 October 1912, with Heeringen note attached; ibid., Admiralty Staff memorandum, 'Direktiven für unser Verhalten gegen Holland und Belgien in einem Kriege Deutschlands mit England und Frankreich', 24 August 1912.

46 ibid., Vol. 4, Moltke to Baudissin, 9 March 1908; ibid., Moltke to Fischel, 2 November 1909; ibid., memorandum by AIV of 23 September 1911.

47 BA-MA, F 2045, PG 66077, Vollerthun memorandum, 'Politische und militärische Betrachtungen über einen englisch-deutschen Krieg', 27 November 1904. (Tirpitz's marginal comments indicate his scepticism at this scheme.) ibid., Bendemann memorandum (copy), Top Secret, 'Gedanken über die augenblickliche kritische Lage', 3 December 1904.

48 BA-MA, F 5587, III, 1.N.10, Vol. II, Büchsel memorandum, 'Denkschrift zum Immediatvortrag über den Aufmarsch und die Verwendung Euer Majestät Flotte im Kriege gegen England im Ms.–Jahre 1905', 20 March 1905.

49 ibid., 'Denkschrift über die Kriegführung gegen England 1906', March 1906. (Audience with the Kaiser held on 3 April 1906.)

50 Quoted in Captain Weniger, 'Die Entwicklung des Operationsplanes für die deutsche Schlachtflotte', *Marine Rundschau* (1930), 3. (This article is the first survey of German operations plans which used the naval records to some extent; but it lacks all references and avoids many delicate political points.)

51 BA-MA, F 5587, II. 1.N.10, Vol. II, Büchsel memorandum, 'Denkschrift zum Immediatvortrag über den Aufmarsch und die Verwendung Euer Majestät Flotte im Kriege gegen England im Ms.–Jahre 1905', 20 March 1906.

52 ibid., Büchsel memorandum, 'Immediatvortrag über O.P. II', 27 March 1906.

53 BA-MA, F 5648, IV–8.3, Vol. I, Tirpitz to Büchsel, 23 April 1906.

54 ibid., Vols. 1–3, which are entitled 'Akta betreffend Schutz und Verteidigung der deutschen Küsten'. British considerations of an assault upon the German coastline are described in great detail in Neil W. Summerton, *The Development of the British Military Planning for a War against Germany, 1904–14*, 2 vols. (unpublished PhD thesis, London 1970), pp. 34–49, 220–97, 320–41, 451–71, 622–8.

55 Kennedy, 'Maritime Strategieprobleme', *passim*.

56 BA-MA, F 5588, III, 1–10ª, Vol. 2, Büchsel memorandum, 8 January 1904. See also BA-MA, Büchsel Papers, N168/8, 'Immediatvortrag. Krieg England und Deutschland' (1903), in which he notes that 'for us the most dangerous tactic of the enemy would be to blockade us from afar and to avoid any offensive action'.

57 BA-MA, F 5587, III, 1.N.10, Vol. 3, Koester to Admiralty Staff, 17 February 1905.

58 ibid., Vol. 4, Baudissin to Moltke, 29 February 1908 and 25 March 1908, and replies of 9 March 1908 and 7 April 1908.

59 ibid., vol. 5, Baudissin memorandum, 'Immediatvortrag zur A.O. an den Chef der Hochseeverbände für den Krieg gegen England 1908', 12 March 1908.

60 ibid., Baudissin memorandum, 'Denkschrift zum Immediatvortrag', 24 October 1908.

61 ibid., Vol. 4, Baudissin notes of 29 October 1908, 31 October 1908 and 2 November 1908.

62 Quoted in Weniger, 'Die Entwicklung des Operationsplanes', 3.

63 BA-MA, F 5587, III, 1.N.10, Vol. 5, Admiralty Staff to Wilhelm (draft), 10 August 1910.

64 ibid., Fischel memorandum of 4 November 1909; ibid., Vol. 5, Prince Henry of Prussia to Baudissin, 31 July 1909.

65 BA-MA, F 2045, PG 66081, memorandum of von Usslar, von Bülow and Vollerthun, presented by Paschen, 17 June 1909.

66 BA-MA, F5587, III, 1.N.10, Vol. 4, Holtzendorff memorandum, 'Denkschrift des Flottenkommandos', 5 November 1909, enclosed in his letter to Fischel of 1 December 1909.

67 ibid.

68 ibid., Fischel to Holtzendorff, 15 December 1909; Hubatsch, *Admiralstab*, pp. 144–6.

69 ibid., Vol. 5, Heeringen to Holtzendorff, 28 December 1911; ibid., Heeringen 'Denkschrift zum Immediatvortrag', 10 January 1912 and 28 January 1912; ibid., Vol 6, Heeringen to Wilhelm, 6 February 1912.

70 ibid., Tirpitz to Wilhelm (copy), 2 December 1912.

71 ibid., Heeringen memorandum, 'Denkschrift zum Immediatvortrag', 28 November 1912; BA-MA, F 2020, PG 65975, 'Entwurf zum Operationsbefehl für den Krieg gegen England', 28 December 1912; Hubatsch, *Admiralstab*, pp. 150–2; Weniger, 'Die Entwicklung des Operationsplanes', 6.

72 BA-MA, F 2021, PG 65977, Pohl memorandum, 'Englische Flottenmanöver 1913' (presented in audience on 13 January 1914); ibid., Pohl memorandum, "Denkschrift zum Immediatvortrag über das strategische Kriegsspiel des Admiralstabes Winter 1913–14' (presented on 26 May 1914).

73 Weniger, 'Die Entwicklung des Operationsplanes', 6–10, 51–5, for a short resumé of the German plans 1912–18.

74 BA-MA, F 5522, II–E. 30, Vol. 3, Pohl minute on Müller to Tirpitz (copy), no. 689 of 30 July 1914.

75 BA-MA, F 2045, PG 66081, memorandum of von Usslar, von Bülow and Vollerthun, presented by Paschen, 17 June 1909, with Tirpitz's comments thereon.

76 Quoted in Steinberg, *Yesterday's Deterrent*, p. 209.

77 BA-MA, F 3419, PG 67346, Knorr to Wilhelm, 20 April 1898 and 13 July 1898.

78 BA-MA, F 5587, III, 1–10, Vol. I, Truppel marginal comment on Scheder memorandum of 5 January 1898.

79 The most detailed documents upon the general policy of commerce-raiding are in BA-MA, F 5167, III, 1–5ᵃ, Vol. I; and BA-MA, F 7639, Vol. 2. Copies of the immediate prewar instructions to German cruisers overseas are reproduced in E. Raeder, *Der Krieg zur See 1914–18. Der Kreuzerkrieg*

in den ausländischen Gewässern, 3 vols. (Berlin 1922–37), Vol 1, pp. 27–31.

80 P. M. Kennedy, 'The Partition of the Samoan Islands, 1898–9 (unpublished DPhil thesis, Oxford 1970), pp. 353–4.

81 For a more detailed discussion of the Admiralty Staff's differences of opinion over strategy with Tirpitz, and the failure to effect any changes, see Kennedy, 'Maritime Strategieprobleme', *passim*.

82 This unco-ordinated strategic planning system stands in obvious contrast to the successful work of the British Committee of Imperial Defence, although it must also be said that the teething problems of this latter body were immense and that it produced less unity on defence policy than German scholars have (rather wistfully) tended to suggest.

83 Weniger, 'Die Entwicklungen des Operationsplanes', 57–9; A. J. Marder, *From the Dreadnought to Scapa Flow*, 5 vols. (London 1961–70), Vol. II, pp. 42–6.

84 BA-MA, F 5587, III, 1.N.10, Vol. 6, marginal comment by Captain Tägert of April 1919 on Heeringen's 'Denkschrift zum Immediatvortrag', 28 December 1912.

9

The Significance of the Schlieffen Plan

L. C. F. TURNER

INTRODUCTION

Few historians would question the immense importance of the Schlieffen Plan which set the pattern for the opening battles and for much of the course of the First World War. Moreover, the plan strongly influenced the decisions taken by political and military leaders in July 1914, and must be regarded as a major factor in the chain of events which plunged Europe into war. Although historians have been referring to the plan for more than forty years, its text was not published until 1956, when Gerhard Ritter produced his outstanding study of the plan and its consequences.[1] The German official histories published between 1920 and 1939 gave only fragmentary information about the plan and, as a result, all discussions of the subject before 1956 reveal serious misconceptions. Ritter's conclusions, and those of Liddell Hart in the preface to the English edition of his book, are open to question on important points, while the publication of new material between 1956 and 1965 calls for a reassessment of some of Ritter's contentions. The purpose of this chapter is to examine the political and military implications of the Schlieffen Plan in the light of Ritter's writings and those of other authorities.

DEVELOPMENT OF THE PLAN, 1891–1906

When Count von Schlieffen became Chief of the German General Staff in 1891, he took over the plans for a two-front war, which had been designed by the elder Moltke and which had been adhered to basically by his successor, Waldersee. As is well known, Moltke was far from being dazzled by his victories in 1870; he did not believe that his rapid triumph over France could be repeated and his operational plans for a future war were marked by extreme caution. In 1879 Moltke outlined his strategy against France and Russia.[2]

If we must fight two wars . . . then, in my opinion, we should exploit in the west the great advantages which the Rhine and our powerful fortifications offer to the defensive and should employ all the fighting forces which are not absolutely indispensable [in the west] for an imposing offensive against the east.

Even Moltke's offensive against Russia was to be of a strictly limited character; the aim was to over-run Congress Poland and achieve a front, 'Kovno-Brest Litovskcourse of the Bug to the Austrian frontier'. When this short front had been reached by the Austro-German armies, reserves were to be switched to the west to deal with the anticipated French invasion of Alsace-Lorraine. By 1879 Moltke had ceased to believe in the possibility of a 'knock-out' against France or Russia. The French were protected by a great chain of fortresses between Belfort and Verdun, while with regard to Russia, Moltke declared: 'To follow up a victory in the Kingdom of Poland by a pursuit into the Russian interior would be of no interest to us.'[3]

Gordon Craig comments on Moltke's awareness of political factors, his appreciation of the role of diplomacy, and his knowledge of the internal conditions of countries opposed to Germany. Craig says: 'Moltke possessed real political insight and in addition he had – despite his differences with Bismarck during the unification period – no hesitation in keeping the Chancellor informed concerning his operational plans.'[4] Moltke's cautious strategy after 1871 fitted in with the pattern of Bismarck's policy.

It is a singular fact that Moltke, the architect of the lightning victories of 1866 and 1870, was almost the only professional strategist of eminence to forsee the deadlock of 1914–18. Perhaps he was influenced by the example of the American civil war which, contrary to legend, he had studied carefully.[5] With advancing age, he became increasingly pessimistic and, in a speech in the Reichstag in 1890, he predicted another seven years' war. Walter Goerlitz summarises Moltke's speech:[5]

If that war should break out which hung like a sword of Damocles over the head of the German nation, then no end to it could be foreseen; for the strongest and best equipped powers in the world would be taking part in it. None of these powers could be completely crushed in a single campaign . . . 'And woe to him that sets fire to Europe'.[6]

It is clear that Schlieffen also dreaded a long-drawn war, but his solution was to be of a very different character from that of the old field-marshal.

Count von Schlieffen was born in 1833, served in the Uhlans of the Guard, and was admitted to the General Staff in 1865. He gained a reputation as a staff officer in 1866 and 1870, and became head of the military history section of the General Staff in 1884. Profoundly versed in strategy and tactics and steeped in the history of war, he lacked Moltke's breadth of view, gift for expression and cultural and political interests. As Chief of Staff between 1891 and 1905, he devoted himself to an intense study of the technical problems of warfare, and the younger generation of staff officers regarded him with awe and admiration. In a narrow professional sense, he trained staff officers of very high quality and such pupils as Ludendorff and Kuhl have paid tribute to his exceptional gifts. Ludendorff described Schlieffen as 'one of the greatest soldiers who has ever lived',[7] while Kuhl says he was 'the most imposing personality with whom I came into contact in my long career of service'.[8] Proud, reserved and sarcastic, he drove himself as ruthlessly as his staff and his capacity for work seemed limitless. He frequently continued his labours until midnight, and then spent a couple of hours reading military history to his daughters. Craig says:

> Like many great soldiers after him, he prided himself on being completely 'unpolitical', forgetting Clausewitz's wise dictum that 'war admittedly has its own grammar but not its own logic', which must be supplied by politics. Few objective critics would deny that Schlieffen was a superb grammarian; but that unfortunately was not enough.[9]

Ritter has analysed the various steps by which Schlieffen discarded the plans of the elder Moltke and gradually committed himself to a gigantic offensive in the west.[10] Extremely dubious of the efficiency of the Austrian army, he feared that an offensive against Russia would either founder against the defences along the Narew and the Niemen, or that the Russians would merely withdraw into the interior of their 'enormous empire', where the German communications 'would be as unfavourable and vulnerable as anyone could imagine'. By 1897 Schlieffen had ceased to inform the Austrians of the details of his plans and had decided to concentrate on a crushing offensive against France.

On 2 August 1897 Schlieffen declared in a memorandum that a break-through of the French fortifications between Belfort and the Belgian frontier was impossible and that 'an offensive which seeks to wheel round Verdun must not shrink from violating the neutrality of Belgium as well as of Luxembourg'. At first his operational plans did not envisage any wide sweep through Belgium, and the advance of the German right wing was restricted to the area south of the Meuse. By June 1904, however, Schlieffen was expressing doubts 'whether a movement extended to Mézières would be enough to force the French to evacuate their fortified line'. He felt inclined to move the bulk of the German army north of Verdun, and attack the line Verdun-Lille. This was the genesis of the plan set out at length in Schlieffen's detailed memorandum dated 31 December 1905.

Ritter publishes this famous memorandum in full,[11] and pays tribute to its 'breadth and boldness' and 'the careful attention to tactical and strategical detail'. Schlieffen envisaged that the German right wing would violate the neutrality of Holland as well as Belgium and would cross the Meuse north of Liège. Sweeping through the Dutch province of Limburg and leaving forces to mask the Belgians in the fortress of Antwerp, the right flank would be extended as far as Dunkirk. The line Verdun-Dunkirk was to be attacked by thirty-five army corps, while only five corps, based on Metz, were to contain the French in Lorraine. Schlieffen wrote: 'It is essential [to the progress of the whole of the operations] to form a strong right wing, to win the battles with its help, to pursue the enemy relentlessly with this strong wing, forcing him to retreat again and again.'

The essence of the plan was that the French left flank was to be constantly enveloped by the strong German right, and forced back successively from the river lines of the Meuse, the Aisne, the Somme, the Oise, the Marne and the Seine. Schlieffen feared that the bulk of the French army might withdraw into central France, and declared: 'By attacks on the left flank we must try at all costs to drive the French eastward against their Moselle fortresses, against the Jura and Switzerland.' He appreciated the problem posed by 'the colossal fortress of Paris', and proposed that the German right flank should extend as far as the mouth of the Somme at Abbeville, in order to envelop Paris from the west and south. Yet he was clearly uneasy about the large numbers of troops required to invest the French capital and commented: 'We shall find the experience of all earlier conquerors confirmed, that a war of aggression calls for much strength and also consumes much, that this strength dwindles constantly as the defender's increases, and all this particularly in a country which bristles with fortresses.' Indeed in an earlier draft, Schlieffen went so far as to declare, 'Before the Germans reach the Somme or the Oise they will have realised, like other conquerors before them, that they are too weak for the whole enterprise.'[12]

Commenting on the plan in his preface to Ritter's book, Liddell Hart says: 'It was a conception of Napoleonic boldness, and there were encouraging precedents in Napoleon's early career for counting on the decisive effect of arriving in the enemy's rear with the bulk of one's forces.' However, he criticises Schlieffen for not appreciating that 'while his troops would have to march on their own feet round the circumference of the circle, the French would be able to switch troops by rail across the chord of the circle'. Moreover, the advancing German right would be sorely handicapped by demolished railway tracks and bridges. Ritter himself is severely critical of the rigidity of the plan – so different from the flexible methods of the elder Moltke – and he deplores the tremendous political and military risks which Schlieffen was prepared to run in an enterprise whose success appeared doubtful even to its author.

Liddell Hart admits that Schlieffen deserves credit for his emphasis on the need for heavy field artillery to shatter the French and Belgian fortresses, but he criticises his lack of attention to technical details. Schlieffen never mentions barbed wire, pays little attention to the deadly effect of machine-guns, and ignores the French quick-firing 75 mm artillery. Possibly Schlieffen felt that such details were out of place in a strategic memorandum, and it is clear that he was painfully aware of the grave supply problems, which would embarrass his right wing. As regards provisions, Schlieffen hoped that the troops could live on the country and, in his essay *Der Krieg in der Gegenwart* published in 1909, he stresses the value of motor transport for ammunition supply.[13]

Neither Ritter nor Liddell Hart do justice to the scope and subtlety of Schlieffen's plan, and they fail to discuss the degree to which it was based on 'the Cannae conception'. Ritter does refer to Schlieffen's *Cannae Studien*, but he makes no attempt to relate his discussion of the plan to Schlieffen's analysis of Cannae, which he regarded as the supreme example of a battle of annihilation. The essential feature of Cannae was Hannibal's withdrawal of his weak centre before the main Roman attack, his crushing of the Roman wings, and his encirclement of the greater part of their army.[14] Although Schlieffen only intended to attack on one wing, the parallel between Cannae and his plan of 1905 is very close.[15] Gordon Craig says of Schlieffen:

> He convinced himself indeed, under the influence of Hans Delbruck's description of the battle of Cannae in his *History of the Art of War*, that the highest achievement of strategy was the crushing attack in the flank and rear of an enemy which had enabled Hannibal, in that battle, to destroy a numerically superior Roman army. To duplicate Cannae had, Schlieffen believed, always been the objective of the great commanders of the past, and the Germans must strive to duplicate Cannae in their war against France.[16]

It is arguable, however, that the real strategic threat posed to the French by Schlieffen's plan was not the very powerful force allotted to the thrust through Belgium, but the weak detachment assigned to the defence of Lorraine. Liddell Hart himself wrote in 1930:

> . . . if a French offensive pressed the left wing back towards the Rhine, the attack through Belgium on the French flank would be all the more difficult to parry. It would be like a revolving door – if a man pressed heavily on one side the other side would spring round and strike him in the back. Here lay the real subtlety of the plan, not in the mere geographical detour.[17]

Just as Hannibal's weak centre had drawn the Romans into a 'sack', Schlieffen hoped that, as his offensive developed through Belgium, he might entice French armies eastwards towards the Rhine. On this point the memorandum of December 1905 says that if the French were to thrust between Metz and Strasbourg, or cross the upper Rhine into Germany, 'it can only be welcome to the Germans'. Schlieffen proposed to open the campaign in Lorraine with an attack on Nancy, in the hope of luring the French into a counter-attack. He said:

> The more troops the French employ for the counter-attack, the better for the Germans. But the latter must not allow themselves to be engaged in prolonged actions, but must realise that their task is to draw as many troops as possible after them . . .

Schlieffen was confident that he would be able to hold the vital pivot of Metz, and that the threat of his encircling right wing would force the French to halt their invasion of Germany before they could seriously interrupt his main communications.

From a purely military and strategic point of view, the plan has much to commend it, and offered a real prospect of forcing a decision in the west and avoiding the agonising trench war deadlock of 1914–18. Like every great military operation, it involved serious risks but Liddell Hart exaggerates considerably when he says in his preface that 'the basis of Schlieffen's formula for quick victory amounted to little more than a gambler's belief in the virtuosity of sheer audacity'. The best justification for Schlieffen's plan of 1905 is to be found in the French Plan XVII put into force in 1914. While two French armies attacked in the Belgian Ardennes, the French first and second armies in Lorraine were committed to a major offensive towards the Saar. If the Germans had withdrawn before this onslaught – counter-attacking from Metz at an appropriate moment – it is very doubtful whether Joffre would have been able to switch reserves to the Paris region in time to launch an effective counter-stroke on the Marne.

Not all historians share the highly critical attitude of Liddell Hart and Ritter towards the Schlieffen Plan. Gordon Craig says: 'The daring of this conception must arouse a reluctant admiration, and it is probably true that, if this plan had been carried out in 1914 in its original form and under the direction of an energetic and stubborn commander-in-chief, it would have achieved an overwhelming initial success.'[18] Walter Goerlitz is rather critical of the rigidity of the plan, and Schlieffen's failure to allow for 'that element which Clausewitz has designated as "Frictions", that is to say, the unexpected incidents and unforseen developments which he held to be characteristics of every war'. However, Goerlitz concedes:

> Yet when the excellence of the Imperial Army of 1914 is taken into account and the cold efficiency of the General Staff, there can be no doubt that if it had been carried out in its original form by a man of, say, Ludendorff's brutal energy, it would have achieved an overwhelming initial success. France would have been hurled into the dust. The question would then have arisen whether England or Russia would have given up the struggle, and we can now almost certainly say they would not.[19]

Schlieffen's critics are on much firmer ground when they condemn the immortality of the plan, the political folly of violating Belgian neutrality, and the almost reckless indifference to British intervention. In his memorandum of December 1905, Schlieffen did not refer to the British army at all – apart from mentioning a possible British landing at the Channel ports – but in an appendix prepared in February 1906, he discussed the role of a British Expeditionary Force of 100,000 men.[20] He thought that the British would probably land at Antwerp and predicted, 'They will be shut up there, together with the Belgians.' Ritter makes a fair comment on Schlieffen's attitude:

> It is clear that Schlieffen had little respect for the fighting power of British infantry – as little as had the London military attaché [Count von der Schulenberg], who was actually looking forward to 'giving them a reception they will remember for centuries'. But is it not strange that in this whole plan there is no thought of the British Navy and the danger of a sea

blockade? . . . But Schlieffen had not the least use for the German Navy either, though its development reached a new and decisive stage in 1906.[21]

In framing his plan, Schlieffen was influenced purely by technical military considerations, although the Russian disasters in the war with Japan doubtless gave him the confidence to plan to hurl almost the entire German army at the French. However, he cannot be accused of keeping the political authorities in ignorance of his plans, and one of the great merits of Ritter's book is his demonstration of this vital point. He traces with great care the successive steps by which the German government was induced to consent to the violation of Belgium and Holland.[22] The elder Moltke never even considered the possibility of a German march through Belgium, and was highly sceptical of predictions that France would take the initiative in entering that country. Moltke wrote in 1887: 'If, incidentally, anything could spur England into action, it would be the occupation of Belgium by the French Army.' In the same year Bismarck inspired an article in the semi-official *Post*, which declared that 'Germany would never open a war with the violation of a European treaty'.

As noted above, it was in 1897 that Schlieffen first expressed the view that a successful invasion of France required a turning movement through Belgian territory. He was on terms of close friendship with Baron von Holstein of the Foreign Office, and it may well be that Schlieffen discussed the political implications of the plan with him as early as 1897.[23] In May 1900 Schlieffen appears to have made a formal approach to the Chancellor, Prince Hohenlohe, and declared that 'in the event of a two-front war, success might possibly depend on Germany's not allowing international agreements to restrain her strategic operations'. Ritter believes that 'Schlieffen acted correctly and gave Hohenlohe an opportunity to object to his politically dangerous plan'. It is true that the archives of the German Foreign Office are completely silent on the subject but, as Ritter points out, it was 'a military secret of the first order'.

Neither Hohenlohe nor his successor, Bülow, raised any objections to the development of the plan, which of course required the construction of an intricate network of railway lines and sidings along the Dutch and Belgian frontiers. Curiously enough Ritter does not mention this aspect, but it was patent enough to contemporary observers. Winston Churchill relates[24] that he attended a meeting of the Committee of Imperial Defence during the Agadir crisis in 1911 at which 'overwhelming detailed evidence was adduced to show that the Germans had made every preparation for marching through Belgium'. Churchill says: 'The great military camps in close proximity to the frontier, the enormous depots, the reticulation of railways, the endless sidings, revealed with the utmost clearness and beyond all doubt their design.'

In his highly unreliable memoirs, Prince von Bülow, Chancellor from 1900 to 1909, describes a conversation with Schlieffen 'in 1904 or 1905':

He felt that in the case of a war with France and Russia, we must first try to overthrow France. The surest way to do this was by way of Belgium. I said I was well aware of that. Already, as a Bonn Hussar, I had studied Clausewitz . . . and learnt the phrase, 'the heart of France lies between Brussels and Paris'. But, I added, we could only pursue this course for the gravest political reasons and then only if Belgian neutrality had already been violated by our enemies.[25]

Bülow declares that he drew Schlieffen's attention to the views expressed by Bismarck in 1887, and continues:

Count Alfred Schlieffen, with whom both before and after this conversation I was on the best of terms, twisted his monocle several times in his eye, as his habit was, and then answered: 'Of course. It's still the same to-day. We haven't grown stupider since then.'

Bülow also relates a singular conversation with the Kaiser on 28 January 1904.[26] According to this account, the Kaiser, who had just been talking to King Leopold II, told Bülow that he had warned the Belgian king that in case of necessity the German army would not hesitate to cross Belgian territory. The Kaiser is recorded as saying:

I told him, too, that I could not be played with. Whoever, in the case of a European war, was not for me, was against me. As a soldier I belonged to the school of Frederick the Great, the school of Napoleon the First. As, for the one, the Seven Years War had begun with the invasion of Saxony, and as the other had always with lightning speed forestalled his enemies, so should I, in the event of Belgium's not being on my side, be actuated by strategical considerations only.

Ritter regards Bülow's account as exaggerated, but admits that it is partially confirmed by Baron van der Elst, a Belgian diplomat. The relevant volume of *The Holstein Papers*, published in 1963, contains a very interesting document, which the editors of *Die Grosse Politik* did not choose to include in that collection. This is a memorandum drawn up by Hans Adolf von Bülow, First Secretary of the Brussels legation, on 30 December 1904.[27] The Kaiser explained to the secretary in a conversation at the Neue Palais on 29 December, why he did not propose to return the state visit of the King of the Belgians in January 1904. The Kaiser expressed concern about the presence in Brussels of 'a large number of unsafe French elements', who might insult his person. The memorandum continues:

The main reason, however, why His Majesty did not at this time intend to pay a return visit to Belgium was the fact that King Leopold still owed His Majesty a reply to the question submitted to him in January, as to what attitude he, the King, intended to adopt in case an armed conflict should break out between Germany and France or Germany and England.
    In explanation His Majesty told me in this connection that he had categorically demanded of the King during a lengthy conversation in

January of this year, that he, the King, should give him a written declaration now in time of peace to the effect that in case of conflict Belgium would take her stand on our side, and that to this end the King should amongst other things guarantee to us the use of Belgian railways and fortified places. If the King of the Belgians did not do so, he – His Majesty the Kaiser – would not be able to give a guarantee for either his territory or the dynasty. We would then, if the case arose, immediately invade Belgium and the King would have to suffer all the – to him – harmful consequences . . .

It may be doubted whether in the whole of his extraordinary career, the Kaiser ever displayed greater irresponsibility than in this conversation with King Leopold II. Moreover, the episode indicates that by 1904 the German government had decided on the violation of Belgian neutrality regardless of the attitude of France.[28] Of course Prince von Bülow endeavours to make out that he acted the part of a wise statesman and says that he warned the Kaiser in their conversation on 28 January 1904 that 'we must certainly not be the first to violate the neutrality of Belgium, which had been guaranteed by international justice'. The fact remains that in none of the drafts of the Schlieffen Plan drawn up in 1905 is there any suggestion that the German invasion of Belgium and Holland was dependent on a prior infringement of Belgian neutrality by the French army.[29] Bülow's assertion of innocence is effectively demolished by Draft II which says, 'It is necessary to violate the neutrality not only of Belgium but also of the Netherlands', and adds the significant footnote, 'Discussed with the Chancellor'.[30] More honest than Bülow, Bethmann-Hollweg never denied that he had known of the contemplated violation of neutrality 'long before the war'.[31]

SCHLIEFFEN, HOLSTEIN AND THE MOROCCAN CRISIS, 1904–1906

In 1952 Peter Rassow published an article in *Historische Zeitschrift*[32] in which he asserted that Schlieffen's memorandum of December 1905 was inspired directly by the Moroccan crisis of that year, and that both Schlieffen and Holstein were then urging a preventive war with France. Although Gordon Craig does not accept this interpretation of the memorandum, he takes the view that Holstein was strongly in favour of preventive war and that 'Schlieffen was in a war-like mood in 1905'.[33] Ritter does not dispute that Schlieffen was impressed by the dismal showing of the Russian army against Japan, and admits that he may have indulged in bellicose talk. However, he argues with considerable conviction that 'there is no reliable documentary evidence for the statement that Graf Schlieffen urged the Kaiser or Bülow to make war against France during the Morocco crisis'.[34]

Ritter is even more emphatic that Holstein was not in favour of pushing the Moroccan crisis to the point of war. He draws attention to Holstein's memorandum of 3 June 1904,[35] which shows no desire to make war over Morocco, but is deeply concerned with Germany's prestige. Holstein said:

' . . . if we now allow our feet to be stepped on in Morocco without a protest, we simply encourage others to do the same somewhere else.' Ritter interprets German policy in 1904–5 as a determined effort to shatter the Anglo-French *entente*, to demonstrate to France the worthlessness of British friendship, and to induce her to join a continental alliance of Germany, France and Russia.

On this question, E. E. Kraehe writes:

> Yet on one issue Ritter comes to the rescue of Schlieffen and Holstein. With a brilliant analysis of available sources and sequence of events, he concludes that neither man desired or advocated preventive war during Russia's involvement with Japan in 1905. The risk of the plan, he contends, make even less sense with Russia out of the picture than on the assumption of a two-front war. Despite this penetrating observation, the question remains where other writers, especially Gordon A. Craig and Peter Rassow, left it – undecided. One feels that Ritter is here demanding an excessive degree of documentary proof, more at least than he himself deems necessary when arguing that Schlieffen kept the political authorities well informed of his plans (pp. 95–7).[36]

The relevant volume of *The Holstein Papers*, published in 1963, contains no document indicating a desire on Holstein's part for preventive war.[37] On the contrary, the documents confirm Ritter's interpretation of Holstein's policy. With regard to Schlieffen's attitude, the evidence is necessarily inconclusive because 'there is not a single letter from Schlieffen in the Holstein Papers, and only a few insignificant letters from Holstein have been found in the Schlieffen Papers'.[38] In view of the close relationship between the two men, it is of course significant that Holstein should have destroyed every letter he received from Schlieffen. However, some documents in *The Holstein Papers* refer to the attitude of the German military leaders, and throw a good deal of light on German policy.

In a memorandum dated 22 October 1904, Holstein refers to the desire of 'the military party' for war with France,[39] and adds: 'The military are always the same in every country. Only here they have no political influence.' In a letter from Bülow to Holstein, dated 15 December 1904,[40] the Chancellor refers to the opinion of Count von der Schulenberg, the military attaché in London, that a British attack on Germany was 'imminent' and 'inevitable'. Bülow says:

> In the light of Schulenberg's view of the situation in London we should here clarify amongst ourselves certain major questions. (1) In case of an English attack on us, is France also to be drawn into the war? The argument against this is that the General Staff thinks France is a very serious adversary, more so than in 1870, that a move against France could bring in Russia against us unless we had previously come to some sort of agreement with her; that perhaps even Italy might side with England and France. The argument in favour is that if the war remained confined to ourselves and England, we are practically powerless against England. By capturing our colonies and shipping, destroying our navy and trade and paralysing our industry, England could within a forseeable time force us

to a disadvantageous peace. But if France is involved, and particularly if we also bring in Belgium and Holland, we increase our risk, but we would at least have the chance of achieving military successes, obtaining guarantees and exercising pressure for our part . . .

On 28 June 1905 Holstein wrote to Prince von Radolin, the German ambassador in Paris, and quoted Schlieffen's opinion that the French were calling up reservists and strengthening their frontier garrisons.[41] Holstein said:

For the time being the Chancellor wants to prevent counter-measures being taken – I think he is definitely right in this, because once that starts, both sides will drive each other further and further; but if the French continue with their preparations, it will not be possible to stop our military from taking steps here too, otherwise the responsibility becomes too great. Let us hope for the best.

A telegram from Holstein to Joseph Maria von Radowitz, German delegate at Algeciras, dated 16 January 1906, says that 'the Kaiser openly declares that a German war on account of Morocco is absurd',[42] while in a letter to Radolin on 7 February 1906 Holstein said: 'His Majesty is telling everyone that he wants peace, and France will certainly not provoke a war. It is difficult for us to negotiate *for this reason* . . . '[43] On 22 February 1906, Bülow wrote to Holstein, 'Neither public opinion, Parliament, Princes, or even the army will have anything to do with a war over Morocco'.[44]

With regard to Schlieffen's attitude, this somewhat inconclusive evidence must be supplemented by documents from *Die Grosse Politik*. On 19 April 1904 Prince Lichnowsky, at Bülow's request, asked Schlieffen for his official opinion on the effect of the Russo-Japanese war on the balance of power.[45] Schlieffen believed that although Russia had not yet drawn many troops from her western frontier, yet she was in a most unfavourable position to wage war in Europe, and added: 'If therefore we should be faced with the necessity of a war with France, the present time would undoubtedly be advantageous for that purpose.' In June 1905 Bülow asked Schlieffen for an estimate of Russian military power in the light of the impending treaty of peace with Japan. In his reply, Schlieffen expressed the opinion that within six months of the conclusion of peace, Russia would have as many troops in her western provinces as before the war.[46] While admitting that the efficiency of the Russian army was questionable, Schlieffen concluded: 'Even if the Russian Army gets worse, it must still be reckoned with because of its sheer mass.'

In conclusion, it seems fair to say that Schlieffen was perfectly willing to fight France in 1905, but that Bülow was probably correct in his statement that Schlieffen had never 'recommended a preventive war on any occasion or even sought to incite a war'.[47] Admittedly there was a strong element of threat in Germany's attitude towards France in 1905, and Bülow himself says, 'I did not hesitate to confront France with the possibility of war'.[48] But the publication of *The Holstein Papers* in 1963 seems to prove beyond doubt that neither Bülow nor Holstein wanted war over Morocco, and that both were pursuing a policy of bluff. Such a policy was bound to founder on the temperament of the Kaiser who, when the crisis became dangerous, displayed an almost pathetic fear of war. Early in June 1905, immediately after the dismissal of Delcassé, he appears to have told the French General de Lacroix, 'I haven't the slightest intention of waging war against France on account of Morocco'.[49] In a long letter to Bülow, dated 31 December 1905, he practically begged the Chancellor to preserve peace.[50]

In his biography of Holstein, published in 1965, Norman Rich analyses the Moroccan crisis in detail and concludes as follows:

> At no stage of the Moroccan affair was a military solution ever advocated or seriously contemplated by the German leaders primarily responsible for Germany's Moroccan policy. On the contrary, the Kaiser, Bülow and also Holstein went to extreme lengths to avoid war; they allowed themselves to be miserably duped, and in the end they submitted to a humiliating diplomatic defeat while their army was still capable of dictating the destinies of the states of Europe. Neither the Kaiser's nor Holstein's was a war policy, it was merely a stupid policy, and so far as Germany's national interests were concerned went far to substantiate Talleyrand's famous aphorism: 'It was worse than a crime, it was a blunder.'[51]

MOLTKE, SCHLIEFFEN AND THE PATH TO WAR 1906–1914

Schlieffen retired as Chief of the General Staff on 31 December 1905 and Gordon Craig says that 'for his advocacy of preventive war in 1905, Moltke's most gifted successor lost his post'.[52] Ritter shows that this assertion is quite unfounded; the retirement of Schlieffen was already being considered by the Kaiser in 1904 and was virtually decided in January 1905, when Moltke informed Bülow of the Kaiser's intention to make him Schlieffen's successor.[53] It does not appear that there were any political or even important military reasons for Schlieffen's retirement.[54] The Kaiser was greatly attracted by the splendid appearance of the younger Moltke, his charming manners and lively conversation. He was tired of Schlieffen, who at 72 was a 'taciturn and rather stiff old gentleman'.

The younger Moltke, nephew of the great field-marshal, had shown outstanding personal courage in the battles of 1870, and had held the command of various guards regiments. A conscientious and studious soldier, he did well in senior appointments on the General Staff. Yet he had little confidence in his own abilities, and accepted the post of Chief of Staff with much reluctance. Moltke told Bülow: 'I lack the power of rapid decision; I am too reflective, too scrupulous, or if you like conscientious for such a post. I lack the capacity for risking all on a single throw . . . '[55] As Walter Goerlitz remarks, Moltke was by nature diffident, had strong intellectual interests, and shared with his wife 'an appetite for somewhat exotic types of religion'.[56] Like many weak men, he frequently indulged in extravagant and bellicose talk and wrote to his wife during the Agadir crisis of 1911: 'If we again slink out of this affair with our tail between our legs, if we cannot pull ourselves together to present demands which we are prepared to enforce by the sword, then I despair of the future of the German Reich.'[57] By 1914 he regarded war as inevitable, but Goerlitz says:

> For all that, he looked upon that coming war with horror, and in his darker moments began to despair of any possibility of victory. Believing, as he did, that his own abilities were sufficient for peacetime requirements but incapable of doing justice to more arduous demands, he actually drew some comfort from the Emperor's frequent declarations that in the event of war he would himself assume command in the west.[58]

During the years 1906–12, Schlieffen was devoting his retirement to writing copiously on military history and strategy, and producing revisions of the famous plan he had bequeathed to his successor. Like many old soldiers in retirement, he took a pessimistic view of the situation; he pictured Germany as surrounded by powerful and predatory foes and, in his writings, stressed the gigantic perils menacing her on every side. In January 1909 'an alarming essay' published by him in the *Deutsche Revue* 'contained some expressions which caused anxiety in Belgium'.[59] Schlieffen's pessimism deepened after the Agadir crisis, which he regarded as a severe diplomatic defeat for Germany. He continued to dabble in strategy, and on 28 December 1912 completed a new memorandum, just a week before his death.[60]

In this final memorandum, Schlieffen still stressed the need for an immensely powerful right wing, sweeping as far west as the English Channel and crossing the Somme at Abbeville.[61] He advocated a considerable extension of the German penetration into Holland, but specifically abandoned the 'Cannae conception' and advised attacking along the whole front Belfort-Nijmegen. Schlieffen was very concerned that the German army would not be strong enough for its task; he was most emphatic that Landwehr and Ersatz troops must be employed to the maximum, and should be used for investing fortresses and guarding lines of communication. He now attached considerable importance to the role of the British and feared that, with their help, the Belgians might block the front Namur-Antwerp. In order to force a decision in the west, he proposed the extraordinary step of leaving literally nothing against Russia and declared: 'The *whole* of Germany must throw itself on *one* enemy – the strongest, most powerful, most dangerous enemy: and that can only be the Anglo-French!'

It would be a mistake to attach much importance to the opinions of an octogenarian on the verge of death. Moltke read the memorandum and made some notes on it, but the document had no practical effect on his plans. A note, written in 1923 by Schlieffen's son-in-law, Major von Hahnke, complains that by 1911 Moltke and Colonel Ludendorff, chief of the operations section of the General Staff, 'were foolish enough never to ask Schlieffen's opinion any longer'.[62] They were in fact recasting the whole Schlieffen plan of December 1905, and were introducing modifications which drastically altered its character.

In a memorandum drawn up in 1911, Moltke decided to abandon the projected advance through Holland.[63] He declared that 'a hostile Holland at our back could have disastrous consequences for the advance of the German army to the west', and added: 'Furthermore it will be very important to have in Holland a country whose neutrality allows us to have imports and supplies. She must be the windpipe that enables us to breathe.' Moltke continued:

> However awkward it may be, the advance through Belgium must therefore take place without the violation of Dutch territory. This will hardly be possible unless Liége is in our hands. The fortress must therefore be taken at once [i.e. at the very beginning of mobilization] . . . Everything depends on meticulous preparation and surprise. The enterprise is only possible if the attack is made at once; before the areas between the forts are fortified. It must therefore be taken by standing troops immediately war is declared . . . the possession of Liége is the *sine qua non* of our advance.

By abandoning the wide sweep through Holland, Moltke was imposing a tremendous logistical burden on the German First and Second armies destined to advance north of the Meuse. Until Liège was taken, its outer forts shattered and its four lines of railway brought under German control, no advance into the Belgian plain would be possible. Two German armies must pass through this bottleneck, and everything hinged on its capture in the first days of the war. Accordingly six brigades of infantry and supporting artillery had to be kept permanently on a war footing in the Aachen area.

Moreover, Moltke threw the 'Cannae conception' overboard and, by deploying two powerful armies in Lorraine, completely altered the balance of force between the German right and left wings. Schlieffen in 1905 had proposed to deploy fifty-nine active and reserve divisions north of Metz, and nine to the south of that city. Making use of additional divisions which became available to the German army after 1906, Moltke decided to deploy fifty-five divisions on his right and twenty-three on his left. General J. F. C. Fuller says: 'In percentages the Schlieffen plan represented 100 : 15 and the Moltke plan 100 : 42.'[64] Moreover, Schlieffen had intended to move two corps from left to right as soon as the French troops in Lorraine were effectively entangled.

Moltke's modifications had disastrous effects on the German prospects of victory in 1914. The French Plan XVII fitted into the original Schlieffen Plan like a glove but, by placing powerful armies in Lorraine and driving the French back on their own fortress barrier, Moltke effectively nullified his chances of victory. Moreover, under the impact of the Russian invasion of East Prussia in August 1914, he detached two army corps from his enveloping right wing and sent them all the way across Germany to assist his Eighth Army at Tannenberg – they arrived at the end of August after the victory had already been won. Another army corps and detachments were immobilised in the investment of the frontier fortresses of Maubeuge and Givet, while two others were detached to watch the Belgians at Antwerp – Schlieffen had intended that these tasks should be carried out by

Landwehr and reserve formations. The result was that in September 1914 the German right wing' was too weak to invest Paris from the west and south, and had to wheel inwards to the east of the capital. This presented Joffre and Galliéni with their opportunity for a successful counter-stroke at the battle of the Marne.

Liddell Hart and Ritter both attempt to demonstrate that Moltke's modifications fitted in with Schlieffen's ideas. This can only be done by distorting the significance of certain obscure passages in the early drafts of the plan of December 1905,[65] and by attaching undue weight to the memorandum of December 1912, completed on the eve of Schlieffen's death.[66] Moreover, they argue that it was impossible to make the German right wing stronger in 1914 because of the strain on railway communications. Liddell Hart says:

> In any case the course of events amply proved that the right wing could not have been made stronger than it was, nor its strength maintained as the advance continued – because of the rail demolitions. It is useless to multiply numbers if they cannot be fed and munitioned.[67]

This is a plausible argument, but overlooks the fact that the entire problem of maintaining and supplying the right wing had been enormously aggravated by Moltke's decision to respect Dutch neutrality, and push two whole armies through the bottleneck of Liège. From the very start of their offensive, the German First and Second armies were faced with chronic supply problems, which they would not have encountered if the railways and roads of southern Holland had been at their disposal. Even Schlieffen in his dotage never countenanced the fatuous blunder of trying to maintain more than 600,000 men through the narrow aperture of Liège.

The decision to capture Liège in the first days of the war had the gravest political consequences in 1914. Winston Churchill says:

> Nearly three weeks before the main shock of the armies could begin . . . six German brigades must storm Liége. It was this factor that destroyed all chance that the armies might mobilize and remain guarding their frontiers while under their shield conferences sought a path to peace. The German plan was of such a character that the most irrevocable steps of actual war, including the violation of neutral territory, must be taken at the first moment of mobilization. Mobilization therefore spelt war. None of the Governments except the German and French, and none of the Sovereigns seem to have understood this . . .[68]

The impending coup against Liège was kept a close secret by the general staff, and Bethmann-Hollweg did not hear of it until 31 July 1914. The influence of the modified Moltke-Schlieffen Plan on German policy in 1914 is analysed by Ritter in his *Staatskunst und Kriegshandswerk* and in an article published in *Historische Zeitschrift* in 1961.[69] He first traces the various plans drawn up between 1871 and 1914, and summarises the conclusions presented in *The Schlieffen Plan*. As Ritter points out, by 1913 the strategic position of Germany and Austria-Hungary was becoming very dangerous. In 1905 Russia was in no condition to fight, but by 1913 she was arming fast and was filled with bitter resentment at her humiliation in the Bosnian crisis of 1908–9. In that crisis, Moltke had assured Conrad von Hotzendorf, the Austrian Chief of Staff, of German support, and declared on 21 January 1909, 'The moment Russia mobilizes, Germany also will mobilize, and will unquestionably mobilize her whole army'.[70] Moltke told Conrad, however, that Germany must concentrate first on crushing France, and only then could the bulk of her forces be transferred to the eastern front. Nevertheless he gave Conrad the impression that the German Eighth Army in East Prussia would be strong enough at the outset to launch an offensive from that province against the Russian railway communications running east of Warsaw, thus facilitating an Austrian offensive from Galicia.

Ritter declares that by 1914 Moltke had become extremely pessimistic, and that 'for him the Schlieffen Plan certainly did not appear as a sure recipe of victory'. However, he could not see any practicable alternative. As only one German army could be allotted to the defence of East Prussia, Moltke considered that it was of vital importance that Austria should launch a massive offensive in southern Poland, while Germany was endeavouring to strike down France. By 1914 the prospects of a successful offensive by Austria against Russia were becoming extremely dim. Serbia was now a formidable military power, capable of putting 400,000 men in the field, while Romania had virtually withdrawn from the Triple Alliance. This meant that Conrad could no longer count on 400,000 Romanian troops, who were supposed to cover the right flank of the Austrian armies in Galicia. Ritter says that Moltke's pessimism was shared by Conrad, who believed in the summer of 1914 that the odds were heavily against Austria, but that 'so ancient a Monarchy and so glorious an Army' ought not to perish without putting up a fight.

Perhaps Ritter exaggerates the pessimism of Moltke and Conrad in 1914. At their meeting at Carlsbad in May, Moltke declared that 'delay meant a lessening of our chances; we could not compete with Russia in masses'. Discussing the situation with the Bavarian envoy in Berlin in the spring of 1914, Moltke expressed the view that 'the military situation is from the military point of view favourable to a degree which cannot occur again in the foreseeable future'.[71] It would seem that Moltke was continually fluctuating between pessimism and bluster.

Ritter stresses the importance of the divergent strategic views of Moltke and Conrad in July 1914. On 25 July, when Austria ordered the partial mobilisation of her army, Conrad put into force Plan B, which involved a maximum concentration against Serbia with a minimum of holding forces against Russia. Even when Austria ordered general mobilisation on 31 July, Conrad telephoned to Berlin that the Austrian army would remain on the defensive against Russia and proceed with the punitive action against Serbia.[72] It is true that on 31 July, Conrad seems to have tried to halt the movement of some of his army corps towards Serbia, but 'the Chief of the Field Railways informed him that if utter confusion was to be avoided he must allow "B" to go to its original destination on the Danube frontier, and from there it could be transported to Galicia'.[73] The final upshot of this muddle was the crushing defeat inflicted by the Russians on the Imperial and Royal Army at the battle of Lemberg in September 1914. Gordon Craig says: 'It is difficult to study the campaigns of 1914 without being impressed by the incompleteness of Austro-German planning for their joint military venture and the dearth of their knowledge about each other . . . '[74]

Ritter emphasises that 'in his general attitude Moltke was far from being a warmonger'. It is certainly true that between 26 and 29 July, his attitude was one of restraint and caution; during this period he did nothing to hamper Bethmann-Hollweg's belated attempts to put the brake on Austria and he did not press for general mobilisation.[75] But by the morning of 30 July, when the news of Russian partial mobilisation was received in Berlin, Moltke was becoming desperate. The Moltke-Schlieffen Plan depended for success on the ability of the German Eighth Army in East Prussia, supported by a powerful Austrian offensive in Poland, to hold back the Russian masses, during the six weeks or so while France was being overthrown. However, reports from Vienna indicated that Conrad was concentrating against Serbia, and that the forces he was assigning to Galicia were entirely inadequate for an offensive. This explains the excited conversations between Moltke and the Austrian military attaché on 30 July and the frantic telegrams sent by them to Vienna, which Moltke dispatched on 30 July, urging immediate mobilisation against Russia and promising unqualified German support. As Ritter points out, the tone of these telegrams ran completely counter to the efforts of Bethmann-Hollweg to restrain Austria and persuade her to negotiate. On 31 July those contradictory exhortations drew the sarcastic comment from the Austrian Foreign Minister, Count Berchtold, 'Who rules in Berlin? Moltke or Bethmann?' Berchtold said to the Imperial War Council that morning: 'I have sent for you because I had the impression that Germany was beating a retreat but I now have the most reassuring pronouncement from responsible military quarters.' The council then decided to submit the order for general mobilisation to the Emperor Francis Joseph for signature.[76]

Ritter concludes by dealing with the effects of the Moltke-Schlieffen Plan on German decisions, ultimatums and declarations of war during the period 31 July–3 August. As soon as Moltke learned of Russian general mobilisation, which he did on the morning of 31 July, he not only insisted on the proclamation of a state of 'threatening danger of war' in Berlin, but induced the Chancellor to dispatch an ultimatum to St Petersburg demanding that Russia should cease all military measures against Germany and Austria-Hungary within twelve hours. In the absence of a satisfactory reply, Germany declared war on Russia at 6 pm on 1 August. Ritter explains this 'unbelievable haste' by the need to capture Liège at the very outset of the war. This of course required the immediate presentation of ultimatums in Brussels and Paris, followed swiftly by declarations of war on France. Ritter comments:

In other words: the gamble of the Schlieffen Plan was so great that it could only succeed as a result of a rapid surprise advance by the Germans or by a sudden onslaught on Belgium. In the opinion of the General Staff, Germany was therefore obliged by purely technical necessities to adopt, before the whole world, the role of a brutal aggressor – an evil moral burden which, as is well known, we have not got rid of even today.[77]

Ritter does not discuss the effect of the Moltke-Schlieffen Plan on Franco-Russian policy in July 1914, but it could be argued that it was very significant. By 1911 the French General Staff was well aware of the general character of the plan, and the Franco-Russian military agreement of that year stipulated that Russia should invade East Prussia as rapidly as possible if Germany threw her main weight towards the west. This explains why the French General Staff brought very strong pressure to bear on Russia on 27 July 1914 to order general mobilisation and invade East Prussia at the earliest possible moment.[78] On 29 July Russia ordered the partial mobilisation of her army against Austria but, under pressure from the French ambassador, Maurice de Paléologue, this was converted to general mobilisation on 30 July. At his decisive interview with the Tsar on

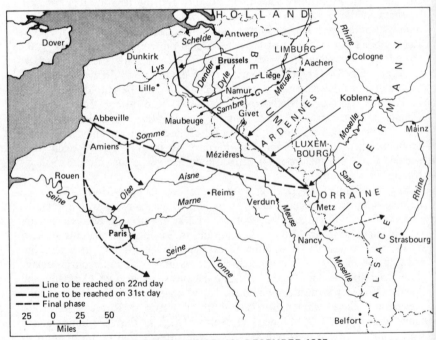

THE SCHLIEFFEN PLAN, DECEMBER 1905

the afternoon of 30 July Sazonov, the Russian Foreign Minister, advanced the sinister but effective argument that 'partial mobilization was a violation of Russian duties under the alliance with France and that it would give Wilhelm II an opening to demand a promise of neutrality from the French Government'.[79]

It will be seen therefore that the Moltke-Schlieffen Plan not only stampeded Germany into committing gross political errors in 1914, but it also accelerated the whole tempo of the crisis in eastern Europe and went far to make a peaceful solution impossible. Ritter's conclusion seems irrefutable:

> German politics . . . now laid itself open to the accusation of the whole world that it was governed and directed by 'unscrupulous' militarists – an accusation which has lain on Germany like a curse and became her doom not only at Versailles but also, even more, at the conferences of Moscow, Teheran and Yalta in 1944–5, when the terrible deeds of Adolf Hitler seemed subsequently to have justified it.
>
> Seen in the light of latter-day events, the Schlieffen Plan appears to be nothing less than the beginning of Germany's and Europe's misfortunes.[80]

NOTES

1 G. Ritter, *Der Schlieffenplan* (Munich 1956). English edn *The Schlieffen Plan* (New York 1958). References are to the English edn.

2 Quoted by G. A. Craig, *The Politics of the Prussian Army 1640–1945* (Oxford 1955), pp. 274–5. The quotation is from Moltke, *Die deutschen Aufmarschpläne 1871–1890* (Berlin 1929).

3 For an analysis of Moltke's plans see Ritter, op. cit., pp. 17–21.

4 Craig, op. cit., p. 276.

5 The Railway Section of the Prussian General Staff set up in 1864 and the Prussian Field Railway Section established in 1866 were modelled on the comparable organisations in the United States army. See J. Luvaas, *The Military Legacy of the Civil War: The European Inheritance* (Chicago 1959), pp. 72 and 122.

6 W. Goerlitz, *History of the German General Staff* (New York 1962), p. 102.

7 E. Ludendorff, *My War Memories 1914–18* (London, 1920), p. 24.

8 Quoted by Craig, op. cit., p. 277.

9 ibid., p. 277.

10 Ritter, op. cit., pp. 22–48.

11 ibid., pp. 134–48. The memorandum bears the date 31 December 1905, but was actually completed in January 1906.

12 ibid., p. 159. The serious differences between Schlieffen and the Prussian ministry of war and Schlieffen's failure to obtain the army increases demanded by his plan are discussed by Ritter in his *Staatskunst und Kriegshandwerk*, Vol. II (Munich 1965), pp. 256–67.

13 Ritter, *The Schlieffen Plan*, p. 51.

14 *The Cambridge Ancient History*, Vol. VIII (Cambridge 1930), p. 54.
15 However, General J. F. C. Fuller has said of Schlieffen, 'The grand tactics he decided upon were not those of Cannae, as so many writers suggest, but of Leuthen.' (*The Decisive Battles of the Western World*, Vol. III, London 1956, p. 195,) Fuller appears to base this opinion of Bernhardi, who criticised Schlieffen for reverting to the linear methods of Frederick the Great (Ritter, *The Schlieffen Plan*, p. 52).
16 Craig, *The Politics of the Prussian Army 1640–1945*, pp. 278–9..
17 B. H. Liddell Hart, *A History of the World War 1914–18*, 2nd edn (London 1934), pp. 68–9.
18 Craig, op. cit., pp. 279–80.
19 Goerlitz, *History of the German General Staff*, p. 135. Of course if the French had stood on the defensive, and used their artillery and machine-guns, the Schlieffen Plan was bound to fail.
20 Ritter, *The Schlieffen Plan*, pp. 161–4.
21 ibid., p. 71.
22 ibid., pp. 78–96. Ritter's principal source for Schlieffen's approach to the German government is Graf Hutten-Czapski, *60 Jahre Politik und Gessellschaft* (Berlin 1936), p. 371f. Count Hutten was confidential adviser to Prince Hohenlohe.
23 N. Rich, *Friedrich von Holstein* (Cambridge 1965), p. 305, says that Holstein's relations with Schlieffen are 'shrouded in a good deal of mystery', but that their relationship was 'close'. Holstein described Schlieffen as an 'honest man and a splendid patriot'. (ibid., p. 378.)
24 W. S. Churchill, *The World Crisis 1911–14* (London 1923), p. 57.
25 Prince von Bülow, *Memoirs 1903–9* (London 1931), pp. 74–5.
26 ibid., pp. 72–3.
27 N. Rich and M. H. Fisher (eds.), *The Holstein Papers, Vol. IV, Correspondence 1897–1909* (Cambridge 1963), pp. 358–9. The editors obtained the document from the German Foreign Office files.
28 In 1910 the Kaiser did indeed visit Brussels and told Baron van der Elst of the Belgian Foreign Office that Belgium had nothing to fear from Germany. The Kaiser said: 'You will have no grounds of complaint against Germany . . . I understand perfectly your country's position . . . I shall never place her in a false position.' (B. Tuchman, *August 1914* (London 1962), p. 109, quoting E. Cammaerts, *Albert of Belgium* (New York 1935), pp. 108–9 and p. 115.)
29 However, there is a mention in Draft I (Ritter, *The Schlieffen Plan*, p. 148) that if the Germans confine their attack to the area between Belfort and the Belgian frontier, 'they run the danger of being enveloped on their right flank through southern Belgium and Luxembourg'. In Draft III (Ritter, op. cit., p. 78) Schlieffen expresses fears that if the Germans do not invade Belgium they will eventually be outflanked by 'an unscrupulous enemy'.
30 Ritter, *The Schlieffen Plan*, pp. 79 and 92. Ritter does not mention this vital point in his brief and inadequate discussion of this problem in *Staatskunst und Kriegshandwerk*, Vol. II, p. 255.
31 Ritter, *The Schlieffen Plan*, p. 94.
32 P. Rassow, 'Schlieffen und Holstein', *Historische Zeitschrift*, Band 173 (1952), 297–313.
33 Craig, op. cit., pp. 283f. This view is accepted by *The New Cambridge Modern History*, Vol. XII (Cambridge 1960), p. 317, which states that

'there is evidence that the German Chief of General Staff favoured a preventive war against France'.

34 Ritter, *The Schlieffen Plan*, pp. 111–12.
35 *Die Grosse Politik der Europaischen Kabinette 1871–1914*, 40 vols. (Berlin, 1922–7), Vol. XX (I), pp. 207–9.
36 E. E. Kraehe, review of *Der Schlieffenplan* by G. Ritter, *The Journal of Modern History*, XXIX (December 1957), 397.
37 Rich and Fisher, *The Holstein Papers*, Vol. IV, pp. 277–451.
38 Rich, *Friedrich von Holstein*, p. 305. There are few references to Schlieffen in *Die Grosse Politik*.
39 Rich and Fisher, op. cit., p. 312.
40 ibid, pp. 317–9. For detailed treatment of German fears of a British attack in 1904–5 see J. Steinberg, 'The Copenhagen complex', *Journal of Contemporary History*, vol. I, no. 3 (July 1966). Incidentally Bülow's letter shows that for him the Schlieffen Plan was not without political attractions.
41 ibid., p. 347.
42 ibid., p. 387.
43 ibid., p. 392.
44 ibid., p. 397.
45 Memorandum by Lichnowsky, 19 April 1904; Schlieffen to Bülow, 20 April 1904, *Die Grosse Politik*, Vol. XIX (I), pp. 174–7.
46 Schlieffen to Bülow, 10 June 1905. *Die Grosse Politik*, Vol. XIX (II), pp. 423–4.
47 Craig, op. cit., p. 283, quoting Bülow's letter to *Süddeutsche Monatshefte*, March 1921. It is true that admirers of Schlieffen like General Groener have declared that he pressed strongly for war in 1905. (I. Geiss, *Julikrise und Kriegsausbruch 1914*, Vol. I (Hanover 1963), p. 43n.) Schlieffen may well have fostered this story in his later years.
48 Bülow, *Memoirs*, p. 104.
49 Rich, *Friedrich von Holstein*, p. 710n, quoting R. Zedlitz-Trützschler, *Zwölf Jahre am deutschen Kaiserhof* (Berlin 1924), p. 174.
50 ibid., pp. 731–2n.
51 ibid., p. 745.
52 Craig, *The Politics of the Prussian Army 1640–1945*, p. 286.
53 Ritter, *The Schlieffen Plan*, pp. 109–11.
54 It is true that the younger Moltke had severely criticised Schlieffen's conduct of manoeuvres, and this may have influenced the Kaiser, yet the basis of Moltke's criticism was that the Kaiser was always allowed to win! Schlieffen was reputed to be a devoted Monarchist but his private letters, first published in 1958 (A. Schlieffen, ed. E. Kessel, *Briefe* (Göttingen 1958), contain severe criticisms of the Kaiser.
55 Bülow, *Memoirs*, p. 176.
56 Goerlitz, op. cit., p. 143.
57 Moltke, *Erinnerungen, Briefe, Dokumente 1877–1916* (Stuttgart 1922), p. 362.
58 Goerlitz, *History of the German General Staff*, p. 144.
59 Bülow, *Memoirs*, p. 76.
60 Ritter, *The Schlieffen Plan*, pp. 168–76, publishes the memorandum in full.
61 In his Preface to Ritter (p. 9), Liddell Hart says that Schlieffen 'contemplated wheeling inwards north of Paris as Moltke did'. There is some

hint of this in 1905 drafts, but there is nothing in the memorandum of December 1905 or the supplementary memorandum of December 1912 to justify this view. Schlieffen repeatedly stressed the importance of crossing the Somme at Abbeville in order to envelop Paris from the west and south.

62 Ritter, *The Schlieffen Plan*, p. 183.

63 ibid., pp. 165–7.

64 Fuller, op. cit., p. 197.

65 Particularly Draft II (Ritter, *The Schlieffen Plan*, p. 154).

66 General Fuller says of the 1912 memorandum that 'Schlieffen's strategical sense must have sadly degenerated in his seventy-ninth year'. (Fuller, op. cit., p. 196n.)

67 *The Schlieffen Plan*, p. 9. This was the argument advanced by Moltke's Chief of Operations in 1914, Colonel Tappen, in *Bis zur Marne 1914* (Berlin 1920), pp. 7f. Ludendorff, who as Chief of Operations 1908–13 bore a heavy share of responsibility for Moltke's modifications, also attempted to argue in this way in his post-war writings and said that 'although Moltke had changed the ratio of strength between the right and left wings by reinforcing the latter, he had not diminished the troop strength of the right wing'. (Ritter, op. cit., p. 54n.)

68 W. S. Churchill, *The World Crisis: The Eastern Front* (London 1931), p. 93.

69 Ritter, *Staatskunst und Kriegshandwerk*, Vol. II, Chap. X, and 'Der Anteil der Militärs an der Kriegskatastrophe von 1914', *Historische Zeitschrift*, Band 193 (1961), 72–91. Ritter's views on the origins of the war are in sharp conflict with those put forward by F. Fischer, *Griff nach der Weltmacht* (Düsseldorf, 1961). For a critical refutation of Fischer's thesis see Ritter, 'Eine neue Kriegsschuldthese?', *Historische Zeitschrift*, Band 194 (1962), 646–68. For a convenient summary of German revisionist writing on the origins of the war see I. Geiss, 'Le déclenchement de la première guerre mondiale', *Revue Historique*, 232 (1964), 415–26.

70 Conrad von Hoetzendorf, *Aus Meiner Dienstzeit* (Vienna, 1921–5), Vol. I, pp. 380–1. Gordon Craig, *The Politics of the Prussian Army 1640–1945*, p. 289, considers that this assurance by Moltke, approved as it was by the Kaiser and Bülow, transformed the Austro-German alliance of 1879 'from a defensive to an offensive instrument'. This seems to exaggerate its general significance, although there is little doubt that Bülow and Moltke wanted Austria to attack Serbia in March 1909 and vainly urged her to do so.

71 L. Albertini, *The Origins of the War of 1914* (London 1952–7), Vol. II, p. 487.

72 Ritter, article, *Historische Zeitschrift* (1961), pp. 86–7.

73 Liddell Hart, *History of the World War*, p. 76. For a detailed discussion of this problem see chapter 10 below.

74 G. A. Craig, 'The World War I alliance of the Central Powers in retrospect', *The Journal of Modern History*, XXXVI (September 1965), p. 339.

75 See L. C. F. Turner, 'The role of the General Staffs in July 1914', *The Australian Journal of Politics and History*, XI (December 1965), 312–15. According to Geiss, Moltke asked Jagow, the Foreign Secretary, at the end of May or early in June 1914, 'to start a preventive war as soon as possible, because militarily the situation for Germany was constantly deteriorating'. (I. Geiss, 'The outbreak of the First World War and German

war aims', *Journal of Contemporary History*, vol. I, no. 3 (July 1966), p. 81. Of course 'Jagow refused'. Moltke's naive request should not be taken too seriously; it runs completely counter to his conduct in July 1914.

76 Conrad, op. cit., Vol. IV, pp. 152–3; S. B. Fay, *Origins of the World War* (New York 1938), Vol. II, pp. 506–10; and Ritter, *Staatskunst und Kriegshandwerk*, Vol. II, pp. 321–2.

77 Ritter, article *Historische Zeitschrift* (1961), pp. 89–90.

78 L. C. F. Turner, op. cit., pp. 320–2.

79 Albertini, op. cit., Vol. II, p. 571n, p. 578, p. 616, p. 621, and pp. 625–6. Paléologue's activities throughout the July crisis are open to the gravest suspicion, and he seems to have acted as the agent of the French General Staff rather than as the representative of France.

80 Ritter, *The Schlieffen Plan*, p. 88.

Moltke and Conrad: Relations between the Austro–Hungarian and German General Staffs, 1909–1914

N. STONE

The eastern front of the First World War remains, as Winston Churchill called his book on it, 'the unknown war'. Whereas in the west, politics were dominated by the military events, the reverse happened in the east: the gigantic struggles which took place from the Baltic to the Black Sea now seem to have been but a prelude to the Revolution in Russia and the collapse of the Austro-Hungarian Empire. There has been little interest in the military aspects of the eastern conflict.

The one battle which has attracted much attention in the west is that of Tannenberg – the 'Cannae of East Prussia', celebrated in military histories and Nazi junketings. It was indeed a spectacular battle, destroying as it did an entire Russian army, and creating the reputation of Hindenburg and Ludendorff. However, for all this laudatory attention, the battle seems to have been rather over-rated. It occupied less than a fifth of all troops engaged at that time in the east, and it is curious that so little regard should have been accorded to the fate of the other four-fifths. Tannenberg acquired its fame largely because it prevented 'the barbarian hordes' from invading the German Reich; hence the hero-worship of Hindenburg and his Chief of Staff. In fact a good part of the work which procured Tannenberg was done by the Austro-Hungarian army in the south.

It had been planned before the war began that Austria-Hungary should take upon herself the greater part of the eastern fighting, while the Germans turned upon France. Negotiations between the allied General Staffs had opened in 1909, at the height of the Annexation crisis, and a joint agreement had been reached to cover the event of a war with France and Russia. The German Chief of Staff, Moltke the Younger, was anxious that the entire German army should seek an absolute victory in France, leaving but a small force to protect Germany from a Russian invasion. This plan naturally required considerable allied assistance, since the small German army in the east could not hope to contain large Russian forces unless Austria-Hungary promised to divert them. The Germans on their side therefore worked to obtain such a promise from Austria-Hungary. The Austro-Hungarian General Staff, whose chief was Franz Baron Conrad von Hoetzendorf, had different ideas. The essential aim of any Austro-Hungarian plan should be to destroy Serbia before attacking Russia. However, Austria-Hungary recognised that Germany must try to secure victory in France, and therefore agreed to take a principal share in the eastern conflict. The General Staff negotiations turned upon these questions: Austria-Hungary must give adequate support in the east, but she also insisted that the German army in East Prussia should give her some parrallel help. Under these circumstances it was agreed that both sides, having completed their mobilisations, would launch an offensive into Russia. The German Eighth Army, in East Prussia, would encompass the defeat of the Russian Second (in the event defeated at Tannenberg); the Austro-Hungarian forces in Galicia would destroy the Russian armies in southern Poland. Conrad promised Moltke that he would take the offensive as soon as he could after war had been declared; Moltke promised Conrad that his force in East Prussia would attack as well, in order to relieve his ally of any extra pressure. This agreement, reached only after considerable trouble, was reinforced by a further stipulation that German troops would arrive in the east within six weeks of beginning the campaign in France.

In the event, both sides tried to evade these promises: the Germans with considerably greater success than Austria-Hungary. The Germans elected not to attack from East Prussia, and Tannenberg, foreseen in the correspondence as an offensive victory, turned out to be the most spectacular defensive one of the war. On his side, Conrad tried to deal with the Serbians before making his promised attack on Galicia: but since the Germans had not fulfilled their part of the bargain, he had to suspend his Serbian plans in order to send vital troops to the east. The Germans did not, of course, finish their campaign in the west as Moltke's ranting confidence had allowed his allies to believe: and German troops did not arrive to the assistance of Austria-Hungary, in significant numbers, until the spring of 1915. Germany had thereby won this competition in *deutsche Treue*; and Austria-Hungary bled to death in order to defend Berlin.

The Austro-Hungarian alliance with Germany, concluded in 1879, was originally planned as an instrument of conservative diplomacy. It was not to be supplemented by any military conventions: Bismarck was careful not to encourage Austro-Hungarian ambitions by granting them military sanction. He was reluctant even to allow conversations between the respective miltary authorities, although these did in fact take place. The German Chief of Staff, Moltke the Elder, uncle of the later Chief of Staff, had decided that if war broke out between Germany and her French and Russian neighbours, the German army would stand on the defensive against France while undertaking a limited offensive in the east, against Russia. This naturally demanded some co-operation with Austria-Hungary, and Berlin was anxious to discover whether her ally intended to play an active part in the campaign, or whether she would be content to defend the Carpathian line. Conversations were opened in 1882, and both sides expressed satisfaction at their outcome. Vienna learned that Berlin intended to send large forces against Russia: the Germans were glad to hear that the Austro-Hungarian army would launch an offensive from Galicia. Writing of these conversations to the Emperor Francis Joseph, Archduke Albert said, 'I can report with considerable satisfaction that, even without prior consultation between Vienna and Berlin, Field-Marshal von Moltke and General Count Waldersee expressed exactly the same views of our eventual joint operations against Russia as have been held here for years'.[1]

Neither Vienna nor Berlin changed these informal arrangements for the next decade: then, harmony was impaired. In 1891 Count Schlieffen became Chief of the German General Staff in succession to Waldersee: and he decided to alter the balance of Germany's strategy. In 1892 he drew up a memorandum in which he argued that Germany must seek absolute victory in a short campaign, and that this could be certain only against France. The German army should concentrate against France, not Russia: necessarily, it would have few troops to spare for East Prussia. This plan gradually became more emphatic: by 1897 Schlieffen had added an injunction that the Germans must march through Belgium in order to conquer France: 'A German army which seeks to wheel round Verdun must not shrink from violating the neutrality of Belgium as well as that of Luxembourg.'[2] A concentration of this kind altogether disturbed the agreements which had been made with Austria-Hungary, and at once relations between the two staffs deteriorated. Beck, the Austro-Hungarian Chief of Staff, first met Schlieffen at the funeral of the elder Moltke, in 1891: and he was unfavourably impressed to find the German 'taciturn' and 'hardly forthcoming'.[3]

Preoccupied as he was with his schemes against France, Count Schlieffen tried to make Beck undertake the real burden in the east. By 1896 he had even suggested that an Austro-Hungarian army should be directly sent to defend Prussian Silesia – a project which Beck indignantly rejected. As one authority says, 'Clearly the allies were now to be saddled with the main burden of the war with Russia, and their Army to be split up in the great spaces between Silesia, Lemberg, and Czernovitz'.[4] When Beck refused to commit his forces in this way, Schlieffen allowed the exchanges to lapse. He claimed that 'Austria need not worry, for the Russian army intended for Galicia will not march until the die has been cast in the west. And the fate of Austria will be decided not on the Bug but on the Seine'. In the autumn of 1896 he told his military attaché in Vienna, 'It is unnecessary to try to obtain further information from Beck'.[5] The suspension of these exchanges lasted until 1909, and during the interval each of the allies framed its plans with no more than cursory reference to those of the other.

Relations between the two armies remained distant for some years and it was not until January 1909 that they were fully resumed. The initiative came from Vienna, at that time menaced by a prospect of war with Russia and Serbia. The Austro-Hungarian Chief of Staff, Conrad, sought and obtained permission from his Foreign Minister to find out from Germany how she intended to act in the event of war with Russia. Accordingly, on 1 January 1909 Conrad addressed a request for information to Moltke, who had succeeded Schlieffen in 1906, and enclosed an exposé of his own views on the situation.[6]

The Austro-Hungarian General Staff had elaborated a complicated series of plans. Austria-Hungary had to count on the hostility of most of her neighbours: most pressing was the possibility of war with Serbia, Montenegro and Russia, but other chances of war existed as regards Italy, a traditionally unreliable ally, and, more remotely, Turkey and Romania. However, Conrad's great preoccupation was the Belgrade–St Petersburg combination, and it was against this that he laid his plans. Three possibilities occurred to him for solution. Serbia and Montenegro might conceivably declare war on the Monarchy and then be left in the lurch by a Russia frightened by Germany; on the other hand Russia and her two Balkan allies might simultaneously declare war on the Monarchy; and, most likely of all, the Monarchy might declare war on Serbia and Montenegro while Russia intervened only some time afterwards. There were therefore two difficult problems: how could Austria-Hungary destroy the Serbian army, and at the same time defend herself against a possible Russian intervention? On the one hand, Conrad must secure himself enough force to destroy Serbia; on the other hand, he must be prepared at any time to devote enough of his strength to the defence of Galicia. Austria-Hungary was not rich in military railways, and these problems were difficult to solve.[7]

However, the General Staff did work out a plan which seemed to provide the necessary flexibility. Conrad decided that he must have a minimum defence force both in Galicia and in the Balkans. These defence forces could be converted to offensive ones by the addition of an extra twelve divisions. If war with Serbia alone appeared likely, these twelve divisions should move to the Balkan theatre; if war with both Russia and Serbia evidenced itself, then these twelve divisions should be transported to Galicia. In the first case, they would make up, together with the minimum defence force, sufficient strength to destroy Serbia; in the second, they would make it possible to launch a powerful offensive against Russia. These three projected groups were given special names: the minimum defence group for the Balkans – about ten divisions – was called Minimalgruppe Balkan; the minimum defence group in Galicia – about thirty divisions – was to be called A-Staffel; and the twelve divisions whose weight could add decisive strength either to the conquest of Serbia or to the maintenance of a powerful attack from Galicia, were called B-Staffel. These three groups could be mobilised singly or together – in other words, Austria-Hungary could, if necessary, perform only partial mobilisation against Serbia, while, at least in theory, this partial mobilisation did not automatically entail mobilisation against Russia. There was one complication in this system, and it was a very serious one. If partial mobilisation were ordered, and both the Minimalgruppe Balkan and the B-Staffel proceeded to Serbia, then B-Staffel could not, with the existing complications of mobilisation, be speedily reversed to meet a danger of war with Russia. Unless Russia chose to clarify her position in a short time after the declaration of war against Serbia, then B-Staffel would not be able to reach Galicia in good time, and the thirty divisions of A-Staffel would alone have to cope with a Russian attack. Conrad's aim in his correspondence with the Germans was to discover whether, to lessen this danger, they would take on enough of the work in the east: if they gave such a promise, then Conrad could also safely take the offensive in Galicia, whether B-Staffel were present or not.[8]

On the German side, matters were less complicated by such anxiety to avoid responsibility for international disturbance. If Germany and Russia came to blows, the German General Staff must assume that France would actively side with the Russians: Germany would therefore seek to destroy France before attacking Russia. No mobilisation plan existed by which Russia alone could be faced: at the very outbreak of war with Russia, the German army, dominated by its inexorable timetables, must unconditionally move to the Belgian and French frontiers. It does not seem to have occurred to the German planners that this movement must unfailingly present the French extremists with a reason of indisputable validity for counter-mobilisation in favour of Russia. Gradually, the proportion of the German army intended for the West was increased from two-thirds to four-fifths and eventually to eight-ninths: the frontier with Russia was to be covered only by the thirteen divisions of the Eighth Army in East Prussia, and an army corps of inexperienced soldiers loosely attached to the left wing of the allied army. Under these circumstances, Moltke was anxious to secure from his ally an assurance that she would take the burden of the eastern conflict while the Germans sought absolute victory in France. Austria-Hungary must therefore be induced to take the offensive in Galicia.

Conrad's letter of 1 January 1909[9] made clear the Austro-Hungarian terms for such an offensive. He outlined the various possibilities which existed, above all that of Russian intervention when Austria-Hungary was already involved against Serbia. He promised to have at least thirty divisions in the Galician area, and announced that these divisions would attack if given an assurance of German co-operation. However, if Russia intervened some considerable time after the mobilisation against Serbia, Conrad could not promise that his divisions in Galicia would be joined in good time by troops from elsewhere: this would occur 'only after three months, counting from the first day of mobilisation': and therefore German support was imperative. This letter also contained technical details in some volume.

Moltke's reply on 21 January[10] was more liberal with encouragement than with information. He suggested that the two Staffs should consider above all the basic principles of their co-operation. He agreed with Conrad that war might be imminent, that 'the moment may arrive when the patience of the [Austro-Hungarian] Empire with Serbian provocation may come to an end . . . in that case the Monarchy will have no alternative but to march into Serbia. I believe that possible active intervention by Russia will occur only after the Austrian invasion of Serbia: this would be the *casus foederis* for Germany'. He was concerned with the complications which German mobilisation must have as regards France, and was convinced that, although France was not at all anxious to have war, she would not stand by while Germany defeated Russia. Germany would somehow force France to clarify her position in this respect. Moltke told Conrad that he intended leaving only the smaller part of his army in the east, in the event of a two-front war, since a quick decision in the war was to be obtained only against France, and his colleague would agree that to split forces would be a disaster. No mention was made of the projected violation of Belgian neutrality; but Moltke seemed confident of victory. 'There is good cause to foresee that Germany, should victory be decided in her favour, will have strong forces within reasonable time for direct support,' he claimed. He told Conrad to fear nothing from Italy, whose army was in a pitiable condition, and announced that 'a final decision on the Western frontier will have taken place by the time events on the Austro-Hungarian frontier have taken a similar course' – a restatement of Schlieffen's 'Austria need not worry'. However, Moltke did not believe that the Powers would go to war: too much was at stake to be hazarded over a conflict in the Serbian cause, and Russia would not intervene.

As far as the strategic details went, this letter left Conrad little better off. Moltke had confined himself to optimistic generalisations and had confirmed Conrad's fear that Moltke was prepared to send only a small part of his forces to the east. The Austro-Hungarian Chief of Staff did not share Moltke's confidence as regards Italy; and Romania, though full of loyal utterances, was as yet questionable support. Conrad endeavoured in his reply, dated 26 January,[11] to find out more precisely from Moltke the determined strength of the German Eighth Army, and to stress the benefits which must accrue to the allies from a German attack. Again he reviewed the various possibilities – France neutral; France and Russia declaring war simultaneously with Serbia; France and Russia intervening only after the war with Serbia had begun. Conrad told Moltke that if he could, he would send both A- and B-Staffeln to the Russian theatre, but said that in the last case B-Staffel might be irrevocably committed in Serbia. In this event he would have only the thirty divisions of A-Staffel in Galicia, which, in order to mount an offensive, must have some German assistance. Conrad's position would be most critical, he said, in 'the most difficult, but, if Russia intends to intervene at all, the most probable case', in which Russia and France hung back 'until such time as the Monarchy has engaged considerable forces in Serbia without being able to withdraw them and send them to Galicia'. Here, Conrad said he could only hope that German support would arrive from the west within forty days of mobilisation, since he did not expect 'to pull out [his forces from Serbia] in the middle of a decisive operation' within fifty days of mobilisation. He suggested accordingly that if Moltke could not give him such an assurance, he would do better to stand on the defensive in Galicia and with the other hand to destroy Serbia. To clarify his position, he said, he required an answer to three questions: what would Germany do if France remained neutral; what would she do in the east if both France and Russia entered the war; and how soon could he, Conrad, expect German troops to arrive in the east after the decision in France?

This letter cannot have been satisfactory to Moltke. The Schlieffen Plan required that Austria-Hungary undertake the somewhat thankless task of defending Germany's back door. If Austria-Hungary elected, as Conrad suggested, to adopt a defensive attitude, then the way was clear for numbers of Russian troops to invade Silesia or even Prussia itself. Conrad must therefore be told that Germany had not forgotten the east; he must be placated with assurances of confidence and support. Moltke's reply of 24 February[12] gave such assurances in liberal measure. He agreed with Conrad that the most likely, and the most dangerous case would be a Russian intervention after war with Serbia had begun. Nevertheless, he urged Conrad to take the offensive, even if at the time he was involved in a Balkan war. He would be supported by eight Romanian divisions situated in Moldavia and 'I believe unreservedly that these German forces [the thirteen divisions in East Prussia] are strong enough to bind on their own $19\frac{1}{2}$ Russian divisions'. On the question of German reinforcement after the war in the west had been decided, he could give no precise answer, since 'here the enemy is also a determining factor' – unusual generosity – and added, 'If France takes the offensive, the decision will come, in my opinion, within three weeks after mobilization. If the French Army awaits our attack in the presumable position behind the frontier fortresses, then I reckon on a decision within four weeks'. He assured Conrad that at all events Austria-Hungary need not particularly worry: she would not be let down and, if Conrad and Moltke together dealt with Russia, then 'the Serbian affair will solve itself for Austria as a matter of course'.

On this letter, Conrad added a pencilled note: 'Certainly: but what am I to do if already tied down in Serbia?'; and his next letter, dated 8 March,[13] endeavoured to extract a more satisfactory answer from Moltke. He urged the German Chief of Staff to make some form of attack in the east, and again declared Austro-Hungarian willingness to undertake an offensive in Galicia even if B-Staffel were already involved in the Balkans, provided that there were some co-operation. If B-Staffel had a chance to move to Galicia, he would of course unconditionally attack, since 'the decision against Russia also involves the decision in the Balkans'. However, he insisted on a German attack in the east, and thought that ten German divisions should cross the Narev into Russian Poland. He next considered 'the most difficult yet the most probable case' – a much used phrase – that France and Russia would not intervene until the Monarchy was already fully committed to a Serbian campaign. Conrad stressed that the Monarchy's best course, in this event, would be to fight a defensive battle based on the San and Dniester rivers: his letter contained a sketch of this position for A-Staffel. He said he regarded this course with abhorrence, alleging his 'decided dislike of any hesitancy' and his 'conviction of the great value of the initiative'; he expressed a willingness to attack, even with only thirty divisions, provided that Romania co-operated and that Germany undertook to deliver an offensive from East Prussia. If pinned down in northern Poland and Bessarabia, the Russian armies would not have so much to spare for Galicia, and the Austro-Hungarian army might be able to win a good success there. Conrad held out a tempting prospect to the Germans: the German attack would defeat the Russian army of the Narev (which was eventually beaten at Tannenberg), while Austria-Hungary performed similar triumphs of arms over the Russians in southern Poland (here, in 1914, the reverse took place). 'This would be a most successful opening of the camapign' and would be a good preparation for the arrival of a victorious force from France and the Balkans.

Conrad had prepared this letter, and passed it through the necessary channels to Moltke, when Moltke's next letter, dated 3 March, reached him. This was a purely technical study,[14] giving details of expected Russian strength, but it prompted Conrad to a still more adamant insistence on this German attack.[15] Dated 8 March, this second letter made clear Conrad's concern that the Eighth Army would have a mere ten divisions with which to make an attack: but this problem he left to the Germans. A routine inquiry was circulated among his staff to consider aspects of this question, but without attempting any answer to it. The central point of the correspondence had been reached: if Germany promised to attack over the Narev in the early phase of the war, then Austria-Hungary would unconditionally attack in Galicia, whether or not she was already involved in Serbia. If the Germans could not give this assurance, then the Austro-Hungarian army would be content to defend the line of the Carpathians and the rivers San and Dniester, unperturbed by the fate of Berlin.

In his reply, dated 19 March,[16] Moltke gave in to Conrad's demands, and promised that his Eighth Army in East Prussia would make the required offensive. He agreed with Conrad that this attack would be an 'effective support' for the Austro-Hungarian offensive in the south. 'I will not hesitate to make the attack to support the simultaneous Austrian offensive. Your Excellency can count absolutely upon this assurance, which has been extensively considered . . . should the allies' intentions be disturbed by enemy action, immediate reciprocal information is required.' This was a promise of the most dubious value. Any such attack across the Narev would be, for the Eighth Army, an almost lunatic venture: everything was against it. In his letter, Moltke stressed these difficulties to his colleague: the role of the German Eighth Army was intended to be purely defensive; recent railway construction in Russian Poland indicated that the Russians intended to send large forces against Germany in the event of war; if the ten divisions foreseen for the attack were in fact to carry it out, they would leave the other three divisions of the Eighth Army to face the entire Russian Army of the Niemen alone; and, from the tactical viewpoint, the ten divisions would find severe troubles in their venture – 'Such an attack by weak forces must at all events overcome severe difficulties: it would be threatened on the right flank from Warsaw, on the left from Lomza'. If Moltke really intended to keep his promise, it showed a reprehensible lack of responsibility; if he did not, then it was a gross deceit of his ally. Probably the promise was a genuine one: Moltke was not a man to lend his name to a conscious fraud. The letter was a typical example of Germany's inability to resolve the contradictions of her existence. In the same way as her statesmen failed to combine their western and eastern interests in a viable, coherent policy, her generals were incapable of overcoming the problems of a two-front war. Moltke was much less concerned with the eastern front than was Conrad: eight-ninths of the German army were to attack France, and Moltke's concentration followed theirs. He felt that the entire war would be decided in France: on the Seine would be decided the fate of battles on the Vistula, the Drina and the Bug. Correspondingly, Moltke seems to have treated the east with a certain unconcern – in all his letters he stressed his belief that the decision in the west would inevitably precede that in the east: the Russian army would be slow to mobilise: therefore Austro-Hungarian fears were groundless. If Austria-Hungary insisted on his making an attack across the Narev, it meant little to Moltke to promise this attack. He therefore yielded to Conrad's importunings: and no one was more surprised than Conrad when, on the very morrow of the outbreak of war, Moltke withdrew his promises. However, Conrad was not clairvoyant, and decided to base all future decisions on the letter of 19 March. He informed Moltke to this effect in a letter sent on 10 April 1909.[17]

When he reopened communications in 1910, Conrad again stressed his reliance upon the engagements of the preceding year. He had now secured a concrete promise of assistance from Germany, and he concerned himself with wider considerations. In his letter of 8 January 1910,[18] he told Moltke that he counted on Romania's assisting the Central Powers while Bulgaria and Turkey remained neutral. He was worried that Italy might completely revoke all her engagements to Berlin and Vienna: 'I cannot avoid the impression that the Monarchy must be unconditionally prepared to find Italy suddenly in the ranks of her enemies.' He even mooted a plan for war with Russia, Italy and Serbia, and said that 'the Russian offensive would have to be stopped on the Danube line Vienna-Budapest, until the main forces should be freed from their engagement in Italy'. Moltke's response, on 30 January,[19] displayed great accord: he too did not count on the Italian alliance. Italy, he said, played for Austria-Hungary much the same role as France for Germany: and if it came to a war with Russia, it would clearly be the most effective solution to declare war at once on both France and Italy – but this solution must be dismissed on 'legal, political, and generally humane grounds'. He told Conrad that if war broke out with Russia, the German government would 'demand from the French Government a comprehensive and clear declaration as to how France will behave in the event of war'. This declaration must be made at once, for the decision whether to send the German army to the east or to the west could brook no delay. 'An evasive or ambiguous answer would be considered tantamount to a declaration of war.' Germany must know on mobilisation who was a friend, and who was an enemy. Conrad's reply to this was simple, in all senses. If war broke out with Russia, Austria-Hungary would send a demand to Italy similar to that made by Germany to France, requesting guarantees for Italian neutrality. This exchange shows how far Conrad was anxious not to be outdone by the Germans in a show of force: for it could only be absurd for Austria-Hungary, already at war with Russia and Serbia, to provoke Italy as well. The rest of the 1910 correspondence dealt, more practically, with the possibilities of Romanian help: this, Moltke said in a letter of 30 March,[20] 'would be unquestionably a worthwhile relief for the Austrian right', and Romania would undoubtedly be easily excited at the prospect of recovering Bessarabia. Conrad replied on 9 April[21] that he had arranged matters with Crainiceanu, the Romanian Chief of Staff; and a substantial Romanian force would co-operate from Moldavia.

Correspondence in 1911 went little further than this. On 26 May[22] Conrad addressed a routine inquiry to Berlin on the case of war with Russia alone. He did not lay too much weight on Romanian intervention, since the Romanian army was bound to be concerned with the possibility of Bulgaria's entering the war against her. Moltke replied on 3 June[23] that if France remained neutral, he would naturally concentrate everything against Russia: but this case was so improbable as to be hardly worthy of consideration. Conrad's reply on 10 June[24] emphasised that he expected Romania to co-operate, although the effect of this might be cancelled out by Bulgarian intervention. This concluded the exchanges for 1911, apart from purely formal communications. On 30 November 1911 Conrad was requested to resign his post, since his constant belligerency had upset the Foreign Minister.

Conrad's successor, Schemua, was a nonentity. He did not change any of the arrangements: late in November 1912 he made a journey to Berlin and confirmed with Moltke all arrangements and agreements: for his benefit the General Staff drew up a file of extracts from the Moltke-Conrad letters.[25] In a report which he made of the meeting, Schemua wrote that Moltke had assured him 'not of any hesitant offensive, but a powerful one parallel with ours . . . he said repeatedly that we can rely absolutely upon Germany's support, in complete loyalty to the alliance, if we are threatened by Russia'. Moltke also promised, according to Schemua's report, that German troops would arrive in the east by the fortieth day of mobilisation (4–5 weeks). Schemua had written to Moltke before that he wished all previous engagements to stand, and Moltke had said nothing to indicate a contrary view.[26] In December 1912 Conrad was again appointed Chief of Staff, and his correspondence with Moltke was reopened.

In 1913 the relations of Austria-Hungary with Italy and Romania began to deteriorate sharply. At the end of 1912, Conrad had heard from his Romanian colleague, Averescu, that Romania intended to assist him in the event of a Russian war: and Conrad, in reply, wished Romania all success in the Balkan arena. However, as a result of the Balkan wars, the Balkan balance was upset, and Romania changed sides.[27] The Balkan wars decisively affected her position: through them she acquired Bulgarian territory with the help of Serbia and under the patronage of Russia, and therefore any Bulgarian renascence must adversely affect both Serbia and Romania. The two thus had, at last, a common interest. Thereafter, Austria-Hungary could not count on Romanian assistance in a war against Serbia. Similarly, Italy, despite the optimism of some members of Moltke's staff, began to show conclusively that she would not side with the Central Powers: the Italian military attaché in Vienna left no doubt on this point in Conrad's mind,[28] and Conrad knew that the military conversations which occurred from time to time were no more than window-dressing.

Correspondence in 1913 remained above such disquieting facts. On 10 February,[29] Moltke urged Conrad not to concern himself too far with the eastern difficulties since 'in the outcome of the conflict between France and Germany lies, to my mind, the essential of the whole European war, and even the fate of Austria will be decided not on the Bug, but on the Seine'. Moltke's domination by Schlieffen evidently included plagiarisation of the master's inaccuracies. Moltke counselled Conrad against causing war at that particular moment, since the German people would not understand the necessity for it. But, he added, 'as ever, I am of the persuasion that a European war must come sooner or later, and in the last resort it will be a war between *Germanentum* and *Slaventum*. To prepare for this is the duty of all states which carry the banners of Germanic *Kultur*. The initial attack must come, however, from the Slavs'. Conrad could not reciprocate these childish fantasies: in his reply of 15 February[30] he pointed out that if Moltke's racialist notions were to establish themselves in wartime, then 'we can hardly rely upon our Slavs, who form 47 per cent of the population, to be enthusiastic about a struggle against their allies. As to military details, he stressed particularly that the Monarchy would need active co-operation from both Germany and Romania in the east, or the offensive in Galicia would be prejudiced. He agreed that 'in the present political and military situation the overthrow of France must be the first aim – that I gladly grant'. No doubt his confidence was not increased by the news that Moltke was now reckoning on English intervention at the side of France.[31]

In 1914 relations continued much as before: the military agreements were not altered, but Conrad had resigned himself to the loss of Romania. On 25 March 1914 he addressed a memorandum to Francis Joseph, pleading for 'energetic action' against the faithless Romanian auxiliaries.[32] The military position of the Central Powers was not now as favourable as it had been: Italy was certain not to fulfil any of her commitments – in this at least she was a reliable ally. Moreover, the essentials of the Moltke-Conrad agreements were not affected: it was, until the very moment war broke out, certain that Germany would seek absolute victory in the west; that her Austro-Hungarian ally, whether or not involved with Serbia, would undertake an offensive in the east in order to defend the German rear; and that the German army in East Prussia would undertake an offensive into Russian Poland, parallel with the Austro-Hungarian attack, in order to take some of the weight from Germany's ally. Furthermore, German troops would arrive from the west within a few weeks of mobilisation. There is no record that these engagements were revoked at any time before the war. Conrad met Moltke in the Bohemian spa of Karlsbad[33] a few weeks before war broke out, and was told only that Germany must unconditionally seek success in the west: she had little to spare for the east. To Conrad's question, what would Moltke do if he lost in the west, Moltke replied, 'Well, I'll do what I can. We're not superior to the French'. This was the last communication of the two General Staffs before the crisis broke, and it remained only to test the accord in war.[34]

War broke out on 28 July 1914 with the Austro-Hungarian declaration of war upon Serbia. The Archduke's assassination on 28 June had been judged an excellent pretext for war, and it had remained only to make sure of German support for the step. This had been forthcoming in greater measure than expected, and a ministerial council of 7 July was informed through Hoyos, returning from a mission to Berlin, that the responsible authorities in Germany had urged

> that we should judge what was to happen, that Germany would stand as a friend and ally at the side of the Monarchy. The Reich Chancellor had also added as his personal opinion that he, like the Kaiser, regarded immediate drastic measures by us against Serbia as the best and most radical solution of our Balkan problems, and considers the present moment to be, from the international point of view, more propitious than a later one.[35]

With this assurance, Berchtold decided to send to Belgrade a series of demands designed to be unacceptable. He delayed until 23 July before sending the note. A principal preoccupation here was, of course, that Russia might intervene to save her Balkan protégé, and Conrad was asked on 7 July whether it was possible to mobilise against Serbia and only later, if need be, against Russia. He replied that the army was prepared for this case: it was possible to mobilise partially, but he must know 'by the fifth day of mobilisation' whether Russia would intervene, or his plans would go awry.[36]

For Conrad this was a most important question. It was inherently probable that Austria-Hungary would already have begun her movement against Serbia when Russia decided to intervene. In military terms, this would mean that B-Staffel and the Minimalgruppe Balkan would be enmeshed in Serbia, prepared to carry out the planned defeat of the Balkan enemy. If the attitude of Russia were not clear by the fifth day of mobilisation, then it would be difficult in view of the Monarchy's railway problems, to redirect the vital B-Staffel to Galicia. Conrad had promised Moltke an offensive from Galicia, and it was important to know as soon as possible when Russia would intervene. Conrad himself says he would have preferred to mobilise the entire army at once, without waiting for a Russian declaration: '. . . from the military point of view it would have been desirable to anticipate this danger, to treat the Serbian War as a subsidiary and to begin the war with Russia. But it was impossible to do so merely on a suspicion of Russian intervention.'[37] On 25 July, at 9.23 pm, the Austro-Hungarian army was partially mobilised against Serbia, which had, in the interval, sent the expected 'unsatisfactory' reply to the ultimatum. Conrad's order affected in substance the troops of B-Staffel and the Minimalgruppe Balkan.[38]

The situation demanded close co-operation between the Foreign Ministry and the Chief of the General Staff. It was of the utmost importance from the military point of view that the General Staff should know whether to expect Russian intervention, so that B-Staffel, indispensable in the Galician theatre, should not be irrevocably sent to the Balkans. There seem, however, to have been great gaps in the liaison, and Conrad was largely left to make up his own mind on the possibility of Russian intervention. There are records of several conversations between Conrad and Berchtold, but these exchanges seem to have been vitiated in the first place by Conrad's inability to listen for long to uncongenial information, and in the second by Berchtold's incapacity to assert political control of strategy. Consequently, despite an ever increasing volume of information, Conrad appears to have acted in the hope that Russia would permit Austria-Hungary to extinguish Serbia: a hope no doubt nourished by Berchtold's intimidated silences.

It is difficult to believe that Conrad expected Russia not to intervene. Perhaps he thought that, as in 1909, the Russians would back down in face of a concrete German threat – certainly Conrad, like most people in Central Europe, greatly admired German power, if not its spirit. At all events, it is curious that he should have mobilised B-Staffel against Serbia when it became clear that there were excellent grounds that it would shortly be required in Galicia. On 27 July Conrad heard from Berchtold that consular reports from Russia indicated considerable military activity.[39] These reports continued throughout the 28th, and on the 29th Count Shebeko, the Russian ambassador, told Berchtold that Russia had decided to mobilise her western districts.[40] At 10 pm on the same day Conrad heard from his military attaché in St Petersburg, Prince Francis Hohenlohe, that the Russian army had begun to mobilise.[41] On the 30th, this news was confirmed with reference to the entire Russian army.[42] In consequence of these reports Austria-Hungary decided to mobilise the rest of her army, A-Staffel, intended for Galicia. The order was to be delayed until 1 August, since it was hoped not to embarrass German diplomatic action through any belligerent moves.[43]

However, after the decision had been taken, word reached Vienna from Count Szögyény in Berlin that the German army might mobilise if Russia continued her mobilisation.[44] On 31 July Vienna received word that the Russians had received a German ultimatum to this effect,[45] and Conrad's military attaché in Berlin wrote that Moltke urgently required military co-operation from his ally.[46] A telegram arrived from Moltke stating, 'It is necessary for Austria-Hungary to take counter-measures'.[47] At midday on the 31st, Austria-Hungary therefore ordered the mobilisation of A-Staffel as well. In the afternoon, Vienna heard that Germany had proclaimed a state of danger, and at 6 pm it was heard that Germany would mobilise against Russia.[48] Only one question remained: whether France would be involved in the war. Berlin was naturally anxious to establish that Austria-Hungary would order the mass of her army against Russia, while Germany attacked France, and on 31 July the Kaiser telegraphed to Francis Joseph:

In this great struggle it is of primary importance that Austria should mobilise her main force against Russia and not fragment herself through any simultaneous offensive on Serbia. This is all the more important since a great part of my Army will be engaged against France. Serbia plays, in this gigantic struggle where we stand shoulder to shoulder, a quite subsidiary role, requiring only a necessary minimum of defensive measures.[49]

Early in the morning of 1 August, a telegram arrived from Count Szögyény, announcing that the German Secretary of State, Jagow, had asked him to report as his 'personal hope' that 'the main weight of our military action be directed against Russia'.[50] Within an hour of this, further word arrived from Berlin that the Kaiser had asked the Austro-Hungarian military attaché to pass on 'the highly urgent request' to Francis Joseph and his Chief of Staff 'that all means at their disposal should be turned against Russia, in order to deal with the forces threatening from there'.[51] Francis Joseph replied to the Kaiser's telegram on 1 August, saying, 'As soon as My General Staff learned that you are determined to begin the war with Russia as early as possible, the decision was also established here to assemble the great majority of our troops against Russia'. This part of the telegram was based on a note given by Conrad to the Foreign Ministry officials responsible for the draft telegram.[52]

Conrad's note may have been an exaggeration. It was certainly far from the truth. On 1 August only A-Staffel had been ordered to proceed to Russia: the rest of the army was already bound for Serbia, according to Conrad's orders. If there had been any likelihood of war with Russia, the vital B-Staffel should have gone to Galicia, not Serbia. By 31 July war with Russia had become a near certainty, and even before then it had been more than highly probable. Conrad had promised Moltke that if it came to war with Russia he would send most of his troops to Galicia: but in fact the twelve divisions of B-Staffel were proceeding according to an altogether different plan. Moreover, orders to the contrary did not reach the commands involved until 6 August. This decision resulted in disaster. B-Staffel was not allowed to stay in the Balkans, where it would presumably have inflicted a defeat upon the outnumbered Serbs; but it did not reach Galicia until it was too late to change the situation in the north-east.

After the war, Conrad wrote an apologia for this decision to send the Second Army – B-Staffel – to the Serbian theatre. He represented his decision as 'eine verkehrstechnische Unvermeidlichkeit', a necessary and inevitable consequence of technical considerations. He says that on 31 July it was impossible to send the Second Army to Galicia: it had already started for Serbia, and it could not be reversed without causing chaos in the mobilisation of A-Staffel. Therefore it must continue its predestined course to the Serbian front, and, having arrived there, depart again for the Galician front when the mobilisation lines were clear.

If the change of strategic tasks had occurred two days earlier, the prepared deployment [of both Staffeln, to Galicia] could have been carried out. But now the transports to Serbia were already in movement. To interrupt them and to reverse them at short notice would have caused chaos.

Only a few units of the Second Army could proceed to Galicia by the direct route: the rest must continue towards Serbia. Such was Conrad's 'verkehrstechnische Unvermeidlichkeit'.[53]

In view of certain evidence, this is a strange decision. But it is confirmed by the files and log-books of the railway section in the General Staff.[54] The Austro-Hungarian railways had been prepared for war with Serbia since 20 July, three days before the note was sent, and on 21 July preparations were made for the Balkan mobilisation. Between that day and the end of the month preparations went on in ever increasing scope. The chief of the railway section, Lieutenant-Colonel Straub, was an important man in the General Staff, and most of his log-book entries show records of consultation with Conrad or his deputy, Höfer, or the Chief of the Operations Section, Metzger. There is a curious entry for 29 July: Straub, Metzger and Höfer [Conrad's *Stellvertreter*] met to consider the possibilities for mobilisation against Russia, and 'established a similarity of views' – nothing more specific is recorded. Straub was asked by Conrad when, from the mobilisation timetables, it would be best to mobilise against Russia, and heard from Straub that 1 August would be the most suitable time for mobilisation, naming 4 August as the first day of mobilisation. The evening of 31 July first brought a crisis. When he came home in the evening, Straub had a message from Conrad asking him to return at once. At 9.45 pm he saw Conrad, and was asked

the serious question, what would be my reaction if the 'B'-deployment already in movement were not to be carried out and if everything were to be turned against Russia. I inform His Excellency that this would mean a catastrophe and that it would be impossible to carry out under the technical conditions of the railways.[55]

Later, he says that a reversal of B-Staffel would cause 'endless complications' and enumerates those troop-transports which had already begun to move south.[56] Conrad, composing his memoirs after the war, has left a note on the side of this report to say that he showed Straub the German Kaiser's telegram, but that even here Straub remained adamant. The Second Army could not be reversed to the Galician front. The next day, 1 August, Straub arrived early at his desk, and was again urgently asked whether the Second Army could be reversed: again he said that 'this would be a catastrophe for which I can take no responsibility'.[57] But he told Conrad that B-Staffel could, with careful planning, be sent back from the Balkans in order to take part in Conrad's Galician enterprises. Moreover, no significant time would be lost. Such is the log-book of the railway section of the General Staff, written day by day as events took place. It seems completely to vindicate the truth of Conrad's account.

On the other hand, there is a very great volume of evidence to suggest an altogether different explanation. In the first place, it is most curious that

Conrad should not have restrained B-Staffel in view of the very obvious danger threatening from Russia. He hoped, of course, that Russia would not intervene. But it had been becoming increasingly clear since 26 July that Russia would take military measures to protect Serbia. This was apparently obvious to Conrad, who wrote a report to the Emperor which began, on 29 July, 'The general situation can at any moment take a turning which will directly cause the outbreak of war among the Great Powers'.[58] A similar document, addressed to the Emperor by Archduke Frederick, nominally Commander-in-Chief of the Army, again written on 29 July, indicates that the General Staff were highly concerned with the possibility of Russian intervention.[59] Conrad in his memoirs says that 'only the 30th July brought clarity' to the Russian question.[60] It is certainly curious that Conrad under these circumstances did not hold up the Second Army until some decision had been achieved by the German approach to Russia, of which he was informed in the early evening of 30 July; but no order, to judge from the files of the high command, the Balkan commander and the Second Army command, was made or even mooted by Conrad. To send the Second Army to Serbia when it was clear that the Russian army would at least threaten war, was a decision either of an incredible frivolity or reflected some design on Conrad's part which he was not, after the war, anxious to air: namely, an attempt to evade his promise of an offensive in Galicia.

Again, it is altogether curious that the 'technische Unvermeidlichkeit' should have materialised so severely on 31 July. From the beginning, Conrad had said that 1 August, not 31 July, was the day on which he must know whether or not Russia would intervene, so that he could at will send the Second Army to Galicia. After 1 August, it must carry out its planned advance on Serbia. At the ministerial council of 7 July he had answered that he must know this 'by the fifth day of mobilisation', this being the day on which the Second Army would be irrevocably committed to Serbia.[61] In the order of 25 July, 'the first day of mobilisation' was named as 28 July, on which day the whole mobilisation programme was to be built. Until then, the necessary security precautions and preparations would be made: troops would begin to appear at the regimental depots only on 28 July. The first of August would therefore be, as Conrad himself describes it, 'the fifth day of mobilisation'. That he claimed this day as decisive is corroborated in the papers left by Count Berchtold to describe the proceedings of the council of 7 July. Again, on 28 July, according to his own account, Conrad told Berchtold that 1 August was the last point at which the General Staff could revoke a decision to open the offensive against Serbia: he told the assembled authorities 'that I must know by August 1st whether we would be compelled to begin war with Russia, for, if this did not become clear by then, all transports would start their movement against Serbia'.[62] His own account is corroborated by a telegram sent by the Hungarian minister, Baron Burián, who was present.

In confidence: in a conversation which has just taken place, the Chief of Staff announced that if Russia begins mobilisation by August 1st, he would send the mass of the Army to the North and would regard Serbia merely as a subsidiary theatre. Until then no time is lost. If by August 1st Russia does not intervene against us, then the Serbian war proceeds with all energy and we turn against Russia after striking down Serbia with rapid blows.[63]

Yet it was on 31 July, a day before he needed, by his own and every other extant account, to learn of Russian intervention, that Conrad suddenly discovered that it was too late to recall the Second Army.

Besides, if Conrad really had the pressing intention of recalling the Second Army from Serbia, he would presumably have informed all the relevant military commands of the proposed switch. There is nothing in the records of any of these relevant commands to suggest that Conrad sent them any information at all on this point until considerably later than 31 July. The orders of *Armeeoberkommando* are clear: no instruction was sent either to the Second Army or to Lieutenant-General Potiorek, the commander of the Balkan theatre, that the Second Army was expected to return to Galicia. An order to the Second Army command in Budapest, sent at 8 pm on 31 July – some considerable time after the knowledge of Russian mobilisation had reached Vienna – stated, 'For those formations mobilised before July 30th (for the Case of a Balkan War) the instructions made by the War Ministry and the High Command with regard to Case "B", and especially the transport arrangements for Case "B", are to remain in force', Case 'B' being the movement of the Second Army to Serbia.[64] This order was made after Conrad had learned of Russian mobilisation, after he had learned that Germany intended to send an ultimatum to Russia, but before he had even had any word with Straub concerning the matter. It would seem, then, that whatever Straub's answer Conrad was anxious to send the B-Staffel to Serbia. This order to the Second Army was confirmed by a further one on 1 August: 'Mobilization will be carried on as it began', excepting for a few trivial units.[65] This order was sent in response to an inquiry from the Second Army as to whether its arrangements were to be affected by the outbreak of war between Germany and Russia. Similarly, on the same day word was sent to Potiorek in Sarajevo, who was expecting to command the operations against the Serbian army, and who therefore had a primary right to know whether he could count on the presence of the Second Army, that 'despite the general mobilization, the orders already given are to stand and the deployment against Serbia will be carried out as it began'.[66] The files of the Second Army show no indication of any contrary order until 6 August, and indeed on 4 August it issued an order to begin preparations for a campaign in Serbia – it elaborated details concerning quartering, Serbo-Croat interpreters, an automobile for the commander.[67] It was not until 6 August that any order was received from Vienna: on that day, word arrived in Peterwardein, headquarters of the Second Army, that 'Second Army with Seventh Corps will be transported to the North-Eastern theatre between 18th and 21st August' – an order to be deciphered personally by the army's Chief of Staff.[68] If Conrad did decide on 31 July to send the Second Army to Galicia, he allowed it none the less to base all its calculations on its remaining in the south – indeed, it was specifically ordered to do so.

Moreover, if the records both of the high command and of the Second Army betray no trace of any intention to send B-Staffel to Galicia, there is no such indication either in the log-book and reports of Potiorek, commander of the Serbian front. He above all should have been informed of the alteration in plans, if any such really existed, for he was to undertake the offensive into Serbia, a task manifestly impossible if the twelve divisions of the Second Army were removed to Galicia. But his records up to 6 August show nothing but ignorance. On 1 August one of his units asked if, in view of the general mobilisation, it should change any of its dispositions, preparatory to a purely defensive role in the Balkans: Potiorek ordered against this.[69] On the same day, Potiorek wrote to the high command, 'I am hampered in my work in as much as I do not know whether it is intended, despite the intervention of Case "R", at once to send the Corps designed for Case "B" against Serbia and then turn them with all force against Russia', or whether he must expect B–Staffel to be sent directly to Galicia. He had just heard from the chief of the railway section that the mobilisation towards the Balkan theatre was proceeding without disturbance, which he described as 'a very satisfying piece of news'.[70] On 2 August, writing to the chief of the emperor's military chancellery, Baron Bolfras, he says that there is little to report, that the mobilisation is proceeding well and that the spirit of the troops is excellent. He looks forward 'to showing the world what we can do' against Serbia – in the event he was through Conrad's blunders to show the world only too clearly.[71] His reports of that day show no change in plan, and those of 3 August indeed begin to develop a plan for an attack on Serbia, based on the assurance that the Second Army would take part.[72] The same project is aired on 4 August, in a private letter to Conrad:[73] Potiorek assumes that Serbia will have only weak forces in the west, against his attack, since most of her strength will be gathered in the north to face the Second Army. On 5 August he criticises the high command: 'I am curious to know when the High Command, until now somewhat economical with its release of information, will emerge from its reserve', and adds later, 'By 7 pm the High Command has evidenced itself only through the telegraphic instruction' that a few small reserve units are to prepare for transport to Galicia.[74] Up to midnight on 5 August, Potiorek had therefore heard nothing of significance from Conrad, and until then he had based all his plans on the presupposition that the Second Army would take part in his campaign. Only on 6 August did he receive an instruction: 'The entry of the Monarchy into war at the side of Germany demands the transport of the Second Army to the North-Eastern theatre . . . the despatch of this Army will presumably begin on 18th August.'[75]

The entire picture is complicated, but its essentials are clear. Until 31 July Conrad seems to have acted with a blithe confidence that Russia would not intervene. In fact, all the evidence, as recognised by Conrad himself, suggested that she would intervene: yet even after hearing the news of a

German ultimatum to Russia, Conrad confirmed his order to the Second Army to move to Bosnia and the southern front. Moreover, he did not countermand this instruction until a week had passed: a week in which several decisive pieces of information reached him. The entire 'technische Unvermeidlichkeit' is puzzling, but probably irrelevant to the main issue. It is curious that Conrad should so boldly and so consistently have maintained that 1 August was the latest day on which the Second Army could be reversed to Galicia: he must surely have known that this was an error. He had been in daily communication with the railway experts since 20 July – the log-book of the railway section makes this clear. It is of course always possible that Straub, not Conrad, made the miscalculation, and suddenly discovered on 31 July that it was already too late to reverse the Second Army: but if Straub had made a statement of such disastrous consequences, he would surely have been dismissed and then castigated in Conrad's memoirs. In fact he kept his post, apparently with all success, during the entire war, and received from Conrad nothing but the firmest of accolades. The evidence suggests very strongly that Conrad was determined above all to destroy Serbia – this was, after all, the reason for the outbreak of war. He had in 1909 informed Moltke that he might be involved in Serbia when war broke out, and that it would be impossible to detach his troops in the middle of any 'decisive campaign'. Possibly, therefore, the Austro-Hungarian Chief of Staff pleaded technical difficulties for a decision already determined by his political views: striking evidence that Austria-Hungary was resolved to solve her south Slav difficulties first through, and then despite, a European war.

Without being unduly hypothetical, this was clearly her best course, both militarily and politically. To attempt an offensive in the east could only be hazardous, and by 31 July it was certain that both Italy and Romania would be neutral: [76] therefore Austria-Hungary could not count on any of the auxiliary support so often mooted in the correspondence with the Germans. One of the conditions laid down for an Austro-Hungarian offensive in Galicia had been Romanian support. It was much better for Austria-Hungary at the peace conference to have a total victory over Serbia, even if this did mean sacrificing a partial advantage in Galicia. Besides, if Austria-Hungary did show enough force against Serbia, then Bulgaria would perhaps be enticed to support the Austro-Hungarian attack; and on 2 August, Conrad did sketch a plan for the event of alliance with Bulgaria. Consequently, Conrad allowed the Second Army to continue to Serbia, and ordered his forces in Galicia to adopt a position more suitable for a defensive action. As a later justification of these proceedings, he urged technical difficulties. His explanation is difficult to accept.

If by 6 August Conrad decided after all to recall the Second Army, this was a result of altogether different factors. Between 31 July and 6 August Austria-Hungary made determined efforts to call in Bulgaria. But the Bulgarians made it clear, by 4 August, that they intended to await a decision in the west before committing themselves to the Central Powers: they too believed that the fate of Austria would be decided on the Seine, not on the Bug – certainly not on the Drina. Again, a probably decisive influence on Conrad's recalling the Second Army was that the Germans in East Prussia refused to carry out their promised offensive. The basic disagreement in the correspondence of January – March 1909, and particularly that expressed in Conrad's two letters of 8 March, was that Austria-Hungary would already be involved in Serbia and would therefore be unable to meet the Russians in Galicia with more than the thirty divisions of A-Staffel: it was this case which Conrad saw as the most difficult yet the most probable, in his much repeated phrase, and it was for this case that the Germans were requested to make their attack over the Narev. If the German army in East Prussia took an active role, then it need not matter – or so Conrad thought – that Austro-Hungarian troops should also be engaged in Serbia. This was the case which Conrad tried to assert in July 1914, against all the evidence: the *technical inevitability* arrived as belated reinforcement for his totally untenable propositions. In fact Moltke revoked his promise to attack, concentrated all in the west and agreed with the Eighth Army commander that a defensive position should be adopted in face of the expected Russian offensive. Moltke's revoke forced Conrad to bring support to Galicia: therefore on 6 August the Second Army was recalled to its service on the Russian front.

For the first three days of August, contact between Moltke and Conrad was curiously remote – the military plenipotentiaries sent by the two allies to each other complain in their memoirs that they were told very little of their respective commanders' intentions.[77] On 2 August Moltke wrote to Conrad, enclosing a review of the German plans in the east. The letter reached Conrad on 3 August. It was little more than a general encouragement, in heavily Germanic terms – 'Mit Gott, mein Herr Kamarad!' was its ending. It was, however, accompanied by certain technical details, among them an extract of the order given on mobilisation to the Eighth Army:

The Commander has the order to bind as many as possible of the effectives of the Northern and Western Russian Army Groups, to draw them away thus from the Austrian Army and to make the first battles easier for that Army. If the Russians undertake an early offensive into East Prussia with forces considerably superior to the German Army in the East, then the victory of the Austro-Hungarian Army will be made easier, the more so the earlier the Austro-Hungarian Army begins to advance into Russia.[78]

Moltke, then, declared that the East Prussian army would take the offensive into Russia only if the Russians remained passive opposite Germany and directed their greatest force against Austria-Hungary. Militarily, this was an impeccable decision. It is most curious that Moltke had not thought of it before: in his letter of 19 March 1909 his promise to attack over the Narev had not been conditional upon any such passive Russian attitude. At all events, the Germans in East Prussia would not launch any attack across the Narev.

Conrad had clearly been relying upon their unconditionally making such an attack, and he expected great results from it. A staff map in the 1914 file of the War Archives shows a sketch by Conrad of an attack from East

Prussia together with a plan for an Austro-Hungarian offensive, both launched at the highly vulnerable base of the Polish Salient.[79] Moltke's withdrawal of his promise came as a complete and unwelcome surprise: Conrad had had no indication that the promised German attack would not materialise, and his letter of 14 February had talked happily of 'our intention of making an offensive as soon as possible'.[80] To protect himself from the Russian superiority, made grave by Moltke's revoke, Conrad had belatedly to summon the Second Army from the Serbian front.[81] It arrived some days after the 'decision' had been made in Galicia: as Winston Churchill puts it, 'it left Potiorek before it could win him a victory: it returned to Conrad in time to participate in his defeat'.

Denied his chance of settling accounts with Serbia, Conrad now thought to procure at least a partial victory elsewhere. Only in Russia could the prestige of the dynasty and the army, that quantity for which war had been declared, be redeemed. He informed Moltke that he would take the offensive, in the firm hope that the Germans would repeat Sedan in the west. He was sure that the Germans would send him adequate reinforcements in the east within six weeks, and with this insurance could hazard a great deal. On 3 August he wrote to Moltke, 'May it be granted to our Armies, allied in German good faith (*deutsche Treue*) to emerge with success from this gigantic conflict'[82] – the reference to *deutsche Treue* presumably being intended for press release. Moltke replied on 5 August, his enthusiasm similarly defeating his insight: 'Let loose the Bulgars against the Serbs, and let that pack strike each other dead. Now we have only one goal! Russia! Throw the knout-carriers into the Pripet marshes and drown them there!'[83]

Even in the first days of the war, the military eclipse of Austria-Hungary by Germany had begun. Austria-Hungary had been cast for a thankless part in German schemes, a role which also involved a sacrifice of her own direct interests. As a Great Power, Austria-Hungary was interested in destroying Serbia:[84] as a German satellite, in some respects as tame and cowed as those of a later war; she had to forget her own interests in order to follow German requests as regards the Eastern front. Conrad had tried to evade this role by sleight-of-hand, to plead his technical difficulties and to destroy Serbia before obeying German behests as regards Russia. However, it had been sufficient for Germany to evade her promises for Conrad to be recalled to his own. After 4 August, Conrad's one hope of an early, respectable and independent success was through an attack in Galicia: and even this depended upon an insurance by German reinforcements. In the event, Conrad launched his armies into southern Poland on 23 August. After a few early successes, which in fact drew vital Russian reserves from the East Prussian front, he found that the Russian superiority was much greater than he had expected. By 11 September his offensive in Galicia had collapsed; and there was no prospect of immediate German help in significant proportions. He had therefore to give an order to retreat. By a curious twist of fate, Conrad gave his order to retreat at almost exactly the same hour on the same day as Moltke issued a similar order to his troops on the Marne:

at 5 pm on 11 September 1914. The Battle of Lemberg ended the Austro-Hungarian army as a first-class fighting force, and Germany was never to redeem the judgement of the Marne.[85]

EDITOR'S NOTE

Since writing this important article Dr Stone has done further research on the Austro-Hungarian war planning, which both supplements and corrects some of the details given here. Readers are referred to his article, 'Die Mobilmachung der österreichisch-ungarischen Armee 1914', *Militärgeschichtliche Mitteilungen* (1974), Issue II, pp. 67–95; and to his book, *The Eastern Front 1914–17* (London, 1975).

NOTES

1 H. Schäfer, 'Die militärischen Abmachungen des Dreibundes vor dem Weltkrieg', *Militärwissenschaftliche Mitteilungen* (1922), Heft 9. Further material on these early negotiations is provided by E. von Glaise-Horstenau, *Franz Josephs Weggefährte. Das Leben des Generalstabschefs Grafen Beck* (Vienna, 1930); in R. Kiszling's study of the subject in *Mil. Wiss. Mit.* (1933), Heft 3; and in three admirable works by Gerhard Ritter, *The Schlieffen Plan*, of which there is an English edn (New York, 1958); the first two volumes of his *Staatskunst und Kriegshandwerk*; and a long article, 'Die Zusammenarbeit der Generalstäbe Deutschlands und Oesterreich-Ungarns vor dem ersten Weltkrieg', in *Zur Geschichte und Problematik der Demokratie* (1958), pp. 523–49.
2 The full text of this draft is given in Ritter's *Schlieffen*. The plan became more and more single-minded, until eventually Schlieffen included Holland in his list of condemned neutralities. She won her reprieve in 1914 because Moltke thought her an essential economic outlet.
3 Glaise-Horstenau, op. cit., p. 344.
4 Ritter, 'Zusammenarbeit', 532–3.
5 Ritter, *Schlieffen*, pp. 31–2.
6 F. Conrad (hereafter 'Conrad'), *Aus meiner Dienstzeit 1906–1918*, 5 vols. (Vienna, 1921–5), Vol. I, pp. 369–70, gives an account of the opening of these negotiations and discussions. They were arranged beforehand by Aehrenthal and Bülow, and throughout the resulting correspondence the Foreign Minister, the German Chancellor and the two emperors were shown the letters concerned.
7 Railway construction in the Habsburg Monarchy, particularly in the Balkans, was made excessively difficult by Hungarian obstruction. The Hungarian regime was most anxious to emphasise that Hungary was a separate state and to make her economically cohesive. Consequently, while each half of the Monarchy built up its railways with speed and care, there were very few lines which connected the two. Hungary and Galicia, for example, were connected only by a single-track railway over the Dukla Pass; transport from Vienna to Lwów (Lemberg) went not by the shorter route through Hungary but via Cracow and Prague. These conditions

were still worse in the Balkans, where they were complicated by economic rivalry between Austria and Hungary. Hungary was anxious to integrate Croatia into the other lands of the Crown of St Stephen, and there was therefore no direct and fast railway communication between Austria and Bosnia, except via Budapest. To travel from Laibach (Ljubljana) in Austrian Slovenia to Zagreb in Hungarian Croatia, a distance of some forty miles, took three hours; and any freight to Europe proper had to pass from Croatia via Budapest. The Hungarians seem even to have chosen a somewhat different railway track. The Archduke Charles, later emperor, when returning from his honeymoon in Dalmatia in 1911, had to transfer from his own state coach to one specially brought down from the Hungarian capital, since the Hungarian state railways could accommodate only such a carriage (R. Lorenz, *Kaiser Karl und der Untergang der Donaumonarchie* (Graz/Vienna/Cologne, 1959), p. 100.

8 Winston Churchill's *The Unknown War* (New York, 1931), contains an unsurpassed account of the Austro-Hungarian mobilisation plans and the difficulties they encountered. Information on these comes from a variety of sources, notably Conrad's memoirs; the Austrian official history, E. von Gleise-Horstenau *et al.* (eds), *Oesterreich-Ungarns Letzter Krieg*, 15 vols. (Vienna, 1930–8), Vol. I, pp. 3–15 – this is an official history rare in its kind in fairness and lucidity – Kiszling, *Oesterreichs Anteil am Ersten Weltkrieg* (Graz, 1959); and a dissertation for Vienna University by F. Käs. I have considerably simplified the Austro-Hungarian plans, particularly as regards the exact numbers involved with the three mobilisation plans: these were slightly altered from year to year, and in a strategic study it would be cumbersome to record trivial changes in the operational structure. In July 1914 the strength of the three groups was: A-Staffel, 28½ infantry divisions, 10 cavalry divisions, 21 reserve brigades; B-Staffel, 12 infantry divisions, 1 cavalry division, 6 reserve brigades; Minimalgruppe Balkan, 8 infantry divisions, 0 cavalry divisions, 7 reserve brigades. (The reserve brigades were composed of territorials (*Landsturm*) and untrained conscripts (*Ersatz*): these were not counted as a serious fighting-force.) I do not, in the text, complicate issues by mentioning the cavalry divisions, since each was little more than the size of an infantry regiment, and all but one were intended for Galicia. The First, Fourth and Third Armies made up A-Staffel; the Second Army was B-Staffel; the Fifth and Sixth Armies formed the Minimalgruppe Balkan. Each of the sixteen army corps of the Monarchy were also attached to one of the Staffeln, but the mobilisation of 1914 disrupted these careful apportionings, and B-Staffel lost, in the end, a good part of its original force. The exact strength of the Austro-Hungarian army in 1914 was: 48 infantry and 11 cavalry divisions, 2 *Landsturm* divisions and 41 reserve brigades. The German army contained 90 infantry and 11 cavalry divisions. Much useful information on these points is to be gained from the London War Office series, 'Handbooks on Foreign Armies', prepared for the Intelligence Department of the British War Office.

9 The Moltke-Conrad correspondence is printed almost in entirety in Conrad's memoirs. After the war, when writing these memoirs, Conrad had the use of the original material in the War Archives and his versions are, apart from a few and trivial verbal omissions, correct. This correspondence is still extant, for the great part, in Vienna, and, where possible, I have given the reference of the War Archives, Kriegsarchiv (Wien)

Generalstab Faszikel 89 (a) Operations-Bureau, in addition to the Conrad reference. This archive source contains Moltke's letters as they arrived, and Conrad's letters in their final draft before being made easily legible by a copy-writer. In quoting the original German I do so where the source is entirely unprinted. According to the text of these letters, or to notes appended to the text, they were invariably shown to the Foreign Ministry and the Emperor, both in Vienna and Berlin, before being sent off. I find it difficult to believe that the responsible political authorities ever paid much attention to this correspondence, varying as it does so often from wearisome technicalities to grotesque fantasies. Many of Conrad's comments to Moltke were in flagrant contradiction to his Foreign Minister's views: but I can find nothing to suggest that the Foreign Ministers, particularly Aehrenthal, ever took exception to the contents of any of these letters. I assume that Ahrenthal, after a time, gave up reading the correspondence. The German statesmen were presumably more thorough: but at the same time they were much more intimidated by military minds. Conrad's initial letter of 1 January 1909, referred to in Conrad, Vol. I, pp. 369–75, is in Vienna as Kriegsarchiv Generalstab Faszikel 89 (a) Operations-Bureau Kuvert 1909/I.

10 Conrad, Vol. I, pp. 379–84; Kr.A., ibid., 1909/II.

11 Conrad, Vol. I pp. 384–93; Kr.A., ibid., 1909/III. To this letter is attached as *Beilage III* a document which appears to be a tracing of an operational sketch, apparently sent with the letter. It covers a possible defensive position for A-Staffel in Galicia, with its strength gathered behind the rivers San and Dniester. This was the very plan which Moltke found unwelcome.

12 Conrad, Vol. I, pp. 394–6; Kr.A., ibid., 1909/IV. Conral's pencilled note occurs where Moltke urges Conrad to attack Russia: 'Ist dieses grosse Ziel erreicht, dann wird sich die serbische Angelegenheit für Oesterreich von selber erledigen.'

13 Conrad, Vol. I, pp. 396–9; Kr.A., ibid., 1909/V.

14 This letter, briefly mentioned by Conrad, is Kr.A., ibid., 1909/VI.

15 Conrad, Vol. I, pp. 401–2; Kr.A., ibid., 1909/VII.

16 Conrad, Vol. I, pp. 403–5; Kr.A., ibid., 1909/VIII.

17 Conrad, Vol. I, pp. 405–6; Kr.A., ibid., 1909/IX. Conrad mentions in his memoirs a further letter of 1909, described as *Privatschreiben* (I, 165). Here Moltke regrets that an occasion for war was missed in 1908–9.

18 Conrad, Vol. II, pp. 54–7; Kr.A., ibid., 1910/II.

19 Conrad, Vol. II, pp. 57–60; Kr.A., ibid., 1910/III.

20 Conrad, II, 61–2; Kr.A., ibid., 1910/VIII.

21 Conrad, II, 62; Kr.A., ibid., 1910/IX.

22 Conrad, II, 102–5; Kr.A., ibid., 1911/XVII.

23 Conrad, II, 105–7; Kr.A., ibid., 1911/Geheimnummer 34.

24 Conrad, II, 107–9; Kr.A., ibid., 1911/Geheimnummer 35.

25 Kr.A., ibid., 1912/I.

26 Schemua wrote to Moltke in May to confirm all previous arrangements (Kr.A., ibid., 1912/III) and, on taking up office, had required the file of extracts. On 22 November 1912, he wrote a report of his stay in Berlin with the German Chief of Staff: 'Auch versprach mir derselbe eine nicht nur zuwartende, sondern tatkräftige Offensivaktion parallel mit der unseren. Er betonte wiederholt die bundestreue Gesinnung, dass wir absolut auf Deutschlands Unterstützung rechnen dürfen, wenn Russland

uns bedroht, und dass es ja auch für Deutschland ein eminentes Interesse sei, dass wir nicht geschwächt werden.' On his plans in the west, Moltke gave as his intention 'Den Gegner in West zuerst niederzuwerfen, was er in 4–5 Wochen hoffe, und dann den Ueberschuss an Kraft gegen Ost einzusetzen'. Moltke even talked of strengthening his forces in the east with reserve troops. (Kr.A., ibid., 1912/VII.)

27 Conrad, Vol. III, pp. 49–50. The 1912–13 files contain a plan for Averescu's attention.

28 Conrad, III, 76; Kr.A., ibid., 1913/VIII. The 1914 files contain the text of a military agreement with Italy, concluded in 1913. I doubt if anyone took this very seriously, though Conrad (III, 33 and 88) gives curious evidence of German optimism here.

29 ibid., pp. 144–7.

30 Conrad, Vol. III, pp. 147–51. I have not found the original texts of these letters in the Archives.

31 There are several indications that Moltke was assuming English intervention at the side of France. An Austro-Hungarian military mission, sent by Conrad, reports that Moltke was thinking in such terms. (Kr.A., ibid., Kuvert/1911.) Conrad cites (III, 151–3) a report from his military attaché in Berlin that Moltke 'with regard to England . . . believed that England had pledged herself to France by a written agreement to co-operate in a war against Germany, therefore he had to reckon on her intervention . . . it was a pity that England was so blind'. Again, at the Leipzig anniversary celebrations in October 1913, Moltke declared that 'We must consider England, who will certainly stand at the side of France'. On the other hand, Moltke's military attaché in Vienna told Conrad that German statesmen did not believe England would intervene until two years of war had passed. (Conrad, III, 433 and 167.)

32 ibid., pp. 561–3.

33 ibid., pp. 668–73; Kr.A., ibid., 1914/IV for the text of Conrad's final letter of 14 February, where he regrets that war was not caused in 1908–9 or 1912–13, and describes his fears at the growth of an enemy ring.

34 Moltke came to Karlsbad again at the beginning of July, but it was deemed inappropriate that the two men should meet, in view of a possible press comment on the danger of war. (Conrad, IV, 63.)

35 ibid., pp. 55–6; Oesterreich-Ungarns Aussenpolitik (hereafter Oe.U.A.P.), Vol. VIII, Doc. Nr. 10,076 ('One of the most damning documents on German responsibility for the war', L. Albertini, Origins of the War of 1914, Vol. II, p. 146).

36 Conrad, Vol. IV, pp. 52f.

37 ibid., pp. 110f.

38 Details of the Austro-Hungarin mobilisation procedure are given in the official history, Oesterreich-Ungarns Letzter Krieg, Vol. I, pp. 3–15, and in the introductions to the sections on the summer campaigns in Russia and Serbia. Conrad's memoirs also contain most of the relevant material – the partial mobilisation against Serbia is discussed in Vol. IV, p. 122. In the partial mobilisation 'B' the third corps (Graz) was also mobilised, for fear of complications with Italy: strictly it belonged to A-Staffel. The mobilisation programme was built on the so-called Mobilisation Day, generally two or three days after the mobilisation order was given. For the partial mobilisation against Serbia, 28 July was named as the 'first day of Mobilisation', with 27 July as Alarmtag, a day on which all security

precautions were taken and frontiers closed and the necessary precautions taken to receive *Wehrpflichtige* when they arrive on the Mobilisation Day. For the total mobilisation, on 31 July, 4 August was named as Mobilisation Day, the preceding two days being those of the *Alarm*. Thus for Minimalgruppe Balkan and for B-Staffel the 'fifth day of mobilisation' which Conrad mentions would be 1 August, as Conrad himself recognised (IV, 157). An extremely valuable account of the military programme is given by General Béla von Lengyel, 'Die oesterreichisch-ungarische Heeresleitung 1914', *Allgemeine Schweizerische Militärzeitschrift* (August 1964).

39 Conrad, Vol. IV, p. 132. There is also certain evidence to suggest that the Russians began to mobilise considerably earlier than they made out: at a comparatively early stage in the Lemberg campaign, Austro-Hungarian units took prisoners from Siberian and Caucasian units, which could scarcely, in view of Russia's great transport problems, have reached the west if mobilised only at the end of July.

40 Conrad, Vol. IV, p. 142.

41 *Oe.U.L.K.*, Vol. I, Doc. No. 15; *Oe.U.A.P.*, Vol. VIII, Doc. No. 11,002.

42 Conrad, Vol. IV, 150–1.

43 Conrad advised that it would be better to mobilise on 31 July, but that with 1 August he still had time enough (IV, 150–1). This is curious, as his chief of the railway section advised him that mobilisation against Russia should be delayed, naming 1 August as the more suitable day (Kriegsarchiv A.O.K. 4119, Eisenbahn-Berichte, Tagebuch 20.7.14–31.12.14, report of 30.7.14, 11 a.m.). It seems strange that Conrad should have told Berchtold that 31 July was a more convenient day: perhaps he wished to reduce the time available to Berchtold for further negotiation.

44 Conrad, IV, 152.

45 ibid., pp. 152–3.

46 ibid., p. 152.

47 ibid., p. 153. At the same time Bethmann sent Berchtold a request for moderation, which prompted Berchtold's famous 'Das ist gelungen! Wer regiert in Berlin, Bethmann oder Moltke?'. He could equally have said the same of himself and Conrad.

48 *Oe.U.A.P.*, Vol. VIII, Doc. No. 11,130.

49 ibid., Doc. No. 11,125.

50 ibid., Doc. No. 11,132.

51 *Oe.U.A.P.*, Vol. VIII, Doc. No. 11,134.

52 ibid., 11,204. Conrad's account of the drafting of this reply, and an apparently full text of his recommendations to the Ballhaus, is contained in Vol. IV, pp. 159–60.

53 Conrad, IV, 110–13 and 156–7.

54 Kriegsarchiv A.O.K. 4119, *Eispegel* (code name for the chief of the railway section) *Tagebuch* 20.7.14–31.12.14.

55 Log-book entry of 31 July: 'Es wird nun die ernsthafte Frage vorgelegt, wie ich darüber denke, wenn der im Rollen befindliche 'B'-Aufmarsch nicht geführt werden sollte und alles gegen Russland gebraucht. Ich informiere Seine Excellenz dass dies eine Katastrophe bedeuten würde und dass dies isenbahntechnisch nicht durchzuführen wäre.'

56 Still later in the evening, Straub saw Conrad and declared that there would be 'eine Unzahl von Komplikationen', since too many of the B-Staffel units had already begun to move south – of VIII Corps (Prague)

the vanguard of 9th Division; of IV Corps (Budapest) the vanguards of 31st and 32nd Divisions; of IX Corps (Leitmeritz/Litoměrice) the vanguard of 29th Division; of VII Corps (Temesvár/Timişoara) about a third of both 17th and 34th Divisions. By *vanguard (die Teten)* is meant, I assume, headquarters troops, perhaps in all 2,000 men in each division: thus 15,000 men had already begun movement to Serbia.

57 *Eispegel* entry of 1 August: the reversal would be a catastrophe 'für die ich unter keinen Verhältnissen die Verantwortung übernehmen kann'. General von Lengyel has severe criticisms to make of these pronouncements, and, although I cannot claim to be an expert in military transport, I greatly sympathise with his views. It had been accepted as an integral part of the Austro-Hungarian plans since 1909 and before that it would be possible to reverse B-Staffel provided that the necessity became clear within reasonable time of mobilisation. There is no evidence that railway administration altered its plans: a *Referat* on the subject on 18 December 1913 actually confirmed previous arrangements (Kr.A. Gstb. Faskl. 89(a), Korrespondenz, Kuv. 1914/10) and it seems particularly curious that 31 July was too late to reverse B-Staffel. As General von Lengyel says, 'Die Umleitung dieser Divisionen nach Galizien hatte in den ersten Augusttagen ohne Schwierigkeiten umso besser durchgeführt werden können, als die Divisionen der vom 4. August an mobilisierten und nach Galizien zu führenden 'A'-Staffel den Eisenbahntransport planmässig erst am dritten, beziehungsweise am siebenten Mobilmachungstag, also am 7, beziehungsweise am 11 August anzutreten hatten. Die 'B'-Staffel hatte in ihrer Marschbereitschaft daher vor der 'A'-Staffel einen Vorsprung von 4 Tagen'. (Lengyel, op. cit. pp. 504–5. General von Lengyel's argument seems to me to be unanswerable: until 4 August, even the A-Staffel lines and trains would be entirely clear for B-Staffel to use, and even if headquarters troops had moved to Serbia, it was surely not impossible to send off the units by brigades, under the corps commands, which had not, at that stage, moved off. Moreover, Straub's assurance of 1 August that B-Staffel, even by the Bosnian route, would still arrive on time, is altogether suspect. General von Lengyl contents himself with the reproach that organisation 'dürfte eisenbahntechnisch nicht ganz einwandfrei gewesen sein'. It seems to me not unlikely that certain General Staff officers were so anxious to see B-Staffel destroy Serbia that they arranged their technical details in consequence of this wish rather than any reality. Perhaps this is the meaning of the curious entry for 29 July where Straub, Metzger and Höfer discussed the Russian mobilisation and 'konstatieren die Gleichheit unserer Anschauungen' – the log-book does not in any way clarify this entry. Conrad, as the record shows, does not seem to have been particularly perturbed: he had been pleading since 1907 for the destruction of Serbia, and in any case, at that time, he was sure the Germans would take on an adequate burden of the eastern war. Also, his conscience could be relatively clear, since he had warned Moltke in 1909 that his troops might be engaged irrevocably in Serbia.

58 Kr.A. A.O.K., Op.Nr. 35, 29 July 1914.

59 Kr.A. A.O.K.., Op.Nr. 41, 29 July 1914.

60 Conrad, Vol. IV, p. 275.

61 ibid., p. 54, confirmed in the Berchtold papers. H. Hantsch, *Leopold Graf Berchtold*, 2 vols. (Graz, 1963), Vol. II, p. 579.

62 ibid., p. 137.

63 Conrad, Vol. IV, p. 137, is here confirmed by a telegram from Burián to Tisza on 28 July printed in *Gróf Tisza István összes munkái*, Vol. II, p. 33 (*The Complete Works of Count Stephen Tisza*, 6 vols, Budapest, 1922 –7).

64 Kr.A. Neue Feldakten II, Armee Op. Abteilung 1914, Nr. 25. This order, missing from the A.O.K. files, was sent at 8 pm and received in Budapest by the Second Army at 8.15: 'Es bleiben für die vor dem 30 Juli zur Mobilisierung befohlenen Formationen die für den Kriegsfall B (*Balkan*) getroffenen Anordnungen des Kriegsministeriums und des Armeeober-kommandos sowie speziell die Instradierung für den Kriegsfall B in Kraft.'

65 Kr.A. A.O.K., Op.Nr. 122 of 1 August: 'Aufmarsch wird, wie eingeleitet, durchgeführt.'

66 Kr.A. A.O.K., Op.Nr. 123, 19 August 1914: 'Trotz allgemeiner Mobilis-ierung bleiben die erteilten Befehle aufrecht und Aufmarsch gegen Serbien wird, so wie eingeleitet, durchgeführt.' In the files of A.O.K. for this period there is also an unreferenced paper marked 2 August which seems to be a sketch by a member of the railway section for B-Staffel to move to Galicia. However, there is no evidence on this paper that it was considered, and had it been more than a routine exercise, it would certainly have been at least initialled by Conrad. It does not therefore seem to have more than cursory significance.

67 Kr.A. Neue Feldakten II. Armee Op.Abt. Armeebefehl, Nr. 1 of 4 August 1914.

68 Kr.A. Neue Feldakten II Armee Op.Abt., Nr. 113 (missing from A.O.K. files): 'II. Armee mit 7. Korps, das ab heute dem II. Armeekommando unterstellt ist, wird zwischen 18 August und 21 August auf nordöstlichen Kriegsschauplatz abtransportiert werden.'

69 Kr.A. Nachlässe A–3, Faszikel 5, Tagebuch des Feldzeugmeisters Portiorek, 31 July–6 August 1914, Geh. Nr. 7. I should like here to thank Dr Pebbal of the Kriegsarchiv for his invaluable help with many of the documents connected with the article.

70 ibid.: 'Ich bin . . . in meiner . . . Arbeit dadurch gehemmt, dass ich nicht weiss, ob beabsichtigt ist, tratz des eingetretenen Falles R zunächst mit den für den Fall B bestimmten Korps einen Schlag gegen Serbien zu führen und dann mit ganzer Kraft gegen Russland zu wenden . . .'

71 ibid., Geh. Nr. 8 of 2 August 1914.

72 ibid., Geh. Nr. 10 of 3 August 1914.

73 ibid., Geh. Nr. 11 of 4 August 1914.

74 ibid., Geh. Nr. 13 of 5 August 1914: 'Ich bin sehr begierig wann das A.O.K., das bisher nur als spärlicher Nachrichtenvermittler fungiert, aus seiner Reserve heraustreten wird', and later, 'A.O.K. hat sich bis 7 Uhr nur durch die telegraphische Vrfügung bemerkbar gemacht'. There is considerable evidence that A.O.K. found these sarcasms little to its liking. There was a well-known rivalry between Potiorek and Conrad. Potiorek was a most peculiar commander: in one of his reports (Geh. Nr. 13 of 5 August) he complains that his staff insists on keeping him occupied with details and statistics: he proposes in future to limit his communications with it to short notes. His *Tagebuch* is filled with such notes to his Chief of Staff, and on the most trivial subjects.

75 Oe.U.L.K., Vol. I, pp. 96–7 (Op.Nr. 128).

76 Italy did not formally declare her neutrality until early in August: but it is most unlikely that anyone in Vienna really expected her active assist-

ance: indeed, the Graz Corps had been specially mobilised on 25 July against the case that Italy might feel that her conscience compelled her, too, to defend Serbia. Italy had said several years before that she would have no part in any war with Great Britain, and on 31 July both Berlin and Vienna were prepared to reckon on an English intervention against them. As Jagow told the Austro-Hungarian ambassador on that day (*Oe.U.A.P.*, Vol. VIII, Doc. No. 11,127) it was 'leider sicher, dass England unbedingt sofort gegen Deutschland und Oesterreich-Ungarn losgehen werde, wenn der kriegerische Konflikt mit Frankreich und Russland ausbrechen würde'. Romanian help was also purely a fictitious possibility: Count Czernin from Bucharest reported on 29 July that Romania would unquestionably remain neutral (*Oe.U.A.P.*, Vol. VIII, Doc. No. 10,956). This report did not reach Vienna until the 31st, but even on the 29th, Burián informed Tisza that 'our Romanian ally had just cleared her position, and this is to the good. In the case of a Russian war, she will go neither against us nor with us'. (*Gróf Tisza István összes munkái*, Vol. II, p. 35.)

77 Graf J. Stürgkh, *In deutschen Grossen Hauptquartier* (Leipzig, 1921), p. 12; cf. Freytag-Loringhoven, *Menschen und Dinge, wie ich sie in meinem Leben sah* (Berlin, 1923), p. 195.

78 Conrad, Vol. IV, pp. 318–21; the text of the letter exists as Kr.A. A.O.K. Kuvert, Op.Nr. 1–500: Nr. 15, received by Conrad at 5.30 pm on 3 August. In 1925 the Kriegsarchiv was given a copy of this order to the German Eighth Army; see R. Kiszling *Oesterreichs Anteil*, p. 10, for the effect of this; and August von Mackensen, *Briefe und Aufzeichnungen des Generalfeldmarshalls aus Krieg und Frieden*, ed. W. Foerster (Leipzig, 1938), p. 32.

79 General von Lengyel, op. cit., pp. 504–5, believes that Conrad recalled the Second Army because Russian mobilisation turned out to be much quicker than expected. I cannot accept this explanation: on 5 August, when Conrad sent the orders to Potiorek and the Second Army, there was no evidence that Russia would mobilise so much more quickly than expected. This became clear only some three weeks after the outbreak of war and therefore had little to do with Conrad's initial decisions. Professor Ritter, in his 'Zusammenarbeit' study and also, using almost the same words, in his *Staatskunst* ('Zusammenarbeit', 543, and *Staatskunst*, Vol. II, p. 306) makes a curious defence of Moltke's retraction of his promise to attack. Giving Moltke credit for this 'klüglich' escape clause, he alleges that the promise given in the letter of 19 March 1909 was followed by a reservation that immediate information should be given if enemy action changed one ally's plans: this change occurred, and the reservation therefore operated, he says, through the invasion of East Prussia by the Russian army of the Niemen (Rennenkampf's). In the first place, Moltke withdrew his unconditional promise on 2 August, a day after war had been declared: Rennenkampf did not invade East Prussia until several days later. Also, it would hardly be more creditable to Moltke if we did accept Professor Ritter's defence: in this case, Moltke's letter of 19 March was no more than a promise to Conrad that he would let him know in good time when he intended to let him down. It was assumed in the entire correspondence, and stressed by Moltke in this very letter, that the Russians would mount a large-scale operation against Germany. Conrad's strategic map is: Kr.A. Gstb. Faskl. 89(a), 1914/7.

80 Kr.A., ibid., 1914/14; 'Vorhaben einer ehesten Offensive' is Conrad's phrase, summing up Eastern plans.
81 Orders to this effect were issued on 5 August, reaching the commands on the 6th.
82 Conrad, Vol. IV, pp. 323–4.
83 Conrad, IV, 193–5.
84 Conrad seems to have been acutely conscious throughout this time of the great risks which he and the Monarchy were taking: he knew that this would possibly be 'Oesterreich-Ungarns letzter Krieg'. He told an old friend, Baron von Chlumecky, shortly before the ultimatum was sent, 'In 1908–9 it would have been a lay-down for us, in 1912–13 a game with the odds in our favour: now it is a simple gamble'. (Conrad, IV, 72; a similar, though not identical, version of this remark is given by Chlumecky in his book *Erzherzog Franz Ferdinands Wirken und Wollen* (Berlin, 1929), p. 106.
85 I should like to thank Mr J. M. K. Vyvyan of Trinity College, Cambridge, for his many helpful suggestions in connection with this article.

II

The Russian Mobilisation in 1914

L. C. F. TURNER

This article represents a complete revision of one with a similar title published by the writer in *The Journal of Contemporary History* in January 1968.[1] Moreover, the subject has been approached from a different angle and related more specifically to the Balkan crisis of November 1912. While writing his *Origins of the First World War*,[2] the writer concluded that the significance of the crisis of November 1912 has been much under-rated and its connection with July 1914 largely ignored. November 1912 was not only a dress-rehearsal for July 1914; it also made its own explosive contribution to the final catastrophe. This is particularly true in regard to Russian mobilisation.

Between 1894 and 1912 the Franco-Russian alliance was of a strictly defensive character, but one of the most important consequences of the Agadir crisis of 1911 and the tightening of military and naval bonds between France and Britain was to impart a new and far more confident tone to French diplomacy. The accession to power of Raymond Poincaré in January 1912 represented a victory for the nationalists, and the new Prime Minister proved to be a man of outstanding personality and intellectual power. Henceforth French policy would be guided by a remarkable statesman, who combined a firm belief in the Franco-Russian alliance with a deep hostility towards Germany.

While Germany reacted to Agadir by introducing the *Novelle* and a wide programme of army reforms, the French General Staff was now discarding the cautious defensive plans drawn up between 1906 and 1911 and turning its thoughts to the offensive. In February 1912 General Joffre, the new Chief of Staff, told General Nostitz, the Russian military attaché, that he was preparing for an outbreak of war in the spring and added: 'All the arrangements for the English landing are made down to the smallest detail, so that the English army can take part in the first big battle.' Nevertheless it is clear that the attitude and strength of France's Russian ally aroused serious misgiving. In 1910 General Foch told General Wilson of the British General Staff that if war broke out in the west, he was far from certain whether Russia would honour the alliance but that she would make every effort if war broke out over the Balkans.[3] Foch was sceptical of the efficiency of the Russians while, during the Agadir crisis, the Prime Minister, Caillaux, remarked to those who urged him to take a strong line, 'You forget that the Russian army is worth nothing'. Russia was supposed to have embarked on a great programme of military reforms; the size of her standing army and her great masses of trained reserves appeared impressive but at the Franco-Russian General Staff conference held on 31 August 1911 it was stated that Russia would be unable for two years to wage war against Germany with the slightest chance of success. At a similar conference on 13 July 1912 the Russian representative, General Jhilinski, stressed the inadequacy of Russia's strategic railways and the slowness of her mobilisation. At this conference, Joffre predicted that Germany would commit most of her troops against France and leave only a minimum against Russia. He declared that in the first few weeks of war both France and Russia must launch massive offensives to dislocate the German plan; while recognising that Russia would have to cope with an Austrian offensive in Poland, he urged that all efforts should be concentrated on annihilating the German armies. Yet Joffre realised that the Russian railways were inadequate and that many lines would have to be doubled or quadrupled before a major Russian offensive could be launched against Berlin.

This is not the place to discuss the formation of the Balkan League, and the circumstances which led to the outbreak of the first Balkan war in October 1912. It should be stressed, however, that although the League was brought into being by Russian diplomacy, it is generally accepted by historians that neither the Prime Minister, Kokovtzov, nor the Foreign Minister, Sazonov, had any desire to precipitate a major European war. This seems to be true of all the Great Powers, including Germany and Austria, although General Schemua, Chief of the Austrian General Staff, demanded on 28 September that Austria should order partial mobilisation immediately Serbia declared war on Turkey, and should use military force to prevent a junction between Serbia and Montenegro. However, his request was rejected by the Foreign Minister, Count Berchtold, while the German government initially favoured a strict neutrality.

Under the impact of the Bulgarian and Serbian victories and the collapse of Turkish resistance in the Balkans between 17 October and 8 November, both the Austrian and German political leaders sharply changed their views. There was a feeling in Vienna that some drastic action was required if the Monarchy was not to collapse as a Great Power and, from the beginning of November, Austria began to call up reservists in Bosnia and to take military measures along the Russian frontier. Fritz Fischer has described and has rightly stressed the importance of the visit of the Archduke Franz Ferdinand and General Schemua to Berlin on 22 November 1912 and the significant assurances they received from the Kaiser, Moltke and Bethmann Hollweg.[4] According to Schemua, Moltke 'emphasised again and again' that Austria could call on Germany if threatened by Russia, while the Austrian ambassador quoted the Kaiser as saying that to protect Austria's prestige 'he would not even fear a world war and that he would be ready to enter into a war with the three *entente* powers'. It appears therefore that if Russia had mobilised in strength to support Serbia's claim to an Adriatic port, Europe would have been on the verge of a major catastrophe. In fact Russia did come very close to mobilisation.

In contrast to the cautious attitude of Kokovtzov and Sazonov, the Russian Ministry of War and General Staff had shown from the onset of the crisis a disposition to play with fire. In October they had ordered a 'trial mobilisation' which involved a wide calling up of reserves in Russian Poland, while early in November they decided to retain with the colours some 400,000 conscripts eligible for release, thus increasing by one-fourth the number of men under arms. The Tsar was then at his hunting-lodge at Spala in Poland and, in the opinion of the British ambassador, 'the presence of the Grand Duke Nicholas and other generals at the Imperial shooting party . . . had tended to give a chauvinistic turn to his policy'.[5] On returning to Tsarskoe Selo, Nicholas II listened too readily to the proposals of General Sukhomlinov, his highly irresponsible Minister of War.

On 22 November 1912 the Tsar presided over a conference attended by Sukhomlinov and the commanders of the Warsaw and Kiev military districts, at which they decided to mobilise the entire Kiev district, with part of the Warsaw district, and to prepare to mobilise the Odessa district. This was in fact the embryo of the famous 'partial mobilisation' with which Russia dabbled with such disastrous consequences in July 1914. It is only fair to point out that on 19 November, Austria-Hungary had decided to strengthen her garrisons on the Russian frontier, and that the visit of the Austrian Heir Apparent and Chief of Staff to Berlin on 22 November had aroused considerable excitement in St Petersburg.

All the telegrams for the Russian partial mobilisation were prepared on 22 November, but the Tsar decided that it would be as well to call a conference of his senior ministers before the orders were dispatched. Accordingly Kokovtzov, Sazonov, Rukhov, the Minister of Communications, and General Jhilinski, the Chief of Staff, were summoned to Tsarskoe Selo on 23 November for discussions with the Tsar and Sukhomlinov. Nicholas II outlined the plan of the Minister of War and stressed that the measures were directed only against Austria, and that no menace was intended towards Germany. He said: 'The Minister of War wanted to dispatch these orders yesterday, but I asked him to wait another day.' Kokovtzov comments in his memoirs:

> We . . . looked at each other with the greatest amazement and only the presence of the Tsar restrained us from giving vent to the feelings which animated all of us.
> I spoke first, and had to struggle to retain my composure. I stated frankly that the Minister of War and the two commanders apparently did not perceive what danger they were preparing for Russia in planning this mobilization – a danger of war with Austria and Germany, and at a time when in consideration of our national defense every effort should be made to avert this catastrophe.[6]

Sukhomlinov remained silent but the Tsar argued that these were purely precautionary measures directed only against Austria, and that he wished to avoid war with Germany. Kokovtzov responded that 'no matter what we chose to call the projected measures, a mobilization remained a mobilization, to be countered by our adversaries with actual war.' The Prime Minister concluded with 'an impassioned appeal to the Tsar not to permit the fatal error the consequences of which were immeasurable, since we were not ready for war and our adversaries knew it well'. Sazonov declared that he was 'simply overwhelmed' by the impending catastrophe, and that in any case Russia had no right to order a partial mobilisation without consulting France. In the end Nicholas II yielded reluctantly to these appeals and cancelled the proposed mobilisation.

According to Kokovtzov, Sazonov said to Sukhomlinov after the Tsar's departure: 'Doesn't your conscience tell you that had the Tsar not decided to call us here today and had he not given us a chance to rectify the evil you very nearly brought about, your folly could not have been mended?' Sukhomlinov replied: 'We shall have a war anyway; we cannot avoid it and it would be more profitable for us to begin it as soon as possible.'

Sazonov's rebuke to Sukhomlinov was well merited, for the military situation in eastern europe was extremely critical. Austria had put her troops in Bosnia and Dalmatia on a war footing and was strengthening her Galician garrisons at Cracow, Przemysl and Lemberg. There seems little doubt that a Russian partial mobilisation on the scale envisaged by Sukhomlinov would infallibly have produced Austrian counter-measures on a very large scale and would probably have led to Austrian general mobilisation. The remorseless process of mobilisation and counter-mobilisation might well have followed the same fatal course as in 1914.

Although Balkan affairs were to give rise to grave tensions in the coming months, the risks of a general European war now diminished perceptibly. By mutual agreement in March 1913 Russia released her reservists, while Austria reduced her troops in Galicia to a normal level. Nevertheless the November crisis had contained the ingredients of a great explosion, and it is surprising that standard histories say so little on the subject. It is true, however, that until the publication of Kokovtzov's memoirs, historians were not in a position to measure the gravity of the threat to peace in November 1912. The Russian edition of these memoirs was published in Paris in 1933, while a condensed and revised English edition appeared in the United States and Britain in 1935.

Publishing in 1938, E. C. Helmreich made use of Kokovtzov's memoirs and described the conference at Tsarskoe Selo on 23 November in general terms, but he was essentially a diplomatic historian, unversed in military affairs, and his account is unenlightening and inadequate.[7] Luigi Albertini referred to the conference, but dated it 10 Sepetmber 1912 and failed completely to appreciate its significance.[8] This has deceived subsequent historians, such as A. J. P. Taylor, who have ignored the conference altogether and therefore present a very misleading account of the diplomatic situation in November 1912. When Fritz Fischer published his elaborate work on the origins of the First World War in 1969, he commented on the Kaiser's assurances to Franz Ferdinand on 22 November 1912, but he said nothing at all about the conference at Tsarskoe Selo on 23 November.[9]

In the course of the conference of 23 November, Kokovtzov made the following very important point, which was also endorsed by Sazonov:

> . . . in such a mobilization we assumed a great responsibility not only for Russia but also for France, since under the terms of our military agreement with our ally we had no right to undertake any such measures without coming to an understanding with her. This evidently had been overlooked by the Tsar's advisers, who in adopting this course of action would have destroyed the military covenant and thus permitted France to repudiate her obligations to us. I said that the Minister of War had not even the right to discuss such a matter without a preliminary understanding with the Minister of Foreign Affairs and myself . . .[10]

The attitude of France in the 1912 crisis has been analysed in detail by Albertini, who adopted a highly critical attitude towards Poincaré and his 'broadened interpretation' of the Franco-Russian alliance.[11] If the reports of Isvolski, the Russian ambassador in Paris, are to be accepted, it is certainly true that Poincaré made dangerous statements calculated to encourage those Russians who disagreed with the cautious policy of Kokovtzov and Sazonov. It is obvious that in November 1912 France did not give Russia any authority to mobilise, but she did not discourage her from adopting a venturesome policy in the Balkans. There is documentary proof to support Isvolski's statement that Poincaré said to him on 12 September 1912 that 'the experts viewed the chances of the Dual Alliance [i.e. France and Russia] in a general outbreak with great optimism'.[12] This proof is to be found in the report of the French General Staff, produced at Poincarés request on 2 September 1912, and demanded by the French Prime Minister on returning from his visit to Russia in August.[13]

Asked to assess the probable consequences of military intervention by Austria in the Balkans, the French General Staff gave as its considered opinion that such intervention would put Germany and Austria 'at the mercy of the *entente*'. The General Staff based its view on the argument that Austria would have to engage at least seven of her sixteen army corps in the Balkans, that this would fatally weaken her forces deployed against Russia in Galicia, and that because of the relative weakness of the German army in East Prussia, the Russians would be able to mount 'une offensive très dangereuse dans la direction de Berlin'. If the Germans strengthened their forces on the eastern front, the French army with British support would enjoy a substantial superiority in Lorraine; moreover, Austrian action in the Balkans might well lead to a rupture with Italy. The French General Staff doubted whether Germany would permit Austria to indulge in a Balkan adventure but, if she did, a general war would result in which 'the Triple Entente would have the best chances of success and might gain a victory which would enable the map of Europe to be redrawn'. On 13 September 1912 Poincaré circulated this report to the French ambassadors in London, Paris, Vienna, Rome, Constantinople and St Petersburg.

Having considered the crisis of 1912 at length, this article will now glance at significant Franco-Russian moves in 1913, and then pass on to the 1914 crisis. Parallel with the turmoil of the Balkan wars, the French adoption of the Three Years Military Service Law and the very substantial expansion of the German army, the year 1913 witnessed important developments in Franco-Russian military relations. These provide a vital link between the crisis of November 1912 and that of July 1914.

Russia's military strength expanded very considerably in 1913. Very large sums were allotted by the Duma to augment the artillery and reserve stocks of munitions, while French loans of 400–500 million francs a year were to be devoted to the development of strategic railways in western Russia.[14] In August 1913 General Joffre visited Russia and the French ambassador, Delcassé, reported to Paris that the Chief of Staff was very satisfied with the progress in railway construction and impressed by the growing efficiency of the Russian army.[15]

In September 1913 the Franco-Russian Military Convention assumed its final form.[16] Article II laid down that in case of German mobilisation or 'pour tout acte de guerre de l'armée allemande', France and Russia were free to mobilise immediately and without previous consultation. The article added: 'Mais en cas de mobilisation partielle, ou même générale, de l'Autriche ou de l'Italie seules ce concert est indispensable.'

Article III discussed basic strategy. France undertook to concentrate virtually her entire army against Germany and to commence offensive operations on the eleventh day of mobilisation. On behalf of Russia, General Jhilinski, her Chief of Staff, declared that at least 800,000 men would be deployed on the Russo-German frontier and would begin offensive operations on the fifteenth day of mobilisation. The article confirmed the opinion expressed at the conferences of 1910, 1911 and 1912 that 'Germany will direct the greatest part of her forces against France and leave only a minimum of troops against Russia'. The article stated: 'Le plan des alliés doit donc être, de tâcher d'attaquer simultanément des deux côtés à la fois, en exerçant le maximum d'efforts combinés.' As it was 'essential for the French armies to be able to have a marked superiority over the German forces in the west', an early Russian offensive against Germany was of vital importance. The need for Russia to deploy numerous formations against Austria was recognised but, in preliminary discussions, Joffre stressed that it was 'l'anéantissement des forces de l'Allemagne qu'il faut poursuivre à tout prix et dès le début des opérations'.

The Franco-Russian convention confirms the degree to which all military thinking in Europe was dominated by the implications of the Schlieffen Plan. Moreover, historians have failed to stress sufficiently how the potential application of that plan would lead automatically to intense military activity in eastern Europe. Russia would have to invade East Prussia as soon as possible to relieve pressure on France, while Austria would be compelled to attack in Russian Poland to bring relief to the German Eighth Army in East Prussia. Just as the French General Staff was desperately anxious that

Russia should launch a major offensive against Germany, so Moltke, the German Chief of Staff, never ceased to stress to Conrad von Hoetzendorf, his Austrian opposite number, the need for a massive Austrian thrust from Galicia.[17] The urgent need of both France and Germany for rapid mobilisation and early offensive action by their eastern allies accelerated the whole tempo of the crisis of July 1914.

A remarkable feature of the Franco-Russian convention is that it ignores the strategic problem which would be posed by an Austrian invasion of Serbia. This is particularly surprising in view of the memorandum of the French General Staff of 2 September 1912, which stated that a large-scale operation by Austria in the Balkans would have the effect of putting Germany and Austria 'at the mercy of the *entente*'.[18] In the event of Austrian action against Serbia, a rapid Russian mobilisation was unnecessary and indeed positively undesirable. There were excellent reasons for Russia to delay mobilisation until a substantial portion of the Austrian army was entangled in operations against Serbia. The possibility that Russia might do this was a source of great anxiety both to Moltke and to Conrad and in February 1909 Moltke had agreed with the Austrian Chief of Staff that 'the most likely and the most dangerous case would be a Russian intervention after war with Serbia had begun'.[19] It would be interesting to know to what extent the Russian General Staff was aware of Conrad's Plans 'R' and 'B' (after all, Colonel Redl, Chief of Staff of the Prague army corps, who committed suicide in May 1913, is supposed to have betrayed the Austrian plans to the Russians). What is certain from its memorandum of 2 September 1912 is that the French General Staff had a clear concept that Plan 'B' would involve the deployment of seven Austrian army corps in the Balkans, and would gravely weaken the Austrian forces available for operations in Poland. Why then did the French representatives ignore this vital point in their strategic discussions with the Russian General Staff? It would be idle to speculate on the matter; the fact remains that Joffre and his advisers threw away Russia's military trump card against Austria and concentrated on the simple theme of getting the Russian army into action as quickly as possible against Germany.

The Liman von Sanders crisis at the end of 1913 provided Kokovtzov with his last opportunity to influence Russian policy. A meeting of Russian ministers held on 13 January 1914 discussed the imposition of military or diplomatic measures against Turkey.[20] Admiral Grigorovich, the Navy Minister, thought it would be possible to occupy Trebizond under cover of naval bombardment and hold it as a pledge until Turkey revoked Liman's appointment. Kokovtzov thought this would lead to war with Germany and asked: 'Is war with Germany desirable and can Russia wage it?' Sukhomlinov and Jhilinski, the Chief of Staff, 'categorically declared that Russia was perfectly prepared for a duel with Germany, not to speak of one with Austria'. Kokovtzov reiterated his opinion that 'a war at present would be the greatest misfortune that could befall Russia'. The council adopted his view and decided to endeavour to reach a settlement by negotiation.

Influenced by reactionary circles at Court, the Tsar dismissed Kokovtzov from his post at the end of January and replaced him by Goremykin whom the British ambassador, Sir George Buchanan, describes as 'an amiable old gentleman, with pleasant manners, of an indolent temperament and quite past his work'. In the next international crisis, Russia would have to rely on the mercurial Sazonov guided by such advice as he might receive from her ignorant and irresponsible military chiefs.

This article will not attempt to deal in detail with the crisis of July 1914, which has been covered at length in so many histories. The writer's views on the crisis have been summarised in his *Origins of the First World War* and it would be superfluous to duplicate them here.[21] Comments will be made, however, on crucial points relating to Russia's mobilisation measures.

In the first place it should be noted that, in contrast to 1912, Russia was acting in the closest concert with France. The confidence of the French General Staff in 1914 was certainly greater than in 1912 when it had advised Poincaré on 2 September that in a general European war 'the Triple Entente would have the best chances of success and might gain a victory which would enable the map of Europe to be redrawn'. In 1912 France was represented at St Petersburg by George Louis, a cautious and prudent diplomat, who had exercised a restraining influence on Russian policy. In 1914 the French ambassador was Maurice de Paléologue, formerly Political Director at the Quai d'Orsay, and a close friend of Poincaré, who had specially arranged his appointment. A man of brilliant intellect and great persuasive powers, an ardent patriot who longed to restore the 'glories of France', Paléologue fully represented the *réveil national* and the aggressive confidence of the French General Staff. According to Paléologue, the Prime Minister, Doumergue, said to him before his departure in January 1914:

War can break out from one day to the next . . . Our allies must rush to our aid. The safety of France will depend on the energy and promptness with which we shall know how to push them into the fight.[22]

It is interesting to note that Paléologue visited Paris in June 1914 in order to see the new Prime Minister, Viviani. He warned him against the repeal of the Three Years Military Service Act and stressed the disastrous effects such a course would have on Russian public opinion and the maintenance of the alliance. They met on 18 June; according to Paléologue's own account, Viviani was won over by his argument that war was imminent and Paléologue then said: 'You are determined, then, to prevent any tampering with the Military Service Act? I may assure the Emperor Nicholas of this?'[23] It is clear from the above and from Paléologue's memoirs that he enjoyed the full confidence of the Tsar, Sazonov and the Grand Duke Nicholas, commander of the St Petersburg garrison and Commander-in-Chief on the outbreak of war. Paléologue's relations with Sukhomlinov were cool, but his military attaché, General de Laguiche, appears to have been in close rapport with the Russian General Staff.

Although the French government has never published any report on the conversations of Poincaré and Viviani with Russia's leaders and ministers between 20 and 23 July 1914, it is clear that during this visit to St Petersburg Poincaré promised Russia the full support of France in the impending international crisis. The British ambassador, Sir George Buchanan, reported to Grey on 24 July regarding Poincaré's visit, and said that he had been informed confidentially by Sazonov and the French ambassador that there was full agreement between France and Russia and that they had decided 'to take action at Vienna with a view to the prevention of a demand for explanations or any summons equivalent to an intervention in the internal affairs of Serbia which the latter would be justified in regarding as an attack on her sovereignty and independence'.[24]

Russian moves towards mobilisation between 24 and 26 July cannot be considered in isolation, but must be appraised within the context of the Franco-Russian alliance and the intimate relations which now existed between the key political and military figures of France and Russia.

Sazonov heard of the Austrian ultimation to Serbia at 10 am on 24 July and at once exclaimed, 'C'est la guerre européenne!' He immediately telephoned the news to the Tsar, who commented characteristically: 'This is disturbing.' After a tense discussion with the Austrian ambassador, Count Szapary, Sazonov sent for General Janushkevich, Chief of the General Staff, and discussed plans for a partial mobilisation of the Russian army. Standard histories of the crisis convey the impression that the concept of partial mobilisation originated with the Foreign Minister, and Albertini describes it as 'this bright idea of Sazonov's'. It is obvious, however, that Sazonov, who was pathetically ignorant of military affairs, was merely reviving the scheme for partial mobilisation already formulated by Sukhomlinov in 1912 when Russia had come perilously close to plunging Europe into a major war.

It is significant that Sazonov was contemplating something like a partial mobilisation before the delivery of the Austrian ultimatum. On 18 July he told the British ambassador, Sir George Buchanan, that 'anything in the shape of an Austrian ultimatum at Belgrade could not leave Russia indifferent, and that she might be forced to take some precautionary military measures'. It is highly probable that he discussed this question with the military leaders before 24 July, and that Sukhomlinov then submitted in extended form the proposal for partial mobilisation which he had already formulated in 1912.

The proposal considered by Sazonov and Janushkevich on the 24th was to mobilise the military districts of Kiev, Odessa, Moscow and Kazan, but to refrain from mobilising the districts of Warsaw, Vilna and St Petersburg in order to avoid alarming Germany. Sazonov certainly seems to have regarded this as an admirable way of exerting pressure on Austria; he did not understand that a partial mobilisation involving thirteen Russian army corps along her northern border would compel Austria to order general mobilisation, which in turn would invoke the Austro-German alliance and require general mobilisation by Germany. Sazonov's ignorance was shared by Jagow, the German Foreign Secretary, who told the British ambassador on 27 July that 'if Russia only mobilized in the south, Germany would not mobilize, but if she mobilized in the north, Germany would have to do so'. Jagow repeated the same statement to the French ambassador on the 27th and Albertini rightly describes his behaviour as 'a tremendous blunder', because 'partial mobilization would have led to war no less surely than general mobilization'.

Janushkevich was incapable of giving Sazonov sound advice. He had only been in office for five months and Sir Bernard Pares, who knew him personally, says 'he had nothing to recommend him but the personal favour of the Tsar'. Commenting on a letter written by Janushkevich in the summer of 1915, the Minister of Agriculture, Krivoshein, wrote: 'The extraordinary *naïveté* or, to be exact, the unforgivable stupidity of this letter written by the Chief of Staff makes me shudder'.

Much ink has been expended by historians in debating the question whether the concept of partial mobilisation was a fatal military blunder and would have thrown the Russian army into dire confusion. The writer has examined the evidence in some detail in his article of January 1968.[25] One may balance the view of General Dobrorolski, chief of the mobilisation section of the Russian General Staff, that 'partial mobilization was simply folly', against the opinion expressed by Sukhomlinov himself in 1922 to the German historian, Alfred von Wegerer, that 'it would have been quite possible to carry out a partial mobilization'. This writer now believes that the whole argument about partial and general mobilisation is largely irrelevant. It is true that following on the discussions between Sazonov and Janushkevich, the Russian Council of Ministers decided on the afternoon of 24 July to request the Tsar to authorise in principle the mobilisation of the Military districts of Kiev, Odessa, Moscow and Kazan.[26] However, the crucial Russian decision was taken on 25 July and went far beyond this.

A Russian Imperial Council, presided over by the Tsar and attended by the Grand Duke Nicholas and General Janushkevich, assembled at Krasnoe Selo on the morning of 25 July. The Grand Duke had given Joffre personal assurances that Russia would invade Germany as rapidly as possible; he was on bad terms with Sukhomlinov, but got on well with Janushkevich, who served as his Chief of Staff in 1914–16 and was very much under his influence in the July crisis. The Council approved the decisions taken on 24 July and adopted various resolutions. These included the return to winter quarters of troops on manoeuvres, the recall of officers on leave, and the promotion of cadets to be officers. Although the actual order for partial mobilisation was still to be suspended, the Council decided to introduced immediately 'The Period Preparatory to War', over the whole of European Russia. This corresponded with the German *Zustand drohender Kriegsgefahr* ('State of Threatening Danger of War'), and involved taking many measures preparatory to mobilisation. Janushkevich sent out the relevant orders at 1 am and 3.26 am on 26 July, and thereby set in train a whole succession of military activities along the German and Austrian frontiers.

As a result, all fortresses in Poland and western Russia were placed in 'a state of war', frontier posts were fully manned, censorship and security measures were tightened, harbours were mined, horses and wagons were assembled for army baggage trains, depots were prepared for the reception of reservists and all steps were taken to facilitate the impending mobilisation. These orders, already in force throughout European Russia, were extended on 27 July to include the military districts of the Caucasus, Turkestan, Omsk and Irkutsk. Fay says: 'These secret "preparatory measures" . . . ordered before dawn of the 26th, enabled Russia, when war came, to surprise the world by the rapidity with which she poured her troops into East Prussia and Galicia.'

On 25 July Paléologue informed Paris that the Tsar had approved in principle the mobilisation of thirteen army corps against Austria, and on the 26th his military attaché, General de Laguiche, reported as follows to the French Ministry of War:

> Yesterday at Krasnoe Selo the War Minister confirmed to me the mobilization of the army corps of the military districts Kiev, Odessa, Kazan and Moscow. The endeavour is to avoid any measure likely to be regarded as directed against Germany, but nevertheless the military districts of Warsaw, Vilna and St Petersburg are secretly making preparations. The cities and governments of St Petersburg and Moscow are declared to be under martial law . . . The Minister of War has reiterated to us his determination to leave to Germany the eventual initiative of an attack on Russia . . .[27]

Although the order for mobilisation had yet to be promulgated, this singular document indicates that Sukhomlinov regarded the mobilisation proclamation as a mere formality which would follow automatically after the preliminary measures covered in 'The Period Preparatory to War,' had been completed. This adds significance to the statement of General Dobrorolski, chief of the mobilisation section of the Russian General Staff, who says of the situation in Russia on 26 July: 'The war was already a settled matter, and the whole flood of telegrams between the governments of Russia and Germany represented merely the stage setting of a historical drama.'[28]

It seems difficult to dispute that Russian general mobilisation did in fact begin on 26 July, with the full knowledge and tacit approval of the French ambassador and French military attaché, and that Paris was kept fully informed of this development. This statement does not affect in any way the question of the guilt and responsibility of the German and Austrian governments, or mitigate the folly of Bethmann Hollweg on 25–26 July in pressing Berchtold to declare war on Serbia a soon as possible in order to confront Europe with a *fait accompli*. Albertini is perfectly correct in saying that 'Austria declared war on Serbia against the advice of the Austrian Chief of Staff and under German pressure'.[29]

There seems little doubt that neither Sazonov nor the Tsar appreciated the significance of what was happening in Russia between 26 and 29 July. It is probable that Sazonov only wanted to frighten Austria, while Nicholas was so naïve that he telegraphed to Wilhelm II at 1.20 am on 30 July:

'The military measures which have now come into force were decided upon
five days ago for reasons of defence on account of Austria's preparations. I
hope from all my heart that these measures won't interfere with your part
as mediator which I greatly value.' This telegram produced an explosion in
Berlin and the Kaiser commented: 'So that is almost a week ahead of us
. . . That means I have got to mobilize as well.'[30]

Needless to say Russia's military preparations between 26 and 29 July
attracted much attention in Germany. At 3.25 pm on 26 July, Pourtalès, the
German ambassador, had telegraphed to Jagow that Major Eggeling, the
German military attaché in St Petersburg, had reported that mobilisation
had certainly been ordered for the military districts of Kiev and Odessa,
but it was doubtful whether this had been done for Warsaw and Moscow.
On the evening of the 26th Pourtalès interviewed Sazonov and was assured
that 'no mobilization order of the sort had been issued' but the 'certain
military measures' had been taken.[31]

On the evening of 26 July Sukhomlinov sent for Major Eggeling and gave
him his 'word of honour that no mobilization order had yet been issued'.
He asserted that only preparatory measures were being taken, but that 'not
a horse was being requisitioned, not a reservist called up'. If Austria invaded
Serbia, the districts of Kiev, Odessa, Moscow and Kazan would be
mobilised, but in no circumstances would this be done at Warsaw, Vilna or
St Petersburg, as 'peace with Germany was earnestly desired'. Eggeling's
report continues:

Upon my inquiry as to the object of the mobilization against Austria, he
shrugged his shoulders and indicated the diplomats . . . I got the impression
of great nervousness and anxiety. I consider the wish for peace genuine,
military statements in so far correct, that complete mobilization has
probably not been ordered but preparatory measures are very far-reaching.
They are evidently striving to gain time for new negotiations and for
continuing their armaments. Also the internal situation is unmistakably
causing serious anxiety.[32]

Eggeling warned Sukhomlinov that 'even mobilization against Austria
alone must be regarded as very dangerous'.

The diplomatic activity of the French government between 23 and 29
July was virtually paralysed by the absence of Poincaré and Viviani on
their return voyage from Russia, but General de Laguiche's telegram of 26
July, reporting on Russia's military preparations, raised the whole question
of the Military Convention between France and Russia and produced a
prompt response from the Ministry of War. At the request of General
Joffre, Messimy, the Minister of War, communicated with Laguiche at
St Petersburg on 27 July and, in his own words, 'urged with all my might
that, in spite of the slowness of Russian mobilization, the Tsar's armies
should as soon as possible take the offensive in East Prussia'.[33] On 28 July
Joffre and Messimy saw Colonel Ignatiev, the Russian military attaché in
Paris, and impressed on him that France was fully prepared to fulfil her
alliance obligations.

The pressure which Joffre and Messimy were exerting in St Petersburg was calculated to drive the Russian General Staff into demanding general mobilisation. Moreover, Paléologue continued to exert all his influence in favour of extreme measures. On 27 July Viviani had telegraphed to him from the warship *France*, stressing the need to make every effort to secure a peaceful solution. So far from advocating this course to Sazonov, Paléologue assured him on the 28th of the 'complete readiness of France to fulfil her obligations as an ally in case of necessity'.

Although historians have frequently asserted that the Russian General Staff was driven into demanding general mobilisation, because of the technical impossibility of carrying out partial mobilisation, yet this belief is of doubtful validity. Partial mobilisaton would have imposed some delay on a general mobilisation but, in any case, the Russian General Staff – in contrast to Sazonov – never seems to have taken the partial mobilisation concept very seriously. On the afternoon of 28 July Janushkevich presided over a conference attended by Danilov, the Quartermaster-General, Dobrorolski, the chief of the mobilisation section, and Ronzhin, the chief of military transport. Danilov says in his account:

> The result was that General Janushkevich, visibly convinced by our argu-ments [i.e., in favour of general mobilization], consented to ordering the preparation of two drafts of Imperial *ukazes*, one for general mobilization, one for partial mobilization . . . These two drafts were to be submitted simultaneously to the Tsar, accompanied by a special report.[34]

Meanwhile news of the Austrian declaration of war on Serbia at 11 am had reached St Petersburg, and during the afternoon Sazonov discussed the matter with Paléologue. Albertini comments:

> Sazonov's idea had been to resort to partial mobilization only when Austrian troops crossed the Serbian frontier, but now, obeying the dictates of his impulsive temperament and, as Baron Taube puts it, the 'pathological nervosity of his nature', he decided to proclaim it forthwith, possibly in the belief that the invasion of Serbia would follow immediately. Far from dissuading him from this course, Paléologue, who was always hinting at the inevitability of a European war brought on by Germany, must now have approved Sazonov's decision and promised full French solidarity.[35]

Sazonov had an interview with the Tsar on the evening of 28 July but, before leaving for Peterhof, he discussed the situation with Janushkevich, who urged him to press for general mobilisation. Nevertheless after seeing Nicholas II, Sazonov dispatched the following telegram to Berlin, repeated to Vienna, Paris, London and Rome:

> In consequence of the Austrian declaration of War on Serbia, we shall tomorrow proclaim mobilization in the districts of Odessa, Kiev, Moscow and Kazan. Inform the German Government of this, and lay stress on the absence of any intention on the part of Russia to attack Germany.[36]

Significantly that night Janushkevich sent a very different telegram to the commanders of all military districts: '30 July will be proclaimed the first day of our general mobilization. The proclamation will follow by the regulation telegram.'[37]

On the morning of 29 July Janushkevich discussed the situation with Sazonov and then went to Peterhof, where he induced the Tsar to sign the *ukazes* for partial and general mobilisation, while leaving for a final decision the question of which type of mobilisation would be implemented.[38] To judge from Janushkevich's telegram to the military districts, he had no doubt that general mobilisation would carry the day. That afternoon he saw Major Eggeling and gave him a solemn assurance 'that up to that moment, 3.00 pm, nowhere had there been mobilization, that is, the calling up of a single man or horse'. That same afternoon, however, Dobrorolski was getting the signatures of the Minister of War, Navy Minister and Minister of the Interior, to the *ukaze* for general mobilisation. The necessary telegrams were also prepared, ready for dispatch to the farthest parts of the empire.

Two events seem to have swung Sazonov over to supporting general mobilisation. The first was the news received on the afternoon of the 29th of the bombardment of Belgrade by Austrian monitors, and the second was a communication from Pourtalès at about 7 pm, when the German ambassador passed on a telegram from Bathmann Hollweg: 'Kindly impress on M. Sazonov very seriously that further progress of Russian mobilisation measures would compel us to mobilise and that then European war could scarcely be prevented.'[39]

It was in vain that the ambassador assured Sazonov that this was 'not a threat but a friendly opinion'. The Foreign Minister was so disturbed that he telephoned the Tsar for permission to convene a conference with the Minister of War and Chief of Staff to decide on mobilisation. The conference took place between 7 and 9 pm in Janushkevich's office, and the official diary of the Russian Foreign Ministry records:

> After examining the situation from all points, both the Ministers [i.e., Sazonov and Sukhomlinov] and the Chief of the General Staff decided that in view of the small probability of avoiding a war with Germany it was indispensable to prepare for it in every way in good time, and that therefore the risk could not be accepted of delaying a general mobilization later by effecting a partial mobilization now. The conclusion reached at this conference was at once reported by telephone to the Tsar, who authorized the taking of steps accordingly. This information was received with enthusiasm by the small circle of those acquainted with what was in progress.[40]

This was perhaps the most important decision taken in the history of Imperial Russia and it effectively shattered any prospect of averting a great European war. From a purely military point of view, there was no immediate necessity for the Russian mobilisation order. Russia had introduced 'The Period Preparatory to War' on 26 July and had thus gained several days advantage over Germany, who was not to proclaim *Kriegsgefahrzustand* until the 31st. The Austrian partial mobilisation of eight army corps on 25 July was in no sense a direct threat to Russia; on the contrary, the more the Austrians committed themselves to the Balkans, the weaker their position would be in Galicia, where their northern frontier would be more vulnerable to a Russian attack. Nor was Serbia in imminent danger. The bombardment of Belgrade by Austrian monitors was a futile operation, for Conrad had told Berchtold that he could not begin his invasion of Serbia until 12 August. Of course the ignorant and impulsive Sazonov was unaware of these factors, but Sukhomlinov and Janushkevich should have known better.

The rest of the story can be briefly summarised, since it is dealt with at great length in the standard accounts. Between 9.30 and 10 pm on 29 July, General Dobrorolski was at the Central Telegraphic Office in St Petersburg ready to dispatch the general mobilisation order to all military districts and commands. He was just about to do so when Janushkevich telephoned him to say that the Tsar had cancelled general mobilisation and substituted partial mobilisation instead. The Tsar's change of mind resulted from a telegram from the Kaiser received at 9.40 pm. Saying 'I will not be responsible for a monstrous slaughter', Nicholas insisted on the cancellation. The partial mobilisation order was telegraphed to the relevant military districts at midnight.

Matters had gone so far, however, that even partial mobilisation had a fatal effect on the explosive situation. Moltke was driven to drastic action by the news of Russian partial mobilisation, coupled with reports that Conrad was concentrating against Serbia and would stand on the defensive in Galicia; by 1 pm on 30 July he was pressing Bethmann Hollweg for the immediate proclamation of the *Kriegsgefahrzustand*. Failing to achieve this, he brought pressure on Vienna to order general mobilisation and effectively nullified Bethmann Hollweg's efforts to bring about a peaceful solution. Meanwhile in St Petersburg, Sazonov, Sukhomlinov and Janushkevich exerted all the pressure in their power on the Tsar, and that afternoon Sazonov won his reluctant consent to the proclamation of general mobilisation. The significance of the Tsar's change of mind has been much exaggerated; the fatal decision had been taken on 29 July, for partial mobilisation would have led to war as surely as general mobilisation.

This article has concentrated on the actual mobilisation measures taken by Russia, in concert with France, in 1914. The writer wishes to stress strongly that these measures must be seen against the background of July 1914 as a whole, and in no way excuse the German and Austrian policies which precipitated the crisis. Moreover, to a very considerable degree, the alacrity with which Russia moved towards mobilisation is to be explained by the Schlieffen Plan, and the very urgent need of France to get the Russian army into action as rapidly as possible. Nevertheless it is well to remember that the writings of Fischer and Geiss on Germany's policies and her will towards expansion and war must be balanced against the aggressive attitude of the French nationalists, the confidence of the French General Staff, and the extraordinary mélange of chauvinism, corruption and political and military incompetence which characterised the Russia of Nicholas II.

NOTES

1 L. C. F. Turner, 'The Russian mobilisation in 1914', *Journal of Contemporary History* (January 1968), 65–88.
2 L. C. F. Turner, *Origins of the First World War* (London, 1970 and New York, 1970; reprinted 1972).
3 J. C. Cairns, 'International politics and the military mind: the case of the French Republic 1911–14', *Journal of Modern History* (September 1953), 275.
4 F. Fischer, *Krieg der Illusionen: Der Deutsche Politik von 1911 bis 1914* (Düsseldorf, 1969). English translation, *War of Illusions* (London, 1975), pp. 156–8. References are to the English edn.
5 G. Buchanan, *My Mission to Russia* (London, 1923), Vol. I, p. 126.
6 V. N. Kokovtzov, *Out of My Past* (London, 1935), p. 345.
7 E. C. Helmreich, *The Diplomacy of the Balkan Wars, 1912–13* (Cambridge, Mass., 1938), p. 149.
8 L. Albertini, *The Origins of the War of 1914* (London, 1965), Vol. I, pp. 402–3. The same error occurs in the Italian edn, *Le Origini della Guerra del 1914* (Milan, 1942), Vol. I, p. 423.
9 See also the very inadequate reference to this question in F. R. Bridge, *From Sadowa to Sarajevo: The Foreign Policy of Austria-Hungary, 1866–1914* (London, 1972), p. 348.
10 Kokovtzov, op. cit., p. 346.
11 Albertini, op. cit., Vol. I, Chap. 7, sections 7 and 8.
12 ibid., Vol. I, p. 373.
13 The report is reproduced in *Documents Diplomatiques Français, 1871–1914*, 3rd ser., 1911–14, Vol. III (Paris, 1931), no. 359. The document is mentioned briefly by Fischer, *War of Illusions*, p. 425, quoting a Russian source (the work of A. V. Ignatiev, published in Moscow in 1962).
14 For details of the loans see Fischer, *War of Illusions*, p. 426. The French loans were officially approved on 27 June 1913 and were subject to two conditions – the construction of strategic lines must begin at once and the peacetime strength of the Russian army must be increased. In October 1913 a plan was inaugurated to increase the peacetime strength of the Russian army by 480,000 recruits; the programme was to be completed in 1917.
15 *Documents Diplomatiques Français, 1871–1914*, 3rd ser., 1911–14, Vol. VIII (Paris 1935), no. 62, Delcassé to Pichon, 21 August 1913.
16 ibid., Vol. VIII, no. 79. Convention signed by the Russian Chief of Staff, Jhilinski, and the French Chief of Staff, Joffre, 9 September 1913.
17 G. Ritter, 'Der Anteil der Militärs an der Kriegskatastrophe von 1914', *Historische Zeitschrift* (1961), 72–91. See also Chapter 10 of this book.
18 See p. 256 above. See also the very pertinent comments of Albertini, op. cit., Vol. II, p. 482. Fischer, *War of Illusions*, pp. 488–92, completely ignores the fact that a rapid Russian mobilisation against Austria, in the event of her attacking Serbia, was unnecessary and undesirable.
19 Stone, Chapter 10 above, pp. 225–30.
20 For details of the conference see Albertini, *The Origins of the War of 1914*, Vol. I, pp. 547–9. Incidentally Fischer, op. cit., p. 428, regards the

outcome of the Liman von Sanders crisis as a 'diplomatic defeat' for Russia. This view seems hard to justify.

21 L. C. F. Turner, *Origins of the First World War*, Chapters 5 and 6.

22 M. Paléologue, *Journal 1913–14* (Paris, 1947), p. 269.

23 Georges Michon, *The Franco-Russian Alliance 1891–1917* (London, 1929), pp. 274–5. Michon is quoting from Paléologue's article in the *Revue des Deux Mondes* of 15 January 1921. See also Fischer, *War of Illusions*, pp. 431–2.

24 G. P. Gooch and Harold Temperley, *British Documents on the Origins of the War 1898–1914*, Vol. XI (1926), no. 101, p. 80.

25 L. C. F. Turner, 'The Russian mobilisation in 1914', 72–4.

26 The Council was held after Sazonov had lunched with Paléologue and the British ambassador, Buchanan, who says in his report: 'The French ambassador gave me to understand that France would not only give Russia strong diplomatic support, but would, if necessary, fulfil all the obligations imposed on her by the alliance.' According to Buchanan, Paléologue used strong language and gave the impression of being more decided than Sazonov. (*British Documents . . .*, Vol. XI, no. 101, pp. 80–1.)

27 *Documents Diplomatiques Français, 1871–1914*, 3rd ser., 1911–14, Vol. XI (Paris, 1936), no. 89.

28 S. Dobrorolski, *Die Mobilmachung der Russichen Armee 1914* (Berlin, 1922), pp. 21–2.

29 Albertini, op. cit., Vol. II, p. 457n.

30 ibid., Vol. II, p. 560; Vol. III, pp. 2–3.

31 I. Geiss, *Julikrise und Kriegsausbruch 1914* (Hanover, 1963–4), Vol. II, p. 33 and pp. 39–40.

32 ibid., Vol. II, p. 52.

33 R. Recouly, *Les Heures tragiques d'avant guerre* (Paris 1922), pp. 69–70.

34 Y. Danilov, *La Russie dans la guerre Mondiale (1914–17)* (Paris, 1927), pp. 37–8.

35 Albertini, op. cit., Vol. II, p. 538.

36 Geiss, op. cit., Vol. II, p. 206.

37 Albertini, op. cit., Vol. II, p. 545. This important telegram was not published by Geiss. S. B. Fay, *The Origins of the World War* (New York, 1935), Vol. II, p. 314, shows that the telegram was dispatched to the Warsaw military district at 7.20 am on 29 July.

38 Albertini, op. cit., Vol. II, pp. 545–8. There is some doubt whether the Tsar signed the *Ukaze* for partial mobilisation; it is certain that he signed the one for general mobilisation.

39 ibid., Vol. II, p. 553.

40 Geiss, op. cit., Vol. II, p. 304.

Select Bibliography

The following list is intended solely as a guide for further reading and is in no way an exhaustive bibliography of the literature upon this topic.

L. H. Addington, *The Blitzkrieg Era and the German Staff 1865–1941* (New Brunswick, New Jersey, 1971).

L. Albertini, *The Origins of the War of 1914*, 3 vols (London, 1952–7).

R. J. Art, 'The influence of foreign policy on seapower: new weapons and Weltpolitik in Wilhelmian Germany', *Sage Professional Paper in International Studies*, vol. 2 (1973).

Sir George Aston, 'The Entente Cordiale and the military conversations', *The Quarterly Review*, CCXLII (1932).

T. Baecker, 'Blau gegen Schwarz. Der amerikanische Kriegsplan von 1913 für einen deutsch-amerikanischen Krieg', *Marine Rundschau*, 69, Heft 6 (1972).

C. Barnett, *Britain and Her Army 1509–1970. A Military, Political and Social Survey* (London, 1970).

V. R. Berghahn, 'Zu den Zielen des deutschen Flottenbaus unter Wilhelm II', *Historische Zeitschrift*, 210 (1970).

V. R. Berghahn, *Der Tirpitz-Plan. Genesis und Verfall einer innenpolitischen Krisenstrategie* (Düsseldorf, 1972).

V. R. Berghahn, *Germany and the Approach of War in 1914* (London, 1973).

V. R. Berghahn and W. Deist, 'Kaiserliche Marine und Kriegsausbruch 1914. Neue Dokumente zur Juli-Krise', *Militärgeschichtliche Mitteilungen*, Issue 1 (1970).

B. Bond, *The Victorian Army and the Staff College* (London, 1972).

B. Bond (ed.), *Victorian Military Campaigns* (London, 1967),

K. Bourne, *Britain and the Balance of Power in North America 1815–1908* (London, 1967).

K. Bourne and C. Boyd, 'Captain Mahan's "War" with Great Britain', *United States Naval Institute Proceedings*, 94, no. 7 (1968).

W. R. Braisted, *The United States Navy in the Pacific 1897–1909* (Austin, Texas, 1958).

W. R. Braisted, *The United States Navy in the Pacific 1909–22* (Austin, Texas, 1971).

V. Bueb, *Die 'junge Schule' der franzosische Marine: Strategie und Politik, 1875–1900* (Boppard, 1971).

J. Butler, 'The General Board of the Navy', *United States Naval Institute Proceedings*, LVI (1930).

J. C. Cairns, 'International politics and the military mind: the case of the French Republic', *Journal of Modern History*, 25 (1953).

R. D. Challener, *The French Theory of the Nation in Arms 1866–1939* (New York, 1955).

R. D. Challener, *Admirals, Generals and American Foreign Policy 1898–1914* (Princeton, New Jersey, 1973).

R. Chickering, *Imperial Germany and a World Without War* (Princeton, New Jersey, 1975).

G. A. Craig, *The Politics of the Prussian Army 1640–1945* (Oxford, 1955).

G. A. Craig, *War, Politics and Diplomacy* (London, 1967).

J. B. Crowley, 'Japan's military foreign policies', in J. W. Morley (ed.) *Japan's Foreign Policy 1868–1941. A Research Guide* (New York/London, 1974).

P. M. de la Gorce, *The Frence Army. A Military Political History* (New York, 1963).

J. K. Dunlop, *The Development of the British Army 1899–1914* (London, 1938).

E. M. Earle (ed.), *Makers of Modern Strategy* (Princeton, 1952).

L. L. Farrar, Jr., *The Short-War Illusion* (Santa Barbara/Oxford, 1973).

F. Fischer, *Germany's Aims in the First World War* (London, 1967).

F. Fischer, *War of Illusions. German Policies from 1911 to 1914* (London, 1973).

J. F. C. Fuller, *The Conduct of War, 1789–1961* (London, 1972).

A. Harding Ganz, 'Colonial policy and the Imperial German Navy,' *Militärgeschichtliche Mitteilungen*, Issue 1 (1977).

I. Geiss, *July 1914* (London, 1967).

C. A. Gemzell, *Organisation, Conflict and Innovation. A Study of German Naval Strategic Planning 1888–1940* (Lund, 1973.).

N. H. Gibbs, *The Origins of Imperial Defence* (Oxford, 1955).

J. Gooch, 'The creation of the British General Staff 1904–14', *Journal of the Royal United Services Institute for Defence Studies*, CXVI, no. 662 (1971).

J. Gooch, *The Plans of War. The General Staff and British Military Strategy c. 1900–16* (London, 1974,)

J. Gooch, 'Sir George Clarke's career at the Committee of Imperial Defence', *Historical Journal*, XVIII, no. 3 (1975).

J. Gooch, 'Great Britain and the defence of Canada 1896–1914', *Journal of Imperial and Commonwealth History*, III (1975).

D. C. Gordon, 'The Admiralty and the Dominion Navies 1902–14', *Journal of Modern History*, XXXII, no. 4 (1961).

D. C. Gordon, *The Dominion partnership in Imperial Defence 1870–1914* (Baltimore, 1965).

W. Görlitz (ed.), *Der Kaiser* (Göttingen, 1965).

J. A. S. Grenville and G. B. Young, *Politics, Strategy and American Diplomacy: Studies in Foreign Policy 1873–1917* (New Haven, 1966).

R. F. Hackett, *Yamagata Arimoto in the Rise of Modern Japan 1838–1922* (Cambridge, Mass., 1971).

P. G. Halpern, *The Mediterranean Naval Situation 1908–14* (Cambridge, Mass., 1971).

W. S. Hamer, *The British Army. Civil-Military Relations 1885–1905* (Oxford, 1970).

M. P. A. Hankey, *The Supreme Command*, Vol. I (London, 1961)

H. H. Herwig, *The German Naval Officer Corps. A Social and Political History 1890–1918* (Oxford, 1973.).

H. H. Herwig, *Politics of Frustration. The United States as a Factor in German Planning 1888–1941* (Boston, 1976).

M. Howard, *Studies in War and Peace* (London, 1971).

M. Howard, *The Continental Commitment. The Dilemma of British Defence Strategy in the Era of two World Wars* (London, 1972).

M. Howard (ed.), *The Theory and Practice of War* (London, 1965).

W. Hubatsch, *Der Admiralstab und die obersten Marinebehörden in Deutschland 1848–1945* (Frankfurt am Main, 1958).

A. Iriye, *Pacific Estrangement. Japanese and American Expansion 1897–1911* (Cambridge, Mass., 1972).

D. D. Irvine, 'The origin of capital staffs', *Journal of Modern History*, X, No. 2 (1938).

F. A. Johnson, *Defence by Committee: The British Committee of Imperial Defence 1885–1959* (London, 1960)

J. Joll, *1914: The Unspoken Assumptions* (London, 1968).

G. Jordan (ed.) *Naval Warfare in the Twentieth Century: Festschrift for A. J. Marder* (London, 1977).

D. Judd, *Balfour and the British Empire* (London, 1968).

P. Kelly, 'The *Naval Policy of Imperial Germany*' (PhD Thesis, Georgetown University, 1970).

P. Kemp (ed.), *The Papers of Admiral Sir John Fisher*, Vol. II (Navy Records Society, CVI, London, 1964).

P. M. Kennedy, 'Tirpitz, England and the Second Navy Law of 1900: A Strategical Critique', *Militärgeschichtliche Mitteilungen*, issue 2 (1970).

P. M. Kennedy, Maritime Strategieprobleme der deutsch-englischen Flottenrivalität, in H. Schottelius and W. Deist (eds.), *Marine und Marinepolitik im kaiserlichen Deutschland 1871–1914* (Düsseldorf, 1972).

P. M. Kennedy, 'Mahan versus Mackinder: Two interpretations of British sea power', *Militärgeschichtliche Mitteilungen*, Issue 2 (1974).

P. M. Kennedy, *The Rise and Fall of British Naval Mastery* (London, 1976).

M. Kitchen, *The German Officer Corps 1890–1914* (Oxford, 1968).

I. Lambi, 'Die Operationspläne der Kaiserlichen Marine bis zur Auflösung des Oberkommandes in europäischen Gewässern in Jahr 1899', in J. Hütter, R. Mayers and D. Papenfuss (eds.), *Tradition und Neubeginn* (Cologne, 1975).

R. Langhorne, 'The naval question in Anglo-German relations 1912–14', *Historical Journal*, XIV, no. 2 (1971).

D. E. Lee, *Europe's Crucial Years. The Diplomatic Background of World War I* (Hanover, New Hampshire, 1974).

H. I. Lee, 'Mediterranean Strategy and Anglo-French Relations 1908–12', *Mariner's Mirror*, 57 (1971).

B. H. Liddell Hart, 'French military ideas before the First World War', in M. Gilbert (ed.), *A Century of Conflict 1850–1950. Essays for A. J. P. Taylor* (London, 1966).

S. W. Livermore, 'The American naval base policy in the Far east 1850–1914', *Pacific Historical Review*, XIII (1944).

E. W. B. Lumby (ed.), *Policy and Operations in the Mediterranean 1912–15* (Navy Records Society, CXV, London, 1970).

W. J. McDermott, 'The immediate origins of the Committee of Imperial Defence: a reappraisal', *Canadian Journal of History*, VII, no. 3 (1972).

W. J. McDermott, '*British Strategic Planning and the Committee of Imperial Defence 1871–1907*' (PhD thesis, University of Toronto, 1971).

W. McElwee, *The Art of War. Waterloo to Mons* (London, 1974).

R. F. Mackay, 'The Admiralty, the German Navy and the redistribution of the British Fleet 1904–5', *Mariner's Mirror*, 56 (1970).

R. F. Mackay, *Fisher of Kilverstone* (Oxford, 1973).

J. P. Mackintosh, 'The role of the Committee of Imperial Defence before 1914', *English Historical Review*, LXXVII (1962).

A. J. Marder, *The Anatomy of British Sea Power. A History of British Naval Policy in the Pre-dreadnought Era 1880–1905* (New York, 1940).

A. J. Marder (ed.), *Fear God and Dread Nought. The Correspondence of Admiral of the Fleet Lord Fisher of Kilverstone*, 3 vols. (London, 1952–9).

A. J. Marder, *From the Dreadnought to Scapa Flow*, Vol. I, *The Road to War 1904–14* (London, 1961).

P. Masson, 'La Politique navale française de 1890 à 1914', *Revue Maritime*, 251 (1968).

H. R. Moon, '*The Invasion of the United Kingdom, Public Controversy and Official Planning 1888–1918*', 2 vols. (PhD thesis, University of London, 1968).

A. Moritz, *Das Problem des Präventivkrieges in der deutschen Politik während der ersten Mavokkokrise* (Frankfurt, 1974).

L. Morton, 'War Plan Orange: a study in military strategy', *World Politics*, XI, no. 2 (1959).

I. H. Nish, 'Admiral Jerram and the German Pacific Fleet, 1913–15', *Mariner's Mirror*, 56 (1970).

N. d'Ombrain, 'The Imperial General Staff and the military policy of a "continental strategy" during the 1911 international crisis', *Military Affairs*, XXXIV, no. 3 (1970).

N. d'Ombrain, *War Machinery and High Policy. Defence Administration in Peacetime Britain 1902–14* (Oxford, 1973).

P. Padfield, *The Great Naval Race. Anglo-German Naval Rivalry 1900–14* (London, 1974).

R. A. Preston, *Canada and 'Imperial Defense'* (Durham, NC, 1967).

D. B. Ralston, *The Army of the Republic: The Place of the Military in the Political Evolution of France 1871–1914* (Cambridge, Mass., 1971).

B. Ranft, 'The *Naval Defence of British Sea-Borne Trade, 1860–1905*' (DPhil thesis, University of Oxford, 1967).

B. Ranft (ed.), *Technical Change and British Naval Policy 1860–1939* (London, 1977).

P. Renouvin, 'The part played in international relations by the conversations between the General Staffs on the eve of the world war', in A. Coville and H. Temperley (eds.), *Studies in Anglo-French History* (Cambridge, 1935).

G. Ritter, *Der Schlieffenplan, Kritik eines Mythos* (Munich, 1956).

G. Ritter, 'Die Zusammenarbeit der Generalstäbe Deutschlands und Oesterreich-Ungarns vom dem Erstern Weltkrieg', in *Zur Geschichte und Problematik der Demokratie. Festgabe für Hans Herzfeld* (Berlin, 1958).

G. Ritter, 'Der Anteil der Militärs an der Kriegskatastrophe von 1914', *Historische Zeitschrift*, 193 (1961).

G. Ritter, *The Sword and the Sceptre. The Problem of Militarism in Germany*, Vol. II, *The European Powers and the Wilhelminian Empire 1890–1914* (London, 1972).

J. Röhl, 'Admiral von Muller and the approach of war, 1911–14', *Historical Journal*, XII, no. 4 (1969).

J. Röhl, *1914: Delusion or Design?* (London, 1973).

J. Röhl, 'An der Schweile zum Weltkrieg: Eine Dokumentation über den "'Kriegsrat" vom 8 Dezember 1912', *Militärgeschichtliche Mitteilungen*, Issue 1 (1977).

H. Rosinski, 'Strategy and propaganda in German naval thought', *Brassey's Naval Annual* (1945).

S. W. Roskill, *Hankey, Man of Secrets*, Vol. I (London, 1970).

W. R. Schilling, 'Admirals and Foreign Policy 1913–19' (PhD thesis, University of Yale, 1953).

D. E. Showalter, *Railroads and Rifles: Soldiers, Technology and the Unification of Germany* (Hamden, Conn., 1975).

F.–C. Stahl, 'Der Grosse Generalstab, seine Beziehungen zum Admiralstab und seine Gedanken zu den Operationsplanen der Marine', *Wehrkunde*, XII Jg. (1963), Heft. I.

F.–C. Stahl, 'Armee und Marine im kaiserlichen Deutschland', in *Die Entwicklung des Flottenkommandos* (Bd. IV, Beiträge zur Wehrforschung, Darmstadt, 1964).

J. Steinberg, *Yesterday's Deterrent. Tirpitz and the Birth of the German Battle Fleet* (London, 1965).

J. Steinberg, 'The Copenhagen complex', *Journal of Contemporary History*, I, no. 3 (1966).

J. Steinberg, 'Germany and the Russo-Japanese war', *American Historical Review*, LXXXV, no. 7 (1970).

Z. Steiner, *Britain and the Origins of the First World War* (London, 1977).

N. Stone, 'Die Mobilmachung der österreich-ungarischen Armee 1914', *Militärgeschichtliche Mitteilungen*, Issue 2 (1974).

N. W. Summerton, 'The Development of British Military Planning for a War against Germany 1904–14', 2 vols. (PhD thesis, University of London, 1970).

A. J. P. Taylor, *The Struggle for Mastery in Europe 1849–1918* (Oxford, (1954).

A. J. P. Taylor, *War by Time-table. How the First World War Began* (London, 1969).

L. Trainor, 'The Liberals and the formation of Imperial defence policy 1892–5', *Bulletin of the Institute of Historical Research*, 42 (1969).

L. C. F. Turner, 'The role of the General Staffs in 1914', *Australian Journal of Politics and History*, XI, no. 3 (1965).

L. C. F. Turner, *Origins of the First World War* (London, 1970).

L.C.F. Turner, 'The edge of the precipice: a comparison between November 1912 and July 1914', *RMC Historical Journal* (Royal Military College of Australia), 3 (1974).

J. E. Tyler, *The British Army and the Continent 1904–14* (London, 1938).

A. Vagts, 'Hopes and fears of an American-German war, 1870–1915', Part I, *Political Science Quarterly*, LIV (1939); Part II, ibid., LV (1940).

J. H. Wallach, *Das Dogma der Vernichtungsschlacht. Die Lehren von Clausewitz und Schlieffen und ihre Wirkungen in zwei Weltkriegen* (Frankfurt am Main, 1967).

E. Wegener, 'Die Tirpitzsche Seestrategie', in H. Schottelius and W. Deist (eds.), *Marine und Marinepolitik im kaiserlichen Deutschland 1871–1914* (Düsseldorf, 1972).

S. F. Wells, Jr., 'British strategic withdrawal from the Western hemisphere, 1904–6', *Canadian Historical Review*, XLIV (1968).

Captain Weniger, 'Die Entwicklung des Operationsplanes für die deutsche Schlachtflotte', *Marine Rundschau*, 35 (1930).

B. J. Williams, 'The strategic background to the Anglo-Russian Entente of August 1907), *Historical Journal*, IX, no. 3 (1966).

S. R. Williamson, *The Politics of Grand Strategy. Britain and France Prepare for War 1904–14* (Cambridge, Mass., 1969).

K. Wilson, 'To the western front: British war plans and the "military entente" with France before the First World War,' *British Journal of International Studies*, 3 (1977).

Index